1670

FOOD DEHYDRATION

Second Edition
Volume 1
Drying Methods and Phenomena

some other AVI books

Food Technology and Engineering

TECHNOLOGY OF WINE MAKING, 2ND EDITION   *Amerine, Berg and Cruess*
DAIRY LIPIDS AND LIPID METABOLISM   *Brink and Kritchevsky*
FUNDAMENTALS OF FOOD ENGINEERING, 2ND EDITION   *Charm*
SYMPOSIUM: PHOSPHATES IN FOOD PROCESSING   *Deman and Melnychyn*
THE TECHNOLOGY OF FOOD PRESERVATION, 3RD EDITION   *Desrosier*
ECONOMICS OF FOOD PROCESSING   *Greig*
PRINCIPLES OF PACKAGE DEVELOPMENT   *Griffin and Sacharow*
ENCYCLOPEDIA OF FOOD ENGINEERING   *Hall, Farrall and Rippen*
DRYING OF MILK AND MILK PRODUCTS   *Hall and Hedrick*
FOOD PROCESSING OPERATIONS, VOLS. 1, 2, AND 3   *Joslyn and Heid*
QUALITY CONTROL FOR THE FOOD INDUSTRY, 3RD EDITION, VOLS. 1 AND 2
    Kramer and Twigg
HANDBOOK OF SUGARS   *Junk and Pancoast*
BAKERY TECHNOLOGY AND ENGINEERING, 2ND EDITION   *Matz*
CEREAL TECHNOLOGY   *Matz*
BREAD SCIENCE AND TECHNOLOGY   *Pomeranz and Shellenberger*
FOOD SCIENCE   *Potter*
SOYBEANS: CHEMISTRY AND TECHNOLOGY, VOL. 1   *Smith and Circle*
POTATO PROCESSING, 2ND EDITION   *Talburt and Smith*
THE FREEZING PRESERVATION OF FOODS, 4TH EDITION, VOLS. 1, 2, 3 AND 4
    Tressler, Van Arsdel and Copley

Food Chemistry and Microbiology

LABORATORY MANUAL FOR FOOD CANNERS AND PROCESSORS, VOLS. 1 AND
    2   *National Canners Association*
MICROBIOLOGY OF FOOD FERMENTATIONS   *Pederson*
FOOD ANALYSIS: THEORY AND PRACTICE   *Pomeranz and Meloan*
YEAST TECHNOLOGY   *Reed and Peppler*
FOOD ENZYMES   *Schultz*
PROTEINS AND THEIR REACTIONS   *Schultz and Anglemier*
CARBOHYDRATES AND THEIR ROLES   *Schultz, Cain and Wrolstad*
CHEMISTRY AND PHYSIOLOGY OF FLAVORS   *Schultz, Day and Libbey*
LIPIDS AND THEIR OXIDATION   *Schultz, Day and Sinnhuber*
PRACTICAL FOOD MICROBIOLOGY AND TECHNOLOGY, 2ND EDITION   *Weiser,*
    Mountney and Gould
FUNDAMENTALS OF DAIRY CHEMISTRY   *Webb and Johnson*

Food and Field Crops Technology

SYMPOSIUM: SEED PROTEINS   *Inglett*
CORN: CULTURE, PROCESSING, PRODUCTS   *Inglett*
HANDLING, TRANSPORTATION AND STORAGE OF FRUITS AND VEGETABLES,
    VOL. 1   *Ryall and Lipton*
GRAIN STORAGE: PART OF A SYSTEM   *Sinha and Muir*
POTATOES: PRODUCTION, STORING, PROCESSING   *Smith*
EGG SCIENCE AND TECHNOLOGY   *Stadelman and Cotterill*
TREE FRUIT PRODUCTION, 2ND EDITION   *Teskey and Shoemaker*
BYPRODUCTS FROM MILK, 2ND EDITION   *Webb and Whittier*

FOOD DEHYDRATION

Second Edition
Volume 1
Drying Methods and Phenomena

Edited by WALLACE B. VAN ARSDEL, B.S.
Consultant, Assistant Director Emeritus,
Western Regional Research Laboratory,
U.S. Department of Agriculture,
Albany, California

MICHAEL J. COPLEY, Ph.D.
Consultant, Director Emeritus,
Western Regional Research Laboratory,
U.S. Department of Agriculture,
Albany, California

and ARTHUR I. MORGAN, JR., Ph.D.
Director,
Western Regional Research Laboratory,
U.S. Department of Agriculture,
Albany, California

WESTPORT, CONNECTICUT
THE AVI PUBLISHING COMPANY, INC.
1973

Contributors to This Volume

BARTA, E. J., Ph.D., Consultant, Formerly Chemical Engineer, Western Regional Research Laboratory, U.S. Department of Agriculture, Albany, California

BROWN, A. H., M.S., Chemical Engineer, Western Regional Research Laboratory, U.S. Department of Agriculture, Albany, California

COPLEY, M. J., Ph.D., Consultant, Director Emeritus, Western Regional Research Laboratory, U.S. Department of Agriculture, Albany, California

KING, C. JUDSON, Ph.D., Professor of Chemical Engineering, University of California, Berkeley, California

LAZAR, M. E., B.S., Chemical Engineer, Western Regional Research Laboratory, U.S. Department of Agriculture, Albany, California

LOWE, EDISON, B.S., Mechanical Engineer, Western Regional Research Laboratory, U.S. Department of Agriculture, Albany, California

MORGAN, A. I., Jr., Ph.D., Director, Western Regional Research Laboratory, U.S. Department of Agriculture, Albany, California

RASMUSSEN, Clyde L., M.S., Application Economist, Western Regional Research Laboratory, U.S. Department of Agriculture, Albany, California

VAN ARSDEL, W. B., B.S., Chemical Engineer, Assistant Director Emeritus, Western Regional Research Laboratory, U.S. Department of Agriculture, Albany, California

WHITE, ELIZABETH D., Ph.D., Agricultural Economist, Marketing Economics Division, Economic Research Services, U.S. Department of Agriculture, Albany, California

Preface to the First Edition

This volume is designed to be the first of a pair of books dealing with food dehydration. It is devoted to an exposition of the underlying scientific principles, while the second volume will describe dehydration technology, both as applied in the many kinds of drying equipment and processes and as reflected in specific methods for dehydrating particular food commodities.

Although the technical and scientific literature relating to the phenomena and operation of *drying* is very extensive, few books have dealt with the subject comprehensively, and none of the recent ones is in English. The two-volume "Trocknungstechnik" (1956, 1959), by O. Krischer and K. Kröll, is by far the most complete treatment of drying theory and drying equipment that has been published anywhere. Food dehydration is given some attention (especially the dehydration of potato pieces), but primary emphasis is placed on the drying of industrial materials and products. The only other fairly recent book, by A. W. Lykow (in Russian, 1950, translated into German, 1955), is concerned mainly with industrial drying and gives only secondary attention to the problems of food dehydration. The present volumes, on the other hand, are directed specifically at these food problems.

Two books on the subject of food dehydration have been published during the past twenty years, both in English: "Drying and Dehydration of Foods," by the late Harry W. von Loesecke (Reinhold Publishing Corporation 1943, Second Edition 1955), and "The Dehydration of Food," by T. N. Morris (Chapman and Hall, London, 1947). Both are highly condensed summaries of current technology. Neither book makes any attempt to go deeply into the underlying principles of drying.

An important contribution to the literature on principles of food dehydration was the bound volume of papers presented at a symposium held in Aberdeen, Scotland, March 25–27, 1958, under the auspices of the Society of Chemical Industry. The general title of the symposium was "Fundamental Aspects of the Dehydration of Foodstuffs." The present volume makes extensive use of the ideas presented there.

Most of the published work on principles of dehydration, whether of foods or of industrial products, has appeared in the pages of the scientific and engineering journals. Important contributions have also been published in paper-back bulletins issued by the British Department of Scientific and Industrial Research and by the U.S. Department of Agriculture. The British Ministry of Agriculture, Fisheries, and Food has very recently published a slender hard-cover book which specifically describes the "Accelerated Freeze-drying" method of dehydration.

The author's purpose in this volume is to present in one place a rather complete description of the physical phenomena of drying; a discussion of the significance of the phenomena in the light of current physical and chemical theory; a presentation of the quantitative relationships between such factors in air drying as temperature, humidity, and velocity; a discussion of the several kinds of difficulty with product quality related to the drying conditions; and a survey of the application of these principles in each of the dozen or more different drying methods employed for food dehydration. The author's presentation of principles has naturally been colored by his own experience, most of which has been gained through contact with the wide-ranging research on vegetable dehydration and the somewhat less extensive work on egg dehydration and fruit dehydration carried on at the Western Regional Research Laboratory of the U.S. Department of Agriculture from 1941 onward. The tray drying of piece-form materials receives special emphasis.

After an introductory chapter on the history and present status of the food dehydration industry, the physical and thermal properties of humid air are summarized, humidity measurement and the use of the psychrometric chart are discussed. The phenomena of heat transfer and mass transfer, as seen in a body undergoing drying, are described next, with particular attention to the mechanism of water transport within the moist body. The next section considers the characteristics of the organic materials we use for food, both as they affect the drying behavior of the material and as they may be responsible for some kinds of damage to product quality inflicted by the drying operation itself. Drying phenomena observed in experiments under controlled laboratory conditions are then analyzed, and the quantitative relations between drying rate and various environmental factors are presented. Thermodynamic relationships within typical air convection driers are next derived, applied first to formulation of procedures for estimating the drying time to be expected in a particular drier under specified conditions, and then more generally to description of the theoretical behavior of common types of tunnel drier. In the concluding section the general principles stated in preceding sections are applied in discussion of the theoretical behavior of other types of driers used for dehydrating various foods.

The student who approaches the technical literature of drying for the first time may get the impression that the big work has all been done, the important discoveries made, and the theoretical basis of dehydration practice thoroughly understood, so that only details remain to be filled in. Nothing could be further from the truth. The field is full of puzzles, inconsistencies, disputed observations, and conflicting interpretations. An enormous amount of well-designed experimental work needs to be done, leading into many lines of theoretical inquiry and technological advance. Only the simpler practical drying methods are now accessible to theoretical analysis. In equipment design and process operation, empirical procedures have so far been much more useful than the predictions of basic physical theory. In the long run this situation will undoubtedly be reversed; understanding of the real mechanism of drying processes will point the way to major practical developments.

The author gratefully acknowledges his debt to the numerous present and past colleagues at the Western Regional Research Laboratory who have contributed so greatly to development of many of the ideas expressed here. Special thanks are due to his long-time associates, W. D. Ramage and M. J. Copley, both of whom read the first draft of the manuscript and made important suggestions for its improvement.

W. B. VAN ARSDEL

Albany, California
June 4, 1962

Preface to the Second Edition

The first volume of the Second Edition of *Food Dehydration* contains information on the technology of food dehydration—its physical basis, the kinds of equipment used, and characteristics of the operations employed in a food dehydration plant. The quick rise of freeze drying to a place of prominence is recognized by the appearance of a new separate chapter on that drying method alone.

The second volume, consisting of 12 chapters, is specifically directed toward the commercial dehydration of major food commodities, such as potatoes, other vegetables, fruits, juices, milk, meat, eggs, etc. In addition, new chapters have been supplied to give an introduction to two topics related to the traditional field of food dehydration—the drying of cereal grains which are initially too high in mean moisture content to be stored safely, and the production and use of the limited group of food materials which have such a combination of properties at an intermediate level of water content as to be edible and palatable, but nevertheless to have only a low water vapor pressure (low water activity) so as to be reasonably stable in storage without refrigeration.

Numerous new publications in the technical journals are referred to in the bibliographies of these volumes, but apparently no new books in the fields of food dehydration or drying in general have been published. However, an extensively revised edition of the major technical book on drying was published in Germany by Springer-Verlag in 1963. This is *Die wissenschaftlichen Grundlagen der trockningstechnik* by Otto Krischer.

W. B. VAN ARSDEL
M. J. COPLEY
A. I. MORGAN, JR.

Albany, California
August 1972

... It is always a process of heating or cooling that dries things, but the agent in both cases is heat, either internal or external. For even when things are dried by cooling, like a garment, where the moisture exists separately it is the internal heat that dries them. It carries off the moisture in the shape of vapour (if there is not too much of it), being itself driven out by the surrounding cold. So everything is dried, as we have said, by a process either of heating or cooling, but the agent is always heat, either internal or external, carrying off the moisture in vapour. By external heat I mean as where things are boiled; by internal, where the heat breathes out and takes away and uses up its moisture. So much for drying. . . .

Aristotle (ca. 335–322 B.C.)

Contents

CHAPTER 1

W. B. Van Arsdel | Introduction

SCOPE

As in the 1st Edition of this work, the two volumes will present a statement of the principles and practices of food dehydration, written by specialists who are familiar with the equipment and procedures used.

The scope will be somewhat broader than that of the 1st Edition because of the inclusion of chapters on the drying of harvested cereal grains sufficiently to assure their safe storage, and on the growing appreciation of the usefulness of certain intermediate-moisture food products for special purposes. As in the earlier edition, however, it does not include such other important dry food products as dry biscuit- and cake-mixes, dry beans and peas, and tree nuts. The fruits and vegetables discussed are only those which have significant commercial importance in the United States and Europe.

We do not insist on a rigidly limited definition of "dehydration" or "dehydrated," and often use the words as synonyms of "drying" or "dried." A "dehydration plant," however, is always more than just a "drier;" it includes also various other facilities and pieces of equipment, sometimes costing much more than the drier itself; these would cover the means used to handle the raw material into the plant; prepare it by cleaning, cutting, scalding, or other preliminary operations; and handle, inspect, package, and store the dry product. In this sense a study of the dehydration of a food commodity may be a great deal broader than just a study of drying.

ANCIENT USE OF DRYING TO PRESERVE PERISHABLE FOODS

The drying of foods in order to preserve them during seasons of abundance for consumption during seasons of shortage is an ancient art; its origins are unrecorded, but many of its practices have been handed down even into the present day, and in some cases form the basis of modern food manufacturing processes. Sun-dried dates, figs, apricots, and raisins must have been almost as highly prized by the aboriginal inhabitants of the Mediterranean Basin and Near East as the wild honey which was the other principal sweet. Mankind's unremitting search for things edible undoubtedly led to countless minor discoveries and inventions that by trial-and-error gradually broadened the list of traditional food processing methods. Salaman (1940) believes that "chuño," prepared from native potatoes in the Andean highlands, may have been invented as long as 2000 or 3000 yr ago, and is possibly the first food product ever to be specially processed by man for storage into the hungry winter and spring months. Pemmican, air-dried lean venison or buffalo meat, mixed with fat, was invented

1

by pre-Columbian American Indians. Diemair (1941) says that the household preservation of fruits, vegetables, and mushrooms by drying has been common in many primitive cultures. See also Brothwell (1969).

The first record of the artificial drying of foods, according to Prescott and Proctor (1937) appears in the 18th Century. J. Graefer, according to a British patent of 1780, treated vegetables with hot water, then held them under drying conditions. Eisen dried vegetables on racks in a stove-heated room. Vegetables dried by Edwards according to British Patent No. 8597 of 1840 are said by Allen *et al.* (1943) to have been shipped to British troops in the Crimea (1854-1856), but the quality left much to be desired. One of the prime needs was a diet that would prevent scurvy among the troops; the dried vegetables then available proved to have little or no antiscorbutic activity when finally consumed. Eventually it was found that scalding the vegetables before drying improved their stability.

E. N. Horsford (1864), who was Professor of Chemistry at Harvard University, was a strong advocate of the use of dried vegetables in military rations, and was responsible for the procurement of a considerable amount of dehydrated food which was used by the Union troops during the War Between the States (1861-1865) (Miles 1961). "Erbswurst," pea sausage, which contains condensed pea soup, was used in German rations during the Franco-Prussian war of 1871.

Prescott (1919) says that during the Klondike gold rush, dried potatoes were imported from Germany. Onions dehydrated by W. A. Beck, at the Pajaro Valley Dehydrating Co. in Watsonville, Calif., were also shipped to the Klondike; hermetically sealed cans opened 50 yr later had kept the contents pungent and edible (Anon. 1959). Dried vegetables produced in Canada were shipped to South Africa for the British forces in the Boer War (1899-1902), and some of the unused supplies were consumed by the British expeditionary force in France early in World War I (Prescott 1919). Relatively small amounts were produced in the United States during that war. According to Chace *et al.* (1941) about 4500 tons of dehydrated vegetables were shipped to the U. S. forces overseas. The 1920 U.S. Census showed some 5500 tons of dehydrated vegetables processed in the United States in 1919; materials included green beans, cabbage, carrots, celery, potatoes, spinach, sweet corn, turnips, other vegetables, and soup mixture. The industry was much further advanced in Europe; in 1914 there were 488 dehydration plants in Germany and by 1916 this had increased to 841 plants. Prescott makes the remark, "War seems to be a great stimulator of methods of food preservation." Chace *et al.* (1941) list 96 U.S. patents on various aspects of dehydration dating between 1915 and 1940. Falk *et al.* (1919) described extensive research done during the first war on the vacuum drying of various foods, including meat and fish.

Fruit dehydration experienced a somewhat different history in the United States, mainly because it was based largely on traditional sun-drying methods. Some of these are still widely used, with only minor improvements in technique and appropriate modernizing in materials handling, packaging, and quality maintenance. A major change occurred, however, in the dried prune industry. In the States of Oregon and Washington, where weather during the harvest is not dependably dry, various types of artificially heated driers had come into use. According to Cruess (1938) the "Oregon tunnel" was invented by Allen about 1890, and was widely known and used. Prune producers in California, equipped only for sun drying, became convinced of the economic necessity of artificial dehydration after experiencing serious losses from untimely fall rains in 1918 and 1919. Engineers and research workers associated with the University of California (Ridley 1921; Cruess and Christie 1921A, B; Christie and Ridley 1923; Christie 1926, revised by Nichols 1929) worked with industrial equipment builders and developed a very simple "tunnel" design which eventually became almost standard in the prune-growing area and exerted a strong influence on the design of many of the vegetable dehydrators built during World War II.

Even before the Second World War other drying methods were being vigorously investigated and developed. Drum drying had been applied to whey and buttermilk, soup mixtures, and tomato flakes and powder. Spray drying had come into extensive use on milk products, especially nonfat milk, and was being increasingly used to make certain egg products, particularly dried egg yolk, because of the economy and convenience of dried egg in commercial baking. A few fruit products were being vacuum dried to low moisture content for a relatively small civilian market. Several attempts had been made to produce and market other dehydrated foods, such as pumpkin and squash powders and onions, but without lasting success until about 1923, when a new group undertook onion and garlic dehydration in California (Pardieck 1960). By 1941, dehydrated onion production was solidly established in the civilian market; the products had found steadily expanding use, especially for remanufacture in a variety of other processed foods; several plants were in regular production.

Enormous logistic problems were encountered by the opposing forces in World War II; armies of millions of men had to be supplied, maintained, and fed in every quarter of the globe, from the Arctic to the tropical jungle. Among all the possible food preservation methods, dehydration especially commended itself to military planners because of its space- and weight-saving possibilities. Rapid expansion of dehydrated food production facilities was undertaken by all the warring nations. Coordination of planning and execution of needed research on dehydrated foods was achieved early between the United States and the British Commonwealth nations. In the United States a Joint Dehydration Committee made decisions on behalf of the War Production Board, the Agricultural Marketing Administration, and the Office of the Quartermaster General, regarding production goals, location, design, and construction of plants, and allocations of scarce materials and equipment. Intensive research was undertaken by the USDA, concentrating on vegetables and eggs at the Western Regional Research Laboratory in Albany, Calif., and on meat at the Department's laboratories in Beltsville, Md. A vast expansion of plant capacity for dehydrating some six vegetables and spray drying whole egg was quickly carried out. According to von Loesecke (1955) there were 139 vegetable dehydration plants in the United States in 1943, and they produced 115 million pounds of dry product, worth nearly 50 million dollars. Pardieck (1960) says that by the end of the war some 375 companies, located in 34 states, were set up to dehydrate vegetables. Peak rate of production was reached with an output of 132 million pounds of dehydrated potatoes and 76 million pounds of other vegetables in 1944 (Anon. 1961). The German dehydrated potato industry reached a maximum production of 66 million pounds in 1944 (Völksen and Wegner 1951).

As might have been foreseen, not all of the hastily built new plants, many of them using makeshift equipment, were successful in getting into satisfactory production; likewise, not all of the dehydrated product delivered overseas was acceptable after months of storage under field conditions. In egg dehydration, particularly, the stability of the whole egg powder was found to be so unsatisfactory that by the summer of 1943 all production had been stopped and intensive search for a remedy had been undertaken by public and private agencies in the United States, Canada, and Great Britain. Greatly improved procedures were discovered and put into large-scale use before the end of the war.

While the new dehydration plants were being designed and built, much effort was put into training a large number of people in the complex technology of food dehydration. Training schools provided a large group of managers and superintendents with the basic knowledge and empirical practices developed by the small previously existing industry. Official dehydration manuals, concerned mainly with the technology of vegetable dehydration, were published and widely disseminated in the United States (USDA 1944), Great Britain (1943 and 1946), Australia (1944), and New Zealand (1944). These manuals, although now long out of print, and in some respects outdated by various technical advances, still represent the most complete published statement of the detailed technology of vegetable dehydration. The British experience was summarized in a book by Morris (1947). The U.S. manual was supplemented by several bulletins published by members of the staff of the USDA Western Regional Research Laboratory and by a Management Handbook (USDA 1959).

Many people in the new dehydration plants realized that the industry would experience severe cutbacks at the end of the war. An interbureau committee of the USDA and the War Food Administration estimated even before the end of the war (Samuels 1945) that from 25 to 30 million pounds of dehydrated vegetables (including potatoes) might be sold in the peacetime market. That output had already been reached 10 yr later, after a period of little activity, and was surpassed in every year after 1955 by an increasing amount; totals reported by the Canner/Packer Yearbook (Anon. 1967) for 1963 were 83,000 tons of dehydrated potato and 47,000 tons of "other vegetables." Current practices for vegetable and fruit dehydration for military procurement, applicable to an emergency, were outlined in a widely disseminated *Management Handbook* (USDA 1959), prepared by the staff of the Albany laboratory at the request of the Quartermaster Corps. This was supplemented by the publication of the first edition of the present work (Van Arsdel and Copley 1963, 1964).

Dehydrated egg production continued to increase for a few years after the end of the war, reaching 47,000 tons in 1950 (Anon. 1967), mainly because of relief shipments abroad; but in 1951, production dropped to only 9000 tons. The sudden loss of production was chargeable mainly to discovery of occasional contamination of the product with *Salmonella* organisms. Effective control measures were eventually worked out, but it was about 1960 before a fairly stable production level of about 25,000 tons per year was again reached.

Production of nonfat dry milk (already an important industry before the war, the product of which has continued to be by far the largest dehydrated food item) increased steadily; from 320,000 tons in 1945, it rose to nearly 1 million tons by 1965 (Anon. 1967).

In general, the producers of dried onion and other such specialties who had developed a prewar business continued to expand their markets in many lines of processed food manufacture. A few well-financed and well-located potato plants made a determined and successful bid for a new civilian market, and several potato products developed during the early postwar years have come ahead fast, especially granules and flakes for instant mashed potato. There has been limited commercial production of foam-mat-dried and vacuum-puff-dried orange juice concentrate. Spray-dried and freeze-dried coffee extracts have achieved wide success. Dry mixes for various kinds of cake, pie, and other desserts have become an important outlet for dehydrated egg products. Freeze-drying, generally agreed to be the most costly practical method for removing water from a food product, is, nevertheless, being applied commercially not only to make a high-quality coffee extract, but also to produce dry shrimp and pieces of chicken meat and mushrooms which will rehydrate in water very quickly. (See Chap. 6.)

Highly developed techniques of formulation, manufacture, packaging, advertising, and merchandising have combined to bring dehydrated foods out into the main stream of modern large-scale food processing.

BIBLIOGRAPHY

ALLEN, R. J. L., BARKER, J., and MAPSON, L. W. 1943. The drying of vegetables.
  I. Cabbage. Soc. Chem. Ind. Trans. *62T*, No. 10, 145–160.
ANON. 1959. Gentry Serenader *10*, No. 7, 1.
ANON. 1961. Canner/Packer Yearbook *130*, No. 10, Sept. 25.
ANON. 1967. Canner/Packer, Yearbook *136*, No. 10, 71, Sept. 25.

AUSTRALIA DEPT. OF COMMERCE AND AGRICULTURE. 1944. Dehydration of Vegetables–Factory Manual. Commonwealth Food Control, Melbourne.

BROTHWELL, D., and BROTHWELL, PATRICIA 1969. Food in Antiquity. Praeger Publishers, New York, Washington.

BRITISH DEPT. OF SCIENTIFIC AND INDUSTRIAL RESEARCH, and MINISTRY OF FOOD. 1943. Dehydration. U.K. Progress Rept., London.

BRITISH MINISTRY OF FOOD. 1946. Vegetable Dehydration. H.M. Stationery Office, London.

CHACE, E. M., NOEL, W. A., and PEASE, V. A. 1941. Preservation of fruits and vegetables by commercial dehydration. USDA Circ. 619.

CHRISTIE, A. W. 1926. The dehydration of prunes. Calif. Agr. Expt. Sta. Bull. 404. Revision by P. F. Nichols, Dec. 1929.

CHRISTIE, A. W., and RIDLEY, G. B. 1923. Construction of farm dehydrators in California. J. Am. Soc. Heating, Ventilating Eng. 29, 687–716.

CRUESS, W. V. 1938. Commercial Fruit and Vegetable Products, 2nd Edition. McGraw-Hill Book Co., New York.

CRUESS, W. V., and CHRISTIE, A. W. 1921A. Dehydration of fruits–a progress report. Calif. Agr. Expt. Sta. Bull. 330.

CRUESS, W. V., and CHRISTIE, A. W. 1921B. Some factors of dehydrator efficiency. Calif. Agr. Expt. Sta. Bull. 337.

DIEMAIR, W. 1941. The Preservation of Foodstuffs. F. Enke Verlag, Stuttgart. (German)

FALK, K. G., FRANKEL, E. M., and MCKEE, R. H. 1919. Low temperature vacuum food dehydration. Ind. Eng. Chem. 11, 1036–1040.

HORSFORD, E. N. 1864. The Army Ration, 2nd Edition. D. Van Nostrand Co., New York.

MILES, W. D. 1961. The Civil War–chemistry and chemists. Chem. Eng. News 39, No. 14, 108–115; No. 15, 116–123.

MORRIS, T. N. 1947. The Dehydration of Food, with Special Reference to Wartime Developments in the United Kingdom. Chapman and Hall, London.

NEW ZEALAND DEPT. OF SCIENTIFIC AND INDUSTRIAL RESEARCH. 1944. Vegetable Dehydration. Auckland.

PARDIECK, J. B. 1960. My four decades in dehydration. Activities Rept., QM Food Container Inst. 12, Second Quarter, 142–147.

PRESCOTT, S. C. 1919. Relation of dehydration to agriculture. USDA Circ. 126.

PRESCOTT, S. C., and PROCTOR, B. E. 1937. Food Technology. McGraw-Hill Book Co., New York.

RIDLEY, G. B. 1921. Tunnel driers. Ind. Eng. Chem. 13, 453–460.

SALAMAN, R. N. 1940. The biology of the potato, with special reference to its use as a wartime food. Chem. Ind. 59, 735–737.

SAMUELS, J. K. (Editor) 1945. Post-war adjustments in processing and marketing dehydrated fruits and vegetables. Inter-Bur. Comm. of Post-War Planning, U.S. Dept. Agr. and War Food Admin.

SELTZER, E. 1964. Progress in food dehydration, 1939 to 1964. Food Technol. 18, No. 9, 117–120.

U.S. DEPT. OF AGR. 1944. Vegetable and Fruit Dehydration–A Manual for Plant Operators. Misc. Publ. 540.

U.S. DEPT. OF AGR. 1959. Management Handbook to Aid Emergency Expansion of Dehydration Facilities for Vegetables and Fruits. USDA Western Util. Res. Develop. Div., Agr. Res. Serv., Albany, Calif.

VAN ARSDEL, W. B., and COPLEY, M. J. (Editors) 1963, 1964. Food Dehydration, Vols. 1 and 2. Avi Publishing Co., Westport, Conn.

VÖLKSEN, W., and WEGNER, H. 1951. Potato Drying. Neumann Verlag, Radebeul and Berlin. (German)

VON LOESECKE, H. W. 1955. Drying and Dehydration of Foods, 2nd Edition. Reinhold Publishing Co., New York.

CHAPTER 2

E. D. White | # Dehydrated Foods in the United States

Production of dehydrated foods in the United States expanded vigorously after World War II until the early 1960's.[1] Commodities which enjoyed a large market growth during this period were nonfat dry milk, potatoes, onions, and garlic. In general, the commodities with the most market growth were those that did not have competing processed alternates.

Since 1966, the total production of the industry has been relatively stable, with an increase in some commodities, especially dried eggs, and a decline in production of other commodities, such as nonfat milk. Dairy products, however, have accounted for about 60% of the total dry weight of dehydrated foods produced since 1966 (Table 2.1). In 1970 over 3,776 million pounds of dehydrated foods were produced (dry weight basis) with a wholesale value exceeding $1.4 billion.[2]

About $1/2$ of the dehydrated foods produced are used by remanufacturers whose principal customers are the food service outlets (USDA 1969). The food dehydration industry also supplies dried foods directly to food service outlets, as well as to retail markets for use in households and for campers and other sportsmen. The federal government purchases dehydrated foods for the military and for federal food distribution programs.

Freeze-dried products are used where better quality is desired than that provided by other drying methods. Because of the higher cost of processing, however, the use of freeze-dried commodities is restricted.

Some of the advantages of dehydrated foods are: (1) lower transportation and storage costs; (2) no refrigeration costs in comparison with fresh or frozen foods; (3) prolonged shelf-life; and (4) compatibility with other ingredients in dry food mixes.

Some of the disadvantages of dehydrated foods are: (1) high unit processing costs, especially for freeze-dried foods; (2) poor quality of texture and flavor in some foods; (3) unsatisfactory rehydration of some items; and (4) the need for unique processing methods for most products.

---

[1] The dehydrated foods discussed in this chapter do not include cereal grains or grain products, dry beans or peas, tree nuts, or dry active yeast. Fruits which are usually sundried are included since some of these are mechanically dehydrated. "Dehydrated" and "dried" are used interchangeably in referring to the foods.

[2] These are low estimates since production figures and/or dollar values for many commodities are not available. Average wholesale values are best estimates from industry and federal government sources.

TABLE 2.1

PRODUCTION OF DEHYDRATED FOODS,
UNITED STATES, 1966 AND 1970
(Millions of Pounds, Dry Weight Basis)

Food Category	1966	1970
Dairy products[1]	2273	2321
Fruit	892	817
Vegetables[2]	330[3]	373
Eggs	52	75
Meat and poultry[4]	NA	24
Fish	1	1[5]
Coffee and tea	166	165
Total	3714	3776

Source: Annual reports of the USDA Statistical Reporting Service.
[1] Data on some products such as infants' dietary supplements and dessert toppings not available.
[2] Potatoes, onions and garlic only.
[3] 1965 data, 1966 not available for onions and garlic.
[4] Does not include sausage.
[5] 1969 data, 1970 not available.

LOCATION OF DEHYDRATION PLANTS, 1970

Plants which dehydrate dairy products are located predominantly in the North Central area of the United States (Table 2.2). Minnesota and Wisconsin account for 50% of the production of dry dairy products. New York, Iowa, and California also contribute significantly to production.

The plants producing dried egg products are located primarily in the North Central area. These plants, which include all of the major producers, are operated under the USDA grading and inspection programs.

California is the major producer of dried fruits (Table 2.3). Of the vegetables, Idaho accounts for most of the dehydrated white potatoes, while plants in Louisiana and North Carolina produce the dehydrated sweet potatoes. All other dried vegetables are produced in California. Of the 10 plants in California producing other dried vegetables in 1970, 4 produced dehydrated onions and garlic, 4 tomato powders, 3 dried chili peppers, 3 dried carrots, and 2 produced all other vegetable products.

Industry sources indicate that there are about 6 plants which dehydrate or freeze-dry meats and poultry, and 1 which freeze-dries fish. These plants are scattered throughout the United States.

The plants which produce instant coffee are located throughout the United States. Ten of these plants produce freeze-dried coffee (Sivetz 1970). Industry sources indicate that 5 or 6 of these plants also produce instant tea.

TABLE 2.2

NUMBER OF PLANTS PRODUCING DRY DAIRY AND EGG PRODUCTS
BY REGION AND STATE, 1970

	Dairy							
	Whole Milk	Buttermilk	Nonfat Milk		Whey	Malted Milk	Milk Sugar	Eggs[1]
			Food	Feed				
Northeast:								
New York	4	7	16	11	3			
Pennsylvania		3	17	5				
Vermont			3	3				
Subtotal:	4	10	36	19	3			
North Central:								
Illinois	3	3			8			1
Indiana			3					
Iowa		15	16	14	13			1
Kansas								3
Michigan	NA[2]	12	5	3	3			
Minnesota	6	30	44	36	11			3
Missouri		NA[2]	NA[2]	NA[2]	11			5
Nebraska	3	5	6	6	6			4
North Dakota		7						
Ohio		6	9	4				1
South Dakota		4	6	3				1
Wisconsin	5	21	28	16	33	3	7	
Subtotal:	17	103	117	82	85	3	7	19
South:								
Arkansas								1
Georgia								1
Kentucky					5			
Oklahoma		3						1
Texas			3					
Subtotal:		3	3		5			3
West:								
California	3	5	14	14				1
Idaho		3	6	6				
Oregon				3				
Utah			5		3			
Washington			6	3				1
Subtotal:	3	8	31	26	3			2
Other States:[2]	12	15	33	15	20		6	0
Total	36	139	220	142	116	3	13	24

Source: USDA Production of Manufactured Dairy Products, July 1971; USDA Poultry Div.,
List of Plants, April 1970.
[1] Plants operating under federal inspection programs. Includes all major plants.
[2] Less than 3 plants reporting within a state.

TABLE 2.3

NUMBER OF PLANTS PRODUCING DRY PRODUCTS BY COMMODITY, REGION, AND STATE, 1970[1]

	Raisin	Fruit Prune	Apple	Vegetable Potatoes[2]	Other	Meat, Poultry, and Fish	Coffee and Tea
Northeast:							
Maine				1			
New Jersey							5
New York			2	2			1
Pennsylvania							1
Subtotal:			2	3			7
North Central:							
Indiana						1	
Michigan				1			
Minnesota				2			
Nebraska						2	
North Dakota				4			
Ohio							2
Subtotal:				7		3	2
South:							
Florida							2
Louisiana					1[3]		3
North Carolina					1[3]		
Tennessee							1
Texas						1	2
Subtotal:					2	1	8
West:							
California	18	260	6		10	1	6
Idaho				18			
Oregon		46[4]		1		1	1
Washington		1	3	4			
Subtotal:	18	307	9	23	10	2	7
Total	18	307	11	33	12	6	24

[1] Mechanical dehydrators only.
[2] Excludes sweet potatoes.
[3] Sweet potatoes.
[4] Twenty operate intermittently.

DAIRY PRODUCTS

About 2.3 billion pounds of dry dairy products were produced in 1970 (Table 2.4).[3] The wholesale value of this production was around $500 million. This was a slight increase in production from 1966. Except for dry whey and crude milk sugar, however, production of dry dairy products has declined since

---

[3] Data for some dry dairy products are not available such as infants' dietary supplements and dessert toppings; therefore, both production figures and value of production estimates are low.

TABLE 2.4

PRODUCTION OF DRY DAIRY PRODUCTS, UNITED STATES, 1966–1970
(Millions of Pounds, Dry Weight Basis)

Commodity	1966	1967	1968	1969	1970
Nonfat dry milk (food)	1579.8	1678.7	1594.4	1452.3	1442.8[1]
Dry whey (feed and food)	470.9	492.8	495.2	516.3	620.4[2]
Dry whole milk	94.4	74.3	79.8	70.2	68.7
Dry buttermilk	76.2	72.6	70.4	66.5	59.5
Dry skim milk (feed)	26.1	30.3	27.0	24.4	12.0
Malted milk powder	22.9	15.2	20.4	18.6	19.4
Dry cream	0.5	NA[3]	0.8	NA[3]	NA[3]
Dry casein	NA[3]	NA[3]	NA[3]	NA[3]	NA[3]
Milk sugar, crude	NA	NA	83.0	92.9	97.6
Dry ice cream mix	2.0	NA	0.5	0.2	0.1
Total	2272.8	2363.9	2371.5	2241.4	2320.5

Source: USDA Agr. Statist., 1970. USDA, SRS, Manufactured Dairy Products, July 1970.
[1] About 1% was roller dried, the rest spray dried.
[2] About ½ was for animal feed, 326.6 million pounds.
[3] Less than 3 plants reporting.

the peak years of 1962–1965, especially nonfat dry milk. The decline in nonfat dry milk production has been the result of: (1) the production of whole milk has declined from 127 billion pounds in 1964 to 117.4 billion pounds in 1970; and (2) the production of butter has decreased, therefore there is less nonfat milk available. Despite the decline in production, nonfat dry milk represented about ⅔ of the total production of dry dairy products in the United States in 1970.

Dry whey accounted for 27% of the production of dry dairy products in 1970 as compared with 21% in 1966. The production of dry whey has been increasing for a variety of reasons: (1) the production of cheese and cottage cheese has increased, therefore there is more whey available; (2) it is more profitable to dry whey and market it than to treat it as sewage; and (3) new processes and new products have expanded the use of whey as an inexpensive protein ingredient in ice cream, bakery goods, and candy (Mathis 1970). It is expected that dry whey production will continue to increase.

Dry dairy products are a convenient alternative to fresh forms for certain purposes. Food remanufacturers and institutions are major users of these products. Remanufacturers use the dry dairy products as ingredients of dry product mixes, as binders, as flavor carriers, and as nutritive additives. The federal government purchases large quantities of dry milk products for use by the military and for food distribution programs. The purchase of dried foods for these programs is discussed in a later section.

FRUIT

Since 1966, about 3–4% of the total fruit produced in the United States has been processed into dried fruit, either sun-dried or artificially dried. In 1970,

TABLE 2.5

PRODUCTION OF DRIED FRUITS, UNITED STATES, 1966–1970
(Millions of Pounds, Dry Weight Basis)

Year	Apples	Apricots	Dates	Figs	Peaches	Pears	Prunes	Raisins	Total
1966	31.8	13.0	42.6	41.2	6.8	2.6	193.8	560.6	892.3
1967	20.0	7.3	41.6	24.4	3.9	0.4	244.2	362.4	704.2
1968	21.7	7.7	46.0	31.6	5.6	0.8	214.8	529.0	857.3
1969	35.0	13.9	33.0	35.0	8.0	1.3	250.2	449.0	825.4
1970	21.6	12.1	36.2	28.8	5.2	1.1	346.7	365.2	817.0

Source: USDA Crop Reporting Board, SRS, Non-Citrus Fruits; USDA Fruit Situation
TFS-179.

1.5 million tons of fresh fruit were processed into dried fruit with a wholesale value of around $223 million.[4] Raisins and prunes accounted for 87% of the dried fruit production in 1970 (dry weight basis) (Table 2.5). Dates, figs, and apples accounted for another 11%. Apricots, peaches, and pears were a very small proportion of the total dried fruit produced.

Almost all of the dates, prunes, and figs which are grown are dried. About $1/4$ of the grape crop is processed into raisins. Around 18% of the apricot, 3% of the apple, 1% of the peach, and 1% of the pear crops are dried. These percentages have remained fairly constant since 1967 with relatively small fluctuations. Although usually sun-dried, a small amount of apricots, peaches, and pears are artificially dried to conform to specifications of health food outlets. There is little or no freeze drying of fruit at the present time.

In 1965, it was found that the use of dried fruits or berries as ingredients in dry mix formulations was limited to a few specialty products such as puddings, cookies, and crackers primarily because of problems of rehydration and relatively high prices (USDA 1969). Since then, rehydration has been improved but the high prices are still a factor which may limit future market growth in this area.

The civilian per capita consumption of dried fruits has been decreasing since 1954. About 3.9 lb per person were consumed in 1954 as compared with 2.6 lb in 1970. The consumption of fresh fruits has also declined during this period but the consumption of canned fruits, canned juices, and frozen fruits has increased.

VEGETABLES

Potatoes

Of all the dehydrated vegetables, potatoes are produced in the largest volume. In 1970, 365 million pounds of dehydrated potatoes (dry weight basis) were produced (Table 2.6). These had a wholesale value of around $73 million. Since

---

[4] Includes apples, apricots, dates, figs, peaches, pears, prunes, and raisins.

TABLE 2.6

PRODUCTION OF DRIED VEGETABLES, UNITED STATES,
1965–1970
(Millions of Pounds, Dry Weight Basis)

Year	Potatoes	Onions	Garlic
1965	282.3	36.0	11.6
1966	277.4	NA	NA
1967	267.2	NA	NA
1968	318.7	NA	NA
1969	356.8	NA	NA
1970	364.7	86.5	21.9

Source: USDA Crop Reporting Board, SRS, Irish Potatoes; Am.
Dehydrated Onion and Garlic Assoc. (1971).

1965 between 6 and 8% of all potatoes grown in the United States has been processed into dehydrated products. Dehydrated potatoes include instant mashed potatoes (granules, flakes, and buds), slices, and dice. Instant mashed potatoes have accounted for about 90% of the production.

Since 1966, the per capita consumption of dehydrated potatoes has increased from 10.3 to 12.8 lb in 1970 (fresh weight basis). The increased usage of dehydrated potatoes, along with the increased usage of frozen potatoes, chips, and shoestrings has been credited with helping potatoes maintain a steady per capita consumption.

Convenience of preparation and portion control seem to have been the most important factors for the growth of the market for dehydrated potatoes. The two major markets for instant mashed potatoes are food service outlets and the retail market. Food service outlets also use sliced and diced dehydrated potatoes for quick preparation of casseroles, salads, and hash brown potatoes. Remanufacturers use slices and dice in their preparation of processed products such as scalloped and au gratin potatoes, and salad mixes.

Onions and Garlic

The production of dehydrated onions and garlic has about doubled since 1965 (Table 2.6). In 1970, 86.5 million pounds of dried onions and 21.9 million pounds of dried garlic (dry weight basis) were produced.[5] In 1965, production figures indicated that about 14% of the onion crop and about 80% of the garlic crop were dehydrated. In 1970, preliminary estimates indicate that between 20 and 25% of the onion crop and more than 90% of the garlic crop were dehydrated. However, in 1970, 19 million pounds of fresh or frozen garlic and 76 million pounds of fresh or frozen onions were imported, primarily from

---

[5] Average wholesale prices for dehydrated onions and garlic are not available. Based on average 1969 farm prices for the United States, the value of the production would be at least $37 million.

Mexico, and it is possible that part of these imports were dehydrated after arrival in the United States.

A large part of the dehydrated onion and garlic production is used by food processors as seasonings in products such as catsup, chili sauce, and meat casseroles, as well as cold cuts, sausages, potato chips, crackers, and other snack items. Food service outlets also use dehydrated onion and garlic because of their convenience in storage, preparation and use. Small quantities are sold to the retail market and armed forces.

Other Vegetables

Current production data are not available on other vegetables because there are only a few firms which produce these products. In 1965, there was an estimated 30 million pounds of other vegetables produced (USDA 1969). Chili peppers accounted for about $\frac{1}{3}$ of the volume. Carrots, bell peppers, and tomato powder accounted for another $\frac{1}{3}$. The remaining $\frac{1}{3}$ included asparagus, cabbage, celery, chives, corn, green beans, peas, pumpkins, green onions, shallots, parsley, lima beans, dill, mint, horseradish, and some others.

Dehydrated vegetables are produced in several forms—slices, dice, flakes, powder, minced or chopped. Most of these dehydrated vegetables are sold to food processors for use in dehydrated packaged mixes such as soups and sauces, or to add variety to canned, frozen, or dehydrated mixtures such as meat loaf and casseroles. However, since fresh and frozen vegetables are generally preferred, the usage of dehydrated vegetables is usually limited to products where dry ingredients are required.

EGGS

There were 75.3 million pounds of dried eggs (dry weight) produced in 1970 (Table 2.7). These had a wholesale market value of around $90 million. This was 24 million pounds more than was produced in 1966 and was due to the increased production of egg-solid blends.

The proportion of liquid eggs converted to dried eggs has remained relatively

TABLE 2.7

PRODUCTION OF DRIED EGGS, UNITED STATES, 1966–1970
(Millions of Pounds, Dry Weight Basis)

Year	Whole	Albumen	Yolk	Blends	Total
1966	8.1	13.7	12.9	16.8	51.5
1967	13.1	19.2	19.1	19.3	70.7
1968	13.8	13.1	12.9	25.6	65.3
1969	7.5	10.1	11.5	32.0	61.1
1970	8.2	15.0	12.3	40.3	75.3

Source: USDA Agr. Statist., 1970; USDA Egg Products, Mar. 2, 1971; USDA Poultry and Egg Situation *PES-267.*

constant since 1966, between 35 and 38%. However, it is reported that trade sources expect egg solids to become the most important type of processed egg product by 1975 because of improved product characteristics, increased economies, and convenience in handling (Jones 1969).

Of the dried eggs produced, ³/₄ are used by food manufacturers and institutional outlets. Manufacturers use the dried eggs in formulations requiring dry ingredients, such as pie, pancake, and doughnut mixes. Only small amounts of dried eggs are sold in the retail markets.

MEAT AND POULTRY

Because of the small number of firms, detailed production and distribution data on the dehydration of meat and poultry are not reported to avoid disclosing figures for individual companies. What data are available show that in 1970, 24 million pounds of dried meats and 179.3 million pounds of dried or semidried sausage were federally inspected (USDA 1970).[6] These quantities represented less than 1% of all meat and meat products inspected. Information is not available as to what is included in the "diced meat" category.

The types of meat and poultry products which are artificially dehydrated include: (1) chicken flakes, pieces, and powder; (2) turkey flakes and pieces; (3) beef pieces, slices, powder, and chunks; and (4) pork pieces and chops. In 1965, about ²/₃ of the dehydrated meats and poultry were used in convenience foods such as dry soup mixes and meat-flavored dishes (USDA 1969). A small amount was purchased by food service outlets and by the military.

It was estimated that in 1965 about one million pounds of freeze-dried meat and poultry were produced. In fiscal year 1970, it was estimated that the military purchased about 1 million pounds of freeze-dried meat and poultry, plus about 1 million pounds which were included in meat casseroles. Since the military uses most of the freeze-dried meats and poultry produced, it is probable that no more than 3–4 million pounds of freeze-dried meat and poultry were produced in the United States in 1970. Because freeze-dried meats are expensive they probably will be limited to highly specialized uses.

FISH

In 1969, 1 million pounds of fish were dried in the United States for human consumption (Table 2.8).[7] This had a processed value of $3.3 million. This included sun-dried and freeze-dried fish and represented less than ¹/₂% of the total catch by the United States.

In 1967, it was reported that out of the 1.6 million pounds of fish that were dried, 1 million pounds were freeze dried. Since there is now only one plant

---

[6] These are not production figures since some meat is inspected more than one time.
[7] Data for 1970 not available.

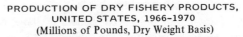

TABLE 2.8

PRODUCTION OF DRY FISHERY PRODUCTS, UNITED STATES, 1966–1970
(Millions of Pounds, Dry Weight Basis)

| | Fishery Products | |
Year	Food[1]	Dried Scrap and Meal
1966	0.9	447.6
1967	1.6	422.4
1968	1.1	470.3
1969	1.0	505.1
1970	NA	553.9

Source: U.S. Dept. Interior, Processed Fishery Products, 1966–1970.
[1] Sun-dried and freeze-dried.

which freeze dries fish, separate figures are not available for 1969. Freeze-dried fish and seafood are used (1) by the military, and (2) as ingredients in products such as dried sandwich mixes. Cod, smelt, tuna, king crab, and shrimp are the only fish and shellfish products which are freeze-dried.

In 1970, 553.9 million pounds of dried fish scrap and meal were produced (Table 2.8). The processed value of this production was $47.6 million. This is used mostly for animal feed and for fertilizer.

MISCELLANEOUS FOODS

Citrus Juices

Two plants in Florida produce instant dehydrated citrus juices for institutional and military uses. They are now exploring the possibilities of expanding sales to the retail markets.

Mushrooms

Less than 1% of the mushrooms grown in the United States are dried, and these are freeze dried. Most dried mushrooms used in the United States by food processors are imported, principally from the Orient. The imported mushrooms are air dried and are much cheaper than the domestic freeze-dried mushrooms. They are used primarily in soup mixes, sauces, and gravies.

Soup Mixes

A variety of dried soups are on the market. Data available for 1963 and 1967 indicate a large increase in shipments during this time period (U.S. Dept. Com. 1970).[8]

	1963	1967
Quantity (million pounds)	46.5	79.2
Value (million dollars)	44.5	76.4

[8] Not production figures since total shipments include interplant transfers.

COFFEE AND TEA

In 1970, 147.7 million pounds of soluble coffee were produced in the United States at a wholesale value of around $370 million. The production of soluble coffee amounted to about 16% of the total roastings. Since 1966, the production of soluble coffee has fluctuated as follows (USDA 1971):

Year	Million Lb (dry wt)
1966	155.3
1967	141.0
1968	147.3
1969	154.3
1970	147.7

At present, most coffee is spray dried. By 1975, some industry sources expect that agglomerated coffee will have almost replaced unagglomerated spray-dried coffee (Maxwell 1970). Several firms have already changed their method of production. Agglomerated coffee is reported to have a better flavor than unagglomerated and is less expensive to produce than freeze-dried.

Freeze-dried coffee usually has a better flavor than spray-dried but costs about twice as much to process. For this reason, although freeze-dried instant coffee has been making rapid gains in the market, some industry sources expect it to level off at about 30–40% of the market from an estimated 25% at the present time (Maxwell 1970). However, other industry sources expect freeze-dried coffee to eventually dominate instant sales (Sivetz 1970).

United States consumption of all coffee has been declining. Factors thought to be contributing to the downtrend of coffee consumption are: (1) an economic slowdown with fewer people consuming coffee in restaurants; (2) price increases; and (3) a decline in consumption of coffee among the younger age due to their "quick snack" style of eating.

Consumption of tea in the United States, however, has been increasing. One factor has been the increased consumption of iced tea which is related to the new "quick" style of eating. Another factor is the increased consumption of instant tea (Gray 1970). In 1970, about 17 million pounds of instant tea were produced (dry weight basis) as compared with 11 million pounds produced in 1966. This amounted to about ⅓ of all tea sold in the United States. In 1970, about 20% of the instant tea produced consisted of instant tea mixes with added sweetener, lemon, and other flavorings.

FEDERAL GOVERNMENT PURCHASES

Military

Purchases of dried foods for the military for fiscal year 1970 totaled 22.4 million pounds of regularly dried foods and 1.7 million pounds of freeze-dried foods (Table 2.9). This represented a substantial decrease from fiscal year 1969,

TABLE 2.9

PURCHASE OF DRIED FOODS FOR UNITED STATES ARMED FORCES, FISCAL YEARS 1969 AND 1970

(Thousands of Pounds, Dry Weight Basis)

Regular Dried	Fiscal Yr 1969	Fiscal Yr 1970	Freeze-Dried	Fiscal Yr 1969	Fiscal Yr 1970
Apple slices	789	–	Beef, diced, raw	–	138
Apple sauce, instant	1,411	855	patties, raw	359	29
Grapefruit juice, instant	594	–	steak, raw	236	–
Orange juice, instant	234	188	Pork chops, raw	126	130
Beans, green	116	14	Chicken, cooked	48	60
Cabbage, raw	–	35	Fish portions, raw	–	31
Garlic	[1]	–	Shrimp, cooked	291	284
Horseradish	44	14	Cottage cheese	81	77
Onions	1,036	434	Beef stew[2]	499	114
Parsley	5	–	Chicken w/rice[2]	499	83
Peppers, green	291	5	Chicken stew[2]	526	120
Potatoes, slices	5,725	–	Pork and escalloped potatoes[2]	570	108
granules	13,128	10,256	Ground beef w/rice[2]	380	108
Soup, chicken noodle	1,286	1,594	Beef hash[2]	499	103
green pea	936	653	Spaghetti w/sauce[2]	499	108
onion	166	545	Chili con carne[2]	630	224
tomato/vegetable	754	892			
Soup/gravy base, beef	1,818	1,658			
chicken	240	570			
Egg mix	1,507	1,371			
Cheese, American processed	746	294			
Ice cream mix	–	180			
Milk, nonfat, dry	–	1,600			
Milk, nonfat, dry, instant	615	500			
Dessert topping	–	750			
Total	31,441	22,408	Total	5,243	1,717

[1] 196 lb.

[2] These items are components of "Food Packet, Long Range Patrol." Each packet contains about 1/3 lb of freeze-dried food.

especially for freeze-dried foods. Purchases of dried fruits, vegetables, and egg mix were decreased in fiscal year 1970, while purchases of dried soup mixes and dairy products were increased. However, few dairy products were purchased in fiscal year 1969 due to a large carryover from the previous year.

Donation Programs

Dehydrated foods are purchased by several agencies in the federal government for distribution to the school lunch program, and to welfare programs which include the needy, the aged, orphanages, and nonprofit hospitals. In addition to those foods purchased by the government and delivered directly to these programs, appropriations are made to the states to assist in the purchase of commodities in the local market. For example, about 80% of the food used in the school lunch program is purchased locally through commercial channels. In 1970, dried foods purchased by the federal government included: nonfat dry milk, mashed potatoes, sweet potatoes, raisins, prunes, scrambled egg mixes, and beverage mixes which included nonfat dry milk.

EXPORTS AND IMPORTS OF DRIED FOOD PRODUCTS

A partial list of exported and imported dried food products for 1970 is shown in Table 2.10. Major exports include nonfat milk, prunes, raisins, potatoes, meat and poultry, and "other" vegetables. It is not known what proportion of "other" vegetables are onions and garlic. Major imports included casein, eggs, dates, mushrooms, cured fish, and coffee. Export-import data on instant tea are not available since it is such a small percentage of total tea shipments. However, data on tea shipments will probably be made available in 1972.

Prior to World War II, the United States produced about 50 million pounds of casein annually and there were about 600 plants in operation (Miller 1971). In 1949, the dairy price-support program went into effect and, as a result, manufacturers found it more profitable to shift from casein production to dry milk production. Since 1955, most of the casein used in the United States has been imported.

FUTURE OF DEHYDRATED FOODS

The overall demand and production of dehydrated foods are expected to continue at present or slightly higher levels for the next several years. While the use of nonfat dry milk has declined in the past few years, the growth in demand for other dried foods such as eggs, coffee, potatoes, onions, and garlic has offset this decline and contributed to a slight increase in total production. The use of dehydrated foods in convenient, quick-cooking dishes for home consumption, as well as for restaurants, institutions, and remanufacturers as a means of reducing preparation costs, will also continue to result in a growing demand for these foods.

TABLE 2.10

EXPORTS AND IMPORTS OF DRIED PRODUCTS,
UNITED STATES, 1970
(Thousands of Pounds, Dry Weight Basis)

	Exports		Imports	
	Lb	Dollar Value	Lb	Dollar Value
Whole milk and cream	13820	4190	1796	188
Nonfat milk (not relief)	212287	52419	–	–
Nonfat milk (relief)	203773	49679	–	–
Buttermilk	–	–	421	76
Casein	4075	3136	135288	30475
Subtotal	433955	109424	137505	30739
Eggs	433	574	2443	1750
Prunes	79049	18415	2130	221
Raisins	140841	25276	1483	211
Apples	1068	463	826	270
Apricots	1037	865	1350	653
Dates	12402	3515	22456	2187
Figs	2054	684	3412	625
Other[1]	11149	2969	1289	476
Subtotal	247600	52187	32946	4643
Potatoes	9454	2250	277	54
Garlic	–	–	170	56
Onions	–	–	70	17
Mushrooms	–	–	948	2567
Other[2]	23847	10998	689	686
Subtotal	33301	13248	2154	3380
Meat and offals[3]	2378	1742	–	–
Poultry[4]	61	86	–	–
Fish and shellfish	9366[4]	8225	1018[5]	889
Subtotal	11805	10053	1018	889
Soup mixes	678	546	–	–
Coffee	4800	9200	36299	47171
Tea	NA	NA	NA	NA
Total	732572	195232	212365	88572

Source: U.S. Foreign Agr. Trade Statist. Rept., 1970. U.S. Dept.
Com., Imports and Exports of Fishery Products, Ann. Sum., 1970;
U.S. Dept. Com., U.S. Exports, Schedule B Commodity and Country, 1970.
[1] Includes peaches, pears, cherries, mixed fruits, bananas, berries.
[2] Excludes dry beans, peas, and lentils.
[3] Does not include pork, ham or bacon.
[4] Salted, smoked or dried.
[5] Dried, unsalted only.

BIBLIOGRAPHY

ADINOLFI, J. 1970. Overview: changing patterns in coffee's public feeding market. World Coffee Tea *11*, No. 4, 50, 52.

AM. DEHYDRATED ONION AND GARLIC ASSOC. 1971. Personal communication. 601 California St., San Francisco.

ANON. 1970. Canner/Packer Yearbook *139*, No. 10, Sept. 25.

BIRD, K. 1967. The food dehydration industry's prospective changes. Speech to Dehydrated Foods Industry Council, Philadelphia (out of print).

BIRD, K. 1969. Key factors in successful new foods. Food Technol. *23*, 1159.

BIRD, K. 1970. New food processes. Machine Design *42*, No. 6, 20, 25–26.

GRAY, F. D. 1970. Tea situation: trends and prospects. *In* Nat. Food Situation, USDA *NFS-134*.

JONES, H. B., Jr. 1969. Processed egg products: a marketing opportunity. *In* Marketing Transportation Situation, USDA Econ. Res. Serv. *ERS-405*.

MATHIS, A. G. 1970. More whey is coming. *In* Dairy Situation. USDA Econ. Res. Serv. *DS-332*.

MAXWELL, J. C., Jr. 1970. Overview: trends in coffee marketing. World Coffee Tea *11*, No. 4, 39.

MILLER, R. R. 1971. Developments and trends in the casein market. *In* Dairy Situation. USDA Econ. Res. Serv. *DS-334*.

MONDSCHEIN, R. 1970. Overview: changes in USA coffee drinking. World Coffee Tea *11*, No. 4, 67, 75.

SCHROETER, R. B. 1971. U. S. imports of horticultural products. USDA *FASM-191-Rev*.

SIVETZ, M. 1970. Overview: trends in coffee technology. World Coffee Tea *11*, No. 4, 33.

U. S. DEPT. OF AGR. 1969. Dehydrated foods–a market perspective. *In* Marketing Transportation Situation. USDA Econ. Res. Serv. *ERS-431*.

U. S. DEPT. OF AGR. 1970. Federal meat and poultry inspection statistical summary for 1970. USDA Consumer Marketing Serv. *CMS-80*.

U. S. DEPT. OF AGR. 1971. National Food Situation. USDA Econ. Res. Serv. *NFS-135*.

U. S. DEPT. OF COM. 1970. 1967 Census of Manufactures: canned, cured, and frozen foods. Bur. of the Census, U.S. Dept. Com. *MC67(2)-20C*.

CHAPTER 3

W. B. Van Arsdel | Drying Phenomena

The *drying* of a liquid or fresh, wet, food substance, the operation which distinguishes *dehydration* from other processes for preserving perishable foods, is only one step in the integrated series of operations required to make a satisfactory and acceptable dehydrated food product. Accompanying Fig. 3.1, for example, illustrates the diversity of the operations used in the manufacture of a dehydrated vegetable, a dried fruit, orange juice powder, freeze-dried chicken meat, and spray-dried whole egg powder.

The behavior of wet materials during drying is analyzed in some detail in this chapter. Chapter 4 gives some of the physical background for that important class of drying processes, air drying; Chap. 5 describes drying equipment; Chap. 6 concerns the special case of freeze drying; and Chap. 8 describes the operations employed in commercial food dehydration plants for handling, cleaning, cutting, blanching, and otherwise preparing the incoming raw material, and for finishing and packing the dry product.

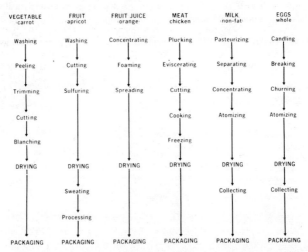

FIG. 3.1. PRINCIPAL OPERATIONS IN THE PRODUCTION OF TYPICAL DEHYDRATED FOODS

PHENOMENA OBSERVED IN DRYING

Evaporation from a Water Surface

Factors which determine the rate of evaporation from the surface of a body of water or a completely wet porous object like a wick have been very extensively studied (see especially Powell and Griffiths 1935; Slesser and Cleland 1962). They include the temperature of the water; the temperature, humidity, pressure, and velocity of the air; and, less importantly, the size and shape of the wet surface and the direction of the air movement with respect to it. The earliest stages of the drying of a wet food material are essentially identical with this evaporation from pure water.

Water Vapor Pressure

A basic property of every moist food substance, and one that is highly important to an understanding of the behavior of the substance upon drying, is its water vapor pressure. If a moist material is held at constant temperature in a small chamber from which the air has been withdrawn by a vacuum pump, and which is connected to a sensitive pressure gage, the gage will register only a small pressure at first, but as a little water evaporates from the material, the water vapor exerts a pressure which builds up to a definite limit. This limit is the equilibrium water vapor pressure of the material at that moisture content and temperature. The water is said to be "sorbed" in the material, and the measured relation between the vapor pressure and the moisture content constitutes a "sorption isotherm." Conversely, the relation shows the "equilibrium moisture content" of the substance at that temperature and water vapor pressure or relative humidity (Labuza 1968).

Moisture Sorption Isotherms of Representative Food Materials.–Extensive measurements of moisture sorption have been reported by Gane (1941, 1943, 1950), Bate-Smith *et al.* (1943), Makower and Dehority (1943), Benson and Richardson (1955), Karel *et al.* (1955), Görling (1954, 1956), Fish (1957), and Notter *et al.* (1959). Curves showing the relation between moisture content (dry basis) and percentage relative humidity for several food products at approximately room temperature are shown in Fig. 3.2, and a family of curves giving the relation for potatoes at temperatures from 20° to 100°C is shown in Fig. 3.3 (Görling 1958). Data for other commodities have been published for wheat by Gane (1941), egg by Makower (1945), garlic by Pruthi *et al.* (1959), egg albumin and gelatin by Benson and Richardson (1955), and carrot, cabbage, and a number of other vegetables, fruits, and miscellaneous products by Gane (1950).

The water content of most fresh foods is so high (generally within the range of 80–95%) that the water vapor pressure at equilibrium is substantially the same as that of pure water. As water is removed by concentrating or drying the product, the vapor pressure falls, at first only slightly, but then more and more steeply. This behavior is illustrated by Fig. 3.4, based on the data of Gane (1943). The scale of moisture content in this diagram reads from right to left in order to let the direction of change correspond with decreasing moisture content, as in drying.

Such diverse food uses as "snack foods," "pet foods," and some kinds of military ration items have recently created a quite large specialty market for

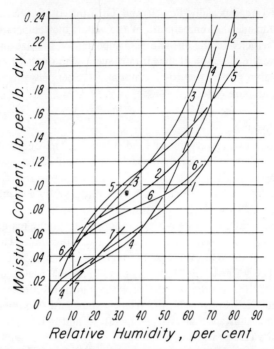

FIG. 3.2. SELECTED WATER SORPTION ISOTHERMS

1—Egg solids, 10°C (from Gane 1943). 2—Beef, 10°C (from Bate-Smith *et al.* 1943). 3—Fish (cod), 30°C (from Jason 1958). 4—Coffee, 10°C (from Gane 1950). 5—Starch gel, 25°C (from Fish 1958). 6—Potato, 28°C (from Gane 1950). 7—Orange juice (from Notter *et al.* 1959).

items of an "intermediate moisture content" (see Chap. 20, Vol. 2). The phrase denotes the class of products which have a relatively low water vapor pressure even at quite high moisture content. Such products can often be held in storage at a desirable soft consistency but without danger of spoilage, even in the absence of refrigeration. Dried fruits, with moisture contents in the range of 18-22% are well-known examples of the class.

Hysteresis in Moisture Sorption.—The phenomenon of hysteresis—that is, the sorption of different amounts of a substance such as water according to whether equilibrium is approached from above or from below—is only imperfectly understood, although it has been extensively studied (Seehof *et al.* 1953). For example, bovine serum albumin, a well-characterized soluble protein, reaches an equilibrium moisture content of about 10% in air of 34% RH at 25°C if it is being dried down from a higher moisture content; but if it is originally drier and is taking up (*ad*sorbing) moisture from air of 34% RH, and at 25°C, the moisture content will rise only to a value of 7%. These 2 distinct equilibrium values, 10

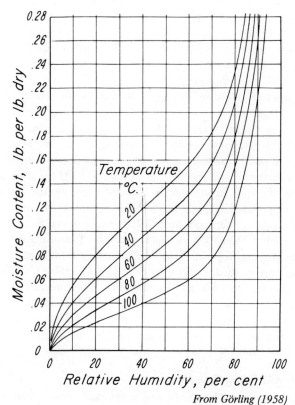

Relative Humidity, per cent

From Görling (1958)

FIG. 3.3. WATER SORPTION ISOTHERMS, POTATO

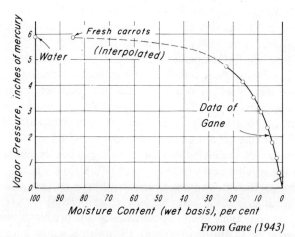

Moisture Content (wet basis), per cent

From Gane (1943)

FIG. 3.4. WATER VAPOR PRESSURE OF CARROT AT 140°F
AS A FUNCTION OF MOISTURE CONTENT

and 7%, can be reproduced again and again if the sample is alternately moistened and redried. Ordinarily, of course, we are concerned only with _desorption_, or drying, which is always the higher of the two equilibrium values. In the preceding paragraphs, unless otherwise specified, we are either dealing with desorption, or the extent of hysteresis is negligible.

The Definition of "Moisture Content."—In view of the complex relationships discussed in the last several paragraphs it is apparent that the term "moisture content" must be defined operationally—i.e., in terms of the exact procedure used physically to determine the quantity. In the absence of a precise definition the meaning is seriously ambiguous. Worse yet, a number of different moisture determination methods are being used, both routinely and for research purposes, and reports of the work frequently fail to identify the method used. Significant differences are possible, especially in the low-moisture region which is especially important for food dehydration. Stitt (1958) has reviewed this entire question and made a critical evaluation of eight methods. The one generally used by workers in the Western Regional Research Laboratory for referee determinations is the vacuum oven method of Makower *et al.* (1946), calling for 40 hr of drying at 70°C for potatoes and carrots, 30 hr at 60°C for cabbage and onions. This method gives a moisture content in dehydrated potatoes about 2% higher than the 6-hr vacuum oven method described in many purchase specifications—e.g., 8% moisture in a sample of potatoes reported by the 6-hr method to contain only 6%.

Constant-Rate and Falling-Rate Phases

Many porous structural materials and some food commodities behave for a considerable time after the beginning of drying as though their surfaces were remaining completely wet. The rate of evaporation from unit surface of the body is then substantially the same as from pure water, and hence can be estimated with a fair degree of accuracy from the air temperature, humidity, and velocity, regardless of the kind of commodity being dried.

In preliminary drying computations, designers often make use of the following facts: (1) convective heat transfer coefficients have been so extensively studied that reasonable values can often be taken from engineering handbooks; and (2) by a happy coincidence, the mass transfer coefficient for evaporation of water into air is approximately equal to the heat transfer coefficient divided by the humid heat of the air. Since under most practical food drying conditions the absolute humidity of the drying air is low, the humid heat is usually only a little higher than the specific heat of the air, 0.24 (Btu)/(lb) (°F), and therefore the mass transfer coefficient, expressed, say, in (lb)/(sq ft) (hr), will be approximately 4 times as large as the heat transfer coefficient (Btu)/(sq ft) (hr) (°F). For example, under conditions of air exposure that would produce a film coefficient for heat transfer of 4 (Btu)/(sq ft) (hr) (°F), which is within a readily achieved range, a rough estimate of the initial rate of water evaporation from a completely wetted object would be given as 16 (lb)/(sq ft)(hr). After a short initial warm-up period, this phase, in which the behavior is that of a completely wet body, is characterized by a steady, unchanging rate of evaporation per square foot of exposed wet surface; hence this is known as the "constant-rate" phase of drying. Sometimes two different, but usually both brief, constant-rate periods are observed, but there is no readily applied way of estimating what the magnitude of the second one will be.

Sooner or later, if drying conditions remain unchanged, the rate of evaporation per unit of exposed surface begins to decrease. This denotes the beginning of the "falling-rate" phase of drying, which continues until all water has been evaporated, at progressively lower rates. The mean moisture content of the body at the time when constant-rate drying ends has sometimes been called the "critical" moisture content for that substance.

The progress of drying is usually observed by frequent weighing of a sample of the material. True drying rate takes into account the shrinkage of exposed surface which usually accompanies drying, but a "gross drying rate" which is simply the rate of loss of weight per unit time is often the only directly observed quantity. The area shrinkage in food materials is usually great enough to cause the gross drying rate to begin to decrease immediately after drying begins, and many materials exhibit no constant-rate phase at all, even when shrinkage is allowed for.

Falling-Rate Phase in Hygroscopic Materials.—Food substances are all "hygroscopic"—that is, when they have come to equilibrium with the surrounding air they contain adsorbed moisture to an extent depending on the temperature, pressure, and humidity of the air. Under drying conditions, water evaporates from such a body at a rate which, in the falling-rate phase, becomes smaller and smaller as the mean moisture content diminishes; that is, the drying rate falls toward zero as the moisture remaining in the body approaches vapor pressure equilibrium with the air surrounding it.

As the drying of a hygroscopic substance progresses under constant drying conditions, the drying rate continues to decrease, but its course may be marked by one or more distinct breaks, or changes of slope in a curve relating drying rate to time or remaining mean moisture content. For example, Görling (1958) shows the drying rate measured in a single slice of potato exposed, on one side only, to an air stream at a temperature of 140°F (Fig. 3.5). The gross drying rate, measured by the loss in weight of the slice, is corrected approximately to true drying rate by use of the change in thickness.

Such abrupt changes of drying rate undoubtedly signal transitions from one type of physical mechanism to another in the internal movement of water through the potato flesh. In practical drying operations these sharp breaks in the rate of drying are usually smoothed out because inequalities of exposure cause

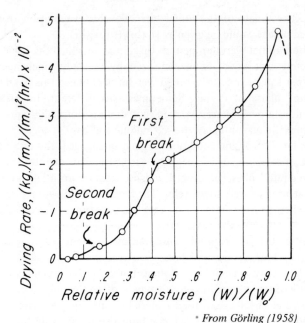

* From Görling (1958)

FIG. 3.5. DRYING RATE OF SINGLE POTATO SLICE

overlapping of different degrees of drying at any one time. For example, see Fig. 3.6.

The Cooling Effect of Evaporation

Approximately 1000 Btu of heat is absorbed when 1 lb of water is evaporated. The resulting strong cooling effect is a major factor in our ability to dry delicate food substances in high-temperature air without scorching the food. While the material is still very wet its temperature will remain lower than that of the air flowing past it, because of this cooling effect, but as the surface of the material becomes partly dry the cooling effect decreases and hence the material temperature rises closer to the air temperature.

Wet-Bulb Temperature.—The temperature indicated by a thermometer in this air stream, with its sensitive bulb kept wet by a thin wick dipping into a water reservoir, is lower than the air temperature because of the cooling effect of evaporation. Under specified conditions, particularly of air velocity around the wet bulb (at least 600 ft per min), and shielding from sources of high-temperature radiation, this is known as the "wet-bulb temperature" of that air. Measurement of the difference between it and the "dry-bulb temperature" of the air (the meaning of this is self-apparent), known as the "wet-bulb depression," is a most important method for determining the moisture content, or humidity, of the air. A related, but not identical quantity, the "thermodynamic

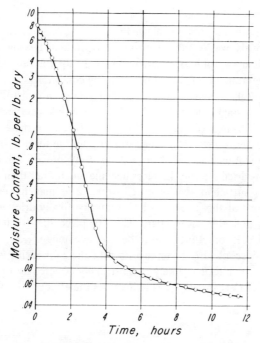

FIG. 3.6. MOISTURE CONTENT AS A FUNCTION OF TIME IN
EXPERIMENTAL DRYING OF CARROT DICE

wet-bulb temperature" (see Chap. 4), occupies a vital position in psychrometric
theory and practice.

CHANGES IN TISSUE DURING DRYING

Shrinkage Effects

A portion of cellular animal or vegetable tissue in its living state exhibits the
property of "turgor," meaning that each cell is distended by its liquid contents
and consequently has taken on a structural stiffness like an inflated toy balloon.
Cell walls are under tension, cell contents under compression. The cell wall
structure possesses strength and elasticity, but, if the unit tensile stress is increased beyond a quite modest value, the structure yields, in part irreversibly.
Upon removal of the stress, the stretched material does not retract all the way to
its original no-load dimensions.

This kind of plastic deformation takes place to some extent in any kind of
drying of animal or vegetable tissue, except perhaps in freeze drying, where the
original dimensions of the quickly frozen tissue are substantially unchanged.

If the cellular tissue is killed, as by blanching or scalding, cell walls may
become more easily permeable, some or much of the turgor may disappear, and
the permanent deformation upon drying may become even greater. The volume

shrinkage may be accompanied by various kinds of damage such as cracking or crushing of the tissue. Unequal shrinkage in different parts of a single piece often produces grotesquely warped and distorted dry product. Drying such a product as macaroni without warping or internal cracking calls for careful adherence to an empirically determined safe schedule of drying conditions.

Effects upon Bulk Density.—The large differences in moisture content that may exist within a single piece of material create shrinkage effects that depend upon the rate of drying. If a piece of a highly shrinking material is dried so slowly that its center is never very much wetter than the surface, internal stresses are minimized and the material shrinks down fully onto a solid core. On the other hand, if it is dried rapidly the faces become much drier than the center and are placed under sufficient tension to give them a permanent set in nearly the original dimensions of the piece; when the interior finally dries and shrinks, the internal stresses pull the tissue apart. The dry piece then contains numerous cracks and holes. It is sometimes said to be "honeycombed."

One consequence of this difference is that the bulk density (measured in pounds per *gross* cubic foot) is likely to be strongly affected by the conditions of drying. Figure 3.7 (Van Arsdel 1951) illustrates the effect with two beakers side

From Van Arsdel (1951)

FIG. 3.7. RELATIVE BULK OF RAPIDLY DRIED AND SLOWLY DRIED POTATO DICE

by side, each containing 250 gm of dehydrated ³⁄₈-in. potato dice. Those on the left had been dried in experiments conducted at the Western Regional Research Laboratory by P. W. Kilpatrick, with air at 150°F and wet-bulb temperature of 85°F; in 3¾ hr the moisture content had been reduced to 0.11 lb per lb dry. The dice in the right-hand picture had been very slowly dried in nearly saturated air to the same final moisture content, total time 15 hr. The bulk density of the latter is almost twice as great as that of the former.

Browning, or "Heat Damage"

The most obvious, and, in some respects, the most troublesome of the irreversible changes that may accompany the drying of a food substance is the color change variously called "browning," "scorching," "burning," or simple "heat damage." As some of these names suggest, it is commonly associated with overheating. Familiar in daily life in the cooking of all kinds of food, it is sometimes highly desired—for example, in the flavorful brown crust formed on a loaf of bread during baking—but in food dehydration it is generally a most serious quality defect. If the degree of browning is not great, the change in color may be the only noticeable effect, but when the change proceeds further the flavor, the rehydration capacity, and the ascorbic acid content may also be adversely affected.

The several kinds of chemical reaction which cause browning have been the subject of extensive research. A frequent cause of trouble is the Maillard group of reactions, in which one or more carbonyl groups (for example, in some of the sugars) reacts with amino groups, as in amino acids or proteins. A complex chain of reactions leads to pink or reddish colorations, and eventually to insoluble brown polymers.

The rate at which browning occurs is increased markedly by a rise in temperature, the temperature quotient of this group of reactions being so high that scorching may seem to occur quite sharply when the substance reaches a certain critical temperature. The damage actually is always the combined effect of temperature and time; a sensitive material may withstand a temperature of 200°F, or even higher, for a few seconds without apparent damage, but be noticeably browned by exposure to 120°F air for 8-10 hr.

The rate of browning also depends on the moisture content of the material. The reactions which give rise to dark products proceed only slowly in the complex but dilute solutions constituting the liquid part of fresh foods. As these solutions are concentrated in the course of drying the reactions go more rapidly. Water itself appears to be necessary for the reactions, however; consequently the rate of browning reaches a maximum at some intermediate moisture content during drying, often in the range of about 15-20% moisture. As complete dryness is approached browning becomes slower and slower; at moisture contents in the range of 1-2% most dehydrated foods are stable for a long time, even at elevated storage temperatures. Other types of quality deterioration (such as oxidative rancidity) then become the limiting factor in practical storage life.

As will be more fully discussed in Chap. 7, the rate of drying of a wet substance can be increased by raising its temperature. But as we have just seen, the rate of browning is strongly dependent on temperature. We might therefore say that a practical drying operation always involves arranging matters so that the drying operation is expedited as much as possible, particularly in order to reduce costs, without causing more than a tolerable degree of browning. In the present state of our knowledge, the only way to arrive at that kind of successful compromise is to carry on a careful empirical study of the process.

Use of Sulfur Dioxide to Retard Browning.—The practice of exposing cut fruits to the fumes of burning sulfur before drying them has been followed since time immemorial; it had been discovered that the "sulfured" fruit could be dried without darkening or loss of its attractive color. Use of a solution of a sulfite (sodium sulfite or metabisulfite) on cut vegetables before drying became standard practice in the British Commonwealth countries and the United States during World War II.

Specifications of United States procurement agencies (military or federal specifications) now call for a range of 350-550 ppm of SO_2 in sliced potatoes, 200-550 ppm in diced potatoes, 200-400 ppm in potato granules or flakes, 25-125 ppm in sweet potato flakes, 200-700 ppm in diced carrots, and 1000-2000 ppm in shredded cabbage. A U.S. Standard for grapefruit juice powder or orange juice powder calls for "not more than 250 ppm of SO_2."

In addition to greatly improved storage stability, the presence of this small amount of sulfite in a blanched, cut vegetable makes it possible to increase the drying temperature, thus shortening the drying time and correspondingly increasing the drier capacity, without exceeding a tolerable small degree of heat damage. For example, operators of tunnel driers producing potato dice believe the finishing temperature in the tunnels can safely be from 5° to 10°F higher in the presence of an allowable level of SO_2 than in its absence.

When a drier is heated directly by the products of combustion of gas or oil, as is very common practice, some "sulfuring" of the product occurs during drying if the fuel contains more than a mere trace of sulfur. In order to avoid exceeding the specification limit of SO_2 content in the dry product, it may sometimes be necessary to restrict purchases of fuel oil for direct heating to sources of supply known to be low in sulfur.

Migration of Soluble Constituents

Water is not the only substance which changes its location within a body as drying occurs. The water in living tissue exists as a solution of scores or hundreds of constituents, some of which are small molecules like simple sugars, while others are very large and highly hydrated structures. During drying, some of the dissolved substances migrate, and change their locations.

When a piece of tissue is dried in a warm air stream, shrinkage in the surface layers puts the deeper layers under compression. This may bring about an outward mass flow of the liquid component of the tissue through pores, cracks, and capillaries. In addition, when moisture content begins to fall at all depths within a piece, obviously moisture must be moving toward the surfaces of the piece. Depending upon the proportion of this outward flow that takes place as liquid, rather than as water vapor, and upon the ability of the tissue cell walls to pass or hold back the dissolved substances, more or less of the latter accompany the liquid toward the outside of the piece. As the solution nears the surface, pure water evaporates from it, leaving behind an increasingly concentrated solution in the outer layers. In the completely dry product, a gradation of percentage of soluble material should be apparent in each piece, the highest concentration being at the surface.

At the same time, a different mechanism will be working in exactly the opposite direction. When surface evaporation raises the concentration of sugars or other solutes in the surface layers, a continuous diffusion of at least the smaller molecules must begin at once toward the deeper layers where the liquid remains more dilute. This displacement will continue only as long as an appreciable amount of liquid remains in the pieces. It will result in an accumulation of solutes near the centers of the pieces.

Both of these physical activities are undoubtedly going on simultaneously in actual systems, but in any particular case we would expect one mechanism or the other to predominate, according to conditions. Decided differences in the properties and quality of the dry product can be made to appear by suitable manipulations of these conditions.

"Case Hardening"

Migration of solutes to the surface of drying pieces may be responsible for an operational difficulty, sometimes very troublesome, known by the picturesque term "case hardening." The same term is often used to denote the condition responsible for the warping and internal checking of green lumber or macaroni during drying, due to improper temperature or humidity control.

Operators of fruit dehydrators, as well as experimenters who had worked on the drying of soap, meat, fish, leather, and other colloidal materials, sometimes found that a drying run would begin normally but then after a time come almost to a standstill, piece surfaces being apparently dry, but piece centers still very wet. Sometimes the formation of a gummy, glassy, or leathery surface layer, substantially impermeable to water, was observed.

In the text above it has been indicated that, under some conditions, the outward migration of solutes may lead to the formation of such resistant surface layers. Although the conditions which lead to serious trouble on this account have not been conclusively defined, as a general rule satisfactory results are obtained by controlling the drying conditions so that material temperature will be relatively high (for example, 120°-130°F) in the early stages of drying, and thus accelerate internal diffusion and redistribution of moisture, but the wet-bulb depression will be relatively small at first (perhaps no more than 20° or 30°F), so that too steep a moisture gradient will not be created just below the surface of the material.

On the other hand, in the dehydration of cut vegetables or apple slices, the phenomenon for which "case hardening" would be an appropriate name apparently does not occur (except, possibly, in moist-type sweet potato pieces). Consequently, instead of controlling drying conditions so as to reduce the initial rate of drying, dehydrator operators purposely use drastic drying conditions (high air temperature, low humidity, high air velocity) from the very beginning. This ordinarily leads to the formation of internal shrinkage cracks, and this "honey-combing" in turn greatly facilitates the late stages of drying. The rule seems to be that we must carry out the early stages of drying as quickly as possible in order to assure a reasonably good drying rate in the final stages.

It is well known that the diffusivity of water in typical food substances is not constant but is strongly dependent on the water concentration; the diffusivity in the range of 5-10% moisture may not be more than one-hundredth as great as it is at 25-30% moisture. The inference has sometimes been drawn that therefore, a nearly dry outside layer on a piece of material must act like a nearly imper-meable skin, preventing further drying, and hence that the formation of such a dry layer must be prevented at all costs. Much theoretical discussion of this point has been published. The conclusion is that *unless there is an irreversible change within the body*, such as would be produced by a chemical reaction or by migration and precipitation of a constituent, the most rapid drying of a piece of material will be accomplished if the best possible drying conditions are main-tained at all times. Purposely circulating very humid air at any stage of the drying would therefore be a mistake; any humidity added to the air would slow the drying, not accelerate it, both immediately and in the long run.

The conflict between this view, and the one frequently held that rapid initial drying is harmful, undoubtedly arises from the widely different structural make-up and composition of the various products that are dried, and particularly their differing behavior with respect to migration of solutes to the surface of a drying piece and tendency to form a glassy or leathery impermeable surface skin there. In the author's opinion, the term "case hardening" should be reserved for in-stances of the latter kind, and not be applied generally to every case of persistent "wet centers." In most cut vegetables, a high gradient of moisture content between surface and center of a piece, which is precisely what is meant by a "wet center," is the very condition that assures the fastest possible drying. It is a desired condition, not a misfortune.

Irreversible Loss of Ability to Rehydrate

The rehydration of a dehydrated food product is too often taken for granted; not infrequently it turns out to be difficult or even quite unsatisfactory. One of the reasons why freeze drying is currently such an important development is that freeze-dried products rehydrate quickly and assume something close to their original moisture content and physical properties.

The process of rehydration after drying can never be a simple reversal of the drying mechanism. Not only were some of the changes produced by drying irreversible, but also the swelling of outside layers occurring as water is reab-sorbed puts severe stresses on the softened outer layers; previously crushed and crumpled structures are unable to come back to their original configurations; and solutes in the tissue leach out into the rehydration water instead of remaining in the tissue and contributing to a recovery of turgor.

A number of studies have shown that irreversible changes of the colloidal constituents of both animal and vegetable tissue do, in fact, occur if the material is held for a period of time at high temperature, even if the exposure is insufficient to produce browning or scorching. The elasticity of cell walls and the swelling power of starch gel, both important for good rehydration, are reduced by heat treatment. Dried meat, which will absorb only a fraction of the water it originally contained, has obviously been damaged by drying; however, even complete regain of original weight does not necessarily mean that the meat has recovered its original structure. The rehydrated product is generally reported to be less juicy, more crumbly, than the original meat.

Loss of Volatile Constituents

When water is vaporized from a food product, the water vapor leaving the drier invariably carries with it at least traces of every other volatile constituent of the fresh food. Ordinarily, the consequence is an unwanted, disadvantageous, and irreversible loss of characteristic flavor. Practically no research specifically directed to a lessening of this loss of volatile flavors has been reported. (But see Menting *et al.* 1970.) There has been some experimentation with the use of activated carbon or other adsorbent to recapture volatile substances carried by the air discharged from a dehydrator, with a view either to returning the recovered substance in order to improve the character of the dry product, or to disposing of it acceptably if it is obnoxious, as it is in the case of onion or garlic dehydration. No such process is presently being used.

The composition of the vapor from such complex systems as we are dealing with here depends on the changing temperature of the material and the vapor pressures of the various volatile constituents at these temperatures; but it also is greatly influenced by the mutual solubilities of the components in water and in one another. Prediction of vapor composition from known values of the individual vapor pressures is not possible. One cannot even say *a priori* that lowering the temperature of evaporation (for example, in the limit, freeze drying) will necessarily result in less loss of desirable aroma constituents per pound of water evaporated than vaporizing the moisture in a few seconds at a high temperature in a spray drier. In the present state of our knowledge, only experiments under the conditions in question can determine which procedure actually gives the better results.

Changes in Moisture Distribution Within the Body

Evaporation of surface moisture from a body starts a process of water transfer from all points within the body to points nearer its surface. The result of the redistribution of moisture is illustrated by Fig. 3.8. (adapted from Ede and Hales

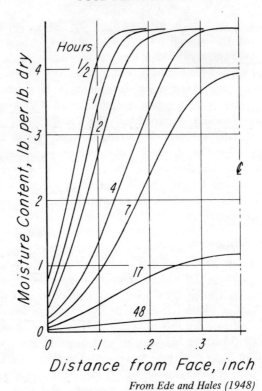

From Ede and Hales (1948)

FIG. 3.8. MOISTURE DISTRIBUTION WITHIN POTATO SLICE
DRIED FROM BOTH FACES

1948), which shows moisture content at different distances from the drying face
of a thick slice of potato after various lengths of drying time from ½ to 48 hr.
Moisture content remains highest at the center of the slice, lowest at its surface.

THEORIES OF MOISTURE TRANSFER

The mechanism of drying has been the subject of scientific study for more
than 100 yr, but is still not thoroughly understood. The external factors related
to it, such as air temperature, pressure, humidity, and velocity, are governed by
relatively simple and well-known laws, but not so the internal transfer of moisture. The following brief description of a typical sequence of physical events as
a piece of vegetable or animal tissue is dried can do no more than suggest how the
leading theories are tied to the observed phenomena.

(1) As water evaporates from the wet surface the diameter of superficial
water-filled pores and capillaries diminishes, solid structural elements pull closer
together under the influence of surface tension, and the effect spreads into
deeper layers of tissue and eventually all the way to the center. Volume shrink-

age is substantially equal to the volume of water evaporated, and the drying rate per unit of surface remains constant.

(2) Structural elements of the body begin to deform by crumpling or folding so as to occupy less space as additional water is removed by evaporation at the surface, but increasing resistance to the deformation is encountered and the water meniscus in capillaries begins to recede into the body. Water vapor also moves to the surface by molecular diffusion through the air in the open capillaries.

(3) The thick layers of water which wedge apart long flexible molecular chains in the wet solid begin to release the most loosely held water molecules into a diffusional flow of water in the direction of lower water concentration—that is, toward the surface—and the progressive thinning of the thick water layers continues until the remaining water, averaging only about one molecule deep, is left adsorbed on the internal surface, not uniformly, but preferentially at the more highly polar groupings in the underlying solid structure. The structural elements, therefore, continue to be drawn closer together, and more volume shrinkage takes place, although by a smaller amount than the volume of water lost.

(4) In the final phase, water molecules adsorbed on the internal surface of solid constituents move by a process of activated diffusion along the solid fibrils or lamellae in the direction of lower surface spreading potential, equivalent to lower vapor pressure. In this process a water molecule which by chance receives a larger than average impetus in its continuous thermal vibration may jump from its adsorption site to a nearby vacant site. Even though these jumps are undirected and random, on the average there will be more vacant sites available in the direction of lower water vapor pressure, so there will be net movement of water in that direction, but more and more slowly as equilibrium with the surrounding humid air is approached.

The physical processes that go on during freeze drying are quite different from those just pictured. They are described in Chap. 6.

Modes of Water Movement

Quantitative descriptions of the phenomena of drying have historically emphasized either one or the other of two quite distinct physical mechanisms as taking part in the mass transfer of water, namely molecular diffusion and capillary flow—that is, flow under the influence of surface forces. The former, as first developed especially by Sherwood and his associates (1929–1936, see below) at the Massachusetts Institute of Technology, assumed that diffusion laws can account completely for the observed phenomena of drying. Fisher (1923, 1935), however, found that account must be taken of surface forces in the drying of fibrous or granular materials; and Lykow (1933) pointed out major disagreements with observed behavior of several materials. Ceaglske and Hougen (1937) vigorously attacked the diffusional analysis as leading to an entirely erroneous idea of the moisture distribution in a body during drying; they based a theory upon the capillary behavior alone. Later writers have tended to accept parts of both mechanisms, but to emphasize one or the other according to whether the materials of principal interest to them are definitely granular like wet sand or clay (Krischer 1938A, B), fibrous like wood (Bateman *et al.* 1939), or more or less structureless wet gels. Lykow (1948, 1950) and numerous other investigators picture practical drying operations as nearly always involving a progression from an initial phase, in which water moves within the wet body readily under the control mainly of surface forces in pores and capillaries, to a final stage in which tightly bound hygroscopic moisture must diffuse through nearly dry solid.

Görling (1958) pictures five distinct physical mechanisms as being involved to some extent in the drying of such materials as potato, wood, or macaroni: (1) liquid movement under capillary forces; (2) diffusion of liquid caused by a difference in concentration; (3) surface diffusion in liquid layers adsorbed at solid interfaces; (4) water vapor diffusion in air-filled pores, caused by a difference in partial pressures; and (5) water vapor flow under differences in total pressure, as for example in vacuum drying under radiation. Marshall and Friedman (1950) recognize the first two of these, and add the following three: (6) flow caused by shrinkage and pressure gradients; (7) flow caused by gravity; and (8) flow caused by a vaporization-condensation sequence. The latter is, of course, related to Görling's number (4); flow would certainly occur, for example, if a temperature gradient existed in the moist body. Lykow (1935) described experiments on thermal diffusion of moisture in colloidal clays, that is, a molecular motion of water in the direction of a temperature gradient, analogous to thermal diffusion in a gas or solution. In his development of drying theory he finds this mechanism is especially significant in determining the extent of transport of soluble materials along with the moisture in a body, as in the drying of dyed sheet leather.

Jason (1958) concluded that the most likely mechanism for molecular diffusion of water through a continuous gel is a surface migration of the higher-energy molecules along molecular fibrils of protein. The computed activation energy, about 9000 calories per mole, is not far from that found by Fish (1957, 1958), for diffusion of water in starch gel.

To the early investigators of drying as a "unit operation" the well-developed theory of heat conduction seemed to offer a straightforward approach to practical design procedures through application of the obvious analogy between the diffusion of heat and the diffusion of moisture. A moist body suspended in an air stream gradually approaches moisture equilibrium with that air in a way that seems entirely analogous to the gradual temperature equilibration of a warm body suspended in a cool air stream. Analytical solutions for the differential equations describing temperature distribution within such a body at any subsequent time were already available—provided the thermal properties of the material were independent of temperature. Lewis (1921, 1922), Sherwood (1929, 1930, 1931, 1932, 1936), Sherwood and Comings (1932, 1933), Gilliland and Sherwood (1933), Comings and Sherwood (1934), Newman (1931), and McCready and

McCabe (1933) developed many consequences of a drying theory based on this analogy. No particular effort was made to scrutinize the intimate physical mechanisms of moisture transfer; moisture movement within the wet body was assumed to take place at a rate proportional to the moisture concentration gradient at any point, just as internal heat flow is proportional to the temperature gradient:

$$G = -D \frac{dC}{dl} \tag{3.1}$$

where

G = mass-velocity of water diffusing (lb)/(hr)(sq ft)
D = diffusivity of water in this material (sq ft)/(hr)
C = instantaneous water concentration at any point within the material (lb)/cu ft)
l = distance measured in the direction of the diffusion movement (ft)
dC/dl = concentration gradient (lb)/(cu ft)(ft)

The minus sign signifies that water moves in the direction of decreasing concentration of water—i.e., from a wetter toward a drier place.

In terms of moisture content rather than concentration,

$$G = D\rho_d \frac{dW}{dl} \tag{3.2}$$

where

ρ_d = density of the moisture-free material (lb)/(cu ft)
W = moisture content (lb)/(lb dry)

Tests of this concept with a variety of materials were only moderately successful, for reasons that will be discussed later. Perhaps the closest approach to confirmation was the work of Jason (1958), which will be described at some length in connection with the phenomena observed in the drying of an isolated piece of wet colloidal material (fish muscle).

Saravacos and Charm (1962) have recently reported experiments on the air drying of potato dice or slices which also appear to be consistent with the molecular diffusion mechanism.

The food materials with which we are dealing in this work are almost without exception hygroscopic and colloidal, and many of them dry to gel-like or glassy solids of poorly defined geometrical shape, frequently "honeycombed," and both coarsely and finely porous. The actual physical systems are so complex as to defy accurate description; and yet, surprisingly enough, investigators have been able to devise comparatively simple mathematical models which simulate observed moisture transfer rates and moisture distributions reasonably well.

Movement of Liquid Water Under Surface Forces.—*The Capillary Flow Mechanism.*—The flow and distribution of water in granular solids were first investigated by Slichter (1898), Buckingham (1907), Gardner (1919), Haines (1927), and other soil scientists in studies of the flow of ground waters. The physical unbalance of forces at an interface between a liquid and a gas or vapor produces the effect of a suction on the liquid, familiar in the rise of a liquid in a capillary tube or wick dipping beneath its surface. If a single such capillary be pictured, as in Fig. 3.9, the maximum capillary rise is determined by Equation 3.3:

$$h = \frac{2\sigma\cos\varpi}{rg\rho} \tag{3.3}$$

where

> h = rise (ft)
> σ = surface tension (lb)/(sec^2)
> ϖ = wettability of the solid; cos ϖ is substantially unity for hydrophilic solids in water
> r = radius of the capillary (ft)
> g = acceleration of gravity (ft)/(sec^2)
> ρ = density of the liquid (lb)/(cu ft)

The maximum rise, it will be seen, varies inversely as the radius of the capillary. At a radius of 0.01 μ (= 10^{-6} cm) the maximum suction would be almost a mile of water, corresponding to a negative pressure of more than a ton per square inch. Capillary pores of this order of size exist in silica gel and doubtless in many solid organic gels as well.

If instead of an open capillary tube a tube full of sand be held with the bottom end dipping below the surface of a container of water, the water will rise through the sand and come to an equilibrium level above the level in the container. Just as in the capillary, surface forces in the curved spaces between sand grains exert a suction on the water; very fine, closely packed grains can exert a

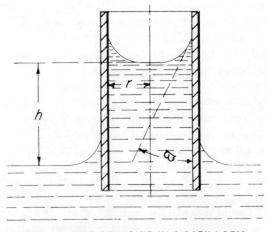

FIG. 3.9. RISE OF LIQUID IN A CAPILLARY

high suction. Equation (3.3) can represent this situation as well as that of a single capillary tube, even if the granular material is a mixture of a wide range of different sizes and shapes of particles; the factor then represents an equivalent mean radius of the open pore spaces. Lykow (1948) gives data, abstracted in Table 3.1, on pore sizes in certain porous materials.

TABLE 3.1

POROSITY OF SELECTED MATERIALS

Material	Volume of Voids per Unit Total Volume (Cm^3/Cm^3)	Proportion of Pores with Radius Less Than 10^{-6} Cm (%)
Birch charcoal	0.936	70.0
Activated carbon	0.870	98.6
Porcelain	0.031	10.9

The simplest model to illustrate this mechanism in action during drying would consist of a flat layer of glass beads in a horizontal pan, with water filling the interstices between beads, and a current of air flowing across the surface of the layer. As water is evaporated there, the "water table" within the layer of beads must fall, air being drawn in between surface beads, leaving wet surfaces but no continuous column of water capable of maintaining a suction.

In most wet granular food materials, soft and easily deformed when wet, the picture would not be so simple. Water keeps the wet body distended, but its interior is under compression because of the surface forces. When any water is removed at the surface of a flat layer of such a substance, these forces draw the weak solid constituents into closer packing, by folding and crumpling them so that they occupy less volume; that is, the layer shrinks. Water at all levels within the layer moves through the gradually narrowing channels between solid structures at velocities dependent on the forces producing the flow and the viscous resistance to this motion; the latter, in turn, is a function of the effective radius of the open channels and the viscosity of the liquid. So long as the shrinkage can occur with little opposition, all the pores and interstices will remain completely full of water. When the solid structure begins to resist further distortion strongly, water in the surface layer of material will begin to be drawn down into the interstices, exerting stronger and stronger suction as the curvature of the liquid surfaces becomes sharper. Eventually air will be drawn all the way to the bottom of the layer, and capillary suction can then no longer be a force producing flow of the remaining water.

Krischer (1938B, 1940, 1942, 1956) regards the early, or high-moisture, stages of drying as being controlled by capillary-flow relationships. He uses the following expression for correlating experimental data on transfer of moisture across unit cross-section area within the body during the stage of pure capillary-flow mechanism:

$$G = -k_w \, \rho_d \, \frac{dW}{dl} \tag{3.4}$$

where

G = mass-velocity of water being transferred (lb)/(hr) (sq ft)
k_w = "moisture conductivity" (sq ft)/(hr)
ρ_d = density of the moisture-free solid (lb dry)/(cu ft)
dW/dl = moisture gradient, 1/(ft)
W = moisture content (lb)/(lb dry)
l = distance perpendicular to the cross-section through which the flow is occurring (ft)

This Ohm's law type of expression, completely analogous to the simple diffusion law, Equation (3.2), simply states that rate of flow is proportional to a potential gradient, here identified as the change in moisture content of the wet body per unit of distance from the surface where evaporation is occurring. The conductivity factor, k_w, lumps together the effects of the distribution of pore diameters within the material and the surface tension and viscosity of the liquid. Experimentally, in any particular solid body, k_w is always found to be strongly dependent on the water content of the material. The relationship may be quite complex, but at high levels of moisture content the resistance to internal flow of water is low and the conductivity is correspondingly high. Görling (1956, 1958) found that moisture conductivity of potato varies with moisture content as shown in Fig. 3.10. While the value remains about constant in the middle range of moisture contents, it falls rapidly toward zero as moisture falls below about 0.3 lb/lb of dry matter.

Experimental studies of moisture conductivity have been made by determining the amount of water removed from various wet bodies by applying a graded series of pressures (Macey 1942), centrifuging (Krischer 1956), or drying under especially simple conditions (Görling 1956). As might be expected, even slight changes in the internal structure of a material, such as those accompanying shrinkage, can change the moisture conductivity by several orders of magnitude.

Diffusional Transfer of Water.—Whether or not the early phases of the drying of a wet body are considered to be governed by capillary flow phenomena, the late phases are indisputably governed by diffusional phenomena. These take place both within the solid fine structure of the moist body and within the capillaries, pores, and small voids, filled with vapor which diffuses outward until, at the open end of a capillary, it is carried away in the rapidly moving air stream. It will be convenient to discuss first the relatively simple case of vapor diffusion through open capillaries. In the view of McCready and McCabe (1933), Krischer (1938, 1942, 1956), Lykow (1948), and some other workers, this represents one of the two major flow mechanisms, capillary liquid movement being the other.

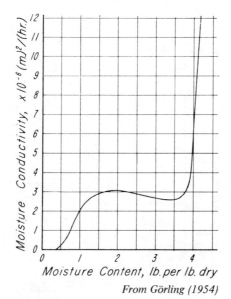

Moisture Content, lb. per lb. dry

From Görling (1954)

FIG. 3.10. MOISTURE CONDUCTIVITY AS A FUNCTION OF
MOISTURE CONTENT IN POTATO

Diffusion of Water Vapor Through Open Spaces. —Krischer (1938) pictures the air within open pores as remaining stationary while diffusing water molecules, which are being continuously supplied by evaporation of liquid water into the pores, make their way through that air from a region of higher water vapor pressure toward the nearest region of lower vapor pressure. The following equation describes the rate of movement:

$$G = -\frac{\mathrm{d}}{\phi} \cdot \frac{1}{R_w T} \cdot \frac{P}{P - p_v} \cdot \frac{dp_v}{dl} \tag{3.5}$$

where

G = mass-velocity of water being transferred (lb)/(hr)(sq ft)
ϕ = a "diffusion resistance factor," dimensionless
d = diffusivity of water vapor in air (sq ft)/(hr)
R_w = gas constant for water vapor, 0.0405 (atm)(cu ft)/(lb)(°R)
T = absolute temperature (°R)
P = atmospheric pressure (atm)
p_v = partial pressure of water vapor (atm)
l = distance perpendicular to the cross-section through which flow is occurring (ft)
dp_v/dl = vapor pressure gradient (atm)/(ft)

The diffusion resistance factor, ϕ, like the moisture conductivity through water-filled pores, k_w, is dependent not only on the geometrical fine structure of the solid material, but also, in hygroscopic materials, very strongly on the

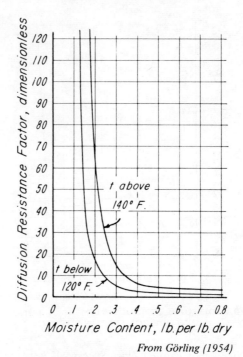

From Görling (1954)

FIG. 3.11. DIFFUSION RESISTANCE FACTOR AS A FUNCTION
OF MOISTURE CONTENT IN POTATO

moisture content. Görling's (1958) results on potatoes show an exceedingly steep increase in the diffusional resistance as moisture content falls below about 0.20 lb/lb dry matter (Fig. 3.11). This resistance also increases quite sharply from one level to another at a temperature of about 140°F. It is not clear from the publications whether Görling's experimental samples were always scalded, or blanched, before drying; if they were not, this change of resistance in the neighborhood of 140°F may have been due to the gelatinization of starch at about that temperature.

Krischer (1956) lists diffusion resistance factors determined by various workers for a large number of building materials, and also tabulates (see Table 3.2) this factor for certain food products, as measured by the Institut für Lebensmitteltechnologie und Verpackung, Munich. The practical usefulness of these figures seems doubtful if, as is likely, the true values of the factor are radically dependent on moisture content of the materials, as Görling's curve shows potato flesh is.

Equations (3.4) and (3.5) can be combined to give the total moisture transfer by both of the major mechanisms (Krischer 1938, 1956):

$$G = -k_w \rho_d \frac{\delta W}{\delta l} - \frac{\mathbf{d}}{\phi} \cdot \frac{1}{R_w T} \cdot \frac{P}{P - p_v} \cdot \left(\frac{\delta p_v}{\delta W} \cdot \frac{\delta W}{\delta l} \right) \qquad (3.6)$$

TABLE 3.2

DIFFUSION RESISTANCE FACTOR FOR CERTAIN
FOOD PRODUCTS

Substance	Density ρ, (Lb)/ (Cu Ft)	Porosity ψ [1]	Diffusion Resistance Factor, ϕ [1]
"Malt coffee"	27	0.725	1.6
"Alete" milk powder	38	0.61	2.5
"Alete" milk powder	53	0.454	3.0
Spray dried nonfat milk	50	0.482	3.3
Dried vegetables	9	0.907	1.7
Egg powder	20	0.80	2.6
Egg powder	21	0.79	2.4
Flour	30	0.69	3.7
Chocolate pudding powder	49	0.5	6.8
Pea sausage, compressed	66	0.322	15.2

Source: Krischer (1956).
[1] Dimensionless.

Diffusional Migration of Water Within the Body.—Marshall and Friedman (1950) regard diffusion of liquid water within the body as important only in single-phase solid systems in which the liquid and solid components are mutually soluble, such as soaps and glues, and to transfer of equilibrium moisture in wood, starch, textiles, and the like. All writers on drying theory have evidently had difficulty in dealing with the liquid diffusion concept in terms of mechanism. Krischer dispenses with it altogether. If such materials as soap, glue, or gelatinized potato flesh were actually homogeneous solid solutions of the components in one another, one might deal with molecular diffusion of the water component through the other component (or vice versa) with some degree of confidence; the conceptual model would seem simple. However, the supposed simplicity vanishes in the light of actual electron micrographs, which show the complex network or lamellar structure that exists in a soap gel, individual muscle fibers, plant cell walls, and the like.

Migration of water within the hypothetical "structureless" wet material can be described in terms of the diffusivity of water in that material and the gradient of water concentration or water content, as stated in Equations (3.1) and (3.2) above. Even in his earliest publications, however Sherwood (1929, 1930) noted that the data on drying of soap give a computed diffusion coefficient whose value must decrease markedly at low levels of moisture content; i.e., diffusivity is not constant. Unfortunately, if this were to turn out to be the case also for other important systems, much of the attractiveness of the simple diffusional model would disappear, because the ready-made analytical solutions of the differential equation, borrowed from heat-flow theory, would no longer be applicable. One line of attack on the difficulty which has met with some success has been to develop the mathematical methods, either analytical or numerical, for obtaining solutions of the differential equation with variable coefficients (Scarborough 1950; Milne 1953; Philip 1955, 1960A, B, 1961; Carslaw and Jaeger 1959). Crank (1956, 1958), in particular, has made extensive investigations of the mathematical procedures that can be used to derive drying rates from known values of the variable diffusivity, and conversely, to find the diffusivity and its moisture-dependence from measurements of drying rate.

Other Mechanisms of Water Movement.—At relatively low moisture contents (i.e., below about 10–15% moisture in many food materials) the water is all adsorbed on the immense internal surface of the high-molecular-weight solid. As will be discussed more fully below, although water molecules are strongly attracted to the solid surfaces, any molecule that by chance experiences an unusually strong thermal vibration may escape that captivity briefly, move at random in a short free path, and come to rest again at a different adsorption site. If there is a gradient of moisture concentration, the process will result in a gradual net transfer of water molecules downhill on this gradient. This is, in fact, the mechanism of "activated" diffusional movement of water within such a body. It has been thoroughly analyzed by Jason (1958). "Flow" seems hardly an appropriate term to describe what happens; even though the forces that determine flow of liquid or vapor through an open channel are still operative even on the molecular scale, they are far overbalanced by the adsorptive force. The essentially discontinuous activity in this model—individual molecules alternating between long periods of rest and short jumps to new positions—bears little resemblance to the usual picture of flow, and the terms "liquid" and "vapor" both become essentially meaningless. The rise in water vapor pressure of moist material as temperature is increased is largely a measure of the rise in number of water molecules possessing more than the threshold activation energy required to break free for a short jump to a new position.

Flow of moisture within a body due to a temperature gradient has already been mentioned. It has been studied especially by investigators of the translocation of moisture through building materials, where it may assume great importance. Lykow (1950) found that in capillary-porous bodies such as clay, moisture diffuses *with* the temperature gradient (i.e., moves from a high-temperature region toward a low-temperature region) at high moisture levels, but below a certain moisture level the movement is in the opposite direction. He attributes this to the greater effect of temperature gradient on the heavier molecules of air in the pores than on the lighter molecules of water vapor. The part played by thermal diffusion during the late stages of vacuum drying of a body heated on one side by radiation (so that a large temperature gradient exists in the body) seems not to have been determined.

Expression of Flow Potential in Concentration or Activity Terms.—As Sherwood and Comings (1932, 1933) had themselves pointed out, the rate of moisture movement through a solid body had not been shown experimentally to be proportional to the moisture gradient. That it actually could not be was deduced by Hougen *et al.* (1940) from the data of Kamei and Shiomi (1937) on the drying of soap, clay, and wood pulp. The distribution of moisture within a body under uniform drying conditions was far different from anything predicted by the diffusional theory as originally presented. Distribution of moisture in $3/4$-in. scalded slices of potato dried in a stream of air at $158°F$ was reported by Ede and Hales (1948) and gave an especially clear picture of the kind of results to be found experimentally (Fig. 3.12). The broken curve on the same figure is the

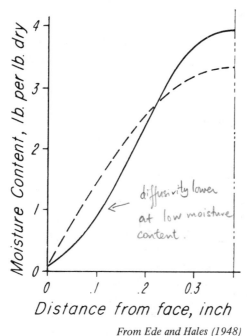

Distance from face, inch

From Ede and Hales (1948)

FIG. 3.12. DISTRIBUTION OF MOISTURE IN POTATO SLICE
DURING DRYING

theoretical distribution predicted by the classical diffusion theory, with diffusivity of moisture assumed constant; the total moisture content of the sample and moisture content at the face are the same for both of these curves.

One especially significant characteristic of the Ede and Hales data, as well as some of the other reported results, is the double curvature and inflection of the plotted moisture distribution curves. Hougen *et al.* (1940) showed that such doubly inflected curves always appeared if there was obviously a capillary flow mechanism; they presented illustrative data taken from experiments on the drying of sand. Indeed, Marshall and Friedman (1950) consider the occurrence of a doubly inflected moisture distribution curve as the infallible criterion for capillary flow mechanism. It was thought that the portion of such a curve that was concave upward must signify an absurd *negative* diffusivity. Van Arsdel (1947) showed, however, that the diffusional flow mechanism could lead to a doubly inflected distribution if diffusivity is markedly lower at low moisture contents than at high, and pointed out that distribution curves similar to those observed were exactly what would be expected if diffusion theory were stated in terms of vapor pressure gradient rather than moisture content or concentration gradient.

Babbitt (1940) had, in fact, reported the results of experiments with fiberboard in which an imposed temperature gradient through the board produced a vapor pressure gradient opposite to the moisture content gradient; water then moved from the warmer, but drier, face to the cooler but wetter face—in other words, *against* the concentration gradient. He concluded that at a moisture content lower than that corresponding to a relative humidity of 75% the vapor pressure gradient controls the rate of moisture movement. At higher levels of relative humidity and moisture content the rate of moisture transfer is no longer proportional to vapor pressure gradient, but is determined by the surface forces acting on liquid in capillaries and pores.

The concept of a pressure gradient as driving force for diffusion of moisture in solids has been much further developed during the intervening years, particularly in conjunction with better pictures of the adsorption phenomena which play the leading role in the relations between water and the hydrophilic polymers which constitute most of our foods. Brunauer *et al.* (1938) had published the now-classic "B-E-T" theory of adsorption of gases in multimolecular layers on solid surfaces. Babbitt (1950, 1951A, B) furnished a definitive description of the diffusional movement of adsorbed layers of a mobile substance like water in and and through a solid which can have a large internal surface. These internal surfaces are pictured as accessible to adsorbed water molecules, but not to mass flow of either liquid or air. The water molecules are in strongly damped thermal vibration. Occasional molecules have high enough energy to leap the potential barrier between adsorption sites and migrate to new sites. There is thus a net movement of water toward the low-pressure side of the solid. The adsorbed layer of water molecules has the thermodynamic properties of a two-dimensional gas under pressure; it exerts a spreading force which is related to the Gibbs free energy of the adsorbed film by the relation:

$$\Pi = - \frac{\delta g_{ads}}{\delta A} \qquad (3.7)$$

where

Π = spreading potential
g_{ads} = Gibbs free energy of spreading
A = area of the film

According to this picture, the space gradient of the spreading potential, $\delta\Pi/\delta l$, is the appropriate term to be equated to the rate of transfer of water through the solid. The potential, in turn, is a function of the number of adsorbed molecules per unit volume, as expressed in the vapor adsorption isotherm.

Similar conclusions were reached by Thomas (1951) in a study of moisture permeability, diffusion, and sorption in organic film-forming materials. Fick's diffusion law is found to be applicable only in the region of low relative humidity, and the rate of permeation depends directly on the vapor pressure difference.

This analysis provides a connecting link with the concept of water vapor pressure gradient as the driving force for diffusion, and answers an objection sometimes raised about the latter, namely that one cannot picture vapor *as such* diffusing through a gelatinous or glassy solid; the spreading pressure of an adsorbed film, however, has been physically familiar ever since Langmuir's classic demonstrations—and the gradient of this pressure varies with temperature and composition in the same way as vapor pressure gradient would.

Van Arsdel's analysis (1947) had shown, through computation of a number of selected hypothetical diffusing systems, that drying rate curves similar to the peculiar rate curves observed in drying carrot and potato pieces to low moisture levels can be duplicated by making relatively simple assumptions about the moisture content-permeability relationship. "Permeability" he defined in terms of rate of water transfer through unit cross-section under unit vapor pressure gradient:

$$G = -\mathbf{P}\,\frac{dp}{dl} \qquad (3.8)$$

where

G = mass-velocity of water diffusing (lb)/(hr)(sq ft)
$\mathbf{P}$ = permeability (lb)/(hr)(ft)(atm)
p = vapor pressure at the point in question (atm)
l = distance measured in the direction of water movement (ft)
dp/dl = vapor pressure gradient (atm)/(ft)

Then the permeability and the diffusivity for water at the point in question are related as follows:

$$\mathbf{P}\,\frac{dp}{dW} = \rho_d \mathbf{D} \qquad (3.9)$$

where

W = moisture content (lb)/(lb dry)
ρ_d = density of the dry substance (lb dry)/(cu ft)
$\mathbf{D}$ = diffusivity (sq ft)/(hr)
dp/dW = slope of the water vapor pressure isotherm

It was also pointed out that in the absence of an internal temperature gradient, the predicted moisture distribution and rate of internal moisture movement will both be exactly the same whether computed from concentration gradient or from vapor pressure gradient, provided the diffusivity and the permeability are related as shown in Equation (3.9). The relation between vapor pressure and moisture content is strongly curved, so either the diffusivity or the permeability or both must vary with moisture content; they cannot both remain constant.

The most detailed study of the behavior of water in a colloidal food material, especially from the standpoint of theoretical interpretation, is the investigation by Fish (1957) of the diffusion and equilibrium properties of water in a clear gel prepared from pure potato starch. This system has the great experimental advantages of good reproducibility, ease of preparation in a solid piece of known shape and dimensions, and a good degree of isotropy; besides, it is not too distant a representative of a large class of food products. Stitt (1958) has also analyzed and commented on the data obtained by Fish in these experiments. Fish (1958) also obtained data on the diffusivity of water in the flesh of scalded potatoes at 1, 25, and 35°C. Figure 3.13 presents his results at 25°C, expressed

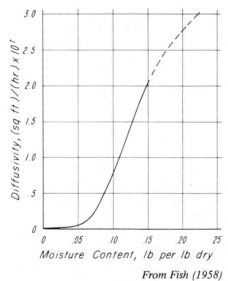

From Fish (1958)

FIG. 3.13. DIFFUSIVITY OF WATER IN POTATO AT 25°C

in engineering units, square feet per hour. The diffusivity is only slightly different from that of water in pure starch gel; this fact indicates that the cell walls and other nonstarch constituents of potato have only a minor influence on the transport of water through the scalded material. The hundred-fold decrease in diffusivity as moisture content falls from $W = 0.15$ to $W = 0.03$ helps to explain the difficulty experienced in drying potato to really low moisture levels.

The only other published data on diffusivity of water in scalded potato, those of Saravacos and Charm (1962), were derived only as a mean over the moisture range 1.0 to 0.1, and for temperatures of 130°F ($D_m = 1.0 \times 10^{-5}$ ft²/hr), 140°,

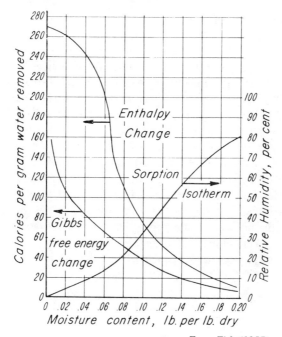

From Fish (1957)

FIG. 3.14. THERMODYNAMIC PROPERTIES OF WATER IN
POTATO STARCH GEL

$150°$, and $156°F (D_m = 2.4 \times 10^{-5} \ ft^2/hr)$; from an Arrhenius-type plot of log D against $1/T$, the activation energy for this diffusion was estimated to be 12,500 cal per gm mole of water transferred in this moisture range.

This extended discussion of the factors which control the internal movement of water in the wet body might be summed up by saying that while this massive and difficult research has succeeded in deepening our understanding of the phenomena of drying, it has accomplished much less of immediate practical usefulness than systematic empirical studies of the effects of external or environmental factors on drying rates. The next generation of research workers may discover how to extend and perfect the theory and use it to make radical improvements on all of our present drying procedures.

Effect of External Factors on Water Vapor Transfer From Wet Body to Surrounding Air

Just as in heat transfer, the principal resistance to mass transfer resides in the thin stationary film of gas and vapor in the near vicinity of the solid surface.

As an approximation, we frequently assume that water vapor at the surface of the moist body mixes immediately and completely with the main air stream, so that the actual environment of the body has exactly the same humidity, temperature, and pressure as that air. This cannot be quite true in any case, and it may be far from exact if velocities and pressures are low and radiative heat transfer is significant; the stagnant film of mixed water vapor and air has a higher water vapor content than the main stream of air. The effective thickness of the film decreases, and the vapor content approaches that of the main stream, as the relative velocity increases. The exact relationships, especially the effects of relative velocity and radiation, have been studied by a number of investigators. (See especially Arnold 1933.) Experimental results are often correlated by use of the Chilton-Colburn (1934) dimensionless "j-factor," which is based on the analogies between heat-, mass-, and momentum-transfer.

During early stage of the drying of very wet bodies the rate at which evaporation can occur is completely determined by the rate at which water vapor can be transferred through the stagnant gas film just outside the water surface and be mixed with the main air stream. For a time the rate of evaporation is even independent of the kind of material being dried.

Marshall and Hougen (1942) concluded that the constant rate of drying can be expressed by the following equation:

$$\left(\frac{dW}{d\theta}\right)_c = k_G \left(\frac{D_p G}{\mu}\right)^n \left(\frac{\mu}{\rho_a \mathbf{D}}\right)^m \left(\frac{P}{p_{am}}\right)\Delta p_w \qquad (3.10)$$

where

k_G = mass transfer coefficient (lb)/(hr)(sq ft)(atm)
D_p = particle diameter (ft)
G = mass velocity (lb)/(hr)(sq ft)
μ = dynamic viscosity of the gas film (lb)/(hr)(ft), and the group $(D_p G/\mu)$ is a modified Reynolds number
ρ_a = density of the gas film (lb)/(cu ft)
$\mathbf{D}$ = diffusivity of water vapor through air (sq ft)/(hr), and the group $(\mu/\rho_a \mathbf{D})$ is a Schmidt number
P = total pressure (atm)
p_{am} = logarithmic mean partial pressure of dry air in the gas film

$$\Delta p_w = p_{wp} - p_{wa}$$

where

p_{wp} = partial pressure of water vapor at the surface of the particle (atm)
p_{wa} = partial pressure of water vapor in the main air stream (atm)

This relation is materially simplified if we take into account the facts that the Schmidt number for air is nearly independent of temperature, the particle diameter is nearly constant, and the ratio (P/p_{am}) is nearly unity;

$$\left(\frac{dW}{d\theta}\right)_c = k_G' G^n \Delta p_w \qquad (3.11)$$

At low partial pressures of water vapor, by Equation (4.5), $p_w = H/0.622$, hence

$$\left(\frac{dW}{d\theta}\right)_c = k_G'' \, G^n \, \Delta H \tag{3.12}$$

Experiments by many investigators have shown that the exponent n in these expressions is approximately 0.80; that is, in the constant-rate phase the drying rate increases as the 0.8 power of the mass air velocity.

Krischer (1956), enlarging upon several of his earlier publications (1938A, B, 1940, 1942), analyzed mass transfer conditions in the boundary layer around solids in terms of Reynolds number, Lewis number, and modified Schmidt, Nusselt, Grashof, and Peclet numbers, and derived a similar defining equation for the mass transfer coefficient, taking "driving force" as the difference between partial pressures of water vapor at the solid surface and in the air stream at a distance.

Removal of water vapor from the vicinity of the evaporating surface is a major factor in successful vacuum drying, and is especially critical in freeze drying. Experimental and theoretical conditions have been discussed by Carman (1948, 1956), Ede (1949), Cooke and Sherwood (1955), and Kramers (1958), among others.

RELATION BETWEEN HEAT AND MASS TRANSFER OCCURRING SIMULTANEOUSLY

In most of the foregoing discussion the tacit assumption has been made that mass transfer and heat transfer can be analyzed separately and the effects simply added to produce a measure of the overall effect. Ever since the investigations of Ackerman and Gnam (1937), Krischer (1942), and especially the derivation of the "phenomenological flow equations" by Onsager (1945), it has been known that this simple additivity is only approximately true. The flow of heat affects the transfer of mass, and vice versa. The principle is stated as follows by Hearon (1950): "when two or more irreversible transport processes, e.g., heat conduction, electrical conduction, or diffusion, take place in a given system, there is mutual interaction between the individual transports." Hall (1953) developed the theory further in a study of "nonequilibrium thermodynamics." So far as our subject is concerned, available evidence indicates that the practical design and operation of dehydrators can be based confidently on the transport relations considered independently of one another. Significant departures would be expected only where large potential differences are involved.

BIBLIOGRAPHY

ACKERMAN, G., AND GNAM, E. 1937. Heat transfer and molecular mass transfer in the same field under large temperature and partial pressure differences. VDI. Forschungsh. 382, Suppl. to Forsch. Gebiete Ingenieurw. Publ. B. *8*, Jan.–Feb. (German)

ARNOLD, J. H. 1933. The theory of the psychrometer. I. The mechanism of evaporation. Physics *4*, 255–262. II. The effect of velocity. *Ibid. 4*, 334–340.

BABBITT, J. D. 1940. Observations on the permeability of hygroscopic materials to water vapor. Can. J. Res. *18* (A), 105–121. NRC No. 907.

BABBITT, J. D. 1950. On the differential equations of diffusion. Can. J. Res. *28* (A), 449–474.

BABBITT, J. D. 1951A. A unified picture of diffusion. Can. J. Phys. *29*, 427–436.

BABBITT, J. D. 1951B. On the diffusion of absorbed gases through solids. Can. J. Phys. *29*, 437–446.

BADGER, W. L., and BANCHERO, J. T. 1955. Introduction to Chemical Engineering. McGraw-Hill Book Co., New York.

BATEMAN, E., HOHF, J. P., and STAMM, A. J. 1939. Unidirectional drying of wood. Ind. Eng. Chem. *11*, 1150–1154.

BATE-SMITH, F. C., LEA, C. H., and SHARP, J. G. 1943. Dried meat. Soc. Chem. Ind. (London) *62 T*, 100–104.

BENSON, S. W., and RICHARDSON, R. L. 1955. A Study of hysteresis in the sorption of polar gases by native and denatured proteins. J. Am. Chem. Soc. *77*, 2585–2590.

BRUNAUER, S., EMMETT, P. H., and TELLER, E. 1938. Adsorption of gases in multi-molecular layers. J. Am. Chem. Soc. *60*, 309–319.

BUCKINGHAM, E. 1907. Studies on the movement of soil moisture. USDA Bur. Soils Bull. *37*.

CARMAN, P. C. 1948. Molecular distillation and sublimation. Trans. Faraday Soc. *44*, 529–536.

CARMAN, P. C. 1956. Flow of Gases Through Porous Media. Butterworth's Scientific Publications, London; Academic Press, New York.

CARSLAW, H. S., and JAEGER, J. C. 1959. Conduction of Heat in Solids, 2nd Edition. Oxford University Press, London.

CEAGLSKE, N. H., and HOUGEN, O. A. 1937. The drying of granular solids. Trans. Am. Inst. Chem. Eng. *33*, 283–312.

CHILTON, T. H., and COLBURN, A. P. 1934. Mass transfer (absorption) coefficients—prediction from data on heat transfer and fluid friction. Ind. Eng. Chem. *26*, 1183–1187.

COMINGS, W. E., and SHERWOOD, T. K. 1934. The drying of solids. VII. Moisture movement by capillarity in drying granular materials. Ind. Eng. Chem. *26*, 1096–1098.

COOKE, N. E., and SHERWOOD, T. K. 1955. The effect of pressure on the rate of sublimation. Proc. 9th Intern. Congr. Refrig. Rept. 2.79, *1*, No. 2, 133–141.

CRANK, J. 1956. The Mathematics of Diffusion. Clarendon Press, Oxford, England.

CRANK, J. 1958. Some mathematical diffusion studies relevant to dehydration. *In* Fundamental Aspects of the Dehydration of Foodstuffs. Soc. Chem. Ind. (London) 37–41.

EDE, A. J. 1949. Physics of the low-temperature vacuum drying process. Soc. Chem. Ind. (London) *68*, 330–332, 336–340.

EDE, A. J., and HALES, K. C. 1948. The physics of drying in heated air, with special reference to fruit and vegetables. G. Brit. Dept. Sci. Ind. Res., Food Invest. Spec. Rept. *53*.

FISH, B. P. 1957. Diffusion and equilibrium properties of water in starch. G. Brit. Dept. Sci. Ind. Res., Food Invest. Tech. Paper *5*.

FISH, B. P. 1958. Diffusion and thermodynamics of water in potato starch gel. *In* Fundamental Aspects of the Dehydration of Foodstuffs. Soc. Chem. Ind. (London) 143–157.

FISHER, E. A. 1923. Some moisture relations of colloids. I. A comparative study of rates of evaporation from wool, sand, and clay. Proc. Roy. Soc. (London) *A 103*, 139–161. II. Further observations on the evaporation of water from clay and wool. *Ibid. A 103*, 664–675.

FISHER, E. A. 1935. Some fundamental principles of drying. Soc. Chem. Ind. (London) *54*, 343–348.

GANE, R. 1941. The water content of wheats as a function of temperature and humidity. Soc. Chem. Ind. Trans. (London) *60*, 44–46.

GANE, R. 1943. The activity of water in dried foodstuffs; water content as a function of humidity and temperature. *In* Dehydration, Sec. X, Part 1. U.K. Progr. Rept., D.S.I.R., Min. Food, London.

GANE, R. 1950. The water relations of some fruits, vegetables, and plant products. J. Soc. Food Agr. *1*, 42–46.

GARDNER, W. 1919. The movement of moisture in soil by capillarity. Soil Sci. *7*, 313–317.

GILLILAND, E. R., and SHERWOOD, T. K. 1933. The drying of solids. VI. Diffusion equations for the period of constant drying rate. Ind. Eng. Chem. *25*, 1134–1136.

GÖRLING, P. 1954, 1956. Investigations to elucidate the drying behavior of vegetable materials, especially potato pieces. Diss. T. H. Darmstadt. *Also in* VDI-Forschungsheft 458, Düsseldorf 1956. (German)

GÖRLING, P. 1958. Physical phenomena during the drying of foodstuffs. *In* Fundamental Aspects of the Dehydration of Foodstuffs. Soc. Chem. Ind. (London) 42–53.

HAINES, W. B. 1927. Studies in the physical properties of soils. IV. A further contribution to the capillary phenomena in soils. J. Agr. Sci. *17*, 264–290.

HAINES, W. B. 1930. Studies in the physical properties of soils. V. The hysteresis effect in capillary properties and the modes of moisture distribution associated therewith. J. Agr. Sci. *20*, 97–116.

HALL, N. A. 1953. Non-equilibrium thermodynamics. J. Appl. Phys. *24*, 819–825.

HEARON, J. Z. 1950. Some cellular diffusion problems based on Onsager's generalization of Fick's law. Math. Biophys. Bull. *12*, 135–159.

HOUGEN, O. A., McCAULEY, H. J., and MARSHALL, W. R., JR. 1940. Limitations of diffusion equations. Trans. Am. Inst. Chem. Eng. *36*, 183–206.

JACOB, M. 1949, 1957. Heat Transfer, Vol. 1 (1949); Vol. 2 (1957). John Wiley & Sons, New York.

JASON, A. C. 1958. A study of evaporation and diffusion processes in the drying of fish muscle. *In* Fundamental Aspects of the Dehydration of Foodstuffs. Soc. Chem. Ind. (London) 103–135.

KAMEI, S., and SHIOMI, S. 1937. A study of the drying of solids. XIX. Moisture distribution in the course of drying. J. Soc. Chem. Ind. (Japan) Suppl. Binding *40*, 257–263.

KAREL, M., AIKAWA, Y., and PROCTOR, B. E. 1955. A new approach to humidity equilibrium data. Modern Packaging *29*, No. 2, 153–156, 237–238, 240.

KRAMERS, H. 1958. Rate-controlling factors in freeze-drying. *In* Fundamental Aspects of the Dehydration of Foodstuffs. Soc. Chem. Ind. (London) 57–66.

KRISCHER, O. 1938A. Fundamental laws of the movement of moisture in bodies being dried; capillary water movement and water vapor diffusion. Z. Ver. deut. Ing. *82*, 373–378. (German)

KRISCHER, O. 1938B. The drying of solid substances, as a problem in the movement of capillary moisture and the diffusion of vapor. Z. Ver. deut. Ing. Verfahrenstechnik Beih. *4*, 104–110. (German)

KRISCHER, O. 1940. Heat, liquid, and vapor movement in the drying of porous materials. Z. Ver. deut. Ing. Suppl. *1*, 17–25. (German)

KRISCHER, O. 1942. Heat- and mass-transfer in a material being dried; the analytic and graphic treatment of the drying of porous hygroscopic materials. VDI Forschungsheft 415, Publ. *B13*, July-Aug. (German)

KRISCHER, O. 1956. Drying Technology, Vol. 1, The Scientific Fundamentals of Drying Technology. Springer-Verlag, Berlin-Göttingen-Heidelberg. (German)

KRISCHER, O., and KRÖLL, K. 1956, 1959. Drying Technology, Vol. 1, The Scientific Fundamentals of Drying Technology (Krischer, 1956). Drying Technology, Vol. 2, Driers and Drying Processes (Kroll, 1959). Springer-Verlag, Berlin-Göttingen-Heidelberg. (German)

LABUZA, T. P. 1968. Sorption phenomena in foods. Food Technol. *22*, No. 3, 15–17, 20, 22, 24.

LEWIS, W. K. 1921. The rate of drying of solid materials. Ind. Eng. Chem. *13*, 427–432.

LEWIS, W. K. 1922. The evaporation of a liquid into a gas. Trans. Am. Soc. Mech. Eng. *44*, 445–446.

LYKOW, A. W. (Also transliterated Luikov, A. V.) 1933. Investigation of the dynamics of drying; equation of the diffusion of humidity during the process of drying solids. Izvest. Teplotekh. Inst. *8*, 1354–1359. (Russian)

LYKOW, A. W. (Also transliterated Luikov, A. V.) 1935. The thermal diffusion of moisture. Zhur. Priklad. Khim. *8*, 1354–1359. (Russian)

LYKOW, A. W. (Also transliterated Luikov, A. V.) 1948. Theory of the kinetics of the process of drying of colloidal capillary-porous bodies. Kolloid. Zhur. *10*, 289–304. (Russian)

LYKOW, A. W. 1950, 1955. Experimental and Theoretical Fundamentals of Drying. Moscow, 1950. (Russian) Veb. Verlag, Berlin, 1955. (German)

MACEY, H. H. 1942. Clay-water relationships and the internal mechanism of drying. Trans. Brit. Ceram. Soc. *41*, 73–121.

MCCREADY, D. W., and MCCABE, W. L. 1933. The adiabatic air drying of hygroscopic solids. Trans. Am. Inst. Chem. Eng. *29*, 131–160.

MAKOWER, B. 1945. Vapor pressure of water adsorbed on dehydrated eggs. Ind. Eng. Chem. *37*, 1018–1022.

MAKOWER, B., CHASTAIN, S. M., and NIELSEN, E. 1946. Moisture determination in dehydrated vegetables. Vacuum oven method. Ind. Eng. Chem. *38*, 725–731.

MAKOWER, B., and DEHORITY, G. L. 1943. Equilibrium moisture content of dehydrated vegetables. Ind. Eng. Chem. *35*, 193–197.

MARSHALL, W. R., JR., and FRIEDMAN, S. J. 1950. Drying. *In* Chemical Engineers Handbook, 3rd Edition. J. H. Perry (Editor). McGraw-Hill Book Co., New York.

MARSHALL, W. R., JR., and HOUGEN, O. A. 1942. Drying of solids by through-circulation. Trans. Am. Inst. Chem. Eng. *38*, 91–121.

MENTING, L. C., HODGSTAD, B., and THIJSSEN, H. A. C. 1970. Aroma retention during the drying of liquid foods. J. Food Technol. (London) *5*, 127–139.

MILNE, W. E. 1953. Numerical Solution of Differential Equations. John Wiley & Sons, New York.

NEWMAN, A. B. 1931. Drying of porous solids. Trans. Am. Inst. Chem. Eng. *27*, 203–216, 310–333.

NOTTER, G. K., TAYLOR, D. H., and DOWNES, N. J. 1959. Orange juice powder: Factors affecting storage stability. Food Technol. *13*, 113–118.

ONSAGER, L. 1931. Reciprocal relations in irreversible processes. Phys. Rev. *37*, 495–526; *38*, 2265–2279.

ONSAGER, L. 1945. Theories and problems of liquid diffusion. Ann. N.Y. Acad. Sci. *46*, 241–265.

PHILIP, J. R. 1955. Numerical solution of equations of the diffusion type, with diffusivity concentration-dependent. Trans. Faraday Soc. *51*, 885–892.

PHILIP, J. R. 1960A. A very general class of exact solutions in concentration-dependent diffusion. Nature *185*, No. 4708, 233.

PHILIP, J. R. 1960B. General method of exact solution of the concentration-dependent diffusion equation. Australian J. Phys. *13*, 1–12.

PHILIP, J. R. 1961. *n*-Diffusion. Australian J. Phys. *14*, 1–13.

POWELL, R. W., and GRIFFITHS, E. 1935. The evaporation of water from plane and cylindrical surfaces. Trans. Inst. Chem. Eng. *13*, 175–198.

PRUTHI, J. S., SINGH, L. J., and GIRDHARI, L. 1959. The equilibrium relative humidity of garlic powder. J. Sci. Food Agr. *10*, 359–361.

SARAVACOS, G. D., and CHARM, S. E. 1962. A study of the mechanism of fruit and vegetable dehydration. Food Technol. *16*, No. 1, 78–81.

SCARBOROUGH, J. B. 1950. Numerical Mathematical Analysis. Johns Hopkins Press, Baltimore.

SEEHOF, J. M., KEILIN, B., and BENSON, S. W. 1953. The surface areas of proteins. V. The mechanism of water sorption. J. Am. Chem. Soc. *75*, 2427–2430.

SHERWOOD, T. K. 1929. The drying of solids. Ind. Eng. Chem. *21*, I, 12–16; II, 976–980.

SHERWOOD, T. K. 1930. The drying of solids. III. Mechanism of the drying of pulp and paper. Ind. Eng. Chem. *22*, 132–136.

SHERWOOD, T. K. 1931. Application of theoretical diffusion equations to the drying of solids. Trans. Am. Inst. Chem. Eng. *27*, 190–200.

SHERWOOD, T. K. 1932. The drying of solids. IV. Application of diffusion equations. Ind. Eng. Chem. *24*, 307–310.

SHERWOOD, T. K. 1936. The air drying of solids. Trans. Am. Inst. Chem. Eng. *32*, 150–168.

SHERWOOD, T. K., and COMINGS, E. W. 1932. The drying of solids. Trans. Am. Inst. Chem. Eng. *28*, 118–133.
SHERWOOD, T. K., and COMINGS, E. W. 1933. The drying of solids. V. Mechanism of drying of clays. Ind. Eng. Chem. *25*, 311–316.
SLESSER, C. G. M., and CLELAND, D. 1962. Surface evaporation by forced convection. I. Simultaneous heat and mass transfer. Intern. J. Heat Mass Transfer *5*, 735–749.
SLICHTER, C. S. 1898. Theoretical investigations of the motion of ground water. U.S. Geological Survey, 19th Ann. Rept. Part 2, 301–384.
SMITH, A. J. M. 1943. Note on physical aspects of drying and some drying characteristics of foods. *In* Dehydration, Sect. X. (Physical Data for Dried Foods) Part 3. U.K. Progr. Rept., D.S.I.R., Min. Food, London.
STITT, F. 1958. Moisture equilibrium and the determination of water content of dehydrated foods. *In* Fundamental Aspects of the Dehydration of Foodstuffs. Soc. Chem. Ind. (London) 67–88.
THOMAS, A. M. 1951. Moisture permeability, diffusion, and sorption in organic film-forming materials. J. Appl. Chem. *1*, 141–158.
VAN ARSDEL, W. B. 1947. Approximate diffusion calculations for the falling rate phase of drying. Chem. Eng. Progr. *43*, 13–24. Also issued as U.S. Dept. Agr. Bur. Circ. *AIC-152.*
VAN ARSDEL, W. B. 1951. Principles of the drying process, with special reference to vegetable dehydration. U.S. Dept. Agr. Bur. Circ. *AIC-300.*

CHAPTER 4

W. B. Van Arsdel
and
M. J. Copley

Properties of Water, Water Vapor, and Air

INTRODUCTION

This chapter is intended to describe and explain the physical laws which underlie the most important class of drying operation, namely air drying. However, although air drying is by far the leader among drying methods, it is by no means the only method, or even always the preferred method. For example, drum drying, or vacuum drying (the latter including freeze drying) are employed for some kinds of operation.

The study of air drying encounters the use of such special terms as "humidity" and "psychrometer," which will be defined and illustrated in this chapter.

The characteristic operation in food dehydration is *drying*, the evaporation of nearly all of the water normally present so that the food product is converted to a dry solid. The nature of the raw material, the kind of product desired, and the characteristics of available processing equipment will modify various stages of a dehydration process drastically—but always there will be a removal of water. The operation of drying is essential to many nonfood manufacturing processes as well, and frequently a liquid other than water is to be vaporized. However, we shall deal here only with processes wherein water is removed by *evaporation*, rather than by pressing, centrifuging, or freezing; where the operation is continued down to dryness, to distinguish it from the *concentration* of a liquid solution or suspension; and where the purpose is recovery of the dry solid, not just the generation of water vapor as in operation of a steam boiler.

PRESSURE-VOLUME-TEMPERATURE-ENTHALPY RELATIONS—THE GAS LAWS

A number of the pertinent properties of water and air are collected in Table 4.1. In most cases the values are given to a greater degree of precision than is required in drier calculations.

The volume occupied by unit mass of a gas or vapor is known as the specific volume; it is the reciprocal of the density. For example, the specific volume of dry air at a temperature of $200°F$ and normal sea-level pressure (1 atm., 14.696 lb per sq in. 29.92 in. of mercury barometric height) is 16.62 cu ft per lb. Water vapor is lighter than air; 1 lb of it occupies about 60% greater volume than 1 lb of dry air at the same temperature and pressure. Moist air is therefore a little lighter than dry air.

Dry air behaves substantially as a perfect gas in this range of temperatures and pressures. Water vapor and moist air depart significantly from the simple relations described by the laws of perfect gases (Goff and Gratch 1945, 1946; Scott

TABLE 4.1

PROPERTIES OF WATER AND AIR
(1 Atmosphere Pressure)

Temperature (°F)	Liquid Water				Water Vapor	Dry Air				
	32	100	200	212	212	32	100	200	212	300
Specific volume[1]	0.0160	0.0161	0.0166	0.0167	26.80	12.39	14.10	16.62	16.90	19.14
Specific heat[2]	1.0074	0.9986	1.0057	1.0076	[6]	0.240	0.240	0.242	0.242	0.244
Thermal conductivity[3]	0.319	0.363	0.393	0.393	0.015	0.014	0.016	0.018	0.018	0.020
Viscosity[4]	4.35	1.90	0.76	0.68	0.032	0.042	0.046	0.052	0.053	0.057
Surface tension[5]	5.19	4.79	4.13	4.04	—	—	—	—	—	—

[1] Specific volume, V, (cu ft)/(lb).
[2] Specific heat at constant pressure, c_p (Btu)/(lb) (°F).
[3] Thermal conductivity, k (Btu)/(hr) (ft) (°F).
[4] Viscosity, μ (lb)/(hr) (ft).
[5] Surface tension, σ [(lb force)/(ft)] $\times 10^3$.
[6] Mean specific heat of superheated water vapor at common drying temperature is 0.440 (Btu)/(lb) (°F).

1958), but the departures are taken into account in most psychrometric tables and charts and are frequently neglected entirely for approximate calculations.

The following "gas laws" are most frequently applied:

Boyle's Law

At a constant temperature the volume of a perfect gas is inversely proportional to the pressure of the gas.

Charles' Law

At a constant pressure the volume of a perfect gas is proportional to the absolute temperature ($^\circ$F + 459.7, symbol $^\circ$R, degrees Rankine).

Dalton's Law

In a mixture of gases each component exerts the same pressure that it would exert if it were present alone at the same temperature in the volume occupied by the mixture (additive pressures). The pressure exerted by any component of a mixture of gases is known as the partial pressure of that component.

Amagat's Law

The volume occupied by a gas mixture is equal to the sum of the volumes occupied separately by each constituent at the same temperature and pressure as the mixture (additive volumes).

Avogadro's Hypothesis

Equal volumes of perfect gases contain the same number of molecules.

A combination of these principles leads to the following general expression for the pressure-volume-temperature relations of gases (including, approximately, moist air):

$$MPV = RT \tag{4.1}$$

The symbols have the following meanings, along with a consistent set of English engineering units:

M = molecular weight (pure component or mean molecular weight of a mixture)
P = pressure (atmospheres)
V = specific volume (cu ft)/(lb)
R = gas constant (atm.) (cu ft)/mole-weight (lb) ($^\circ$R)
T = absolute temperature = $^\circ$F + 459.7 ($^\circ$R)

In these units the numerical value of the gas constant, R, is 0.7302. At the standard conditions of 1 atm. pressure and a temperature of 32°F, or 491.7°R, MV = 358.97; that is, 1 lb-mole of the perfect gas occupies 358.97 cu ft under the standard conditions. Instead of solving Equation (4.1) to determine the volume of a given mass of gas under specified conditions of temperature and pressure, it is frequently more convenient to multiply the volume of the gas under standard conditions by the appropriate ratio:

$$V = V_0 \cdot \frac{P_0}{P} \cdot \frac{T}{T_0} \tag{4.2}$$

remembering that under standard conditions $P_0 = 1$, $T_0 = 491.7°R$.

Again, in a mixture of gases the proportion of any constituent by volume is equal to the ratio of its partial pressure to the total pressure of the mixture and also is equal to the mole fraction of that constituent—i.e., the proportion of the number of molecules of the constituent to the total number of molecules in the mixture. Then if there are x moles of water vapor and y moles of air in a mixture, and since the molecular weights are 18.02 and 28.97, respectively, the proportion of water vapor by weight = $[18.02\ x/(18.02x + 28.97y)]$, and the proportion of air by weight = $[28.97y/(18.02x + 28.97y)]$. The proportion of water vapor by volume, or mole fraction of water vapor, is simply $x/(x + y)$. We shall denote this by the symbol w. Furthermore, in moist air,

$$P = p_a + p_w \tag{4.3}$$

where p_a is the partial pressure of dry air in the mixture and p_w is the partial pressure of water vapor.

The mass of water vapor per pound of dry air in a mixture is

$$H = \frac{p_w}{p_a} \cdot \frac{18.02}{28.97} = 0.622 \frac{p_w}{p_a} = 0.622 \frac{p_w}{P - p_w} \tag{4.4}$$

This quantity is known as the absolute humidity. Under all ordinary outdoor conditions it is a small fraction, rarely greater than 0.02 lb of water vapor per pound of dry air, but in some commercial driers it may rise as high as 0.20 or more. In air conditioning work the absolute humidity is generally expressed as grains of water vapor per pound of dry air (1 lb = 7000 gr.). At low values of humidity we often simplify Equation (4.4) by taking

$$p_a = P - p_w = 1 \text{ (approx)}$$

so that we have

$$H = 0.622\ p_w \text{ (approx)} \tag{4.5}$$

The relation between absolute humidity and mole fraction of water vapor is seen to be

$$H = 0.622 \frac{w}{1 - w} \tag{4.6}$$

The enthalpy of moist air at constant pressure (usually called the "total heat of the air" in the early texts on drying and air conditioning) is defined as the sum of the sensible heat and the latent heat of vaporization of the water in the mixture. At not too high levels of humidity it can be computed with fair accuracy by the following formula:

$$E = c_{pa}(t_a - 32) + H\,[c_{pv}(t_a - 32) + \lambda_{32}]$$ (4.7)

where

E = enthalpy of the moist air (Btu)/(lb dry air)
c_{pa} = specific heat of dry air, very nearly 0.24 (Btu)/(lb) ($^\circ$F) (see Table 4.1)
t_a = temperature of the mixture ($^\circ$F)
λ_{32} = heat of evaporation of water at 32°F, 1076 (Btu)/(lb)
c_{pv} = mean specific heat of water vapor, approximately 0.44 (Btu)/(lb) ($^\circ$F)

Here the enthalpy is measured from 32°F, instead of from 0°F as it is usually shown in charts and Tables used for air conditioning calculations (Goff and Gratch 1945, 1946; ASHRAE 1965, 1966).

The heat of evaporation at temperature t°F can be approximated for many purposes in the range of 50° to 200°F by the linear expression

$$\lambda_t = 1096 - 0.593\,t\text{ (approx)}$$ (4.8)

The humid heat of moist air is defined as the amount of heat required to increase the temperature 1°F in a quantity of the mixture containing 1 lb of dry air.

$$c_s = c_{pa} + H c_{pv}$$ (4.9)

where c_s is the humid heat of the mixture (Btu)/(lb dry air) ($^\circ$F).

The humid volume of moist air is defined as the volume of 1 lb of dry air plus the water vapor accompanying it:

$$V_h = V_a + H V_v = 0.7302\,\frac{T}{P}\left[\frac{1}{28.97} + \frac{H}{18.02}\right]$$

$$= 0.0405\,\frac{T}{P}\,(0.622 + H)$$ (4.10)

Comprehensive Tables of the properties of moist air have been published by Marvin (1941), Goodman (1938, 1939, 1940, 1944), Goff and Gratch (1945), Grubenmann (1958), and ASHRAE (1965, 1966).

VAPORIZATION AND EVAPORATION

The familiar phenomenon of evaporation of water from a wet object may be regarded from the standpoint either of the kinetic behavior of molecules or the macroscopic relations characteristic of the transport properties—that is, heat and mass transfer. We shall have occasion to use both approaches. In general, study of heat and mass transfer is largely empirical and affords little insight into mechanisms, but usually has the more immediate application.

In the German literature on drying, the words "Verdunstung" and "Verdamp-fung" are rather sharply differentiated (Krischer and Kröll 1956, 1959). The former corresponds to our "evaporation," the latter to "vaporization," but we tend to use the words interchangeably. Insofar as they represent shades of meaning, "evaporation" implies that another gas, such as air, besides water vapor is present in the space over the wet surface, while "vaporization" means that only water vapor is present, although perhaps at very low pressure, as in vacuum drying.

According to the kinetic theory, a phase transition like the evaporation or vaporization of water corresponds to the passage of molecules of the evaporating substance from the liquid mass to the vapor phase. This is not a one-way traffic, but is accompanied by the return of some molecules from the vapor to the liquid. On the average, molecules which pass from the liquid to the vapor will be those which possess higher than average velocity and energy, while those that are recaptured by the liquid will be those of relatively low velocity and energy. Whether there will or will not be a net evaporation from the liquid will depend on the temperature at the phase boundary and the temperature gradient through that boundary, the presence of air or other gas along with the water vapor, the presence of dissolved substances in the liquid, and the shape and curvature of the liquid surface.

The rate of evaporation from the surface of water or a completely wet flat porous object like a wick has been very extensively investigated (Carrier 1921; Hinchley and Himus 1924; Sherwood and Comings 1932; Powell and Griffiths 1935; Shepherd et al. 1938; Powell 1940; Smith 1943). It is well known that even a trace of a nonevaporating immiscible liquid which will spread on the water surface, like a film of oil, will reduce the rate drastically, and this ex-pedient is being used to reduce the rate of evaporation from water storage reser-voirs. However, even when the surface is as clean as it can be made experimen-tally, observed rates of evaporation into air are lower by many orders of magnitude than would be calculated by the methods of the kinetic theory, and even under high vacuum the rate is less than 1% of the theoretical. The factor that imposes this limitation is the slow diffusion of water vapor through the stagnant film of adsorbed air at the surface. The reason we are interested is that the *initial* rate of evaporation from the wet surface of a body of typical food material, whether it be liquid or solid, is the same as the rate of evaporation from a water surface if the temperature, pressure, and air velocity are the same. Eventually, as drying progresses, the body ceases to act as though it were com-pletely wet, and the rate of drying decreases.

VAPOR PRESSURE AND HUMIDITY

Saturation, Relative Humidity

When, according to the kinetic picture, the rates of molecular escape from and recapture by the water surface are equal, we have a condition of dynamic equilibrium. The vapor space is said to be saturated with water vapor at whatever temperature prevails there. If conditions remain unchanged, no further net evaporation takes place. Careful experiment has shown that the amount of vapor in any given volume of the saturated space is very nearly the same whether air is also present in that space or not; it is as though it is the *space* which becomes saturated with water vapor.

At saturation, the water vapor exerts a perfectly definite partial pressure, the vapor pressure of water,[1] which rises rapidly as temperature increases. At 212°F the vapor pressure of water is 1 standard atmosphere; that is, 212°F is the boiling point of water. Table 4.2 gives the vapor pressure of water at 10° intervals from

TABLE 4.2

VAPOR PRESSURE OF WATER

Temp (°F)	Vapor Pressure		Temp (°F)	Vapor Pressure	
	Atmos-pheres	In. of Mercury		Atmos-pheres	In. of Mercury
0 (ice)	0.001257	0.0376	160	0.323	9.656
10 (ice)	0.00210	0.0629	170	0.408	12.20
20 (ice)	0.00345	0.103	180	0.511	15.29
30 (ice)	0.00552	0.165	190	0.637	19.02
32	0.00602	0.180	200	0.786	23.47
40	0.00830	0.248	210	0.968	28.75
50	0.01210	0.362	212	1.000	29.92
60	0.01745	0.522	220	1.170	35.0
70	0.02470	0.739	230	1.414	42.3
80	0.03455	1.032	240	1.697	50.8
90	0.0476	1.422	250	2.030	60.7
100	0.0647	1.933	260	2.41	72.1
110	0.0869	2.597	270	2.84	85.1
120	0.1152	3.447	280	3.35	100.1
130	0.1515	4.527	290	3.92	117.2
140	0.1966	5.884	300	4.56	136.4
150	0.2533	7.572	—	—	—

0° to 300°F, both in standard atmospheres and in inches equivalent height of a standard mercury column (Marks and Davis 1929; Keenan and Keyes 1936; Goff and Gratch 1945, 1946; Keyes 1947).

The relative degree of saturation of a vapor space or body of moist air is called the relative humidity. Generally expressed as a percentage, it is defined by Equation (4.11):

$$r_h = 100 \frac{p_w}{p_s} \qquad (4.11)$$

---

[1] The pressure of a vapor in equilibrium with its liquid depends not only on its temperature but also in some measure upon the shape of the liquid surface and the pressure of other gases mixed with the vapor. These secondary effects are not usually significant in drying technology.

where p_s is the vapor pressure of water at the temperature in question. It is also equal to the ratio of the mole fraction of water vapor in the mixture to the mole fraction of water vapor in air saturated at the same temperature and total pressure, expressed in percentage. A relative humidity of zero means that the air contains no water vapor, while a relative humidity of 100% signifies that the air is saturated with water vapor. The average outdoor relative humidity in the United States, winter and summer, is about 65%. On hot afternoons in arid regions it may fall to 10% or even lower. Air that is foggy contains suspended droplets in addition to its saturation level of water vapor.

Absolute humidity, which was defined by Equation (4.4), is likewise an expression of the amount of water vapor in a body of air. Still a third measure is the dew-point temperature, usually referred to simply as the dew point. This is the temperature at which the mixture would just become saturated with water vapor if it were cooled without change in composition or pressure. Thus, if the mixture is already saturated, its temperature is the dew-point temperature, while for air that is only partly saturated or has a relative humidity less than 100% the dew point is lower than the temperature of the mixture.

Absolute humidity and percentage relative humidity are related by Equation (4.12) or Equation (4.13), which follow from Equations (4.4) and (4.11):

$$H = \frac{0.622}{(100 \, P/r_h p_s) - 1} \tag{4.12}$$

$$r_h = \frac{100 \, P}{p_s} \left(\frac{H}{H + 0.622} \right) \tag{4.13}$$

The interaction between air and water vapor in their mixtures, and the departure from perfect gas laws, make this relation somewhat inexact. True relative humidity will be slightly higher than the computed value. At a temperature of $140°F$ and relative humidity about 40%, the discrepancy is about ½ of 1%. The data of Goff and Gratch (1945) allow the difference to be tabulated as a correction factor which can be used in very precise work.

Mean barometric pressure, air temperature, and dew point at selected cities in the United States are given in Table 4.3.

Like the absolute humidity, the dew point remains unchanged if the air is heated or cooled. Absolute humidity also remains constant if the pressure of the air is increased or decreased. It is a particularly useful measure of humidity in drier calculations because it is expressed on a weight basis. A pound of dry air entering a drier, for example, still weighs just 1 lb at any other point in its passage through the system, no matter what changes in temperature or pressure may have taken place or how much water vapor may have been added to it.

Studies of the relation of human comfort to atmospheric conditions have shown that relative humidity correlates closely with comfort. The "feel" of the air, however, is no guide to its usefulness as air supply for a drier. Air that feels very moist on a chilly day, with a temperature of, say, $40°F$, usually will contain

TABLE 4.3

MEAN BAROMETRIC PRESSURE, TEMPERATURE, AND DEW POINT AT SELECTED CITIES IN THE UNITED STATES

Place	Elevation (Ft)	Mean Barometer (In.)	January Mean Monthly		April Mean Monthly		July Mean Monthly		October Mean Monthly	
			Temp (°F)	Dew Point (°F)	Temp (°F)	Dew Point (°F)	Temp (°F)	Dew Point (°F)	Temp (°F)	Dew Point (°F)
Portland, Me.	103	29.87	21	13	43	33	68	61	50	42
Buffalo, N.Y.	768	29.18	24	19	45	35	71	61	53	45
Philadelphia, Pa.	114	29.92	33	23	52	38	76	65	58	47
Nashville, Tenn.	546	29.49	39	32	59	46	79	67	61	49
Charleston, S.C.	48	30.03	51	42	65	54	82	73	68	58
Miami, Fla.	25	30.01	68	58	74	65	82	73	78	69
New Orleans, La.	5	30.04	53	43	68	59	82	73	70	61
St. Louis, Mo.	568	29.43	31	23	57	43	80	65	59	47
Minneapolis, Minn.	838	28.99	14	9	46	33	73	60	50	40
Bismarck, N.D.	1660	28.22	9	6	43	29	71	56	45	33
Omaha, Neb.	1105	28.83	21	15	51	37	75	63	53	42
Denver, Colo.	5283	24.70	31	19	48	33	73	52	52	35
San Antonio, Tex.	794	29.17	52	43	69	58	84	72	71	60
Phoenix, Ariz.	1106	28.74	50	33	69	36	91	56	71	45
Salt Lake City, Utah	4227	25.73	25	22	50	33	77	36	53	26
Boise, Idaho	2858	26.96	28	25	49	34	73	45	50	34
Spokane, Wash.	1900	28.02	9	3	44	27	69	45	44	31
Seattle, Wash.	125	29.92	41	35	51	40	66	52	54	47
Portland, Ore.	154	29.91	39	34	56	46	67	54	54	43
Oakland, Calif.	18	30.01	48	40	56	46	63	54	60	50
Fresno, Calif.	277	29.63	46	42	60	44	81	50	62	47
Los Angeles, Calif.	512	29.35	56	43	60	49	71	59	66	53

less moisture (i.e., have a lower absolute humidity) than air that feels "dry" and comfortable at 80°F. It is almost always a mistake to draw the air supply for a drier from inside the plant building, for that air will usually have a higher absolute humidity than the outside air, even though, being warmer, it may feel much drier. In choosing a location for a dehydration plant, Weather Bureau records of dew point are much more pertinent than the records of relative humidity.

Methods of Measuring Humidity

Among the numerous ways of measuring the amount of water vapor in air, three are sometimes used for the control of drier operation—observation of the contraction or elongation of a hair or other moisture-sensitive fiber surrounded by the air and held taut by a light spring; determination of the temperature (dew point) at which dew forms on a slowly cooled mirror exposed to the air; and determination of the amount of cooling of a wet object exposed to the rapidly flowing air stream (wet-bulb hygrometry). The third of these is by far the most commonly used. Any instrument used to measure the humidity of air is called a hygrometer.

The hair hygrometer, simple in construction and operation, can be made very sensitive and rapidly responsive. The elongation of the hair is a function of the relative humidity of the air around it, nearly independent of air velocity and not very greatly affected by temperature. Constancy of calibration is very difficult to achieve, and readings are unreliable at very high and very low humidities. The dew point hygrometer can be made very precise. In modern instruments a fine thermocouple is brazed to the back of the wafer-thin mirror, and a light-sensitive cell is used to detect fogging of the artificially cooled mirror, supported in the air stream. The instrument has found particular application for determining a trace of unwanted water vapor in highly compressed industrial gases.

Hygrometry by means of the wet-bulb and dry-bulb thermometers, the combination being known as a "psychrometer," has been extensively investigated. According to Arnold (1933) the technique dates back to Hutton, about 1792. Measurements reported by Ferrel (1886) (see also Brooks 1933; Wexler and Brombacher 1951) became the basis for the "psychrometric formula" which was applied thereafter for reduction of Weather Bureau observations:

$$t_a - t_w = 2,730 \frac{p_{sw} - p_w}{P\left\{1 + [(t_w - 32)/1,571]\right\}} \tag{4.14}$$

where

t_a = air temperature (°F)
t_w = wet-bulb temperature (°F)
p_{sw} = vapor pressure of water at the wet-bulb temperature (atm)
p_w = partial pressure of water vapor in the air (atm)
P = barometric pressure in the vicinity of the wet bulb (atm)

This is, of course, an empirical correlation which cannot be expected to apply accurately to conditions very far outside of Professor Ferrel's experimental range. We may convert the terms to others more directly useful in drying calculations by replacing p_w by its value in terms of P and H from Equation (4.4):

$$t_a - t_w = 2,730 \frac{p_{sw} - [HP/(0.622 + H)]}{P\{1 + [(t_w - 32)/1,571]\}} \tag{4.15}$$

or, at a pressure of 1 standard atmosphere

$$t_a - t_w = 2,730 \frac{p_{sw} - [H/(0.622 + H)]}{1 + [(t_w - 32)/1,571]} \tag{4.16}$$

Now at any selected value of wet-bulb temperature, t_w, the saturation pressure, p_{sw}, is fixed and known so that Equation (4.16) may be used to determine any 1 of the 3 quantities (air temperature, wet-bulb temperature, and absolute humidity) if the other 2 quantities are given.

The Sprung psychrometric formula, quoted by Krischer (1939), omits a small term of the Ferrel formula; in terms of degrees Fahrenheit the expression comparable to Equation (4.14) above is:

$$t_a - t_w = 2,720 \frac{p_{sw} - p_w}{P} \tag{4.17}$$

In careful tests made by Flanigan (1960) the most reliable measurements of humidity for the temperature range of $50°-62°$F were obtained with an aspirated psychrometer or a sling psychrometer, neither of which is readily adapted to automatic measurement and control of humidity in industrial operations. Psychrometers in which the wetted wick or sleeve extends into a water-supply reservoir tend to indicate a higher humidity than the true value. The same difficulty is likely to be encountered in carelessly operated psychrometers of any type if the wick is allowed to become coated with dust or crusted from the salts in impure water so that it no longer acts as a true wet bulb. In spite of several elusive sources of error, the psychrometer remains the standard instrument for practical humidity measurement in drying operations. "Wet-bulb depression," the difference between actual air temperature ("dry-bulb temperature") and wet-bulb temperature, is very widely employed as a major factor to be correlated with rate of drying.

Psychrometric Charts

Calculations required in the design of drying equipment or the correlation and analysis of results from drying experiments can be greatly facilitated, and the complex relationships existing in a drier can be readily visualized, by the use of some form of psychrometric chart. Many different forms have been devised. The one that has been most widely used in the United States for following a drying operation was described by Grosvenor (1908) and Carrier (1911), while the one generally used in Europe (and in the United States for many air conditioning calculations), and often known as the i, x diagram, was proposed by Mollier (1923, 1929). The design and use of such charts has been under study for a number of years by a committee of the American Society of Heating, Refrigerating, and Air Conditioning Engineers, and was the topic of an extensive symposium held by the Society in Dallas in 1960. Precisely graduated charts drawn on a large scale for use in computations have been published by Carrier (1940, 1941), Garber (1943), Goodman (1944), Zimmerman (1945), Lykow (1950, 1955), ASHRAE (1965, 1966), Krischer and Kröll (1956, 1959), Grubenmann (1958), and Eckert and Drake (1959). A Mollier-type chart is included in a pocket at the back of this volume.

Fig. 4.1 shows the Grosvenor (1908) diagram on a small scale for the purpose of explanation. Coordinates are rectangular and graduations are uniform, air temperature usually being shown as the abscissa, absolute humidity as the ordinate. In one form of the i, x diagram (Mollier), Fig. 4.2, the ordinate is absolute humidity, graduated uniformly, but the other independent coordinate is enthalpy (sometimes known as "total heat") of the moist air; the symbols commonly used for enthalpy and absolute humidity in European work are i and x, respectively. Lines of constant enthalpy are parallel and uniformly spaced, but are drawn at an acute angle from the lines of constant humidity, instead of perpendicular to them. The remaining variables, for example temperature, are constructed in the resulting oblique network. Lines of constant temperature are straight, but diverge slightly, fan-wise.

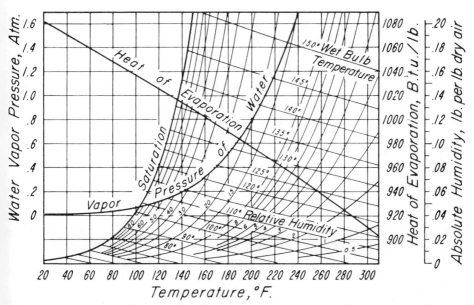

FIG. 4.1. PSYCHROMETRIC CHART, GROSVENOR TYPE

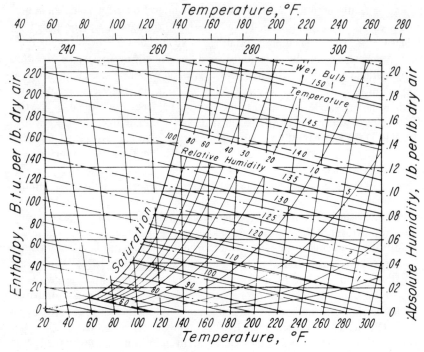

FIG. 4.2. PSYCHROMETRIC CHART, MOLLIER TYPE

The i, x, or Mollier, diagram has the great advantage that it can be used for the simple graphical solution of mixture problems, because the point representing a mixture of two streams of air differing in temperature and humidity falls upon a straight line joining the two points on the diagram, dividing it in the same proportion as the masses of dry air contained in the two streams. For example, if one stream, flowing at a rate of 2000 lb dry air per minute and having $H = 0.080$ lb water vapor per pound dry air, $E = 120$ Btu per pound dry air, is mixed with a second stream flowing at a rate of 1000 lb dry air per minute, and having $H = 0.20$ lb per pound dry air, $E = 60$ Btu per pound dry air, the combined flow of 3000 lb dry air per minute will have $H = 0.060$ lb per pound dry air, $E = 100$ Btu per pound dry air, and the point on the Mollier chart representing this mixture will fall on the straight line between the two points specified, and $\frac{1}{3}$ [i.e., $1,000/(1000 + 2000)$] of the distance from the first of the points to the second. To help avoid mistakes, remember that the point representing the mixture always lies *closest* to the point representing the *major* component in the mixture. The simple mixture rule does not quite hold true in the Grosvenor diagram.

Whichever form of coordinate system is used for the basic chart, at least a third family of lines is almost invariably constructed on it, namely the lines of equal "thermodynamic wet-bulb temperature." The latter will be defined in the next section. Additional curves or families of curves are frequently added in order to facilitate various calculations. Examples are percentage relative humidity or percentage absolute humidity, humid heat, humid volume, heat of evaporation and saturated vapor pressure, shown as functions either of temperature or of absolute humidity.

Applications of the Psychrometric Chart

Conditions During Adiabatic Evaporation.—Any process which takes place without transfer of heat to or from the surroundings is termed "adiabatic." Many drying operations are so conducted that in the section of the equipment where most of the evaporation occurs the heat absorbed by the wet body from the air stream, thus cooling the latter, far outweighs any heat transfer inward by radiation from a furnace or by conduction from the environment; that section of the equipment behaves in a particularly simple way, because of the nearly adiabatic conditions. The heat abstracted from the sensible heat of the air is practically all transformed to the latent heat of the water vapor formed. The enthalpy of the air remains almost unchanged, increases very slightly.

The Thermodynamic Wet-Bulb Temperature.—If the condition of adiabatic evaporation just described is carried to the point of equilibrium through effectively infinite contact between the wet body and the air, the temperature of the air falls and its humidity rises until an equilibrium saturation of the air at the new temperature is attained. This *temperature of adiabatic saturation*, designated by the symbol t^*, is approximately the same as the physically observed *wet-bulb temperature* of the same air, designated t_w, provided the velocity of air past the wet-bulb thermometer is relatively high—on the order of 1000 fpm.—and no high-temperature radiating surface is visible from the thermometer. For this reason the former is also known as the *thermodynamic wet-bulb temperature* (designation t^*). Curves of constant t^* are indicated on both psychrometric charts illustrated here (Fig. 4.1 and 4.2).

The lines of equal thermodynamic wet-bulb temperature on the psychrometric chart are computed from the hypothetical energy balance. Assume an adiabatic system into which flows air of humidity H and enthalpy E. Saturated air at a humidity of H^* and enthalpy E^* leaves the system, and liquid water at the enthalpy E_w^*, corresponding to the temperature of the saturated air leaving the system, is supplied. Then the adiabatic energy balance is as follows:

$$E^* = E + (H^* - H)E_w^* \qquad (4.18)$$

where the asterisk indicates enthalpy or humidity condition at saturation at the thermodynamic wet-bulb temperature. For any chosen value of the thermodynamic wet-bulb temperature, t^*, there is one, and only one, set of values of E^*, H^*, and E_w^*, so all three of these quantities are functions of t^* alone. Now if Equation (4.18) is combined with Equation (4.7) and solved for H, we have

$$H = \frac{-0.240\,(t - 32) + E^* - H^*E_w^*}{0.440\,(t - 32) - E_w^* + 1076} \qquad (4.19)$$

This constitutes the relation between H and t which is plotted on the chart as a family of lines of equal thermodynamic wet-bulb temperature.

Example 1.—Air with an absolute humidity of 0.010 and temperature of 80°F (point A, Fig. 4.3) is heated indirectly to a temperature of 190°F (point B).

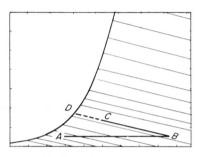

FIG. 4.3. HEATING AND ADIABATIC COOLING LINES ON
PSYCHROMETRIC CHART

The (thermodynamic) wet-bulb temperature, t^*, is then 92°F. This air evaporates water adiabatically from a wet material until the temperature of the air falls to 120°F (point C, like point B, lies on the 92° thermodynamic wet-bulb line). At that point absolute humidity of the air has risen from 0.010 to 0.026. If 1000 lb of water are to be evaporated per hour (1000)/(0.026 - 0.010), 62,500 lb of dry air per hour must be passed over the wet material.

The Evaporation Limit and the Drying Potential.—As is immediately apparent upon looking at the psychrometric chart, the process of adiabatic evaporation can continue to the left along a line of constant wet-bulb temperature until the latter intersects the saturation curve, as at D, Fig. 4.3. In fact, if, as we stipulated in the example, no additional heat is supplied to the air, the fall in temperature from point B to point D represents the maximum amount of heat available for evaporation of water, per pound of dry air circulated. The distance BD represents an unspent working balance of available energy; or, to use another metaphor, the distance of a point on the chart from the saturation curve, measured along an adiabatic cooling curve, is one measure of a *drying potential*. As evaporation proceeds, this potential becomes smaller and smaller, approaching zero as saturation is approached.

Example 2.—Assume that 1000 lb of air, having a temperature of 160°F and a wet-bulb temperature of 95°F, evaporates adiabatically 1 lb of water already at the wet-bulb temperature, 95°F. The latent heat of evaporation of water at 95°F (see curve in Fig. 4.1) is 1040 Btu per lb. In addition to this heat of evaporation the air must also supply the smaller amount of heat needed to raise the temperature of the pound of water vapor from $95°F$ up to the new temperature of the air-vapor mixture. From the psychrometric chart, initial humidity of the air was 0.021 lb water vapor per pound dry air; the initial 1000 lb therefore contained $21/1.021$, or 20.55 lb of water vapor and 979.45 lb of dry air. Then 20.55 lb of water vapor, with a specific heat of 0.44, cools from $160°F$ to the new temperature t_n, and 979.45 lb of dry air, with a specific heat of 0.24, also cools from $160°$ to t_n. The quantity of heat thus given up is balanced by the heat absorbed; 1 lb of liquid water is evaporated at $95°F$, absorbing 1040 Btu, and the pound of vapor is warmed from $95°F$ to t_n, also at a specific heat of 0.44. The resulting equality can be solved for t_n; $t_n = 155.5°F$. That is, the adiabatic evaporation of a pound of water has cooled 1000 lb|of air almost $5°F$.

In air having the initial condition assumed for this example, adiabatic saturation would reduce temperature all the way from $160°F$ to the wet-bulb temperature, $95°F$, a temperature fall of $65°$, corresponding to an increase in humidity from 0.021 to 0.0365, some 15 times as much as in the example. Thus, the drying potential of the air is only slightly decreased. The *evaporative limit* can be taken to mean the maximum number of pounds of water than can be evaporated adiabatically per pound of dry air. In the example this would be 0.0155 lb of water per pound of dry air.

A rough rule of thumb, useful for quick approximations, is that each $5°$ of difference between air temperature ("dry bulb") and wet-bulb temperature makes possible a rise of 0.001 in humidity, or the evaporation of 1 lb of water into 1000 lb of air.

The Cooling Effect of Evaporation.—The high absorption of heat accompanying the evaporation of water (approximately 1000 Btu per lb of evaporation) is, of course, a major factor in our ability to dry delicate food materials in high-temperature air without scorching the food. So long as the material is completely wet it will assume a temperature approximately the same as that of a wet-bulb thermometer in the same air stream—perhaps as much as $150°F$ lower than the air temperature. When the surface is no longer completely wet the rate of evaporation falls and hence the cooling effect decreases; the material temperature rises to near equality with the air temperature. Ede and Hales (1948) give data on the temperature of potato strips during drying in air of $70°C$ temperature, $44°C$ wet-bulb temperature, from which Fig. 4.4 is taken. Air velocity was 10 ft per sec.

Effect of Recirculation on Air Condition.—Many industrial driers are so constructed that a part (sometimes a very large proportion) of the air introduced into the drier is circulated over the moist product again and again before it is exhausted from the equipment. The psychrometric chart enables one to visualize the resulting effect on drying conditions. Figure 4.5 represents the situation on a Mollier-type chart. Point A shows the temperature and humidity of the incoming fresh air. Heating of this air to temperature t' when there is no recirculation takes place along line AB, without change in humidity. If this air is now

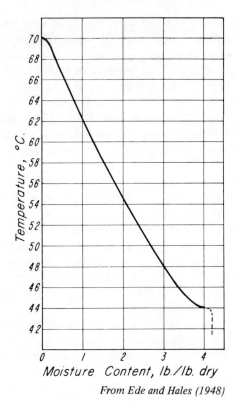

Moisture Content, lb./lb. dry

From Ede and Hales (1948)

FIG. 4.4. TEMPERATURE OF POTATO STRIP DURING DRYING
AT CONSTANT AIR CONDITION

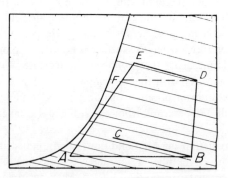

FIG. 4.5. EFFECT OF RECIRCULATION ON AIR CONDITION

brought into contact with the moist material adiabatically, its condition will
change along some such path as line *BC*, and the air will be exhausted at condition *C*. All of the air contacted with the moist material will have been heated
from *A* to *B*; this will have required a quantity of heat proportional to the rise

in enthalpy, and therefore, since the enthalpy scale is uniform, to the length of the line AB. But if only a part of the air at the exit is exhausted, the remainder mixed back with enough fresh air to make up the loss, and then the mixture heated to the same temperature, t', and circulated through the drying chamber, the humidity in the drying chamber will build up until a new equilibrium condition is reached, at some such condition as point D in the figure. As evaporation takes place the air temperature will fall and humidity will rise to the condition of point E. Part of the air at this exit condition will be exhausted and the remainder will be mixed with the make-up fresh air to give condition F. Now the heat to be supplied is the much smaller amount, proportional to the length of line FD, instead of AB.

A mass balance on the water entering and leaving such a dehydrator system leads to the following simple relation:

$$r_d = \frac{H' - H_0}{H'' - H_0} \tag{4.20}$$

where

r_d = proportion of the combined air flow that is recirculated
$1 - r_d$ = corresponding proportion of fresh air introduced
H_0 = absolute humidity of the fresh, or make-up air
H' = absolute humidity of the mixture of recirculated air with fresh air
H'' = absolute humidity of the air as it leaves the drying chamber, to be partly discarded, partly returned

For example, suppose that a dehydrator is operating at a wet-bulb temperature of $100°F$, air going to the drying chamber has a temperature of $165°F$, and at the exhaust stack has a temperature of $137.5°F$. The fresh air drawn in has a temperature of $60°F$ and a wet-bulb temperature of $55°F$. What is the proportion of recirculation, and what is the fresh air intake?

From the psychrometric chart, $H_0 = 0.0080$, $H' = 0.0271$, and $H'' = 0.0337$. Applying the above equation, $r_d = 0.743$, or 74.3%, and $1 - r_d = 0.257$, or 25.7%. If the total circulation of air in the drying chamber is 2000 lb per min, 514 lb per min of fresh air must be drawn in.

Control of the proportion of recirculation in a dehydrator enables the operator to maintain substantially uniform drying conditions regardless of variations in atmospheric conditions. Automatic control of wet-bulb temperature can be accomplished by making the controller operate recirculation dampers.

The reader must not conclude that a high proportion of recirculation of air—or, indeed, any proportion whatsoever—is to be recommended under all circumstances. We have pointed out that increasing recirculation raises the humidity in the dehydrator; at a given air temperature the drying potential of the air is thereby reduced and, as will be discussed later, the drying rate will usually decrease. Several factors must be balanced against one another to arrive at the optimum proportion of recirculation. In some very important and well-designed installations, no recirculation of air takes place.

Effect of Reheating the Circulating Air.—In some types of dehydrator the heating unit is built in sections within the drying chamber and arranged so that air flows over the moist material, then through a heating section, then through another drying section, then another heating section, and so on, in as many as 6 or 8 reheating stages. The air is therefore successively cooled by evaporation of water, reheated, cooled by evaporation again, and so on. As Fig. 4.6 illustrates, wet-bulb temperature of the air rises at each reheating, and absolute humidity of the air finally discarded, shown at point B, may be quite high.

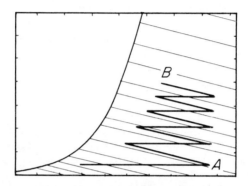

FIG. 4.6. EFFECT OF REHEATING THE CIRCULATING AIR

Humidity and Temperature in a Direct-Fired Drier.—Some driers are heated solely by mixing the products of combustion of an oil or gas burner directly with the circulating air. Combustion of the hydrogen in the fuel increases the amount of water vapor in the circulating mixture and therefore raises the humidity and wet-bulb temperature. The temperatures, humidities, and proportion of recirculation are then related by the following modification of Equation (4.20):

$$r_d = \frac{H' - H_0 - f(t' - t_0)}{H'' - H_0 - f(t'' - t_0)} \qquad (4.21)$$

where

t' = temperature of the mixture of recirculated air with fresh air ($^\circ$F)
t'' = temperature of the air as it leaves the drying chamber, to be partly discarded, partly returned ($^\circ$F)
t_0 = temperature of the fresh, or make-up air ($^\circ$F)
f = coefficient depending upon the composition and heating value of the fuel ($^\circ$F)$^{-1}$

For natural gas, with a heating value of 1000 Btu per cu ft, f will be about 0.000025; for fuel oil, of 15% hydrogen and 18,000 Btu per lb heating value, f will be about 0.000019. The rise in absolute humidity is not, in fact, great enough to have a serious effect on drier performance under most circumstances. The formula states that in a nonrecirculating drier ($r_d = 0$, as in some simple tunnel driers and many spray driers) the incoming fresh air would have to be raised in temperature by about 400°F to cause a rise in absolute humidity of only 0.01 lb water vapor per pound dry air due to combustion of the hydrogen in natural gas.

Construction of Psychrometric Chart for Nonstandard Barometric Pressure

Most published psychrometric charts have been constructed for a standard atmospheric pressure, 1 atm., in most of the charts published in the United States for both air conditioning and drying calculations. Charts in most of the European engineering texts are based on slightly lower pressure of 750 mm of mercury. Most published charts are accompanied by instructions for calculating the correction to be applied to the various psychrometric quantities at a different atmospheric pressure.

As a matter of fact, the standard chart would be of only limited value to a person who needed to make numerous calculations that would be valid for, say, Denver, Colo., at an altitude of 5283 ft and a mean barometric pressure of 24.70 in. of mercury of (0.825 standard atmosphere). Construction of a working chart for any pressure can be accomplished by going back to the numerical relations on which all such charts are based, included among Equations (4.1), (4.4), (4.7), (4.9), (4.10), (4.11), (4.13), and (4.19).

The approximate mean barometric pressure at altitudes up to 8000 ft is shown in Fig. 4.7. In addition to the predictable effect of altitude, actual baro-

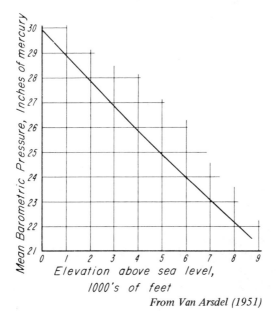

From Van Arsdel (1951)

FIG. 4.7. APPROXIMATE RELATION OF BAROMETRIC PRES-
SURE TO ALTITUDE

metric pressure at any location fluctuates from day to day, with a range of as much as 2 in. of mercury, or more. For very precise calculations relating to a specific time and place, both this variation and the actual pressure within the drier itself must be taken into account.

Effect of External Conditions on Water Vapor Pressure

Capillaries and Drops.—The vapor pressure of a liquid is predictably affected by surface forces such as those which pull a small isolated body of liquid into spherical shape (a drop) or produce capillary rise in a fine tube or wick. Under tension—for example, beneath the liquid surface in a capillary—the pressure of the vapor decreases by an amount dependent on the curvature of the liquid surface; a curvature of 1 μ radius lowers the vapor pressure by only about 0.1%, but a curvature of 1 mμ radius lowers it by about 50%. Under the convex liquid surface of a drop, on the other hand, the pressure of the vapor increases. In both cases the fractional change in vapor pressure is inversely proportional to the radius of curvature of the liquid surface.

The surface tension of water in moist air, 51.8×10^{-4} lb (force) per ft at $32°F$, is somewhat lower at higher temperatures (46.5×10^{-4} lb per ft at $122°F$, 40.3×10^{-4} lb per ft at $212°F$). The radius of droplets produced by atomization into a spray drier is therefore a function of the temperature of the feed liquid. The surface tension is also affected to some extent, generally being increased, by the presence of dissolved substances in the liquid. On the other hand, it can be greatly reduced by the presence of even a small proportion of a surface-active agent such as a soap or other detergent. The effects of such an agent include facilitation of the wetting of a dry surface, the production of foam, and the emulsification of immiscible liquids; a surface-active agent will also increase the rate at which the liquid will penetrate a porous body. The activity is very sensitive to the specific chemical composition of the surface-active material. Reduction of surface tension is always one effect, but other properties are also involved in high detergency. Saravacos and Charm (1962) found experimentally that soaking pieces of various fruits and vegetables in solutions of such surface-active agents as Myveral, Myrj, or sodium oleate caused some increase in drying rate during the constant rate phase, but no change in the equilibrium moisture relations or in the shrinkage during drying.

Vapor Pressure of Solutions.—The water vapor pressure of a solution such as the liquid part of food materials is lower than the vapor pressure of pure water, but the difference becomes substantial only when the concentration of solid becomes high, as in the final stages of drying. This is a reflection of the fact that the molecular weight of substances occurring in solution in foods is generally high. Since vapor pressure lowering is approximately proportional to the number of molecules of solute per unit weight of pure solvent, the relative vapor pressure lowering is small when the molecules are large. Even with a comparatively small molecule, sucrose, having a molecular weight of 342, the vapor pressure of a solution of 10 gm of sucrose per 100 gm of water is lower than that of pure

TABLE 4.4

VAPOR PRESSURE OF GELATIN SOLUTIONS

Gelatin %	VP Percentage of the VP of Pure Water
76	82.5
90	24
92.5	14
95	6
97	2
98	0

water by only about 0.6%. International Critical Tables (Anon. 1928) gives the vapor pressure of solutions of gelatin in water at 25°C as shown in Table 4.4. At the high concentrations of gelatin we are really dealing with water that is sorbed in a colloidal solid, a subject which is covered more extensively in the next section.

The solute molecules in a solution exert an osmotic pressure within the solution, corresponding to a suction or negative pressure in the solvent—in this case, water. Like the vapor pressure lowering, the osmotic pressure of the dissolved substance in dilute solutions is approximately proportional to the number of molecules of solute per unit weight of solvent.

Vapor Pressure of Adsorbed Water.—Molecular forces at the surface of a solid bind molecules of a surrounding gas or vapor more or less firmly into an adsorbed layer; the escaping tendency of a gas or vapor molecule in this layer, that is to say, its fugacity or vapor pressure, is correspondingly reduced. In the case of water vapor in contact with the organic substances of which most foods are composed, the adsorption of one or a few complete layers of water molecules on the solid surface is so strong that the water vapor pressure becomes very low. This tightly bound water is correspondingly difficult to remove. The terms "bound water" and "free water" are, however, hard to define sharply, since the binding energy may have any value between zero and the energy of a valence bond (Kuprianoff 1958). Only that water which exerts full vapor pressure should be regarded as truly "free." A rather large proportion of the moisture content of many raw foods substantially meets this requirement.

BIBLIOGRAPHY

ANON. 1928. International Critical Tables. McGraw-Hill Book Co., New York.
ANON. 1963. Psychrometry. *In* Chemical Engineers' Handbook, 4th Edition. Sect. 15-2 to 15-14. McGraw-Hill Book Co., New York.
ASHRAE. 1965, 1966. ASHRAE Guide and Data Book. Am. Soc. Heating, Refrig., Air Conditioning Eng., New York.
ARNOLD, J. H. 1933. The theory of the psychrometer. I. The mechanism of evaporation. Physics *4*, 255–262. II. The effect of velocity. *Ibid. 4*, 334–340.
BROOKS, D. B. 1933. Psychrometric Charts. U.S. Bur. Stds. Misc. Publ. *143*.

CARRIER, W. H. 1911. Rational psychrometric formulae. Trans. Am. Soc. Mech. Eng. *33*, 1005–1053.

CARRIER, W. H. 1921. The theory of atmospheric evaporation, with special reference to compartment driers. Ind. Eng. Chem. *13*, 432–438.

CARRIER, W. H. 1940. Low and Normal Temperature Psychrometric Charts. Carrier Corp., Syracuse, N.Y.

CARRIER, W. H. 1941. Psychrometric Chart for High Temperatures. Carrier Corp., Syracuse, N.Y.

ECKERT, E. R. G., and DRAKE, R. M., JR. 1959. Heat and Mass Transfer, 2nd Edition. McGraw-Hill Book Co., New York.

EDE, A. J., and HALES, K. C. 1948. The physics of drying in heated air, with special reference to fruit and vegetables. G. Brit. Dept. Sci. Ind. Res., Food Invest., Spec. Rept. *53*.

FERREL, W. 1886. Annual Report of Chief Signal Officer U.S., Appendix 24.

FLANIGAN, F. M. 1960. Comparison of the accuracy of humidity measuring instruments. ASHRAE J. *2*, 56–59.

GARBER, H. J. 1943. Humidity Chart for Air and Water. Suppl. Chem. Eng. Catalog. Reinhold Publishing Co., New York.

GOFF, J. A., and GRATCH, S. 1945. Thermodynamic properties of moist air. J. Am. Soc. Heating Ventilating Eng. *51*, 125–139. *Also in* Heating, Piping, Air Conditioning J. Sect. 17, 334–348.

GOFF, J. A., and GRATCH, S. 1946. Low-pressure properties of water in the range 160° to 212° F. J. Am. Soc. Heating Ventilating Eng. *52*, 95–121.

GOODMAN, W. 1938. New tables of the psychrometric properties of air-vapor mixtures. Heating, Piping, Air Conditioning *10*, No. 1, 1–4, 119–122.

GOODMAN, W. 1939, 1940. Properties of mixtures of air and saturated water vapor for barometric pressures from 22 to 32 in. of mercury. Heating, Piping, Air Conditioning *11*, No. 7, 445–446; No. 8, 505–506; No. 9, 567–568; No. 10, 627–628; No. 11, 689–690; No. 12, 755–756; *12*, No. 3, 185–186; No. 4, 253–254; No. 5, 311–312; No. 6, 373–374; No. 7, 435–436.

GOODMAN, W. 1944. Air Conditioning Analysis–With Psychrometric Charts and Tables. Macmillan Co., New York.

GROSVENOR, W. M. 1908. Calculations for drier design. Trans. Am. Inst. Chem. Eng. *1*, 184–202.

GRUBENMANN, M. 1948. I-x Diagrams for Humid Air. Springer-Verlag, Berlin. (German)

HINCHLEY, J. W., and HIMUS, G. W. 1924. Evaporation in currents of air. Trans. Inst. Chem. Eng. (London) *2*, 57–64.

KEENAN, J. H., and KEYES, F. G. 1936. Thermodynamic Properties of Steam. John Wiley & Sons, New York.

KEYES, F. G. 1947. Thermodynamic properties of water substance, 0° to 150°C. J. Chem. Phys. *15*, 602–612.

KRISCHER, O. 1939. Physical problems in the drying of solid porous materials. Chem. Appl. *26*, 17–23. (German)

KRISCHER, O., and KRÖLL, K. 1956, 1959. Drying Technology, Vol. 1, The Scientific Fundamentals of Drying Technology (Krischer, 1956 1st Edition, 1963 2nd Edition). Drying Technology, Vol. 2, Driers and Drying Processes (Kröll, 1959). Springer-Verlag, Berlin-Göttingen-Heidelberg. (German)

KUPRIANOFF, J. 1958. "Bound water" in foods. *In* Fundamental Aspects of the Dehydration of Foodstuffs. Soc. Chem. Ind. (London) 14–23.

LYKOW, A. W. 1950, 1955. Experimental and Theoretical Fundamentals of Drying. Moscow (1950). (Russian) Veb. Verlag, Berlin (1955). (German)

MARKS, L. S., and DAVIS, H. N. 1929. Tables and Diagrams of the Thermal Properties of Saturated and Superheated Steam. Longmans, Green and Co., New York.

MARVIN, C. F. 1941. Psychrometric tables for vapor pressure, relative humidity, and temperature of the dew point. U.S. Weather Bur. Publ. *235*.

MOLLIER, R. 1923. A new diagram for water vapor-air mixtures. Z. Ver. deut. Ing. *67*, 869–872. (German)

MOLLIER, R. 1929. The i,x diagram for water vapor-air mixtures. Z. Ver. deut. Ing. 73, 1009–1013. (German)

POWELL, R. W. 1940. Further experiments on the evaporation of water from saturated surfaces. Trans. Inst. Chem. Eng. (London) 18, 36–55.

POWELL, R. W., and GRIFFITHS, E. 1935. The evaporation of water from plane and and cylindrical surfaces. Trans. Inst. Chem. Eng. (London) 13, 175–198.

SARAVACOS, G. D., and CHARM, S. E. 1962. Effect of surface-active agents on dehydration of fruits and vegetables. Food Technol. 16, No. 1, 91–93.

SCOTT, A. W. 1958. Some properties of air in relation to dehydration. In Fundamental Aspects of the Dehydration of Foodstuffs. Soc. Chem. Ind. (London) 33–36.

SHEPHERD, C. B., HADLOCK, C., and BREWER, R. C. 1938. Drying materials in trays– evaporation of surface moisture. Ind. Eng. Chem. 30, 388–397.

SHERWOOD, T. K., and COMINGS, W. E. 1932. An experimental study of the wet-bulb hygrometer. Trans. Am. Inst. Chem. Eng. 28, 88–117.

SMITH, A. J. M. 1943. Note on physical aspects of drying and some drying characteristics of foods. In Dehydration, Sec. X, Part 3. U.K. Progr. Rept., D.S.I.R., Min. Food.

VAN ARSDEL, W. B. 1951. Principles of the drying process, with special reference to vegetable dehydration. USDA Bur. Circ. AIC-300.

VAN ARSDEL, W. B. 1963. Food Dehydration, 1st Edition, Vol. 1, Principles. Avi Publishing Co., Westport, Conn.

WEXLER, A., and BROMBACHER, W. G. 1951. Methods of measuring humidity and and testing hygrometers. Natl. Bur. Stds. Circ. 512.

ZIMMERMAN, O. T. 1945. Psychrometric Tables and Charts. Industrial Research Service, Dover, N.H.

CHAPTER 5

A. H. Brown
W. B. Van Arsdel
E. Lowe
A. I. Morgan, Jr.

Air Drying and Drum Drying

INTRODUCTION

Drying, the characteristic operation in *dehydration*, is the more or less complete removal of water from a moist material. The term is usually reserved for those processes which accomplish removal of water by evaporation, rather than by pressure or other physical means.

This chapter considers two of the most widely applied methods for the drying of food substances—air drying and drum (or "roller") drying. The chapter begins with a discussion of the factors which should be considered in the careful selection of a drying method to be employed to accomplish a well-defined task. It goes on to describe the types of equipment available for use in large-scale air-drying operations—fans or blowers for producing air movement, means for heating the air, and instruments for measurement and control. It then describes in some detail the different types of air drier equipment.

Another section of the chapter considers types of drum drier, and describes the applications.

Finally, the chapter contains a brief section on preconcentration of liquid food substances in order to reduce the difficulty and cost of handling a large quantity of dilute material and evaporating the high proportion of water.

SELECTION OF DRYING METHOD

The "best" drying method for a food product is determined by quality requirements, raw material characteristics, and economic factors. The quality required in a finished product, and its necessary physical characteristics, are determined by its end use. A tomato powder, for example, would be made to have different characteristics if it were intended for beverage use than if it were to be used as tomato paste in spiced cookery. The best drying method for a given product is the least expensive one that will provide the needed quality and characteristics in the product. Some drying methods can be ruled out as not practical for products which must sell for a few cents per pound. Food materials range in value from cents per pound for potato solids in the form of granules to dollars per pound for meat solids in the form of chops or steaks. So a drying method may be prohibitively expensive for a cheap product, but quite reasonable in cost for an expensive commodity. Fortunately, many foods can be dried by more than one method; a single food commodity can sometimes be worked into several different end uses by judicious choice of drying methods.

Chapter 3 discusses physical and chemical changes that occur during drying, including effects on the bulk density of the product, and describes harmful effects on food quality, such as excessive stress-cracking due to uneven shrinkage, browning or "heat damage," migration of soluble constituents of the food, "case-hardening" or formation of impervious surfaces, irreversible loss of ability to rehydrate (including denaturation of proteins), and excessive loss of desirable volatile substances. Harper and Tappel (1957), in writing about freeze drying, cited these undesirable changes as consequences of ordinary high-temperature drying. The fact that most of the dried foods produced today are made by air drying suggests that these effects are not all undesirable per se, but are simply factors to be reckoned with in making the optimum product for a given end use. In fact, the optimum for a characteristic like bulk density—that is, weight per unit of gross volume—may be radically different in different markets. For example, sales to institutions and to remanufacturers make up one large market area, sales to consumers make another; for the former, dense products are wanted in order to minimize shipping and storing costs, whereas light, bulky products may be preferred for psychological reasons in the retail market. High density is critically important for foods for military use, particularly in wartime. Furthermore, the appearance of a rehydrated carrot piece may be more important than its flavor in products such as soups or stews. Ready solubility, ease of preparation, rapid rehydration, and other convenience factors are important in the consumer market, but may be much less so in a mechanized remanufacturing plant. Factors such as these must be taken into consideration in determining what drying method shall be used to make products that will be dependably good enough for their intended use but not wastefully better than is warranted by all the facts.

Piece-Form Products

Sun drying, used for large tonnages of fruits, can be very inexpensive in areas where labor costs are low. No costs are incurred to heat or move air. Substantial quantities of apples are dried in kiln driers, where labor requirements are not high, and where the artificial heat supplied and the air movement are both at a minimum. Forced-air drying is capable of making products suitable for many uses. Prunes are commonly dried in tunnels; large quantities of carrots, onions, potatoes, and other vegetables are forced-air dried, largely for use in remanufacturing to other food products. Some of these vegetables are also found in consumer products where a high quality standard is maintained. If the food to be dried is highly susceptible to browning, denaturation, or other deteriorative changes that are temperature-dependent, vacuum drying should be considered. Practical drying rates can be obtained at a lower temperature under vacuum than at atmospheric pressure. However, temperature is not the sole criterion; the extent of deteriorative phenomena depends on time as well as temperature. Thus, if we were to compare air drying with vacuum drying at the same temperature we would find product damage to be much greater under air drying because of the longer time required. The belt-trough drier illustrates the importance of combined time-temperature effects in drying. Its mode of operation enables it to produce better products, using higher temperatures for shorter times, than can be obtained from conventional driers using lower temperatures for longer times. In a vacuum freeze drier, through proper choice of system pressure and rate of supply of heat, conditions can be so maintained that water can exist only in the solid (ice) and vapor phases. Under these conditions, the food pieces are frozen and drying occurs from a receding ice interface within the pieces. Product shrinkage is negligible, heat-induced changes are minimized, and the dry material is porous and readily rehydrated. Freeze drying is a relatively expensive way to evaporate water; it is justified only when the material is highly sensitive to heat or when the particular properties imparted to the product justify the cost for a given end use.

Liquids and Purées

For liquids, purées, or flowable suspensions, other types of drying may be considered in addition to some of those listed for piece-form foods. Some liquid foods are poured into pans and dried in an air stream; for example, a substantial market still exists for pan-dried egg albumin, a highly heat sensitive material. The product is ordinarily hard, dense, and not readily dissolved. Vacuum-drying can be used either to make products that are dense and glassy, or with proper choice of feed material and manipulation of temperature and pressure, the liquid can be made to puff up and trap vapor bubbles in the mass during early stages of drying and then to become solid so that the bubble structure is maintained. The product is composed of flakes and bubble fragments and is much more soluble or dispersible than one obtained by drying to a solid or glassy layer. Liquids or purées can also be freeze dried; the product dissolves or disperses easily in water. Readily dispersed products can also be obtained by air drying if the material is first whipped into a stable foam that is dried in the foam state. Foam-mat drying employs this principle, which has also been applied in the air drying of pans of foamed egg white. Spray drying offers unique features for the drying of liquids, even those that are highly sensitive to heat and oxidation, and can frequently be used where no other method has been able to make an acceptable product at a reasonable cost. In fact, the dollar value of spray-dried foods (especially nonfat dry milk, egg solids, and coffee) is far greater than that of food products dried by all other methods combined. Special techniques, such as foam spraying of eggs and milk, agglomeration of powders after drying, and use of special drier designs, make possible a range of physical characteristics in spray-dried products. Product solubility or dispersibility, as well as product density, is greatly influenced by these techniques and designs.

Drum drying, a short-time, high-temperature method, has been used extensively in the past to dry both foods and feeds, but has been supplanted in large measure by other methods that cause less heat damage and yield products which reconstitute more readily. Drum drying is being used successfully for drying mashed white potatoes, puréed sweet potatoes, tomato concentrate, and homogenized chicken meat. Flowable suspensions, such as moist mashed potato powder, are usually dried in air suspension types of driers.

General Considerations

As outlined in the preceding paragraphs, a wide variety of methods is available for drying food products. Each has a definite effect on the quality and physical properties of the product. Costs are different for different drying methods, and costs vary widely for different products made by the same drying method. An oversimplified cost picture for products that are easily dried might be summarized in the following rough costs per pound of water evaporated: forced-air drying, 0.7¢; drum drying, 0.8¢; spray drying, 1.0¢; vacuum drying, 2.0¢; and freeze drying, 4.0¢. However, other unpublished studies show that the cost of drying by any 1 method may vary as much as 4-fold for different raw materials, nearly as much as the range of drying costs for different drying methods. It is evident that drying costs cannot be used as the primary guide for the selection of the best drying method. Instead, the nature of the material to be dried and the characteristics required in the product must first be carefully considered, so as to establish what drying methods may be applicable to a particular situation. Drying costs may then be used to narrow down the choice of drying method and specific equipment.

Factors other than those discussed in the preceding paragraphs must also be considered in the selection of driers and drying methods. Climate is one. Low ambient air temperatures increase heating costs, high humidities may preclude the drying of hygroscopic products or require installation of dehumidifying equipment for at least the final stages of drying. Sun drying is dependent upon a consistently warm, dry climate during the harvest season. If the operating season of a projected dehydration plant will be short, high capital investment can rarely be justified. A plant intended to air dry a variety of products must be equipped with driers that are versatile. Cabinet or tunnel driers might be considered, depending upon capacity requirements and labor costs, or belt-trough driers within the limitations discussed later in the chapter. If a plant is to process a single material over a long operating season, highly specialized, highly engineered driers can be considered, such as continuous conveyor driers for piece-form foods, or continuous-belt vacuum driers, or spray driers for liquids or purées. The availability of repair parts, equipment service men, and skilled mechanics becomes increasingly important as the drying equipment becomes more complex and expensive. Even in areas where labor costs are high, most manufacturers of freeze driers recommend multiple batch driers to provide versatility, rather than semicontinuous driers to reduce labor costs. The many factors involved in selecting a drier and a drying method must be evaluated for each proposed installation. A review of recent installations, however, suggests that simplicity and foolproofness of operation outweigh low fuel and power costs.

Marshall and Friedman (1950) point out that the high cost of plant-scale drying equipment, and especially the very high cost of shutdown time in a plant geared to continuous long-season production, justify extensive preliminary analysis and appropriate pilot-scale tests while the plant is still in the planning and designing stage. They suggest a four-step approach to the task of deciding upon the purchase of specific drying equipment: (1) pick out from the available descriptions of drier types those which would be suitable for handling the commodity or commodities, both in the prepared wet state and in the final dry state, capable of turning out a dry product of the required quality, and consistent with the other operations to be performed on the material; (2) from the available information on these possibly acceptable types, eliminate those that appear to be far out of line in cost or performance; (3) conduct drying tests on the material in the types of drier that remain on the list, and secure enough data to serve as the basis for writing purchase specifications and securing firm bids; and (4) make a selection on the basis of the price quotations and the results of the drying tests.

MOVEMENT OF AIR IN CONVECTION DRIERS

Use of controlled, forced circulation of air was the most important single element marking the development of modern food dehydration. It represented a radical advance over the immemorial technique of drying foods in the natural circulation of rising hot air around a stove or fire. The modern conveyor, tunnel, spray, or pneumatic drier can be engineered to give high output and economical performance, largely because power-driven fans make possible the dependable, low-cost movement of very large volumes of drying air at controlled high temperatures.

Types of Mechanical Fans

The two classes of air-moving device most used in practical driers differ most obviously in their effect upon the direction of the air flow; in axial-flow fans the air moves through the fan without change in direction, while in centrifugal fans it leaves the fan in a direction at right angles to its entry. This difference leads to quite different space requirements and dictates important features of the drier design. Continuous-conveyor driers almost invariably are equipped with axial-flow fans; spray driers and air-suspension driers with centrifugal fans; truck-and-tray tunnel driers are most often designed for centrifugal fans, but many successful examples utilize some form of axial-flow fan.

For a description and discussion of the design, selection, testing, and performance of different kinds of fans, see such standard reference works as Baumeister (1935); Carrier (1938); Hagen (1951); and ASHRAE (1967). We can do no more in this volume than sketch briefly the general characteristics of fans and their application to various kinds of food drier.

Characteristics of Axial-Flow Fans

Three forms may be distinguished: propeller fans, tubeaxial fans, and vaneaxial fans.

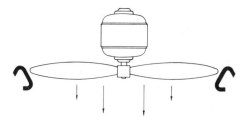

Courtesy of Academic Press and Hartzell Propeller Fan Co.

FIG. 5.1. PROPELLER FAN WITH SPECIAL RING HOUSING

Propeller fans (Fig. 5.1) are the simplest and lowest in cost. They are ordinarily used only to move air against quite low system resistance and where the noise level is not a critical factor, because they are inherently high-velocity fans. In order to perform at all efficiently, the blades must be given good airfoil cross-sections, and the propeller must be surrounded by a ring housing to convert some of the velocity energy into pressure energy. Such fans might be considered for delivery of up to about 20,000 cfm of air at a static pressure not above about 1 in. of water. The operating efficiency can be still further improved by slowing the high-velocity air discharge in a conical expanding duct.

The tubeaxial fan (Fig. 5.2) resembles the propeller fan in that the rapidly rotating airfoil blades impel the air straight through the fan. A cylindrical housing stops the centrifugal spreading tendency of the whirling air flow, and increases the efficiency of the fan. This whirl of the out-flowing air, which also characterizes the propeller fan, may cause some difficulties with uneven drying in some types of dehydrator; the air flow incident on the face of a stack of spaced trays

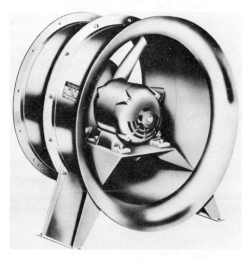

Courtesy of Westinghouse Electric Co.

FIG. 5.2. DIRECT-CONNECTED TUBEAXIAL FAN

in a tunnel drier, for example, will have a strong upward component at some places, a downward component at others, causing major irregularities in the flow of air between trays. Some means of straightening the flow may be necessary, such as an egg-crate type of lattice. Axial-flow fans are available for air flows up to 75,000 cfm and static pressure up to $1\frac{1}{2}$ in.

The vaneaxial fan (Fig. 5.3) is similar to the tubeaxial type except that air guide vanes either before or after the impeller straighten the air flow, eliminating

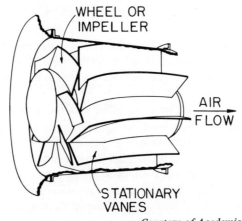

WHEEL OR
IMPELLER

AIR
FLOW

STATIONARY
VANES

Courtesy of Academic
Press and Hartzell Propeller Fan Co.

FIG. 5.3. CUT-AWAY VIEW OF VANEAXIAL FAN

the rotating or screw motion in the air stream and converting more of the kinetic energy to pressure energy; a further improvement can be realized by arranging to discharge the high-velocity air into a conically expanding duct or chamber.

The pressure, power input, and efficiency of a typical vaneaxial fan, operated at constant speed, are illustrated in Fig. 5.4. Here the abscissae represent percentage of wide-open discharge volume, zero being the closed-off condition; the ordinates represent percentage of the maximum power input, and percentage of the static, velocity, or total pressure and the total or mechanical efficiency that would exist at the closed-off condition. Thus, in this type of fan, at constant speed, the static pressure is a maximum at shutoff, decreases as the air flow is allowed to increase, but reaches a slight plateau at about 50% of full discharge, with about 60% of the shut-off pressure. The power absorbed by the fan is relatively constant at different discharge volumes; this kind of fan is, therefore, classed as nonoverloading—the demand on the driving motor is not increased if the fan discharge is opened wide.

Characteristics of Centrifugal Fans

The centrifugal fan (Fig. 5.5) differs in principle from the axial-flow types. Like the latter, it produces pressure in part by conversion of velocity energy, but

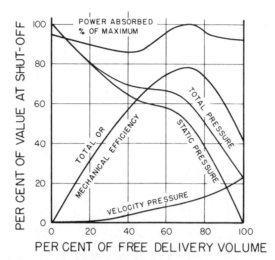

FIG. 5.4. DIMENSIONLESS CHARACTERISTICS OF TYPICAL
VANEAXIAL FAN OPERATED AT CONSTANT SPEED

Courtesy of Buffalo Forge Co.

FIG. 5.5. CENTRIFUGAL FAN

in the main the pressure comes from the centrifugal force created by rotating the enclosed air column at high speed. In the type of centrifugal fan most often used in driers, because of its nonoverloading characteristics, the vanes on the rotating impeller are curved backward.

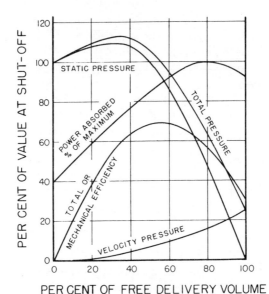

PER CENT OF FREE DELIVERY VOLUME

FIG. 5.6. DIMENSIONLESS CHARACTERISTICS OF TYPICAL
CENTRIFUGAL FAN, WITH BACKWARDLY CURVED BLADES,
OPERATED AT CONSTANT SPEED

Figure 5.6 illustrates the characteristic features of power input, pressure, and efficiency in a typical centrifugal fan with backwardly-curved blades. The static pressure rises appreciably as the volumetric discharge is increased from the shut-off condition, reaching a flat maximum at about 30–40% of free discharge. Power input reaches its maximum at about 80% of free discharge.

Centrifugal fans are made to handle the very large volumes of air, and are widely used in drier systems operating at moderate static pressures. Because the air enters the fan from the side, the fan must be installed with ample clearance on the inlet side (if the fan is single-entry) or on both sides (if the fan is double-entry).

Selection of a Fan

Specific description of the procedure used by engineers when they select the exact fan to be used in a particular drier system would fall outside the scope of this book. The truth is that no procedure, however meticulously applied, can take the place of the experienced judgment of a competent engineer who can weigh imponderables. Fans within a wide range of types and sizes will meet all necessary requirements; choice within that range is the more difficult part. We shall only sketch briefly a procedure for arriving at an initial, or rough screening choice.

The very first necessary item of information, namely the static pressure of the drying system at the desired air flow, will be missing if the system in question is different in size or design from a known system already adequately described. Elaborate model tests and application of aerodynamic laws could supply such information, but drier installations do not usually warrant the expense. The private files of drier manufacturers doubtless contain usable data. Published information, however, is fragmentary, nearly useless; one exception is the publication by Perry *et al.* (1946) of "friction factors" for fruit-drying tunnels of common commercial designs.

Kröll (1959) presents extensive data on the flow resistance of various forms of fittings such as elbows, branches, and expansions or contractions, and gives data on resistances in a cabinet drier. Any drier that is novel in arrangement or design represents, at least in part, a hopeful guess about air flow under actual operating conditions.

The type of fan to be procured will be determined by considering the characteristics outlined in the preceding section, particularly the total air volume to be delivered, the expected operating static pressure, the available space, the need for a nonoverloading characteristic, the degree of importance of quiet operation, and the relative weight of low first cost and low operating and maintenance cost. Remaining to be determined are the size and the rotational speed of the chosen type of fan. These two factors are to some extent interchangeable; because of cost or space conditions a smaller fan, operated at higher speed, may be chosen in preference to a larger, slower one, possibly better in mechanical efficiency. However, substitution of higher speed for larger size is subject to a drastic law of diminishing returns, because the power required to drive a fan of given size varies as the cube of the rotational speed. The conventional arrangement of catalogs issued by fan manufacturers consists of a series of tabulations, each giving the volume discharge of a fan of one particular type, design, and size, and at some one static pressure, over a range of different rotational speeds; the power absorbed by the fan is one of the quantities tabulated for each speed. The range of rotational speeds tabulated usually more than covers the range of good engineering practice; in centrifugal fans with backwardly tipped blades, good practice lies within the range of wheel tip speeds 4600-6000 fpm for static pressures near 1 in. of water, 6800-8500 fpm at pressures near 2 in. By agreement in the industry, all fan characteristics are referred to the handling of air at a single standard condition, namely, dry air at 70°F, density of 0.075 lb per cu ft; here only the air density affects the fan performance directly. The density is related to temperature and pressure as follows:

$$\rho = 1.325 \frac{P}{T} \qquad (5.1)$$

where

ρ = density, lb per cu ft
P = barometric pressure, in. mercury
T = absolute temperature, °R = °F + 460

The well known "fan laws" state the following useful relations: (1) for a fan of given size and constant rotational speed, the volume discharge is independent of air density, but the static pressure and the power absorbed vary directly with the density; (2) for a fan of given size, whose rotational speed is varied in order to maintain a constant static pressure, the fan speed, the volume discharge, and the power absorbed all vary inversely as the square root of the air density; (3) for a fan of given size, whose rotational speed is varied in such a way as to maintain a constant weight of air discharged per unit time, the fan speed, volume discharge, the static pressure all vary inversely as the air density, whereas the power required varies inversely as the square of the density; (4) for a fan of given size, handling air at constant density (for example, the standard density, 0.075 lb per cu ft), volume discharge varies directly as the fan speed, static pressure varies as the square of the speed, and power required varies as the cube of the speed.

Axial-flow and centrifugal fans of the standard commercial designs can be run with the wheel bearings directly in the hot air stream at air temperatures up to about 200°F. If air at a higher temperature is to be handled, the design must be such as to keep the bearings relatively cool.

Distribution of Air Flow in the Drier

Movement of a large volume of air in an orderly, desired path through a drier whose shape is any more complex than a straight cylindrical pipe must be classed as difficult; its mastery is more art than science. A few general principles may be stated, and engineers have succeeded in visualizing poor air distribution in helpful photographs, but by and large, improvement of unsatisfactory air flow in a drier must be brought about by "cut and try," guided by experience and instinct. Some large and expensive commercial installations have finally been abandoned after arduous, but fruitless, efforts to modify the air flow enough to make reasonably uniform drying possible. Aerodynamic studies of flow in a scale model of the drier may well be warranted in important new installations.

First and foremost among the principles to be remembered is the simple, but too often forgotten truth that a current of air possesses inertia and consequently its translational or rotational momentum tends to persist. When a straight, parallel current of air encounters a 90° elbow turn the inertia of the air crowds the flow to the outside of the bend. If an outlet branch is off-center from the supplying pipe, a corkscrew swirl is imparted to the outflow. Novice designers of driers invariably make the mistake of saving floor space by close-coupling the various parts of the unit; the result is that air must make several right-angle changes of direction in a relatively short travel and unless heroic remedial measures are taken, the air flow pattern in the drying section will be severely distorted. Devices known as splitters, baffles, vanes, and commercially in one form as "Ducturns®" (Tuttle and Bailey Div., Allied Thermal Corp., New Britain, Conn.) are employed to maintain some degree of uniformity of distribution in a current of air that is turning a corner. A general principle of good design is that all changes of direction, shape, or velocity shall be "easy," not abrupt. One device sometimes employed to secure uniform flow in a duct is to supply the air into a relatively large "plenum chamber," in which velocities will be low; the discharge from a small opening in the wall of the chamber will be quite uniformly distributed across the opening. Surest of all, but penalized with a substantial sacrifice of static head, is the interposition of a perforated sheet which acts like an orifice plate. This is the remedy of choice in a research or experimental drier, where the cost of the lost power will be inconsequential, and may be worth considering even in a commercial unit if other devices have failed to remedy a bad distribution.

A most illuminating group of photographs illustrating air flow in various types of equipment was published by Kröll (1959). A rapidly moving stream of fine, glittery particles in suspension is viewed in transparent models of different equipment arrangements, with flows at both high and low Reynolds numbers. A conical contraction, a conical enlargement, a slow right-angle turn with added turning vanes, a sharp, square-cornered turn, a series of closely spaced transverse bars simulating the pipes of a bank of heating coils, and a series of spaced shelves parallel to the air flow, are among the arrangements pictured. Some of these illustrations have also been used by Kuprianoff (1962) and by Charm (1963).

SUPPLYING HEAT TO DRIERS

Heating systems used in forced-air driers are of two basic types, direct and indirect. In the direct system, a fuel is burned in the air stream and the products of combustion are mixed with the drying air. In the indirect system, heat is transferred from steam, hot gases, or possibly other hot substances through a metal surface to the air used for drying. Gas or fuel oil is the fuel commonly used in direct heating systems; steam, waste gases from boilers or furnaces, or air streams heated by the combustion of gas, fuel oil, coal, or any available combustible material can be used in indirect heating systems.

Direct Heating

Direct combustion heaters are widely used in forced-air driers. The simplicity of such systems minimizes initial investment; maintenance costs are low in properly designed heaters. Heat transmission losses do not exist and a maximum of heat in the fuel is transferred to the drying air stream. When it is available at a competitive price, gas is the preferred fuel because of the simple construction of the heater, the simplicity of the control equipment, and the ease of handling. Gas is ordinarily burned in a "premix" burner installed directly in the drying air stream. A premix burner is basically a device that maintains the proper ratio of gas to air for satisfactory combustion, regardless of the amount of gas admitted to the burner. This permits regulation of total heat input without separate adjustment of the gas-air ratio. The flame from the premix burner is frequently shielded with an unlined, sheet-metal combustion chamber to prevent air currents from disturbing completion of the combustion. Refractory-lined combustion chambers are not essential to satisfactory burning of gas, but are sometimes used to ensure complete combustion.

Fuel oil is not as easily burned as gas. Unless the combustion takes place at relatively high temperature, some of the oil droplets may be chilled below their ignition temperature, with the result that smoke and soot are carried along with the drying air stream to contaminate the product in the drier. Refractory-lined combustion chambers, properly designed, are needed for the complete combustion of fuel oil. The chamber is frequently sheet steel, lined, and divided into zones with firebrick checker walls. At one end, oil is dispersed into fine droplets by means of any of several available atomizing devices. The zone immediately following the atomizer is heated to incandescence by combustion of the oil, thus providing the temperature needed for rapid combustion of the fuel. The first checker wall, also incandescent, and the following secondary zone and checker wall ensure the burning of oil droplets that may escape from the primary zone.

Fuel oils for direct combustion systems for food driers must be selected with some care. If the oil is too heavy in grade, it will not burn without producing smoke and soot. High sulfur contents must also be avoided. Sulfur dioxide is formed during combustion of the oil, and cases have been reported in which the product being dried absorbed an excessive and variable amount of sulfur dioxide from the stream of drying air. This led, of course, to an unacceptable product.

In direct heating systems, the hydrogen content of the fuel is burned to water vapor that increases the humidity of the drying air stream. A natural gas might contain 80% methane and 15% ethane and have a heating value of about 1050 Btu per standard cubic foot or 18,000 Btu per lb. When 1 lb of this gas is burned, about 1.75 lb of water vapor will enter the air stream. A light fuel oil may contain about 12% hydrogen by weight and have a heating value of about 19,000 Btu per lb. Upon combustion, 1 lb of this oil will release nearly 1.1 lb of water vapor into the air stream.

If we take 0.25 as a sufficiently close approximation to the humid heat of the circulating air in most drying systems, these conditions correspond to an increase in absolute humidity of about 0.000020 lb per lb dry air for each 1°F rise in temperature produced by natural gas combustion, or an increase of about 0.000015 lb moisture per pound dry air for each 1°F temperature rise produced by fuel oil combustion. The increase in humidity of the drying air stream resulting from direct combustion of the fuel is seldom important in tunnel driers and other types of driers commonly used for the drying of piece-form foods. In fact, part of the air flow through a drier may be recirculated to increase the humidity in the drying of some fruits. Milk is often spray dried with air direct-heated by gas, but some other spray-dried products are so hygroscopic that the heating system must be indirect in order to avoid the addition of moisture to the drying air.

Indirect Heating

Two basic types of indirect heating systems are used for heating air to be used for drying. The distinction depends upon whether the heating medium is a condensable vapor such as steam, or a hot gas. In the latter case, the heart of the heating system is a heat exchanger in which the hot gases flow through passages separated by sheet metal from passages through which the drying air flows. Heat is transferred from the hot gas to the metal wall to the drying air, and mixing of the hot gas stream and the drying air stream is entirely avoided. The method used to heat the hot gas entering the heat exchanger has no relation to the drying air. Waste heat from boiler or furnace stack gases may be used to heat the drying air, or furnaces burning gas, oil, coal, wood, or other combustible material may be used. However, the heat transfer coefficients attainable in flue heating systems of this kind are so low (in the range of 2–3 Btu/(hr) (sq ft) ($^{\circ}$F)) that an extensive flue surface has to be provided to supply even a moderate amount of heat to the drying air. Air heaters in which the heat is provided by condensing steam ordinarily take the form of finned coils. These are assemblies of tubing into which steam is fed, arranged so that the condensate can be drained away and removed readily, with thin metal fins or other types of extended surface attached to the outside of the tubing to provide extra heat transfer surface. Such heating coils are manufactured in a wide range of sizes and may be a single coil or several rows of coils deep. Multiple coils are often designed so that 1 coil carries the estimated minimum heating load and is always fully heated, while the remainder of the operating load is carried by 1 or more smaller coils to which the steam supply is regulated by the automatic temperature control. Major manufacturers of steam-air heating coils make coils suitable for steam pressures ranging from 2 to 200 lb per sq in. and temperatures up to 375°F. Recommended practice for such heaters is to provide for an air velocity through the heater, based on the total face area, of 600–800 fpm. Under these conditions, the pressure drop of the air in flowing through the heater will be approximately 0.2 in. of water. These heaters readily provide the air temperatures used in forced-air driers for piece-form foods, but may not be capable of providing temperatures as high as are needed in some spray-drying operations.

INSTRUMENTATION FOR THE FOOD DEHYDRATION PLANT

A well-engineered plant will contain many kinds of measuring instruments as part of its normal initial equipment. Some of the instruments will only indicate the value of some process variable, some will make a continuous record of the variable, and still others will automatically control its value, perhaps making a continuous record at the same time. Instruments deserve scrupulously careful maintenance and protection from accidental or ignorant mishandling; a meter that gives false indications is far worse than no instrument at all. Regular inspection and testing of all the instruments in a plant should be a specific assignment to the technical or engineering staff. The record of these inspections should be kept for several years.

Special problems encountered in the measurement of temperature, pressure, humidity, and air movement will be discussed next and the determination of moisture content of the food material itself during the drying will be considered briefly. The theory or practice of automatic process control will not be presented nor will the various mechanisms used to achieve it be indicated; for these subjects, see such books as Rhodes (1941) or Weber (1941), or handbooks such as Marks (1951) or Perry *et al.* (1963). Kilpatrick *et al.* (1955) described instruments used for control of conditions in tunnel dehydrators.

The instrumental indication of the value of almost any process variable can be displayed or used to bring about corrective action at a great distance by means of telemetry—i.e., remote measurement. Its principles are applied in all remote-reading instruments (Rhodes 1941; Davidson *et al.* 1951). A special problem in food dehydration is telemetry of the temperature in food material on a loaded tray or conveyor being moved through a drying tunnel. A few such measurements have been made by inserting fine-wire thermocouples into pieces of the food at the wet end of the drier, all being connected to a multiple-point temperature recorder at that end, and allowing the wires to be dragged all the way through the drier without disturbing their placement in the food. Usually this is difficult to accomplish without mishaps. A similar problem in the study of air-blast freezing of foods was successfully investigated by Elsken (1960) and Durkee *et al.* (1961). A tiny short-wave radio transmitter was allowed to accompany packages of the food through the tunnel. The frequency of its signal was modulated by the temperature at the transmitter. The telemetry devised by American and Russian scientists to send back information from earth-launched satellites has been based on generally similar principles and has operated successfully under infinitely more difficult circumstances.

Temperature Measurement

Temperature is most often determined by measuring the thermal expansion of a liquid (for example, mercury or alcohol in the bulb of a thermometer), the vapor pressure of a liquid, or the electric potential developed at a thermocouple junction. Many commercial temperature indicating or controlling devices operate on the vapor pressure principle. The liquid-expansion instrument and the thermocouple have nearly linear temperature scales, while the scale of a vapor pressure instrument is crowded at its low-temperature end, very open at higher temperatures.

The temperature indicated by the instrument, of whichever type, is that of the liquid or thermocouple junction in the sensitive bulb, and it can only be inferred that the temperature to be measured, that of the nearby or surrounding liquid or gas, is not far different; we try to arrange matters so that it will be very nearly the same. If a rapid response to changing temperature in an air stream is needed a small sensitive bulb of low heat capacity may be used, provided with copper fins to increase the rate of heat transfer to it from the surrounding air.

If the temperature of a hot lye solution is being measured, the glass or brass thermometer bulb must be protected with an iron thermometer well, and the inevitable lag or error in temperature indication should be minimized by careful design of the well, and by making sure that its sealing liquid does not leak out and that external fittings are well insulated.

The difference in linear coefficient of expansion of two dissimilar metals is employed in many industrial thermometers, thermostats, and thermoregulators. A bimetallic strip, e.g., of spring brass and steel, changes shape when its temperature changes, and a linkage or gear train magnifies the effect. A recently developed electronic device, sensitively responsive to small temperature changes and known as a thermistor, is made of a semiconductive material which has a high negative temperature coefficient of electrical resistivity. It can be applied to temperature measurements on a semimicro scale.

Measurement of surface temperatures, for example the temperature of the drying surfaces of a drum drier, can be accomplished readily, but with only moderate accuracy, by pressing a thermocouple against the surface. Some industrial forms are self-contained portable instruments, with an indicating direct-reading dial and a sensing element made in various forms such as needle-pointed probes, small flat plates, and rollers. Accurate determination of a surface temperature is possible if the body is stationary by employing very fine thermocouple wires, laying them in a shallow groove in the hot surface, and luting them in with a conductive cement (Baker and Ryder 1950).

Any temperature measuring device will be affected by radiant energy incident upon it unless the energy is totally reflected. The thermometer bulbs in the hot end of a gas- or oil-fired dehydrator are especially likely to receive radiation from hot brickwork of the furnace and then give spuriously high readings. Great care should be exercised in the design of dehydrators to place the sensitive elements where they cannot "see" the open flame or incandescent brickwork. Radiation error may also be decreased by putting a mirror-finish on the sensitive bulbs.

The most troublesome errors encountered in temperature measuring instruments are basically failures of communication; the instrument may correctly indicate a temperature at the sensitive bulb, but the operator may mistakenly ascribe it to a different location and therefore read the message erroneously. For example, the air stream coming from a large air heater may be highly stratified into distinct streams at different temperatures. The thermometer reading at one place will then differ greatly from the mean temperature of the whole air stream. Such difficulties as this should be looked for during the acceptance testing of any new drier. They can sometimes be corrected by adjustment of baffles or resistances, but may necessitate more radical steps such as revision of the steam coil sizing and arrangement or transposition of the heaters and the main air-circulating fan. Elimination of uneven air flow through a large cross-section is commonly regarded as easier to achieve than elimination of temperature stratification.

One of the most important uses of thermometers in dehydration work is to serve as the paired sensitive elements of a psychrometer, that is, the wet- and dry-bulb thermometer. This use is discussed more fully in a later section on the measurement of humidity.

Pressure Measurement

Most of the pressure measurements with which we shall be concerned are at or below atmospheric pressure, ranging downward into the realm of high vacuum. We need not devote any discussion to the instruments universely used to indicate and record steam pressure, water pressure, compressed air pressure, and the like, beyond pointing out that in the course of time every such instrument will go out of calibration because of fatigue and creep in the pressure-sensitive Bourdon tube and wear in the multiplying linkage. The technical staff of a plant will need to check and adjust all gages periodically.

Table 5.1 presents the relation between several of the units in which pressure is sometimes expressed. Steam and other service-line pressures are usually stated

TABLE 5.1

EQUIVALENTS OF PRESSURE UNITS

1 atmosphere	760 Torr (mm mercury)
	14.696 lb/sq in. ("psi")
	10,333 kg/sq m
1 lb/sq in.	15.710 Torr
	0.06804 atm
	703.1 kg/sq m
10,000 kg/sq m	735.53 Torr
	0.9678 atm
	14.22 lb/sq in.
1000 Torr (mm mercury)	1.316 atm
	13,596 kg/sq m
	19.34 lb/sq in.
1 in. of water (60°F)	0.002456 atm
	0.03609 lb/sq in.
1,000 ft of air (standard conditions, density 0.075 lb/cu ft)	0.0355 atm
	0.5205 lb/sq in.

at gage pressure in engineering units, i.e., pressure measured from a zero point at one standard atmosphere, 14.7 lb per sq in. The abbreviation "psig" is often used for "pounds per square inch, gage."

Atmospheric Pressure.—Atmospheric pressure is measured by the barometer. The common standard instrument comprises a fairly wide vertical glass tube, sealed at its upper end, filled with mercury and dipping at its lower end into a mercury cistern, and with a brass scale upon which the height of the mercury in the closed tube can be read precisely. Mean barometric height at sea level is 760 mm or 29.92 in. of mercury at a temperature of 0°C, 32°F. The correction to be applied to the reading if the instrument is at a higher temperature is given in

TABLE 5.2

CORRECTION OF MERCURY BAROMETER READINGS TO TEMPERATURE OF 32°F

Temperature of Mercury Column (°F)	Observed Reading of Mercury Column (In.)					
	20	22	24	26	28	30
40	−0.02	−0.02	−0.02	−0.03	−0.03	−0.03
60	−0.06	−0.06	−0.07	−0.07	−0.08	−0.08
80	−0.09	−0.10	−0.11	−0.12	−0.13	−0.14
100	−0.13	−0.14	−0.15	−0.17	−0.18	−0.19

Source: Adapted from Davidson *et al.* (1951).

Table 5.2. In the dehydration plant a good aneroid barometer is an adequate substitute for the mercury barometer. Although this instrument is more rugged than the mercury-in-glass barometer, it too needs careful handling. Before making a reading, the case should be tapped lightly several times, in order to overcome friction at the jeweled pivot. The barometer should be calibrated and its setting adjusted at least once or twice a year by comparison with a standard instrument. The setting must correspond to actual atmospheric pressure at the location of the instrument, not, as in most home barometers, to the computed sea-level pressure which is shown on weather maps. The mean barometric pressure in various cities in the United States is given in Table 4.3 and the mean relation of barometric pressure to altitude is shown in Fig. 4.7, both in Chap. 4.

The static pressure developed by a fan or blower, or the draft in a furnace, is commonly measured by some form of draft gage. This may be a simple U-tube partly filled with water, but many devices of higher sensitivity are also used; for descriptions of several types, see Drew *et al.* (1950), Davidson *et al.* (1951), or Rhodes (1941).

Pressure Difference or Head.—Some form of head meter is very widely employed to determine the velocity of flow of air or other fluid. Techniques for investigation of air flow in a drier are described in a later section but some of the instruments used will be discussed here. "Head," in this context, means a measured difference between pressures at two points in the fluid flow, expressed as the equivalent difference in elevation of the fluid level at the two points. The pitot tube, the venturi tube, the orifice, and the flow nozzle are standard devices for producing a measurable pressure difference that varies in a predictable way with the fluid flow.

The pitot tube (diagrammed in cross-section in Fig. 5.7) displays on a manometer the difference, l, between the impact pressure from the opening which faces directly into the flow and the static pressure, taken from the openings that are finished flush with the surface of the tube. The theoretical relationship is expressed in the law of falling bodies

$$u = \sqrt{2gh} \qquad (5.2)$$

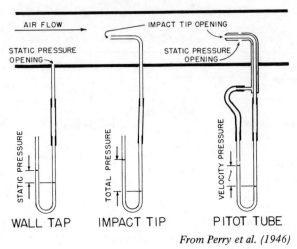

WALL TAP   IMPACT TIP   PITOT TUBE

From Perry et al. (1946)

FIG. 5.7. ONE FORM OF PITOT TUBE

where

> u = fluid velocity, ft/sec
> g = acceleration due to gravity, ft/sec^2
> h = head of fluid, ft

The pressure difference indicated by the manometer is related to the head of fluid by the following expression:

$$h = \frac{l}{12} V\rho \qquad (5.3)$$

where

> l = manometer reading, in.
> V = specific volume of the flowing fluid, cu ft/lb
> ρ = density of the manometric liquid, lb/cu ft

If the pitot tube is used to measure velocity of air in a drier, a very sensitive manometer must be used unless the air velocity is quite high. For example, from Equation (5.2), if the velocity is 900 ft/min h = 3.50 ft of air (at standard gravity, $\sqrt{2g}$ = 8.025). The reading of l from a water manometer [Equation (5.3)] for air of specific volume 17.0 cu ft/lb would be only about 0.04 in. The reading of an actual instrument will depart from this theoretical value by an amount depending on the exact design of the pitot tube and its placement in the air stream (Rhodes 1941) but the correction need not be more than a few percentage points.

The venturi tube, often permanently installed in service supply lines to serve as a flow meter, consists of a conical approach section, in which the flow of fluid is accelerated, a short cylindrical throat of about $\frac{1}{2}$ to $\frac{1}{4}$ the diameter of the entrance pipe, and then a long, gradually diverging cone that finally comes back to the full line diameter. Static pressure taps at the inlet section and the throat are connected to a sensitive manometer (Fig. 5.8). In a venturi tube or other type of restriction of the flow channel, such as an orifice plate or a flow nozzle,

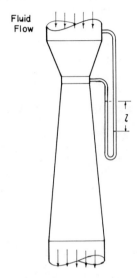

FIG. 5.8. DIAGRAM OF A VENTURI TUBE

the increase in the kinetic energy of the fluid as it is accelerated into the throat is very nearly balanced by the decrease in potential energy of the fluid, shown by a decrease in its static pressure. The equation which represents the decrease in head at the throat takes the following very simple form if the flowing fluid is a liquid (i.e., incompressible):

$$u_2 = C\sqrt{2g\Delta h + u_1^2} \tag{5.4}$$

where

u_2 = fluid velocity at the throat section, ft/sec
u_1 = fluid velocity at the approach section, ft/sec
Δh = change in head, ft
C = a coefficient of discharge, dimensionless, nearly equal to one for a well designed venturi tube

Equation (5.3) applies here if l is the manometer reading, in inches.

The equation for the venturi tube is more complicated if the fluid is compressible, like a gas or vapor. The decrease in head at the throat is then described closely by the adiabatic frictionless flow equations; see Rhodes (1941), or Drew *et al.* (1950).

The venturi tube has the advantage over an orifice plate or flow nozzle that in a properly designed instrument very little loss of energy occurs, so that the increased velocity head at the throat is transformed back into pressure head almost completely in the slowly diverging exit section. We omit discussion of orifice plates and flow nozzles because these devices are not often used to make the flow measurements needed in a dehydration plant. Their characteristics are described in detail in the Rhodes (1941) and Drew *et al.* (1950) references.

Low Pressures.—Low absolute pressures, such as the vapor pressure of a dehydrated food or the pressure in a vacuum chamber, are measured by special techniques. The Bourdon-tube pressure gage, of the familiar industrial pressure gage type, may be constructed to indicate vacuum (usually reading then in inches of mercury, zero on the scale being at atmospheric pressure) as well as pressure, but is not suitable for precise measurement of even moderately high vacuum—that is, moderately low absolute pressure, for example a pressure below about 25 Torr or 1 in. of mercury.

An ordinary U-tube manometer containing a light liquid of very low vapor pressure (such as "Octoil," Distillation Products, Inc., which is used as a sealing liquid in vacuum pumps) is a suitable gage for determination of the water vapor pressures of food products, including dehydrated foods (Makower and Myers 1943). For example, at a temperature of 95°F, in the presence of liquid water, which has a vapor pressure of 42.17 mm of mercury, the pressure reading on an oil instead of a mercury manometer would be more than 13 times as great, about 57 cm of oil.

We shall describe briefly mercury manometers of the Dubrovin and McLeod types, the Pirani gage, and the ionization gage, which are appropriate for measurements in various pressure ranges from about 3 cm of mercury (30 Torr) down to about 10^{-7} Torr.

A manometer of the Dubrovin type described by Legault *et al.* (1948) is well suited to measurement of water vapor pressure in dehydrated foods. The body of the instrument is a glass tube, partly filled with mercury. A glass float, closed at its upper end but open below, and also filled with mercury, is centered within the tube and is guided so as to move up and down freely. Then the height to which the float will rise in the tube will depend on the absolute pressure in the system, and the difference in mercury levels within the float and in the tube provides the reading. The sensitivity of the instrument may readily be made about seven times as great as that of an ordinary mercury U-tube manometer.

The McLeod gage is also a mercury manometer constructed of glass. Various modifications of its form are in use, but all apply Boyle's law that at constant temperature the volume of a gas is inversely proportional to its pressure. A sample of the low-pressure gas whose pressure is to be measured is trapped by mercury in a large side-bulb, *A* (Fig. 5.9) having known volume and provided with a graduated closed capillary stem, *B*. The mercury level is then raised further, filling the large bulb and part of its stem and raising the mercury into side arms *C* and *D*, the former having a capillary of the same known diameter as the one in *B*

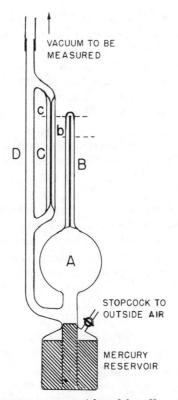

Adapted from Yarwood (1961)

FIG. 5.9. DIAGRAM OF ONE FORM OF McLEOD GAGE

and arranged close beside the latter. The level is raised until the mercury in side-arm C just reaches the level of the top of the capillary in side-arm B. At that point, the level of mercury in capillary B is read; the gas in the top of this capillary is now under a known degree of compression, and a simple formula relates the cross-sectional area of the capillary, the distance between graduations b and c on the two capillaries, the combined volume of bulb A and capillary B, and the initial pressure of the gas:

$$p = \frac{ah^2}{v} \qquad (5.5)$$

where

p = initial gas pressure, mm of mercury
a = cross-section area of the capillary, mm^2
h = distance from b to c, mm
v = total volume, mm^3

The McLeod gage is regarded as the basic instrument for measurement of low pressures, and most other low-pressure or vacuum measuring devices are calibrated against it as the standard.

Two other kinds of instrument sometimes used for measuring low absolute pressures will only be mentioned here because they are best adapted to lower pressures than are applied even in freeze drying. The Pirani gage depends upon the change in thermal conductivity of a gas with change in pressure (Yarwood 1961). The ionization gage determines the relative number of positive ions formed in a low-pressure gas by electrons given off at a heated filament; this number is a function of the pressure of the gas (Yarwood 1961).

Humidity Measurement

Determination of the quantity of water vapor contained in a body or stream of air is a measurement basic to study and control of all forms of convection drying. One method of measuring this quantity, namely wet- and dry-bulb thermometry, or psychrometry, stands out from all of the many others in convenience and direct applicability. We shall discuss some of the other methods first, but only briefly.

Water vapor may be determined quantitatively in air or other gas by the standard procedures of analytical chemistry. A measured volume of the air is dried by passing it through a weighed tube of desiccant such as phosphorus pentoxide; the increase in weight of the desiccant is the moisture content of the sample of air. The temperature and pressure of the sample must be accurately measured. Results may be translated to terms of absolute humidity (and thence to dew point, relative humidity, or other measure of humidity) by applying the gas laws and the known specific volume of dry air. This procedure cannot be used, of course, if the temperature and humidity of the air sample are so high that saturation occurs when the sample is cooled toward room temperature.

The hair hygrometer, which is a familiar instrument in many offices and homes, indicates relative humidity of the surrounding air by changes in the length of a small flat bundle of human hair which is held under tension by a light spring. A multiplying linkage moves a pointer across the scale of relative humidity, reading between 0 and 100%. Equilibrium moisture content of the hair, which has been made fat-free by extraction with a solvent, is attained quickly and the hair shrinks or expands promptly. However, the instrument indication is appreciably affected by the air temperature, there is a hysteresis effect (a different indication for a rising than for a falling humidity), and gradual relaxation of the stress in the hair makes it necessary to recalibrate frequently. The same principle has sometimes been applied to the construction of automatic humidity control instruments, where the sensitive element may be a small piece of wood, but these same difficulties and uncertainties are encountered.

An electric hygrometer, developed by Dunmore (1939) for upper-atmosphere meteorological observation, was modified by Brockington et at. (1949) to determine moisture equilibria in whole-kernel corn, and was further developed by Mossel and van Kuijk (1955) for study of moisture relations of other foods. The common feature of these instruments is a sensitive element consisting of a grid of fine wires coated with an insulating varnish that has the hydroscopic salt lithium chloride dispersed in it. The coating changes its electrical resistance in response to changes of humidity in the surrounding atmosphere. In the Brockington et al. instrument, a microammeter measures the current produced by a small potential impressed across the grid, while in the Mosell and van Kuijk hygrometer, a constant AC voltage produces perceptible heating of the grid and the equilibrium temperature attained is measured. These instruments are well adapted to measurement of high humidities—90% or even higher.

The dew point of an air stream, that is, the temperature to which it must be cooled at constant pressure to become saturated with water vapor, can be determined very precisely, and this is a standard way of determining the humidity of air. One form of dew point hygrometer comprises a thin silvered wafer, mounted on a device which can be controllably cooled by circulating cold liquid or gas, and arranged in the air stream so that its mirror surface can be constantly observed through a window. The temperature of the wafer is indicated by a sensitive fine-wire thermocouple. In operation the mirror device is gradually and steadily cooled until the mirror fogs over. The temperature indicated by the thermocouple at that moment is taken as the dew point of the air. This principle is applicable to air or other gas of extremely low dew point—that is, very low absolute humidity—and is therefore used in testing the dryness of commercial compressed gases. It is incorporated in several industrial instruments, some of which operate automatically by using a photocell and Wheatstone bridge balancing circuit to detect the fogging of the mirror and control the rate of cooling.

The Wet- and Dry-Bulb Thermometer, or Psychrometer.—The absorption of heat which accompanies evaporation of water produces a cooling effect that is readily measurable by a pair of thermometers, one of them indicating the air temperature, the other the temperature of a wet surface in the same air stream. Measurement of the difference between the two temperatures, called the wet-bulb depression, is outstandingly important to the control of drying processes.

The theory and experimental characteristics of the psychrometer have been discussed by many investigators, for example Sherwood and Comings (1932), Arnold (1933), Wexler and Brombacher (1951), Lykow (1950, 1955), and Krischer (1956). The wet-bulb temperature of a stream of air (or other gas) is the temperature at which a dynamic equilibrium is established between the heat inflow from all sources to a wet body in the air stream and the heat absorption at the surface of the body to supply the latent heat of evaporation. The heat inflow comes partly by conduction within the instrument itself, partly by convective transfer from the air stream, and partly by absorption of radiation from surrounding bodies. Wet-bulb temperature indicated by the thermometer or thermocouple is therefore affected by the air pressure and the air velocity past the sensitive element, as well as the temperatures and emissivities of other bodies which can radiate heat to it and, to a minor extent, the construction and arrangement of the sensitive element.

The wet-bulb depression, $t_a - t_w$, is closely proportional to the difference between the vapor pressure of water at the wet-bulb temperature, p_{sw}, and the partial pressure of water vapor in the air stream, p_w, or

$$p_{sw} - p_w = J(t_a - t_w) \tag{5.6}$$

where J is the proportionality factor, nearly constant and nearly equal to 0.5 if pressures are expressed in millimeters of mercury and temperatures in degrees C, and the air is at or near normal sea-level barometric pressure (Walker *et al.* 1937). The factor which most strongly affects the value of the proportionality factor, J, is the amount of heat received by the wet bulb through radiation from the surroundings. These are usually at or above the dry-bulb temperature of the air, hence the effect of radiation is usually to raise the reading of the wet-bulb thermometer. However, the heat transferred to the wet bulb by convection can be increased so greatly by increasing the velocity of the air past the bulb that the heat supplied by radiation will become negligible in comparison. Psychrometers intended for household or office use are usually calibrated in substantially still air. For research or industrial use, however, it is better always to expose the instrument to a sufficiently high air velocity so that J will assume its nearly constant minimum value. According to Walker *et al.* this velocity is about 900–1500 fpm. The air velocity employed in many practical dehydrators lies in this general range. The psychrometer element should therefore be fully exposed to the circulating air, not carefully tucked away in a safely sheltered recess, as too often happens. If the construction or operation of the drier does not allow a good location in the main air stream, a special aspirator should be used to divert a part of that stream over the psychrometer elements at a sufficiently high velocity.

Wet- and dry-bulb temperature readings in relatively still air are best secured by means of an aspirated psychrometer (a battery-operated form is available from many instrument supply houses), or, if there is sufficient free space, by means of a sling psychrometer (Fig. 5.10). The latter consists of two mercury-

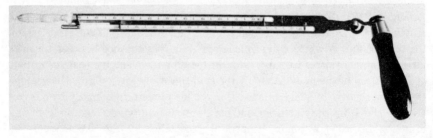

FIG. 5.10. SLING PSYCHROMETER

in-glass thermometers mounted side by side on a light support that is pivoted on a handle so it can be swung in a circle. One of the thermometers projects a little way down below the support; a light cotton fabric sleeve is slipped over the projecting segment. The technique of using the instrument is as follows: A container of distilled water is first brought to a temperature a few degrees above the expected wet-bulb temperature. The fabric-covered end of the "wet" thermometer is dipped in the warmed water for a few moments, then the instrument is swung at a rate of 4 or 5 rotations per second for 10–15 sec. The rotation is stopped and the temperature of the wet bulb is read quickly. Then the instrument is swung again for 10–15 sec and read again. If the second reading is lower than the first, the instrument is swung again and read again. A long flat minimum temperature would be noted if the readings were continued long enough, but ordinarily little change will be observed even in the second or third swing. Finally the reading of the dry bulb will be observed.

Two precautions apply to all psychrometers: Wet the wick only with distilled water, and replace the wick with a clean one frequently. Under the excellent drying conditions that exist in a dehydrator, evaporation from the wick is very rapid; if tap water is used to wet it, soluble salts in the water will soon encrust the wick and produce false readings. Even if distilled water is used, the dust always suspended in the circulating air will soon collect on the wick. Much research has been done to find ways to assure maintenance of a fully wet, clean, sensitive thermometer or thermocouple (Porter and Considine 1950). Regrettably, observation in numerous operating plants discloses many "wet bulbs" which have not been wet for a long time. The operating staff of such a plant has fallen into the habit of disregarding the psychrometer indications.

The water supplied to the wick of a wet-bulb thermometer should be at nearly the wet-bulb temperature of the air. Failure to meet this condition is responsible for erroneous indications in many industrial applications. Particularly objectionable is attachment of the water reservoir to the water service line and operation with a steady flow of cold water through the reservoir.

The fabric used to cover the sensitive bulb or thermocouple should be unsized and defatted, so as to wet easily. It need not be particularly thin. In some industrial instruments a porous alundum sleeve, fitting snugly over the bulb, is used instead of fabric. Keeping the pores from clogging with salts or dust is said not to be a serious problem.

Wet- and dry-bulb temperature units are often used for the automatic control of humidity in circulating air. The dry-bulb unit controls temperature, while the wet-bulb unit either controls a damper which can change the proportion of recirculation of the air or a valve which can introduce a direct water spray or steam spray into the air stream.

Note that the wet-bulb temperature indicated by instruments used as described above has quite a different significance than the "thermodynamic wet-bulb temperature" shown on standard psychrometric charts. The latter represents the hypothetical result of adiabatic evaporation of water, supplied at the same temperature, up to the point of saturation of the air. No question of radiation effects or air velocities arises. As an experimental fact, however, the "physical wet-bulb temperature," determined by the psychrometer with adequate shielding from outside radiation and adequate air velocity, agrees closely with the computed "thermodynamic wet-bulb temperature."

Measurement of Air Movement

Quantitative control of air movement is necessary to the satisfactory operation of any convection drier, and control implies ability to measure accurately. Neglect of this factor has been responsible for many expensive failures of dehydration operations. Quantitative measurements of air velocity (both speed and direction) are often needed. Neither qualitative understanding of flow patterns nor accurate measurement is easy to achieve; a combination of several methods may be required for satisfactory analysis of the performance of a single industrial drier.

The pitot tube (shown in Fig. 5.7) is a basic tool for study of air velocities, but is far more useful for determination of flow through a straight pipe or duct than for mapping flow patterns in a drier. Total volume of flow through a duct is determined by making a velocity traverse. The pitot tube must be accurately positioned parallel to the axis of the pipe; if possible, at least five diameters of straight pipe should lie ahead of the instrument, and straightening of vanes may also have to be placed in the approach section (Davidson *et al.* 1951). The traverse of the duct is usually taken on 2 diameters at right angles, and in a cylindrical duct at least from 12 to 24 readings of velocity head should be taken at points which divide the cross section into from 3 to 6 equal annular areas. An even larger number of equal-area segments should be traversed if the duct is rectangular. The diameter of the pitot tube should be not over 5% of the diameter of the duct, in order to minimize interference with the flow. The velocity at the center of a duct will be higher than the velocity near the perimeter; the ratio of mean velocity to centerline velocity will usually be within the range from 0.77 to 0.92, the exact value depending mainly upon the roughness of the inner surface of the duct. A ratio of 0.91 is frequently used by engineers to provide a rough estimate of total flow from a single reading at the center.

Several kinds of anemometer, or open velocity-meter, are available from instrument supply houses. The Robinson type, in which either 3 or 4 hemispherical cups fastened to spokes a few inches long are pivoted on a vertical shaft, is in general use for measuring wind velocity, but is poorly suited to insertion in a drier. The "windmill" type, on the other hand, is often useful for checking air flow inside full-scale dehydrators. The very light, inclined, multiple vanes are carried on a horizontal shaft which rotates freely in jeweled bearings. A revolution counter and stop watch are used to determine the number of revolutions made by the windmill in a set period of time, and the result is translated to linear velocity by means of a predetermined calibration curve. The instrument is easily damaged by careless handling. Its indications are affected in an indeterminate way if its face is not held nearly perpendicular to the air flow, the inertia of the wheel makes it overrun rapid changes of air velocity, and its case is sufficiently large to cause a perceptible disturbance of the very air flow it purports to measure. If the experimenter himself must enter the drier to make the instrument readings, the air flow pattern will be greatly affected. Nevertheless, much may be learned from intelligent exploration with an anemometer.

The bridled swinging vane type of anemometer, typified by the Alnor Velometer (Illinois Testing Laboratories, Inc., Chicago) is extensively used in installing and testing air conditioning equipment, and may be useful in surveying air velocities within a drier. The light, jewel-pivoted vane within the instrument is swung out against light spring pressure by the impact force of the air stream against the sensitive area, and the equilibrium position of the vane is registered on a scale. Several kinds of external nozzle are available; one averages the impact pressure over a distance of 4 in. or more, others register static pressure or total pressure at the point of test. Pressure readings up to 3 in. of water can be indicated, or velocities from 0 up to 6000 fpm. All of the instruments must be individually calibrated by the maker. As in other anemometers, readings must be interpreted with full regard for the several sources of possible error, particularly the flow disturbances that occur if the operator must accompany the instrument into the drier.

The heated-thermocouple anometer, typified by another Alnor instrument, the Thermo-Anemometer (see also Lowe and Hawes 1949) consists of a fine-wire thermocouple which can be positioned in the air stream by means of a probe, and a standard battery which passes current through the couple; the resulting temperature rise, indicated by the couple itself, depends upon the air velocity. The sensitive area of the instrument is no more than $1/8$-in. sq. It is also very rapidly responsive to even minor fluctuations of air velocity or direction, and consequently does not give useful steady readings in a highly turbulent air stream. It is most useful for exploring slow steady air flows—for example, the air movement above the bed of partly dried material in a bin drier.

Estimation of Air Movement from Fan Characteristics.—Total air flow through a drier, or through a separate stage of a multistage system, can be estimated roughly if the air circulating fan is one of the several standard types and if the static pressure rise across the fan is known. Manufacturers of centrifugal and axial-flow fans publish "characteristic curves" which describe the performance of their equipment. Use of this characteristic, and the size and speed of the fan, in conjunction with the "fan laws" and the conditions of temperature and pressure given for the problem at hand, provide the required value of the total flow delivered by the fan. Most importantly, from this figure one can readily compute the total mass of air being circulated, which is a basic factor in the evaporative capacity of the drier and in the relation between weight of water removed and the consequent decrease in the temperature of the air. The mean air velocity over the wet material can also be computed from the volume of air flowing and the known cross-section dimensions of the air passages in the drier. However, this mean velocity may signify little if the distribution of air flow is very uneven. In a poorly designed drier, the actual air velocity at some parts of a cross-section may be zero, or even be the reverse of the flow in the main stream, because of large eddies, "dead spots," and "back-waters." This subject was discussed earlier in this chapter.

Measurement of Material Moisture Content

Laboratory equipment designed to monitor the change of weight of samples of material in a drier has been described by a number of investigators, for example Ede and Hales (1948), Lykow (1950, 1955), Krischer (1956), and Jason (1958). It consists of a sensitive balance; one of the balance carries the sample in the path of the circulating air. In some designs the weighing is continuous and automatic, but more usually the air flow is interrupted while a weighing is being made.

Much experimental study of drying rates has been carried out in cabinet driers which are not equipped for this weighing in place; instead, an entire tray load of material is periodically removed from the drier, quickly weighed, and then immediately returned to its place in the drier. Various tests of this procedure have shown that the error introduced is acceptably small.

Periodical checks on the moisture content of material in the drier, particularly at about the time when completion of the drying is expected, are made as part of the normal operating routine in commercial dehydration. Here, if the operator is not to be forced to rely entirely on the "feel" of the material (let it be noted that a skilled drier man can make a remarkably accurate estimate by "feel" after he has become familiar with the product) use of one of the rapid moisture determination methods is essential. An answer is needed in a matter of a few minutes, at most. Empirical correlation of an instrument reading with true moisture content is entirely satisfactory for this purpose.

CABINET DRIERS

The cabinet drier may be classified as an air-convection batch tray drier, usually built as an independent "machine," or unit, and intended for relatively small-scale operations. It has two main fields of use. As a single unit or integrated group of units it may be used to produce almost any piece-form, air-dehydrated food, and it may be the drier of choice for the task of preserving a variety of fresh fruits and vegetables during the season in quantities ranging between 1 to 20 tons per day. Driers of this kind were widely used in the United States during World War II to conserve food grown locally by institutions and small communities. The other appropriate application is in laboratory and pilot-scale experimentation on the theory and practice of drying. For example, a properly equipped cabinet drier can be operated to duplicate the drying behavior of a compartment drier or a kiln drier, and can give a close simulation of the performance of a truck-and-tunnel drier or a continuous-conveyor drier. Both types of application find an advantage in the batch nature of the operation. The laboratory experimenter must be able to impose an immediate change in drying conditions at any time throughout the entire mass of his experimental sample, or keep conditions accurately constant for a long time; both of these are things he can readily do with the small batch. The small producer of dried foods can dry each one of many different kinds of fresh produce under the conditions that are optimum for it; each batch can be made large or small within wide limits to suit the occasion; and the drying of a batch can be started and stopped under defined conditions. A continuous operation, in contrast, always encounters a long period of changing conditions every time the system must be started or shut down, and for that reason is always run uninterruptedly for as long a time as is practically feasible.

Main Features of Construction

The size of the cabinet drier ranges from that of the laboratory unit that will stand on top of a table to that of a substantial structure capable of accommodating and drying a ton or more of fresh produce in one batch (Beavens 1944; USDA 1944). Experimental driers have been described and pictured by many investigators, for example Ede and Hales (1948), Lykow (1950, 1955), Krischer (1956), and Jason (1958), as well as the two preceding references. Several equipment manufacturers offer cabinet drier units, complete and ready to be connected to steam and electric power supplies.

A typical drier consists of a framed structure whose walls, roof, and base are well insulated against heat loss, and is equipped with an internal fan that forces the drying medium (usually air) through a heating system and distributes it uniformly across or through one or more trays loaded with the prepared wet material. Removable baffles can be used to direct the air either down through the trays or horizontally between trays. Adjustable dampers are provided to controllably exhaust a part of the air leaving the tray section, make up the loss by admitting fresh air, and recirculate the remainder. One or more tightly fitting insulated doors are provided to give access to the tray section. The material of construction may be light metal panels supporting a rigid insulating material, plywood, hard fiber, cement-asbestos board, etc., preferably fire-resistant and capable of withstanding heavy condensation of warm water on the inside surfaces from circulation of very humid air. Internal baffles, turning vanes, and finally a perforated sheet, are often provided to distribute the air flow uniformly inside the cabinet. Thermometers are installed with the sensitive elements directly in the main air current approaching the drying trays, and often also in the air current leaving the trays. (See earlier discussion on measurement of humidity.)

Most modern cabinet driers are heated by extended-surface steam coils. They can also be heated by direct combustion of gas (Beavens 1944) or, especially in a very small drier, by electrical resistance units. The amount of heat required is a maximum at the very beginning of a run, when evaporation from the moist material is so rapid that air may be supplied at a very high temperature without damaging the material, and when the fresh air damper may be open wide in order to keep the humidity low in the circulating air. A rule of thumb applied by designers is that the heater should be able to deliver from 1200 to 1600 Btu per sq ft of tray surface in the drier. Toward the end of a batch run, when evaporation is very slow, the drier can be run with nearly complete recirculation of air. Inevitable leaks in the system will keep the humidity low. The heat demand is then only a small fraction of what it was at the beginning of the run.

Both centrifugal fans and axial-flow fans are used to circulate the air in cabinet driers. In a small production drier the air flow across trays may be designed for a velocity of 400–1000 fpm, or, if the drier is baffled so as to produce through-flow, a flow of 100–250 cfm per sq ft of tray area. Fans for experimental driers may be designed to deliver air at a velocity from 500 to as high as 1500 fpm between loaded trays. The flow may be made controllable by use of a variable-speed drive.

The trays used for pilot-scale or small commercial operation range from 2 ft square, for 1-man loading and unloading, to 3 × 6 ft for 2-man servicing. Trays may be stacked on one another up to as many as 25 high. If this is done, of course, it becomes difficult to get at the material on one of the trays in order to test the progress of the drying. For experimental work, the cabinet is more frequently designed with a metal frame and guide rails on which any tray can be slid into or out of the drier when the door is opened.

Performance and Cost

The size varies over such a wide range and the required duty is so varied that standards or normals of good performance are hard to set. The least satisfactory element in cabinet drier performance is likely to be the distribution of air flow and temperature across the face of the tray compartment. Changes in the turning vanes, baffles, or screens may have to be made in a new unit until careful tests show that the distribution is acceptably uniform.

KILN DRIERS

Apple rings or slices are the only food materials commercially kiln dried in the United States at present, but hops and chopped green fodder are sometimes dried in similar equipment. Because of the narrow and specialized use in the food field, we present the main discussion of kiln drying in Vol. 2, Chap. 11, on dehydration of fruits. The dry product from the kiln driers is often called "evaporated" apples.

Kiln driers currently in use differ little from the description given early in the

20th Century by Gould (1907). A furnace or burner is located on the ground floor of a small, square two-story building, and the heated air or combustion gases rise through the slotted floor of the second story and through the deep layer of apple rings or slices piled on the floor. The fruit is dried as a batch, but operators periodically enter the kiln and use hand scoops to turn and mix the partly dry product. The traditional kiln relies upon natural draft to provide sufficient circulation of air up through the moist material, but more modern units are provided with a mechanical exhaust fan in the space above the drying floor. If fuel oil is used for heating, the furnace is provided with an extensive array of sheet-iron flues to transfer heat to the drying air.

PNEUMATIC CONVEYING DRIERS

Pneumatic conveying driers are those in which powders or granular materials are dried while suspended in a stream of heated air. Such driers are not used extensively as the sole drying equipment for a food material, but are valuable in specific instances. Since the material entering this kind of drier must be conveyable in an air stream, the incoming material must usually have been dried in other ways to a moisture level below 35–40%.

A pneumatic conveying drier is often integrated with a spray drier to provide a second stage of drying, for example to produce sufficiently dry egg or milk powder. The product obtained directly from the spray drier is normally low enough in moisture content for the commercial market, but special specifications may call for spray-dried milk or egg solids at lower moisture contents than are readily obtained directly by spray drying. In such cases, the powder may be collected from the spray drier and metered into a duct into which a fresh supply of heated air is introduced. The duct leads to a cyclone collector and the powder dries while being conveyed by the air stream, both in the duct and in the cyclone. This type of installation is used to reduce the moisture content of the product by only a few percentage points. Similar systems, using cool air instead of heated air, are used to cool powders before packing them.

Pneumatic conveying driers have found extensive use in the potato granule industry, although little information is available on the design details of the particular driers now in use. One plant is known to use driers similar to that shown in Fig. 5.11, a Rietz P & L Air Lift Drier. In this system, air is heated in the furnace in the lower right portion of the figure and is drawn upward through the body of the drier appearing at the left side of the figure. The air is withdrawn from the top of the drier to enter the cyclone, and is exhausted by the blower mounted above the cyclone. The material to be dried is fed into the air stream near the bottom of the body of the drier and is carried upward through the drier and into the cyclone for collection. A characteristic of this drier is its ability, when air flows are properly adjusted, to classify the material fed to it. The lighter and smaller particles dry more rapidly and are carried over into the cyclone sooner than the heavier and wetter particles. The latter remain suspended

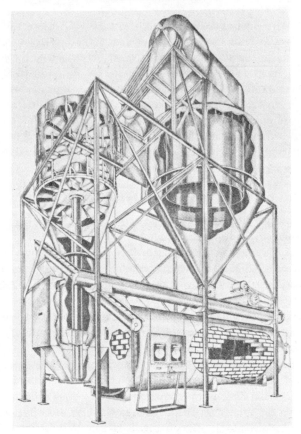

Courtesy of Rietz Manufacturing Co.

FIG. 5.11. AIR LIFT DRYER

in the drier body for a longer time and thus receive the additional drying that they need.

With potato granules, the feed ordinarily enters the drier at 35–40% moisture and the product is discharged from the cyclone at a moisture content in the range of 11–13%. The number and position of the vanes in the body of the drier depend upon the material being dried; fewer vanes than those showing in Fig. 5.11 are probably used with potato granules so as to minimize shattering of the product. A drier of this type is reported by Schanhals *et al.* (1963) to be in operation drying tomato seeds and skins.

An entirely different kind of pneumatic conveying drier is used for the finish-drying of potato granules to a final moisture content of 6%. This is a fluidized-bed drier, originally developed by Neel *et al.* (1954). The fluidized-bed drier resembles a long box or trough with the bottom formed from woven stainless steel cloth or porous ceramic such as sintered aluminum oxide. Another box below the porous surface forms a plenum chamber into which hot air is admitted. Moist potato granules, 11-13% moisture, are fed on top of the porous surface and heated air is fed from beneath, flowing up through the layer of potato granules. When the air flow is properly adjusted, the bed of granules is completely fluidized and has many of the physical properties of a liquid. Addition of a constant-rate feeding device at one end of the trough and an overflow weir at the opposite end is all that is needed to make a simple and effective continuous drier for the finish-drying of potato granules. Similar equipment is also used for the cooling of potato granules before packing. The fluidized-bed drier for potato granules is illustrated in Vol. 2, Chap. 10.

TUNNEL DRIERS

Despite the increasing popularity of continuous driers of various kinds, tunnel driers are still used in the food industry of the United States to some extent because of their simplicity and great versatility, unmatched by any other type of drier. Foods in pieces of almost any size and shape can, so long as they are solids, be successfully dried in a truck-and-tray tunnel; indeed, if solid trays are used, even liquids can be dried. The same drier, without alteration, can be used to handle materials as different as shredded cabbage and whole prunes, although of course, the operating conditions and equipment performance would not be the same.

Tunnel driers, as used for dehydrating fruits and vegetables, have been extensively studied and quite thoroughly described in technical publications; the present discussion will therefore be highly abbreviated. Particularly important publications are those of Perry et al. (1946), Van Arsdel (1951A, B), Kilpatrick et al. (1955), and USDA (1959). The Kilpatrick et al. reference contains an especially full outline of the historical development of this kind of drier.

A tunnel drier is basically a group of truck-and-tray batch driers, operated in a programmed series so as to be quasi-continuous. Truckloads of freshly prepared material are moved at intervals into one end of the long, closely fitting enclosure, the whole string of trucks is periodically advanced a step, and the dried truckloads are removed at the other end of the tunnel. The hot drying air is supplied to the tunnel in any of several different ways, known as the counter-flow, concurrent or parallel-flow, center exhaust, multistage, and compartment arrangements.

In operation, the prepared wet material is loaded in a thin, uniform layer on the drying trays and these are stacked one above another on a low-bed truck or dolly (Fig. 5.12) as high as can be readily handled by a man—about 5-7 ft. The trays are fabricated of wood or light metal, with thin slat or open-mesh bottoms, and are designed so that when they are properly stacked a clear air passage is left between trays (Fig. 5.13). The loaded trucks are pushed either manually or mechanically, one at a time, into the "wet end" of the drier. The passageway which constitutes the tunnel is just large enough to accommodate the loaded

Courtesy of Consolidated Foods Corp.

FIG. 5.12. FLANGE-WHEEL TRUCK

Courtesy of Consolidated Foods Corp.

FIG. 5.13. WOOD-SLAT DRYING TRAYS

trucks; clearances are kept small so that hot air will not circulate uselessly around the stacks of trays but will be forced to flow mainly between trays. A single tunnel may contain as few as 5 or 6 trucks or as many as 15, a maximum working length of about 50 ft; overall length, including space for fan and recirculation port, may be 15–20 ft longer than the drying section. No other type of drier for piece-form materials so successfully exposes a very large area of product to controlled drying conditions within a single moderately-sized piece of equipment. Thus, a 12-truck tunnel, whose 3 × 6 ft trays are stacked 24 high, holds the equivalent of more than 5 tons of fresh produce at one time if the unit loading of trays is 2 lb per sq ft.

Tunnel Arrangements and
Their Preferred Fields of Application

The drying characteristics of a tunnel are strongly influenced by its general design and arrangement, especially the direction of progression of the trucks relative to the direction of the main air flow. In the standard designs all of the air flow may be pictured as directed horizontally between successive trays, although some flow through slat bottom cracks or open mesh bottoms undoubtedly always takes place and is, indeed, advantageous. However, let us neglect this vertical flow component; the main air flow may be directed either parallel to the direction of truck movement or transverse to it. The latter will be considered first.

The arrangement pictured in Fig. 5.14 produces air flow through each truck in a direction across the long axis of the tunnel. It has been called transverse

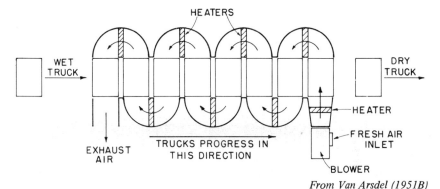

From Van Arsdel (1951B)

FIG. 5.14. TRANSVERSE-FLOW TUNNEL, OR COMBINATION COMPARTMENT AND TUNNEL

flow, but also a combination compartment and tunnel drier because, as is evident from the diagram, a separate heater in each hairpin turnaround of the air stream makes possible independent temperature control at each position; provision for independent control of recirculation at each position, while not shown in the diagram, is usually incorporated in the design. Extreme flexibility of control is offered by such a drier. Material passing through it can be subjected to almost any desired sequence of temperature-humidity-velocity conditions. This characteristic makes the design especially attractive for experimental work, and it has been used in a number of laboratories. An additional advantage is that as a truck advances one step the direction of air flow through it is reversed; the dry material leaving the drier is therefore likely to be more uniform in moisture content than the product from other tunnel arrangements in which one side of a tray is always the leading edge and the other the trailing edge with respect to the air flow.

For commercial use, the transverse-flow arrangement suffers from several disadvantages. Ironically, the very flexibility so desirable in an experimental drier becomes a drawback in a drier installed to do one drying task over and over as economically as possible; the complexities of operation and maintenance are expensive. An unusual degree of care and skill is necessary both in the design and in the construction, for two principal reasons. The 180° turns of the air stream necessitate special provisions to distribute the air uniformly over the whole stack of trays; ordinary splitters or turning vanes are inadequate for this purpose. A perforated sheet is most effective but entails a substantial extra cost for power. The other main reason is that an appreciable pressure difference exists between points only a few inches apart at the junctions between successive compartments, so that airtight seals must be maintained between the ends of the trucks or trays and the tunnel walls. These seals are difficult to maintain in good condition.

In the far more common types of tunnel design, the main air flow is parallel to the direction of truck movement. It may be in the same direction (concurrent, or parallel-flow), or the opposite direction (counterflow), or it may be partly one and partly the other, as in various types of multistage drier.

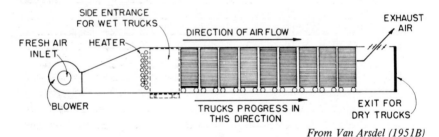

From Van Arsdel (1951B)

FIG. 5.15. SIMPLE CONCURRENT TUNNEL (ELEVATION)

Figure 5.15 illustrates a simple concurrent tunnel; Fig. 5.16 a simple counterflow tunnel. Figure 5.17 shows a more complex counterflow tunnel, designed to allow a portion of the drying air to be recirculated: The essential difference be-

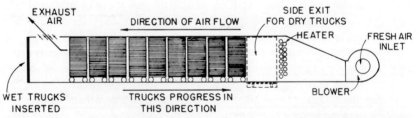

From Van Arsdel (1951B)

FIG. 5.16. SIMPLE COUNTERFLOW TUNNEL (ELEVATION)

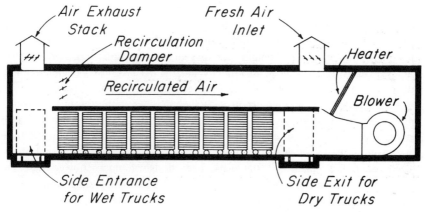

From Van Arsdel (1951B)

FIG. 5.17. SIDE-ENTRANCE COUNTERFLOW TUNNEL WITH VARIABLE RECIRCU-
LATION (ELEVATION)

tween the effects of the two arrangements is that in the concurrent tunnel very rapid initial drying of the material takes place, causing a high moisture gradient within each piece, rapid setting of the outer layers after only a little shrinkage, and formation of internal splits or porosity as the internal flesh finally dries and shrinks; final stages of drying are very slow because not only is the material approaching dryness, but the drying air is relatively cool and moist. In the counterflow tunnel on the other hand, the best drying conditions exist as the material approaches dryness. Unless the evaporative load is very light, initial stages of drying take place in much cooler and more humid air, internal moisture gradients are not so steep, and more nearly unhindered and complete volume shrinkage can take place. For many years, counterflow drying was standard practice for dehydration of fruits such as prunes, which amount to about 90% of the fruit so processed. However, more than half of the current prune crop is dried in parallel-flow tunnels. Air recirculation is common to reduce heat costs.

Several other tunnel arrangements have been used to take advantage both of the high wet-end evaporative capacity characteristic of the concurrent arrangement and the good final drying capability of the counterflow tunnel. The combination generally preferred consists of a concurrent wet end and a counterflow dry end. Various arrangements are diagrammed by Van Arsdel (1951B) and Kilpatrick et al. (1955). In some designs, the trucks are moved straight through a single long tunnel which is divided into sections by one or more movable partitions. Another design, known as "center exhaust," dispenses with partitions and relies upon the placement of the air circulating fan, heaters, and dampers to divide the air flow in the desired way. In some successful installations, a multiple bank of concurrent first-stage tunnels is connected by trackage and switching arrangements with a second bank of counter-flow finishing tunnels; any given truck may be routed into whichever tunnel happens to be scheduled for the next one-step advance. The design which was adopted as standard by the British government for its extensive World War II vegetable dehydration program employed two tunnels of equal length, side by side (British Ministry of Food 1946). The two centrifugal fans were also side by side. A truckload of wet material was introduced into one tunnel at the end nearest the fan, and was moved through the tunnel in a direction concurrent with the air flow; at the far end the truck left the first tunnel, was turned 180° and transferred to the second tunnel, and was moved through it in the counterflow direction. Drying times in the two stages were equal, or nearly so. In some other designs, the concurrent stage (often called the "primary" stage) has been designed much shorter than the counterflow (or "secondary," or "finishing") stage, corresponding to the great difference in drying conditions, particularly the very slow final approach to dryness and the low evaporative duty required of the air in the counterflow stage.

Many other tunnel arrangements have been proposed. One is a closed-cycle system—that is, there is no exhaust to the atmosphere; instead, the exhaust air from the drying section is partially dehumidified and returned to the fresh-air intake. The system has been proposed for onion and garlic dehydration, in order to diminish the nuisance aspect of the highly odorous exhaust from an ordinary tunnel drier. Closed-cycle drying has also been investigated as part of a system for dehydrating foods in an atmosphere of inert, oxygen-free gas, the closed cycle being necessary to diminish the cost of supplying fresh inert gas. At least one commercial plant has used three-stage tunnels successfully. The major advantage of such an arrangement probably is its flexibility with respect to the drying of a wide variety of different products under nearly optimum conditions for each. Unless truck handling is completely mechanized and automatic, the labor cost is relatively high and programming successive operations may be difficult.

Construction of Tunnel Driers

For obvious reasons, modern, direct-heated tunnel driers are almost invariably built of fireproof material such as hollow concrete block, hollow tile, sheet metal, or asbestos-cement sheeting. Most of the tunnels built in the United States in recent years have been of hollow concrete or cinder-block construction. Great care is exercised to get an accurately level track through the tunnel, so as to facilitate movement of the trucks, but it should not be forgotten that the air current itself produces a considerable force on the string of trucks, making it necessary to chock the wheels at the downstream end. Accurate framing of tunnel walls and roof is also necessary in order to maintain the minimum free opening around the stack of trays, generally not more than about 2 in. clearance all around. Many different devices are used to supply mechanical power when the string of trucks is to be moved ahead one step; the simplest is a hand-operated ratchet winch operating a cable whose far end is attached to the last truck. More elaborate devices employ a power winch with a disengaging clutch.

Some tunnels have been completely mechanized. Filled trucks are picked up by a pawl on a conveyor chain, the tunnel door is opened automatically, and the truck is moved periodically by a timing device.

The degree of elaboration and automation designed into the drier ideally depends upon a well informed balancing of the savings in labor cost realized in automatic equipment against savings of maintenance and capital costs obtained in simple, locally built units. If the expected operating season is very short, as it is for most fruit drying tunnels, the choice will usually be the simplest and least expensive tunnel. A strong tendency has been evident in recent years to reduce the complexity of drier design, even in plants operating over a very long season and even in spite of some increase in cost of heat and power, in order to assure simplicity and trouble-free operation.

BELT-TROUGH DRIERS

The belt-trough drier is a continuous through-flow drier with characteristics that make it useful in drying a variety of materials, particularly cut vegetables. It was first described by Lowe *et al.* (1955) and was reported in commercial use only 2 yr later (Anon. 1957). A number of these driers are now in use throughout the world. Patents were issued to Lowe and Rockwell (1956) and to Lowe and Durkee (1959).

The belt-trough drier, shown in Fig. 5.18 consists essentially of an endless,

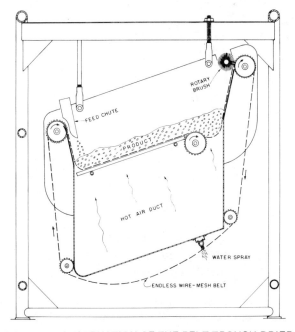

FIG. 5.18. CONSTRUCTION OF THE BELT-TROUGH DRIER

closely woven, metal mesh conveyor belt the width of the drier, supported be-tween two horizontal rolls with a great deal of slack so that it hangs freely. The upper run hangs down only far enough to form a moderately deep trough, and the slack in this run rests lightly on a flat-surfaced hot air grate and a third sup-porting roll. The moist material supplied to the drier forms a flat bed several inches deep in the bottom of this trough. When the mesh belt is driven slowly by means of its supporting rolls, the bed of material slowly turns over, continu-ously exposing new surfaces within the bed to the blast of hot, dry air coming up through the grate at the bottom of the trough. Because of dynamic consid-erations, the trough bottom is slanted at an angle of about $15°$-$20°$ so that the material at the bottom of the bed moves up a gentle slope, works to the top of the bed, and slowly works across and down again on the opposite side. The en-tire belt assembly is also tilted slightly toward one end. The result is that the material in the bed feeds slowly in a generally helical path toward the downside; operation is made continuous by feeding fresh material to the raised end and removing the dried material at an adjustable weir positioned at the low end. The drying air is delivered at a volume high enough to support, but not fluidize, the material in the bed. The material in the drier is thus gently and continuously moved by the air flowing through it and the turning action of the conveyor belt. Food pieces move up the incline in the high temperature zone in the bottom of the trough and return across the top of the bed, surrounded by air that has been greatly cooled by evaporation of water during its passage through the bed. The food pieces undergo this cycle repeatedly as they move the length of the trough.

In typical installations employing the belt-trough, the driers have been set up as a continuous, two-stage operation. Two driers in parallel serve as the first stage, evaporating water amounting to 50-60% of the weight of material fed to the driers. The combined output of these 2 driers is fed to a third drier of the same size that reduces the moisture content to 15-20%. The product leaving the first stage is at the optimum condition for dehydrofreezing (see Chap. 9, Vol. 2). After the second stage of drying, the material is suitable for finish drying in bins to the final moisture content. Air temperatures as high as $275°F$ are used suc-cessfully in the first stage of drying, and as high as $225°F$ in the second stage. The temperatures are to be compared with $200°$ and $160°F$, respectively, as maximum temperatures in conventional driers. Drying times are correspond-ingly shortened—from about 5 hr in a tunnel drier to 55 min in the belt-trough for $3/8$-in. diced vegetables. The high drying temperatures used, the short drying times generally involved, and design features allowing continuous cleaning of the metal conveyor belt all combine to produce dry material of unusually low bac-terial count, an important factor in food dehydration.

The belt-trough drier, operating with an air inlet temperature of $275°F$, is capable of evaporating 25 lb of water per hour per square foot of drying surface when it is fed with material cut small enough so that the moisture can move readily from the interior to the surface of the piece. The standard belt-trough drier, which has a bed 4 ft wide and 10 ft long, thus evaporates 1000 lb of water per hour, and can reduce feed material to half its original weight at the rate of 1 ton per hr. Air leaving the bed in the belt-trough drier is nearly saturated, indicating efficient use of heat. Fuel and power costs for the drier are low, ranging from 0.1 to 0.15¢ per lb of water evaporated under ordinary conditions. The present FOB price of a 4 by 10 ft unit quoted by an equipment concern is about $25,000. Although larger models of this drier have not been built to our knowledge, no problems are foreseen in constructing one with a bed 6 ft wide by 12 ft long; this should provide a capacity 80% larger than that of the standard unit.

Field of Application of the Belt-Trough Drier

Since the belt-trough drier is relatively new, its characteristics and field of application will be discussed in some detail. The drier was originally developed to meet the needs of the dehydrofreezing process in which it is essential that each piece of food material be dried to very nearly the same moisture level. It is not sufficient that a mixture of overdried and underdried pieces be produced at the required mean moisture content. This uniformity is also advantageous when belt-trough driers are used for the major portion of the drying if the product is to be fully dehydrated. Products from conventionally operated tunnels or conveyor driers are not uniform in moisture content, and much of the time spent by the material in bin finishing driers is occupied by equalization of moisture content and drying of the wettest pieces. When the uniformly-dried material from the belt-trough is put into the finishing bin, drying time for finish drying and heat damage therein are minimized. For the reasons outlined, the belt-trough drier has proved capable of making dehydrated vegetables of better quality than those produced by more conventional air driers, products that actually sell at a premium price.

The belt-trough drier is not, however, universal in its application. High evaporation rates and efficient use of the drier depend on piece sizes that are small enough to permit ready movement of moisture from the interior to the surfaces of the cut piece. Sizes and shapes of cut vegetable having a small enough dimension, including $3/8$-in. dice and half-dice, are quite suitable for the belt-trough. Capacity of the drier would be greatly reduced if it were drying pieces with large dimensions, such as apple wedges.

The belt-trough drier also has limitations in regard to piece shape and piece size distribution. As mentioned earlier, the material in the bed of the drier is slightly supported, but not fluidized, by the drying air. This characteristic permits the drying of reasonably soft materials without mashing of pieces or significant rounding of cut edges. However, the partial suspension of pieces in the air stream requires reasonable uniformity of piece size. Large pieces will not be supported adequately, while fine pieces may be blown entirely out of the drier. Again, since the bed is partly supported by the drying air and uniform mixing of the material in the bed is essential, piece shape is important. The optimum shape of piece for drying in the belt-trough drier would be spheres of uniform size; peas are processed commercially in the belt-trough. As mentioned earlier, $3/8$-in. dice and half-dice and similar shapes are easily handled. The behavior of materials in the drier can sometimes be surprising. Blanched potato, cut into pieces $3/32 \times 3/4 \times 3/4$ in. or $1/8 \times 1 \times 1$ in., has been handled in the belt-trough drier, although some piece breakage was encountered. These shapes and sizes were handled successfully only because the air stream forced the pieces to stay on edge. Red and green peppers, onions, and pimentos cut by a dicer can be dried satisfactorily. In contrast, the drier is not suitable for apple rings or onion slices. Apple rings break, onion slices separate into onion rings that become entangled to the extent that drying becomes impossible. The drier is also not suitable for fruits that become very sticky on the surface as drying proceeds. In this case, the bed of material will not move properly and the surfaces of the pieces are marred. This seems to be a characteristic of the stickiness of the mixture of natural sugars found in fruits. Glacéd melon dice, with all surfaces wetted with a concentrated solution of sucrose, were dried in the belt-trough drier with no difficulty. The drier was also found to be an excellent cooler for glacéd fruit pieces.

General guides such as those outlined above are based on several years of experience with this drier. Some products are obviously suitable for it; experimental trials must usually be made to determine whether a particular material can or cannot be dried successfully in the belt-trough drier.

CONTINUOUS-CONVEYOR DRIERS

The through-flow continuous-conveyor drier represents the completely mechanized development of equipment for drying pieces of a food material in warm circulating air, a refinement and improvement on the ancient art of drying food products on trays. Conveyor driers are being used in more and more food dehydration plants in the United States, and are now being applied to the drying of materials which have conventionally been dried on trays in tunnels, such as apple, beet, carrot, onion, potato, and sweet potato pieces. Primary reason for the swing in that direction has been the substantial saving in cost of handling the prepared food into and out of the drier and of maintaining the drying surface in good condition, but advantages of product quality are also claimed. The conveyor drier is best adapted to the large-scale drying of a single commodity for the whole operating season; it is not well suited to operations in which the raw material or the drying conditions are changed frequently, because of the complexity of producing fully satisfactory product during the many hours of startup and shutdown (USDA 1959).

The modern conveyor drier is also a highly sophisticated piece of precision machinery, adapted to manufacture by experienced designers and builders, but not at all suitable for fabrication in the field from locally available construction

materials and by contractors who have not made a specialty of similar equipment. The conveyor drier can properly be called a "machine." The type of
design, precision of construction, and degree of finish effectively ruled this kind
of drier out of consideration in the United States during World War II, because
of the chronic shortage of critical materials and machine building skills.

Principle and Main Features

Figure 5.19 is a diagrammatic elevation and cross-section of a widely used
type of conveyor drier. Wet material supplied to the spreader device at the left-
hand end is loaded evenly and in a relatively deep layer (3-6 in.) on the surface

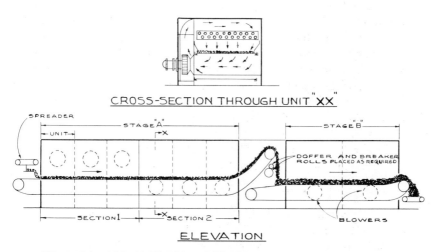

CROSS-SECTION THROUGH UNIT "XX"

ELEVATION

FIG. 5.19. DIAGRAM OF TWO-STAGE CONTINUOUS CONVEYOR DRIER

of a slowly moving conveyor belt. This may be fabricated of woven metal mesh,
but more often presents the flat upper surface of a succession of flat, hinged, or
interlocking perforated plates, each as long as the width of the conveyor and
usually no more than 6-8 in. wide. The working surface of a single stage of the
conveyor may be from 30-60 ft long, and from 6-10 ft wide, and usually at
least 2 stages are combined in series into a single drying operation, as in the illustration. The belt extends beyond the body of the machine at both ends, to
provide for the loading and unloading operations, and returns within the body.
The hot drying air flows through the layer of wet material and through the
meshes or perforations in the conveyor, generally up-through in the first section
and down-through in succeeding sections, although sometimes the drier is designed to produce up-through and down-through flow in alternate sections in
order to improve the uniformity of drying of a thick layer of wet material. Flow
is always down-through in the last 1 or 2 sections so as to prevent light-weight,
nearly dry pieces from blowing out of the bed. This through-flow of air has long

been known to be a highly effective method (Marshall and Hougen 1942; Brown and Van Arsdel 1944, 1951; Marshall and Friedman 1950; Kröll 1959).

Specific equipment arrangements of many kinds have been described in the technical literature and in scores of patents. Variations on the principle of continuous-conveyor drying have attracted the attention of many able engineers, particularly in Europe, where "drying machines" are more nearly commonplace than in the United States. The following major features characterize recent installations here.

The drier is arranged with a hot air plenum supplying air under some pressure above the belt in the first section, below the belt in following sections, and is constructed with minimum clearances around the belt so that nearly all of the air goes through the layer of material. This makes it possible to attain a high rate of air flow even through a thick layer on the belt, and to maintain satisfactory tonnage capacity from the drier within a reasonable floor space. Some European designs dispense with tight construction and forced through-flow of air, and economize instead on floor space by super-imposing several separate belts in one housing so that material enters on the top belt, travels back and forth within the housing, and leaves on the bottom belt. Air circulates more or less freely within the entire housing.

The reversal of direction of air flow through the layer of material, up-through in the first section, down-through in later sections, helps to equalize the drying as between top and bottom of the layer.

Sectionalizing the drier makes it possible to control air temperature, humidity, and velocity independently in several stages to give optimum output and quality. The type illustrated in Fig. 5.19 is three-section. The first section can be supplied with air at high temperature and moderate humidity because rapid evaporation from the wet material keeps its temperature down. The final stage can be operated with very dry air at a low enough temperature to avoid damage during the long, slow approach to the desired final level of moisture content. As noted in the later section on bin driers, the last stage of the conveyor may be constructed to serve as a continuous-bin drier.

Construction of the drier as two separate conveyors in series, as in Fig. 5.19, makes it possible, as shown in that illustration, to discharge the partly dry material at the end of the first stage, mix it, and repile it in a deeper layer for its passage through the second stage. This is an important feature. Not only does the mixing aid in making a uniform product, but the repiling makes possible a great saving in the floor space required. For example, potato strips originally piled on the conveyor in a layer 4 in. deep will shrink by the time they reach the end of the first stage to a layer less than 2 in. deep; some 90% of the original moisture will have been evaporated, but more than $1/2$ of the total required drying time is still to go. If, at this point, the material is repiled to a depth of 10–12 in., the conveyor area needed for the second stage will be only $1/5$ or less of that which would have been necessary without the repiling.

Centrifugal fan wheels are ordinarily used. As indicated in Fig. 5.19, 2 or 3 such fans may all discharge into the common plenum above or below the belt. A large proportion of the air passing through the layer of moist material recirculates into the fan; part of it may be diverted by dampers into the next section, to be replaced by heated fresh air. The intense turbulence in the plenum effectually equalizes the air condition within the section. The fact that air temperature is uniform makes it necessary to control this temperature at a level which is safe to apply to the moist material *leaving* the first section and already partly dry.

Space or cost considerations may dictate the use of high-pressure steam heat and extended-surface transfer coils, but the recently built vegetable dehydrators employ direct heating by combustion of natural gas in the circulating air.

Sizes and Capacities

The cost of a well-engineered conveyor drier, designed for sanitary operation with only stainless steel surfaces coming in contact with the food, is so substantial that all possible measures are naturally taken to extract from it the utmost in performance. Prepared material is loaded heavily on the belt, the air flow through the layer is kept high, especially during the early stages, and air temperatures are maintained at as high a level as can be used without causing heat damage. The conveyor drying is terminated while the moisture content is still as high as 10–15%, in order to transfer the long, slow, final approach to dryness, which demands but little evaporative capacity, to much cheaper equipment, such as bins.

Total residence time of product in the conveyor drier may be as short as 2–3 hr. At $2^{1}/_{2}$ hr, the rate at which prepared wet material can be supplied to a drier whose working surface is 8 ft wide and 75 ft long, and loaded at the rate of 10 lb per sq ft, is 2400 lb per hr, or 28 tons per 24-hr day. This corresponds to a plant input of 35 tons of a raw material whose preparation loss is 20%. Three such conveyor units would serve a plant whose daily capacity would be nominally 100 tons.

No specific information has been published on the installed cost of continuous-conveyor driers engineered to dry food materials acceptably on a large scale. McCormick *et. al.* (1963) estimate that the price (as of 1960) of a type 304 stainless steel drier, including heaters, fans, motors, and drive, ranged from $90 per sq ft of drying surface for a drier 10 ft wide, 50–60 ft long, up to $140 per sq ft for a unit 8 ft wide, 20–30 ft long. The cost of controllers and feeders may add $5,000 to $15,000. Industry sources have estimated that a recent installation of a stainless steel conveyor drier for sliced onions, with capacity of 15,000 lb of product per 24 hr, cost $225,000 including all services, controls, and cost of installation.

Operating Experience

The drying conditions suitable for various fruit and vegetable materials are discussed in the commodity chapters of Vol. 2. First-stage temperatures range from 200° to 260°F in the first section, 160° to 220°F in the second; second-stage temperatures range from 130° to 180°F. No information on suitable relative humidities or wet-bulb temperatures is available. Satisfactory drying conditions for a particular raw material can be determined experimentally in pilot tests by use of an analogue procedure, as described in Chapter 7.

Special mechanical devices are used at the loading end of a conveyor drier to secure a uniform load of material across the entire working surface. Care must be taken to avoid either crushing or matting the soft material or creating thick or thin spots. Thick spots receive too little air, remain wet. In a lightly loaded area product may be blown aside, creating a hole through which much of the air will escape. The surrounding material for several feet on every side will receive too little air and will dry too slowly.

Some soft, starchy or sugary materials may benefit by being subjected first to very rapid surface drying in such equipment as the belt-trough drier so that the working surfaces of the conveyor drier will remain clear and free of sticky buildup. Automatic brushing of the return side of the conveyor removes most adhering pieces of product, but scrupulous manual cleanup should be carried out each time the drier is shut down. The dust and small, light fragments of product which invariably accumulate within and around the drier must also be cleaned out frequently.

BIN DRIERS

Bin driers are used, particularly in the drying of piece-form vegetable products, to complete the drying operation after most of the moisture has already been removed in a tunnel drier or its equivalent. Typically, a bin drier would be used to reduce the moisture content of a partially dried cut vegetable from the 10-15% range (lower in the case of onion slices and possibly cabbage shreds because these products are so limp when they are both warm and somewhat moist that they will pack into a solid mass under only slight pressure) down to about 3-6%. Bin driers are widely used for this purpose because they can do the job of removing a small amount of tightly bound moisture from the pieces more economically than any other type of dehydrator. The long time required, ranging up to as much as 36 hr in some cases, does not entail much cost because the equipment tied up is relatively inexpensive.

Bin drying also serves several other purposes. The product discharged from the main drying tunnel or conveyor may range widely in moisture content, containing decided "wet spots" and "dry spots." The redistribution of pieces of the material as the bin is loaded, and the long holding of the entire batch in warm flowing air, assist in bringing about substantial equalization of the moisture (USDA 1959). The moisture content of the finished product can thus be more closely controlled at a level below, but close to, a specified maximum. The capacity and operating flexibility of preceding driers are improved when bins are used for final drying. The bins themselves also serve as storage reservoirs to smooth the flow of product between the drying units and the finishing and packaging units of a plant. Broad features of the design and operation of bins, as used for the finishing stage in vegetable dehydration, were described in a dehydration manual (USDA 1944).

Main Features

The bin drier is extremely simple in construction and operation, but mathematical description of the process is so difficult that only approximate theories have been worked out (Van Arsdel 1955). Substantially the same problems are encountered in the drying of grain harvested at too high a moisture content. Many kinds of farm grain drier are used (USDA 1952), some of them doubtless applicable to vegetable dehydration. See also Vol. 2 of this work. A typical unit consists essentially of a metal or wooden box equipped with an air inlet at the bottom and a wire mesh deck or false bottom with an air supply duct below it, arranged so that warm dry air can be passed up through the nearly dry product piled on top of the deck. Interior dimensions are usually in the range of 3–4 ft wide, 5–8 ft long, and 5–6 ft deep, although larger bins have been used successfully.

Portable Bins

In a portable bin system, the comparatively small bins are mounted on wheels, and after loading, are pushed up to and connected to a stationary air supply duct (Fig. 5.20). A single fan and heater supply warm drying air for the entire system. The product is unloaded by disconnecting the bin from the air source, and upending the bin by means of an electric hoist or fork lift to dis-

Courtesy of Idaho Potato Growers, Inc.
FIG. 5.20. PORTABLE DRYING BINS IN A POTATO DEHYDRA-
TION PLANT

charge the product into a hopper. Portable bins with independent air-blower-heaters have been used to a limited extent, but are thought to be unduly complex and expensive.

Stationary Bins

Product is usually moved into and out of fixed bins by conveyor. The bottom of the fixed bin opens to discharge the product onto a conveyor beneath it.

Stationary bins require less total floor space, labor, and maintenance, and can be larger in size than portable bins. The latter, on the other hand, have greater flexibility and convenience of operation, are less expensive to construct, reduce the handling and conveying of material and thus minimize breakage of the brittle product and consequent production of fines, and are easily cleaned.

Continuous Bins

Several types of continuously operating finishing bin have been proposed. Stack- or column-driers are used routinely for large-scale grain drying. However, the irregular and distorted shapes of the individual pieces of dry cut vegetable invariably cause arching, jamming, and failure to feed smoothly and uniformly down through columns designed like grain driers, even with the assistance of vibration. The difficulty appears to have been overcome in one recent design, which is essentially no more than a very slowly moving conveyor carrying a deep bed of the product above a warm air grate, and having an open end at the end of the conveyor. An unloading device continuously rakes small portions of the dry outgoing product into the discharge conveyor. This, it will be seen, makes the finishing bin basically the last stage of a continuous-conveyor drier system.

Bin Operation

Drying conditions required for bins handling vegetable pieces have not been closely defined in the published literature, but for onion slices the recommended incoming air temperature falls within the range of $100°-130°F$; for potato dice the temperature may be somewhat higher, up to about $140°F$. The partial pressure of water vapor in the incoming air must be well below the equilibrium vapor pressure of the finally dried vegetable at the chosen temperature. In onion dehydration plants, where a final moisture content of not over 4% is required and bin drying is to be carried out at $120°F$, the air supply to the bins is dehumidified if its absolute humidity is above 0.003 lb per lb dry air. In humid producing areas, dehumidification of the drying air may invariably be necessary. The investment in dehumidification equipment may be reduced by using the desiccated air in only half of the bins, and operating the other half as a first stage, either with warmed outside air, or with the air exhaust from the second stage.

Pressure Required for Air Flow.—A slow flow of air up through the bed of material suffices for satisfactory drying, because the evaporation rate under these conditions is inherently low. A flow of 80–100 (cu ft)/(min) (sq ft) of bin cross-section has often been specified in bin designs. The static pressure required to produce this flow of warm air through a deep bed has been determined by Spaugh (1948). If the bed is not so deep that the lower layers are compacted by the weight above them, the pressure required is proportional to depth and the following relation holds for bins of commercially large cross-section:

$$P = \rho_a C U^n$$

where

P = static pressure per unit depth, in. water/ft
ρ_a = air density, lb/cu ft
C = an empirical coefficient
U = air flow velocity, cu ft/min/sq ft cross-section
n = an empirical exponent

Spaugh's measurements gave values of the exponent n ranging from 1.60 to 1.80, averaging about 1.70. Table 5.3 gives observed values of the coefficient C for

TABLE 5.3

RESISTANCE OF DEEP BEDS OF DEHYDRATED VEGETABLES TO
THROUGH-FLOW OF AIR

Produce	Coefficient C
Potato half-dice, $\frac{3}{8} \times \frac{3}{8} \times \frac{3}{16}$ in.	0.0033
Carrot full dice, $\frac{3}{8} \times \frac{3}{8} \times \frac{3}{8}$ in.	0.0047
Carrot half-dice, $\frac{3}{8} \times \frac{3}{8} \times \frac{3}{16}$ in.	0.0067
Shredded cabbage	0.0060
Flaked onions	0.0262

various dehydrated vegetables. Krischer (1956) and Kröll (1959) present an extensive theoretical study of the flow of air through deep beds of granular materials, and tabulate experimental values for many of them—not, however, for dehydrated vegetables.

Determining End Point.—In a batch bin of the usual type, with air supplied beneath a false bottom, the additional drying starts at the bottom and gradually moves upward through the bin. At any time during the process a gradient of moisture will exist in the bin, and the mean moisture level of the entire contents will be higher than that of a sample taken at the bottom, lower than that of a sample taken at the top (Van Arsdel 1955; Kröll 1959). This inherent characteristic introduces some difficulty into such control of bin operation as to enable the operator to stop when the mean moisture level of the contents reaches the desired figure. One method would be to use a long sampling "thief," mix the sample, and determine its moisture content by means of one of the rapid empirical instruments. Another method proposed by Bouyoucos and Marshall (1945), involves keeping track of the accurately determined temperature difference between bottom and top of the bin; this difference gradually decreases as the drying progresses, and an empirical correlation can be used to convert the result to mean moisture content of the entire bin load.

SPRAY DRIERS

Spray drying is basically a simple operation. The fluid to be dried is dispersed into a stream of heated air, moisture evaporates into the air stream, the dry particles are separated from the air and collected, and the moist, cool air is exhausted. In practice, both the design and the operation of spray driers are highly specialized arts, particularly for difficult products. Many different types of spray driers are manufactured, with various combinations of atomizing devices, air-flow patterns, heating systems, and collecting systems. These are needed to meet the requirements imposed by the materials that are spray dried.

Spray drying may be used in preference to other methods of drying for several reasons, a dominant one being product quality. With some feed materials, no other drying method has been able to yield a satisfactory product at an acceptable cost. Feed materials that are easily damaged by heat or oxidation can frequently be handled acceptably in a properly designed and operated spray drier. Some foods when dried yield powders that are hygroscopic as well as thermoplastic, but if a spray drier is designed to inject cool and/or dry air as needed to cope with these problems, satisfactory products can be collected. Desired characteristics in the dry powder may point to spray drying as the method of choice. For consumer products such as instant coffee, a product of low density is preferred for psychological reasons. The desired product is also relatively coarse and uniform in particle size so that it will dissolve easily in water. Specialized types of driers are made to impart particular characteristics to the final product. The commodity chapters of Vol. 2 elaborate on specific requirements for spray driers for various food products.

The elements of a spray drier system are shown in Fig. 5.21. The essential elements are an air heater, a drying chamber, a system for dispersing the material to be dried into droplets in the drying chamber, a system for collecting the dry particles from the drying air, and one or more blowers for moving the air through the system.

The air may be heated by direct firing of gas or fuel oil in the air stream, or heated indirectly through a heat exchanger. Indirect heating is frequently used

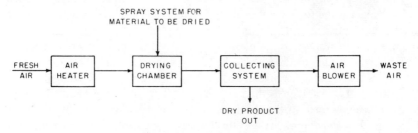

FIG. 5.21. ELEMENTS OF A SPRAY DRIER SYSTEM

in the food industries to avoid contamination of the food with carbon or dirt from the fuel, and to avoid contact by the food with combustion products that could impart foreign flavors or odors.

The Drying Chamber

The primary function of the drying chamber is to provide intimate mixing of hot air with finely-dispersed droplets of the material to be dried, in such a way that drying proceeds adequately and that the dry particles have the desired characteristics. The drying chamber takes many forms, ranging from a horizontal box to tall, vertical towers, and may have a relatively simple or a very complex flow pattern for both the air and the feed droplets. Spray driers are ordinarily classified as to type according to the relative flow directions of the spray stream and the drying air stream. Seltzer and Settelmeyer (1949) and Smith (1949) classified air drier types approximately as follows: (1) horizontal cocurrent; (2) simple vertical-downward cocurrent, (a) where air has straight-line flow, (b) where air has rotary motion; (3) complex vertical-downward cocurrent or mixed-flow; (4) vertical-upward cocurrent; and (5) vertical countercurrent. These different arrangements are shown in Fig. 5.22. Many other arrangements

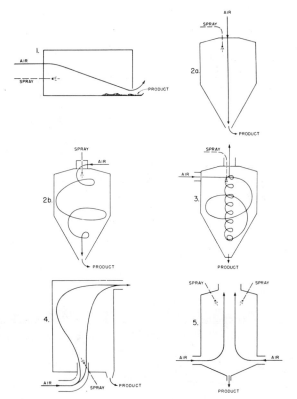

FIG. 5.22. TYPES OF SPRAY DRIERS

are found in practice, particularly in the mixed-flow classification. Such arrangements are characterized by one or more reversals of the direction of air flow.

Atomization

Only three systems have found extensive use for dispersing the material to be dried into droplets in the drying air. These are: pressure spray heads, two-fluid nozzles, and centrifugal atomizers. Pressure spray heads are designed to use the energy in a high-pressure fluid to disperse the fluid into droplets. The head is basically a small orifice immediately preceded by an internal core that imparts a spinning motion to the fluid passing through the head. The feed material enters the spray head at pressures ranging from several hundred to several thousand pounds per square inch, the pressure depending upon the size of orifice and core, the desired droplet size, and the rate at which the fluid must be fed to the drier. Interchangeable orifices and cores allow variations in the capacity of a pressure spray head; several heads may be used in one drier to provide needed capacity. Feed pumps for pressure spray heads may range from positive displacement gear-type pumps for the lower pressure ranges to multiple-piston pumps for the higher ranges.

Two-fluid spray nozzles are those which employ the energy of an auxiliary fluid stream to atomize the material being fed to the drier. The auxiliary fluid may be compressed air, or less commonly, steam. Operating pressures with the two-fluid nozzle are low, not more than several pounds per square inch with some designs. The physical construction of a two-fluid nozzle is relatively simple. A common model provides a tube-like orifice to direct the stream of feed material into the drier. The auxiliary fluid stream (air or steam) enters through an annular or concentric orifice surrounding the feed orifice. The auxiliary fluid tears the feed stream into bits, thus effecting atomization. The two-fluid nozzle has the disadvantage of producing a wide range of droplet sizes; it is not an acceptable system for some types of products.

Centrifugal atomizers, as implied by the name, use the centrifugal force developed in a rotating system to provide much of the energy needed to atomize the feed material to the drier. Several physical configurations are found in centrifugal atomizers. One form is a series of tubes arranged as spokes of a wheel, the feed entering at the hub, flowing outward through the tubes, and being atomized as the fluid streams interact with the surrounding air. A second form is basically a saucer or bowl, the feed again entering at the center and flowing outward in a thin layer. The sheet of fluid flows over the edge of the rotating bowl and is atomized as it encounters the surrounding air. Numerous variations of the centrifugal atomizer are in commercial use, comprising hollow baskets with vanes, slots, ridges, steps, and other features designed to accelerate the fluid and to disperse it in thin layers or droplets into the surrounding air for completion of atomization. Centrifugal atomizers range widely in size and in rotational speed. A laboratory spray drier employs a 2-in. disc driven at a rotational speed as high as 50,000 rpm by an air turbine. Electric motor drives are commonly used for the larger centrifugal atomizers. A spoke-type atomizer, approximately 30 in. in diameter, is directly driven by a 3450 rpm electric motor. Most of the disc or basket types of centrifugal atomizer range from 6 to 14 in. in diameter and are driven at speeds up to 15,000 rpm. Belt drives from conventional electric motors are commonly used for these, although one company mounts the centrifugal atomizer directly on the shaft of a special type of electric motor that is supplied with high-frequency electrical power to obtain high rotational speeds.

Mechanism of Atomization and Product Characteristics.—The physical mechanisms involved in atomization of a fluid have been studied by a number of investigators. A wide range of particle sizes is observed in most spray-dried products, yet drier size is determined by the trajectory and drying time of the largest particles in the original spray. Atomization has consequently been investigated in an effort to find out how to atomize a fluid into droplets as uniform in size as possible. Success in this effort would lead to more uniform products, both in particle size and in characteristics; it would also ensure more even drying of the feed material, and better utilization of the drying chamber and its air supply. Although study has yielded much information on the process of atomization, no way has been found to produce, in large-scale operation, an aerosol, or liquid dispersion in air, that is completely homogeneous in particle size.

If a fluid leaves a nozzle in viscous or laminar flow, surface tension forces will tend to break the jet into droplets. Duffie and Marshall (1953) show frames from high-speed motion pictures in which the jet is breaking into droplets that oscillate from elongated cylinders to flat discs. If drying is rapid, and the droplet becomes rigid before sphericity is attained, both disc- and dumbbell-shaped particles are found in the product. "Satellites," droplets much smaller than the larger droplets, are formed in the process and lead to the fines that are commonly found in spray-dried powders. If the jet is in turbulent flow, radial forces in the jet help to break up the fluid into droplets, even in a vacuum (Marshall and Seltzer 1950). When the fluid is forced out into an air stream which differs appreciably in velocity from the fluid stream, frictional forces also contribute to the breakup of the fluid stream. Photographic evidence shows that the thin sheet of fluid leaving a pressure nozzle waves like a flag and breaks up into droplets and into ligaments that subsequently break up into droplets. The sheet can also roll into a hollow tube that breaks up into a hollow sphere and solid satellites (Fogler and Kleinschmidt 1938; Marshall 1954; and others). Photographs of two-fluid atomizers (Marshall 1954), show that the auxiliary fluid tears the fluid being atomized into ligaments that subsequently break up into large and small droplets. Further, evidence is presented to show that an air jet can blow a liquid droplet into a bag shape that ruptures to form a coronet of satellite droplets, usually accompanied by two much larger droplets. Marshall (1954) shows photographs of several events that occur during fluid atomization from a spinning disc. Depending upon operating conditions, the fluid can leave the disc as droplets, as ligaments that subsequently break up in the air stream to form droplets, or as sheets that break up into droplets and ligaments. Various combinations of these forms occur when operating conditions are less than perfect. In an earlier study on centrifugal atomizers (Friedman *et al.* 1952), effects of design, fluid viscosity, density of feed, and surface tension of feed were investigated. Although a general correlation of these factors with rate of rotation of the disc was obtained, no evidence was found that special disc designs offered advantages over standard cup-shaped or vaned discs.

It is not surprising that the many events occurring during atomization in combination with a wide range of fluid properties and drying characteristics lead to a variety of kinds of particles in spray-dried products. A study by Charlesworth and Marshall (1960) on a number of inorganic salts and coffee extract led to an excellent description of the types of particles that can be obtained from different materials under different drying conditions. Rigid, fractured, cracked, spongy, shrivelled, and inflated particles were observed and related to the rigidity, porosity, and pliability of the materials during various stages of drying. Duffie and Marshall (1953) observed a variety of particle types. These included sodium sulfate, which formed hollow, crystalline spheres, with inblown holes; potassium nitrate, which formed spherical aggregates or thin-walled balloons; a dye, that formed hollow spheres; corn syrup, that formed clear solid spheres; gelatin, that formed collapsed, shriveled spheres that were prune-like in appearance; and potassium sulfate, that formed hollow spheres with a hole in each, apparently blown outward. The dispersibility of the powder may be strongly affected by the particle shape. When such a range of particle types can be obtained with simple feed materials, it is easy to see why much study is necessary to obtain products with desired characteristics with complex foods as feed materials.

Powder Collectors

Product collecting systems used by different manufacturers vary widely in type. Settling chambers may be used in which the powder falls out of the air stream as its velocity or flow direction is changed. Cyclone collectors are also commonly used. These are cone-shaped devices in which the air enters tangentially at the top, swirls around and downward, and then reverses direction to exhaust through a central outlet at the top. The powder in the air stream is thrown out to the walls of the cyclone by centrifugal force developed by the spinning air and falls down the walls to be removed through an outlet at the bottom of the cyclone. A third type of product collector is the bag filter. In this type, exhaust air, from which much of the powder has been removed by other types of collectors, passes through fabric bags which filter out the remaining powder. Many bags in parallel may be needed to recover the product from the exhaust air. In a typical "bag house" mechanized systems are used to clean the bags continuously and to dump the recovered products into hoppers for removal from the system.

A variation on the common or dry cyclone collector is the wet cyclone collector used by at least one manufacturer of spray driers. After the exhaust air has been cleaned by settling chambers and cyclones, the air enters a wet cyclone. The liquid feed material for the drier is sprayed into the top of the wet cyclone to scrub remaining powder from the exhaust air from the drying chamber. By this means, high recovery of product is obtained, and otherwise waste heat in the exhaust is recovered and used in the spray concentration of the fluid material being fed to the drier.

Some spray-drier systems may require careful study before the operation of the collection system will become clear. Some are designed so that the drying chamber itself is used as a product collector. In these, much of the product falls to the bottom of the drier and is continuously removed by sweeping devices combined with mechanical or pneumatic powder conveying systems. The partially cleaned exhaust air may then pass through one or more cyclone collectors before being discarded, or through cyclones followed by bag filters. Cyclones are omitted in some cases, the partially-cleaned exhaust air from the drying chamber passing only through bag filters before being discarded.

The best collection system for a spray drier is determined by many factors. Collection systems represent substantial capital investment as well as operating and maintenance costs. Powder carried out and lost in the exhaust air stream from a spray drier is a direct loss that must be charged against the operation. Collection systems are sometimes used to classify the product into desirable and undesirable fractions depending upon their physical characteristics. Some products can be returned to the drier feed for recovery if necessary; others would suffer from quality loss and therefore cannot be returned. According to Seltzer and Settelmeyer (1949), large-diameter dry cyclones are not efficient in collecting light density food products, losses being particularly high for particles less than 40 μ in diameter. For example, 2 cyclones in series, each 8 ft in diameter, recovered 87 and 3% respectively of the powder entering with the air. Cyclones 20 in. in diameter recovered 97% of the powder entering with the air, the powder having an apparent bulk density of 0.2 and containing 25% of particles less than 20 μ in diameter. Since collection efficiency increases as diameter decreases in a cyclone, many cyclones of small diameter have been installed in parallel by some manufacturers. One maker claims good recovery on particles as small as five μ in diameter. Use of small-diameter cyclones is limited, however, by other problems, such as bridging and plugging of the cyclones by the powder being collected. Wet scrubbers and bag filters are stated to recover from 95 to 98% of all solids fed to them in an air stream.

Spray Drier Costs

Investment costs for spray-drying plants vary widely, depending upon capacity, complexity, materials to be dried, permissible drying temperatures, and sanitary requirements. Most spray driers for food products are designed so that they can be cleaned thoroughly and rapidly. Corrosion-resistant metals such as

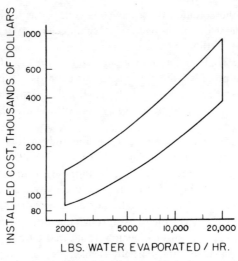

FIG. 5.23. SPRAY DRIER COSTS

stainless steel are frequently used, both to resist corrosion from food products and to provide easily cleaned surfaces. Typical costs, based upon data reported by Marshall and Friedman (1950) and brought up to December, 1962, by the equipment cost index published by *Chemical Engineering*, are shown in Fig. 5.23. Costs are shown as a range, because of the variety of products that can be spray dried under widely different operating conditions. The lower limit is based on a mild steel drier for a material that is not difficult to dry and is not highly heat sensitive. The upper limit reflects special materials of construction such as stainless steel, low inlet temperatures, requirements for coarse atomization, and other factors involved in the spray drying of certain food products. The distribution of total costs among the various components of a spray-drying system was reported by Laster (1953) for several direct-fired spray driers operating on food products. He reported that the heating system comprised 20% of the total cost, the atomizing equipment 4%, the drying chamber 52%, the product recovery system 10%, the air handling equipment 8%, and instrumentation 6%. An indirect heating system would, of course, comprise a larger percentage of the total cost than would a direct heating system.

Costs outlined above could easily be increased by special features for spray driers intended to handle particular food materials. Patsavas (1963) outlines several such features, including provisions for cooling the walls of the drier to reduce heat damage to product deposited on the walls or to prevent melting of product on hot walls; special air distribution heads for parallel cocurrent driers for coffee extract; auxiliary cool air inlets at the bottom of the drying chamber to sweep out and cool the product; and special separating cones which allow the product to fall out of the humid drying air into conditioned air in the bottom of the cone. Such cones or their equivalent are essential for food products that are highly hygroscopic and are sticky at moderate temperatures and moisture contents.

No attempt will be made in this chapter to discuss spray-drying costs. Capital charges vary substantially, depending upon the complexity of the spray-drying system required to handle a particular product as outlined in the preceding paragraphs. Operating costs are strongly influenced by permissible drying temperature for a particular food, because the water evaporating capacity of a given spray drier is directly related to the allowable hot air inlet temperature. Evaporative capacity and air requirements (hot, cool, and conditioned) are related to the hygroscopic and melting characteristics of a given food product. Powder yield per hour from a given spray drier is nearly directly related to the concentration of solids in the feed material going to the drier, yet allowable concentration is limited to that which can be satisfactorily atomized. This limit varies widely, from a few percentage of solids in a pectin solution to 70% or more of solids for juices containing little fiber.

General

Although spray driers have undergone steady development, particularly in regard to specific products and specific physical properties needed for a product, only one radically different drier has been developed in the past 30 or more years. As described by Ziemba (1962) and Hussmann (1963), this drier, developed by Birs A.G., Basel, Switzerland, is characterized by its huge size, 50 ft in diameter and 220 ft high, and low temperature of drying air. The material to be dried is sprayed from the top and falls countercurrent to a slow-moving stream of air to effect drying. The air, at the point of entry, is dehumidified to 3% or less relative humidity and has a temperature not exceeding 86°F. Air flow and spray size are adjusted so that the particles are exposed to the air for about 90 sec for drying as they fall through the drier. Cyclone collectors, and presumably filters, are used to collect the product. The drier is reported to handle tomato, lemon, orange, peach, potato, and other products, including dairy items. Reported capacity is 800 lb of tomato powder per hour, starting from a concentrate containing 28–30% solids. Initial investment is obviously high, but heat requirements are moderate. Product quality is reputedly high. Examination of a sample of tomato powder made by the Birs process indicated a much more dense product than those obtained from spray driers operating at elevated temperatures. There appears, however, to be little use of the system at the present time.

An opposite approach is the experimental adaptation of a jet spray drier to food products, reported by Bradford and Briggs (1963). The jet spray drier is basically a tube, in this case 8 in. in diameter by 6 ft in length. Primary air at high temperature, 600°–650°F, was forced under pressure into one end of the tube, concentrically around the feed nozzle. The primary air thus served as the heat source as well as the energy source for atomizing the feed material. Much larger quantities of secondary air at room temperature were fed into the same end of the tube to reduce the exhaust temperature to the desired level. The investigators reported that "whole milk has been dried without affecting flavor or other properties" and expressed optimism that the drier can be used for other foods. Advantages of the system include the small size relative to conventional spray driers and a very short drying time; disadvantages include higher power consumption than conventional spray driers. Total costs for the jet spray drier as compared to the conventional spray drier have not been established.

PAN DRIERS

The pan drier may be defined as an air convection drier constructed to hold pans of a liquid material which is to be evaporated to dryness in a batch operation. It is therefore a specialized kind of cabinet drier.

Pan drying is apparently used in commercial food dehydration for only one task—evaporation of egg white to dryness in circulating warm air. We accordingly only mention it here; the process and product are discussed in Chap. 16, Vol. 2.

DRUM DRIERS

Drum driers are simple in principle but become physically complex as the basic drier is modified for particular products. A drum drier comprises one or more rolls or drums which are hollow and fitted so that a heating medium, usually steam but occasionally water, or special high-temperature heat-transfer liquid, can be circulated through the drums. The drums are mounted to rotate about the symmetrical axis and are customarily driven with a variable speed drive. Some type of feeding device is used to apply a thin, uniform layer of the material to be dried on the hot drum surface. A knife or doctor blade is also fitted to the drum at an appropriate location. The feed material is applied on the periphery and is dried as the heated drum rotates toward the doctor blade which scrapes the thin layer of dry material from the drum surface. General descriptions of the equipment, especially as it is applied in the chemical manufacturing industry, have been published by Van Marle (1938), Marshall and Friedman (1950), Kneule (1959), and Kröll (1959).

Types of Drum Driers

Drum driers are classified by type as single-drum, double-drum, and twin-drum, arranged as shown in Fig. 5.24. The single-drum comprises only one roll. A double-drum drier comprises two rolls which rotate *toward* each other at the top. The double-drum drier is conventionally operated with the spacing between the two rolls carefully adjusted to control the thickness of the layer of feed material applied to the drums. The twin-drum drier is similar in appearance to the double-drum drier, but is quite different in its operation and in the products that

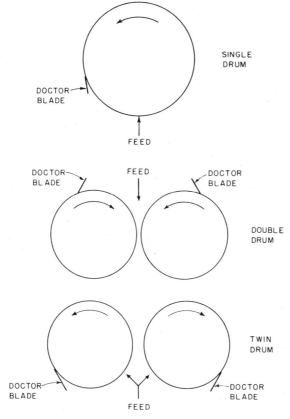

FIG. 5.24. TYPES OF DRUM DRIERS

it handles satisfactorily. The two drums occupy the same general position as in the double-drum drier but rotate *away* from each other at the top and are not spaced closely together.

These basic arrangements are used in many ways, depending upon the needs of the process. Drum driers are conventionally fitted with hoods to collect and exhaust the water vapor evolved during the drying operation. When necessary, the drier may be totally enclosed to protect personnel against toxic products or vapors, to prevent cross contamination when different driers are used on different products, or to allow recovery of toxic or valuable vapors from the drying operation. The entire drier may be further enclosed so that the system can be operated under vacuum. A vacuum drum drier is used only when the product is heat sensitive and must be dried at lower temperatures than is practical at atmospheric pressure. In the food industries, the atmospheric drum drier is most commonly found, although the vacuum drum drier has been used for certain specialty products.

Feeding Systems

A variety of devices is employed to apply the feed material to the drum for drying. The variety arises largely from the need to apply a uniform layer of materials differing widely in characteristics to the drying drum. The single-drum drier is conventionally fed from beneath. In the simplest form, the drum merely dips into a pan of the feed material, which may be constantly stirred to assure uniformity. Feeds that cannot tolerate prolonged exposure to heat may be dip-fed from a very small pan constantly supplied with fresh material. When a dip feed is unsatisfactory, various rotating devices can be used to splash or spray the feed material onto the drum in a uniform layer. With feeding systems such as these, a spreading knife may be used to improve the uniformity of the deposited layer. A small, unheated, auxiliary roll has been used to apply a uniform layer of tomato paste to single-drum driers (Anon. 1942). Feeding arrangements for the double-drum drier are usually simple. Clear liquids that are not too viscous are fed from a perforated pipe located above the trough formed between the two drums of the drier. For viscous liquids, or for those containing appreciable amounts of suspended matter, the feeder may comprise an oscillating pipe that deposits the feed along the trough formed between the two drums of the drier. Twin-drum driers are fed by dip or splash systems located underneath the drums, or by flow systems located above the drums. Spreaders are used as needed.

Applications of Drum Driers in the Food Industries

Only the single- and double-drum driers have been employed extensively in the food industries. In years past, skim milk was conventionally dried on single-drum driers and enormous quantities were produced on them. The spray drier has since largely supplanted the drum drier in the dairy industry for food products, but whey, distillers' solubles, and many other products are still drum dried for use in feeds. A new use for the single-drum drier has, however, developed in recent years, out of work done by the Eastern Regional Research Laboratory. Large quantities of mashed potato flakes are now dried, both in this country and abroad, on a special version of the single-drum drier. The general arrangement of the potato flake drier is shown in Fig. 5.25. Auxiliary small rolls driven at the same surface speed as the main roll are located around the periphery of the main roll. The smaller rolls, part of the feeding system, are used to apply and reapply the mashed potato to the drying drum. This application has been described by Cording et al. (1957) in a paper that outlined the effects of operating variables on product density and on production rate. Anon. (1942) reported the drying of tomato on a single-drum drier.

Double-drum driers are in commercial use for drying applesauce, milk, pre-cooked cereals, mashed white potatoes, mashed sweet potatoes, gelatinized starch, molasses and honey, and purées of tomato, pumpkin and banana. Brekke and Talburt (1950) reported the use of a double-drum drier in making fig powder, and other workers at the Western Regional Research Laboratory have

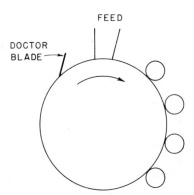

FIG. 5.25. POTATO FLAKE DRIER

used a modified double-drum with good results on applesauce and purées of prune, cooked dry beans, cranberry, blueberry, apricot, peach, and other foods. Success has been reported in drum-drying mixtures of applesauce with strawberry, raspberry, loganberry, cranberry, blueberry, black currant, and banana (Anon. 1968).

Special Techniques for Drum Drying Various Foods

Special techniques are required for drum drying different products, particularly fruit purées, tomato paste and other feeds containing large amounts of sugars. Under practical drying conditions, the sugars in these feeds will usually be sticky and may actually be molten when the feed has dried and the sheet is ready to be peeled from the drum. Such materials pile up on the doctor blade as a molten mass and cannot be removed continuously. Molasses and honey are exceptions (Klis 1963). In some cases, semimolten or thermoplastic materials can be removed from the drum by guiding the sheet over take-off rolls and using cooling air jets to support and solidify the sheet of product.

Lazar and Morgan (1966) modified a standard double-drum drier so that difficult-to-dry foods could be dried satisfactorily thereon: (1) Provision of high velocity air flow countercurrent to the drum rotation to accelerate drying and to evaporatively cool the product on the drums. This increased drying capacity and reduced scorching of the product. (2) A chilled air blast was directed on the product just preceding the doctor blades. This hastened solidification of melted or thermoplastic products and aided in peeling a continuous sheet from the drums. (3) Variable speed take-off rolls were installed and were driven at $\frac{1}{2}$ to $\frac{1}{3}$ of the surface speed of the drying drums. (4) Low humidity air was supplied to the peeling zone and to the product collection area. This prevented absorption of moisture by hygroscopic products.

The relationship of the surface speed of the take-off rolls to that of the drying drum deserves special emphasis. When the take-off rolls turn at a lower surface speed than the drums, the product sheet is crinkled and resembles crepe paper. The crinkled structure provides ready access to water so that rehydration is much faster and easier than is the case with the flat product sheet that is produced when the take-off rolls turn at the same or a higher surface speed than the drying drums. No universally satisfactory arrangement for handling different products has been devised; each is an individual case.

With new developments in drum drying, quality of the products has been greatly improved, making the products competitive with those dried by other methods. Drum drying is one of the cheapest drying methods available.

Drum Drier Investment and Operating Costs

The costs for drum driers shown in Fig. 5.26 are adapted from those given by Lapple *et al.* (1955) and are in agreement with those given by Marshall and Friedman (1950), both corrected for price increases up to December, 1962. The lower line refers to atmospheric drum driers of the single-drum, twin-drum,

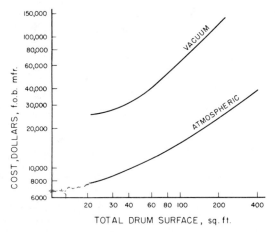

FIG. 5.26. DRUM DRIER COSTS

or double-drum type. The upper line refers to vacuum drum driers of the single-drum type, although Lapple comments that the data are probably applicable to other types of vacuum drum driers. The indicated prices are FOB the manufacturer's plant and apparently apply to driers with cast iron drums; they include a feed mechanism, the drive, and conveyors. Lapple indicates that chrome plating of the drums (as of December, 1954) will cost an additional $24 per sq ft for drum areas below 185 sq ft, and $36.50 per sq ft for larger drum areas. He further comments that an additional 10% should be allowed for a variable speed drive, and that the installed cost is roughly twice the FOB cost. Operating costs for drum driers for food have not been published, but would obviously depend highly upon the particular product, the moisture content of the feed, and the requirement for final moisture content. Marshall and Friedman state that the operating labor for drum driers should not exceed $\frac{1}{2}$ man per drier if proper controls are provided, and that maintenance costs on drum driers may be as much as 10% of the installed cost of the drier.

FOAM-MAT DRYING

The general scheme for foam-mat drying is shown in Fig. 5.27. This is a method of dehydrating food liquids developed about 1960 at the USDA's Western Regional Research Laboratory (Morgan *et al.* 1960-1963). The liquids

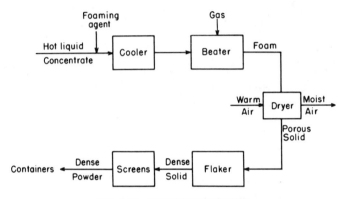

FIG. 5.27. FOAM-MAT DRYING

are first foamed, then spread out in thin mats on some support, and then dried in warm air streams. The foam structure persists during drying so that the dried mats can be easily scraped off the support and readily crumbled up into tiny pieces. The solid pieces so produced also have a foamy fine structure which promotes rapid rehydration by the user. Commercial use has so far been restricted to fruit juices.

Advantages

Foam-mat drying offers the advantages of air drying—cheapness and accessibility. Foam structure offers peculiar advantages in spreading, in drying, in surface removal, in crumbling up, and in rehydration of the product. The liquid foams are stiff and can be extruded, shaped, and placed accurately. High quality dried products are obtained by uniform treatment. Overheating is inevitable when liquid thickness varies significantly, because drying rate is very sensitive to thickness of the layer or piece. Layer thickness must be very small, probably 0.1-0.5 mm, for drying times of a few minutes in 150°F air streams. It seems hopeless to achieve very thin liquid layers with, say, less than 20% variation in an industrial machine. The results had therefore been poor quality in air driers and high final moisture in vacuum driers.

Foam is an escape from the dilemma of thickness control. When liquid density is sufficiently reduced, the thickness for any surface loading is so increased as to make practical the desired percentage uniformity. Furthermore, with stiff foams, flow is so slow that surface irregularities do not cause dangerous layer thinnings after application and before complete drying.

A liquid layer usually dries at the rate water can find its way through the previously dried material at or near the free surface where the water is evaporating. A layer of foam dries much more rapidly than the same amount of unfoamed liquid under the same external conditions. This is because liquid moves more easily through a dry foam structure than through a dense layer of the same material. This is due to capillary action along the dry interstices; also, evaporation inside bubble spaces followed by gaseous diffusion through the thin outer dry walls aids rapid drying. A sponge dries more quickly than a potato. Bread dries faster than meatloaf. The foam structure decreases drying time to about $1/3$ what it would be for liquids under conditions of interest in food dehydration. To acquire processing efficiency and the product quality and convenience advantages, the liquid must not only be foamed, but the foam must persist through drying to a great extent. Only certain foams have this durability.

Disadvantages

Foam-mat drying is usable only on liquids. Some liquids do not foam readily. Others collapse during drying. In many cases, therefore, it becomes necessary to add a foam stabilizer for foam-mat drying. A number of edible stabilizers have been found useful. This means that such powders cannot be sold as pure substance. Labels include such statements as "vegetable gum added" or "soluble protein added." Only a few foods, such as whole milk, contain enough foam stabilizing solutes naturally.

Another difficulty arises from the thin mats which must be used. Layers thicker than about 3 mm take longer to dry than the time that most foams will remain stable. The result is that much surface must be installed for a practical production. The consequence of this is a higher cost than spray or drum drying, although lower than vacuum or freeze drying.

Processing Factors

In order to reduce the load on a drier, feed should be concentrated in an evaporator if possible. Concentrates, furthermore, form stiffer, more stable foams for foam-mat drying. Too highly preconcentrated food, on the other hand, yields solids so dense that the final moisture cannot be easily removed in the drier. Good feed solids concentrations are 30% for tomato and 55% for orange.

A stabilizer seems to fill either of two needs—bulk stiffening or film forming. Stiffening is needed for feeds of low insoluble solids content or low bulk viscosity. Methyl cellulose or guar gum can stiffen most foams well when used at about 0.5% DSB. Film forming is needed for feeds poor in surface active solutes. Glyceryl monostearate, soluble soya protein, or egg albumin have usually been satisfactory. In a few cases, only sucrose fatty esters were usable. Continuous foaming consists of adding the stabilizer, injecting the right proportion of gas, subjecting the two-phase mixture to high-shear mixing, and cooling the foam at least enough to remove the heat of mixing. The correct density of foam is the highest density consistent with a stable foam. Foam densities of 0.4–0.6 g per ml are normal. This actually consists of spherical bubbles, averaging 0.1 mm in diameter, dispersed in a continuous liquid. Light froths, which consist of larger gas spaces separated by nearly planar liquid walls, are not suitable. Air foams seem to make as good product as inert gas foams (Hart et al. 1963).

Foams must be spread into mats 2–3 mm thick. These layers will dry in 10–20 min while keeping the product below 135°F. Thinner layers dry much faster but contain less material. The result is a production rate limit of 0.3–0.4 lb powder per hour per square foot of surface installed. Drying rate is sensitive to air velocity over or through the mat only while the foam is still quite wet. As the product becomes nearly dry, the drying rate is most sensitive to air relative humidity. At least two drying stages seem desirable. The first might use 300 fpm of 220°F cocurrent air flow, the second using 50 fpm of 135°F countercurrent air flow.

When the product has a low hot-sticky temperature, as citrus powders do, the mats must be cooled with dehumidified air before scraping of the drying surface. Scraping must be sufficiently complete so that the surface can be reloaded without washing, in order to avoid losses of product.

Equipment

Two types of driers have been built. Neither seems to have a clear advantage as yet. In one case, foam is dried on a belt, in the other it is dried on trays.

Foams are spread or extruded onto stainless steel belts up to 4 ft wide. The belts may be perforated with 1/8-in. holes on 3/16-in. centers. The foam mat extruded onto this perforated surface spans the holes without dropping through. The belt passes over an air jet which pierces the mat above each hole and heaps up the displaced foam around the hole like a little crater (Fig. 5.28). The drying air then flows up through the belt and foam, coming into good contact with an extended foam surface. The air is side ducted in such a way that it passes a number of times through the belt in the drier—first cocurrent, then countercurrent to belt movement (see Fig. 5.29).

Another belt foam-mat drier uses an unperforated belt (Fig. 5.30). This version, known as Microflake, uses thinner mats and shorter residence times. In addition to cross or longitudinal air flows, heat can be added by condensing

FIG. 5.28. FOAM CRATERING

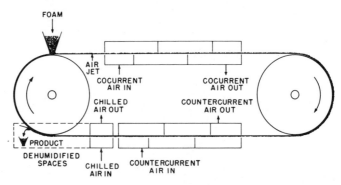

FIG. 5.29. PERFORATED BELT DRIER

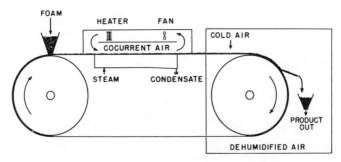

FIG. 5.30. UNPERFORATED BELT DRIER

atmospheric steam on the bottom of the belt. The belt acts as top of boxes into which the steam is admitted, the condensate being wiped off by the downstream side of the boxes. This method is said to achieve higher production rates at the cost of a higher percentage of exposed surface to weight ratio in the product.

Foams may be extruded onto perforated trays up to 4 by 4 ft in size. Both stainless steel and aluminum have been used. The $1/8$-in. hole on $3/16$-in. center pattern has been applied to trays as well as belts. The trays pass continuously end to end under the foam extruder and over the cratering air jet. They are then inserted one at a time at the bottom of a vertical stack of trays inside a duct which forms the drier. The trays move up the drier and leave the top—dry. Flat trays may be moved by stubs attached to roller chains, only the stub extending through a slot in the wall of the drier. Alternatively, the trays may have a self-stacking shape. The trays then rest on each other in the drier. The stack can be pushed upward from below and latched into position. A new tray is inserted below and the dryest tray is dragged off at the top. The trays are cooled, scraped, and returned continuously for reloading. In this version, somewhat better product is obtained through thicker layers and slower drying. The more complicated apparatus requires more sophisticated, if not more, labor. It has been made fully automatic. See Rockwell et al. (1962).

Product Characteristics

A critical moisture content must be reached in drying to permit handling of the product. A somewhat lower moisture, about 1% for citrus powders, is needed for storage stability. About 2% moisture is required by tomato powder. These low moistures can be reached only by using countercurrent drying and good foams. Such low moistures require a dehumidified packing space. The product, once cooled below 100°F, must remain in air below 15% RH. Moisture contents are usually determined by the Karl Fischer method.

The dry product often has a bulk density of 0.3 gm per ml. This can be raised as high as high as 0.8 gm per ml by compacting the powder between strong, warm steel rolls. The extent of densifying is determined by balancing reduced rehydration rates against smaller container costs. Where a foamy rehydrated product, or a floating powder is undesirable, densifying is necessary (Morgan et al. 1959). Another compacting device used is the pelletizer. For bite-sized doses, or for simulated berries, the pelletizer has proven useful.

Foam-mat-dried products have storage requirements equal to the same materials dried other ways. Fruit powders must be protected from humidity, especially if storage temperatures are above 85°F. In addition, tomato powder must be protected against oxygen content above 1%. Aluminum or Saran films, cans, or glass have been used.

Present Use

Foam-mat driers have been sold by four equipment manufacturers: FMC Corp. of San Jose, Calif.; Chemet Engineers of Pasadena, Calif. (Lawler 1962);

AMF of Stamford, Conn.; and TAG of Berlin. A number of users have constructed their own units, such as Foamat Foods of Corvallis, Ore., Kikkoman Foods of Tokyo, and Gerber Foods of Fremont, Mich. At present, orange, grapefruit, pineapple, berry, and tomato powders are being made. For details see Bates (1964), Ginnette et al. (1963) and Graham et al. (1965). Potato mash is foamed by some processors before drying to granules or aggregates. The quantity of fruit powder foam-mat dried is small, probably less than 3 million pounds per year total in 1970.

Prospects

Uses will grow only slowly until new product classes are found. The high raw material value of fruit solids makes sales of these products difficult. The uses in which only dry products can compete are expanding slowly—dry soup mixes, drink powders, bakery ingredients, fruit-cereal mixtures, or dry dessert items. If dry whole milk can become popular, a sudden expansion might occur. If European and Japanese consumers continue to lean toward dry products over frozen, an important penetration of this fruit juice market might take place. The instant coffee and tea trend toward freeze drying may slacken. Producers could reduce charges by foam-mat drying at the cost of mentioning a stabilizer on the label. Any of these events would rocket the method to high use.

CONCENTRATORS FOR HEAT-SENSITIVE MATERIALS

Many of our important food commodities contain such a large proportion of water that there is a strong cost incentive to concentrate them before packaging, transporting, or storing them; if a completely dry product is needed, a preliminary concentration is almost invariably carried out because water removal is less expensive by evaporation than by drying. Since concentration can obviously be an economically essential part of the process leading to dry foods, this section is devoted to a review of developments in food evaporators in the past 15–20 yr and a description of special types now available.

For many years, liquid food materials were concentrated in conventional evaporators, modified to some extent to improve sanitation and to provide access for cleaning. Common types included the vacuum pan, the calandria evaporator, and side-arm evaporators with either natural or forced circulation. Some of these types, as well as more modern ones, are outlined and described by Moore and Hesler (1963). Such evaporators are customarily operated under vacuum and are combined into double- and triple-effect systems to improve heat economy. Improved versions of these evaporators are still widely used for the concentration of skim milk, whey, and other food products that are not highly heat sensitive. Stainless steel is the common material of construction, and great care is taken in design to make all surfaces contacted by the product smooth, easy to clean, and accessible for inspection. Many of these evaporators are now approved for in-place cleaning without disassembly. Cleaning is accomplished by chemical solutions admitted through sprays strategically located within the evaporators. Progress has also been made in improving the efficiency of evaporators by compounding them into multiple-effect systems, by mechanical or thermal recompression of vapors for reuse, or by application of a refrigeration cycle both to supply heat and to condense vapors.

The advent of frozen orange concentrate brought on the first major effort to concentrate a highly heat-sensitive material in large volume. Many equipment manufacturers entered the field, as well as noncommercial research groups, and a variety of designs emerged. The trend was toward evaporation at low absolute pressures so that liquid temperatures were maintained in the range of 50°-100°F. It was necessary to minimize hydrostatic head in the liquid and to reduce resistances to fluid flow in order to attain the required temperature conditions. The most widely used evaporator for orange juice was one in which the juice was fed to the top of a tube bundle heated externally by low-pressure steam or warm fluids. The juice was fed so that it ran down the inside of the heated tube in a film; tubes were of relatively large size so as to permit vapor to flow with little pressure drop. A vapor separator was located below the tube bundle to separate the evolved vapor from the concentrated juice. Juice within a stage was usually recirculated while a part of the juice stream was pumped to another evaporator stage for further concentration. Steam jet ejectors were commonly used to recompress evolved vapors for reuse in the systems as well as for producing the needed vacuum. In practice, the steam used to produce the vacuum, by conversion of its kinetic energy, was more than was required as a carrier of latent heat to evaporate water from the juice. This led, of course, to further efforts to improve heat economy.

Low-temperature evaporation, such as is used for orange juice, did not prove to be the answer for other products such as tomato, peach, pear, and apricot juice or purée. These products contain a great deal of suspended material and become extremely viscous as they are concentrated—so much so that they cannot be handled satisfactorily in the orange juice type of evaporator. Further, the requirements of the various industries are quite different. The processing season for orange is long, perhaps 9-10 months out of the year, while the processing season for tomato, pear, peach, and apricot is measured in weeks. Heat economy is more important for the former; for the latter, the need is for evaporators that will maintain the highest possible evaporation capacity during the short season so that down-time will be minimized and output maximized.

About the same time that engineers were developing the low-temperature types of orange juice evaporator, others were working with systems that employed high temperatures for exceedingly short residence times, the HTST system. The systems evolved proved to be satisfactory for heat-sensitive products as well as those containing large amounts of suspended solids, and in recent years have superseded the low temperature evaporator for the concentration of orange juice. The use of the HTST evaporator avoids the necessity of a separate heat treatment to inactivate the enzymes that would otherwise cause loss of cloud and gelation of the concentrate (Cook 1971). Such systems are inherently single-pass rather than recirculating; in the latter, different portions of the material in process are subjected to different process conditions. The importance of a single-pass operation for heat-sensitive products and the implications of recirculation are discussed by Moore and Hesler (1963) and Dedert and Moore (1963).

Fouling of Evaporators

A characteristic of fluid foods is their tendency during concentration to leave a solid deposit on heated surfaces that they contact. In heat exchangers and evaporators, this is called "fouling." Fouling increases the resistance to heat transfer and leads to a loss in heating or evaporating capacity. Further, fouling continues to occur as operation of the equipment proceeds, so that the loss of evaporating capacity is progressive. Continuing research, carried on by the Western Regional Research Laboratory, has yielded information on the mechanism of fouling, particularly with respect to tomato. Morgan and Wasserman (1959) showed that the material deposited on evaporator tubes during evaporation of tomato juice, tomato paste, and grape juice is high in nitrogen content, indicating that the protein in these materials plays an important part in the fouling process. They also showed that the degree of disintegration of the tomato tissue influences both heat transfer coefficients and fouling rates. In their experiments, the more extensively disintegrated tomato fouled the evaporator tubes faster and consistently yielded poorer heat transfer coefficients. This was attributed in part to the release of protein from the disintegrated cells. Effects of individual components in the feed were studied with a synthetic tomato juice. The influence of protein on fouling was verified, and the presence of fiber in the feed was shown to increase fouling rates markedly. The heat processing of tomato prior to evaporation was shown to influence fouling rate; fouling rates were higher with tomato preprocessed to retain the pectin than with tomato preprocessed to degrade the pectin. Heat treatment during concentration was also shown to reduce the tendency of the tomato to foul evaporator tubes.

A number of significant findings were made that should guide the design of food evaporators for optimum performance. The temperature of the metal surface over which the feed passes has the greatest effect on the fouling rate; the rate increases with increasing temperature. For the same tube-wall temperature, fouling is faster during warming of the feed than during boiling of the feed. Fouling rate increases as the fraction of vapor increases in the vapor-liquid mixture passing through the evaporator tube. Fouling rate also increases with increasing concentration of solids in the feed. Fouling rates were considerably higher when downflow was used in the evaporator tubes than when upflow was used. The conclusions to be drawn regarding evaporator design for long-tube evaporators for tomato and presumably other foods are: (1) fouling is unavoidable, hence ample tube surface must be provided; (2) feed should be preheated outside the evaporator section so that boiling occurs throughout the evaporator section; (3) upflow is preferable to downflow; (4) evaporator sections should be so related to vapor separators as to maintain the vapor fraction in the tubes below 20% by weight—that is, a highly attenuated froth; and (5) highest permissible temperatures should be used so as to keep viscosity at a minimum. These conclusions suggest that an effective evaporator should be single-pass and should consist of a series of evaporator sections, each followed by a vapor separator. A further factor affecting evaporator performance was reported by Kilpatrick and Breitwieser (1961). Using a recirculating upflow evaporator with preconcentrated tomato as feed, consistently higher heat transfer rates were obtained and maintained in evaporator tubes that had been highly polished than in tubes having a rougher surface—normal pickle-finish. Heat transfer rates with nonfouling feeds were higher in the pickled tubes than in the polished tubes, but with feeds that fouled the evaporator tubes, fouling was faster and more extensive on the rougher tube surfaces.

Developments in HTST Evaporators

Empirical development of high-temperature short-time (HTST) evaporators for foods preceded the studies outlined above. An example of the HTST processing of fruit juices to recover volatile flavor essences was reported by Milleville and Eskew (1946). Brown *et al.* (1951) reported the characteristics of a flash evaporator which employed preheating of the feed material by steam injection ahead of the evaporator section. This system was characterized by the ability to employ high temperatures (300°F and above if desired) and extremely short processing times, less than 1 sec being required to preheat, concentrate, and cool the material in process. This led to several commercial installations for essence recovery and concentration of various products, including apple, grape, and strawberry juice and tomato, apricot, and peach purées. These installations have been described by Anon. (1953), O'Connell and Nowlin (1954), Nowlin and Henwood (1955), Havighorst (1956), and Anon. (1956).

Several other designs of evaporators have appeared in recent years which are single-pass, avoiding product recirculation, and which emphasize short processing times. One of the first, described by Havighorst (1956) and Anon. (1956), was used in manufacturing tomato paste. This evaporator comprised four stages, each employing both upflow and downflow in the evaporator sections, with vapor separators between stages. Similar evaporators are challenging the low-temperature evaporators that have dominated the orange concentrate industry. Milleville (1962) and Anon. (1963) reported on a three-stage, single-pass evaporator employing both upflow and downflow in the evaporator sections, with vapor separators between stages. The unit was designed to produce orange concentrate at $72°$ Brix and employs thermo-recompression of vapors to obtain double-effect economy in steam consumption. Liquid temperatures ranged from $170°$ to $120°F$ in the various stages, and the throughput time was 3 min. Orange concentrate at $60°$ Brix was rated at top quality, and satisfactory orange concentrate at $85°$ Brix was made on a test basis.

Another HTST evaporator, developed for citrus juice, has been briefly described by Anon. (1963). This is a downflow type, using several stages of evaporation with vapor separators between stages, and is single-pass in construction. The unit is designed so that the feed is superheated at all times with respect to the individual evaporator sections. This means that the feed is boiling throughout each evaporator section. In the case of citrus juice, fluid temperatures range from $175°$ to $110°F$ and retention time is in the 1-2-min range. This evaporator is downflow rather than upflow; otherwise it meets criteria established by Morgan and his co-workers (1959, 1960-1963).

Another HTST evaporator, novel in concept and extremely compact, has been developed from the plate-type heat exchangers long used in the milk industry and more recently in many other industries. The plate-type heat exchanger consists of an assembly of nearly flat stainless steel plates separated by gaskets and clamped together. The plates and gaskets are ported so that the heating medium flows between alternate plates while the fluid to be heated flows through the space between the pairs of heated plates. As an evaporator, 4 plates comprise an evaporator section where the fluid flows upward between 2 plates, downward between 2 plates, and discharges into a vapor duct common to all evaporator sections. The duct leads to a vapor separator where the vapor can be reused as desired to obtain multiple-effect economy. Lawler (1960) described this evaporator as used for orange concentrate. The installation used two effects to produce concentrate at $65°$ Brix with a retention time of about 1 min. The first effect was single-pass, using a heating medium at about $160°$- $170°F$; the second effect employed a limited amount of recirculation and a heating medium at about $120°F$. Holdup was remarkably low, amounting only to about 5 gal. in each effect. The unit is reported to concentrate apple and pear juices from 12 to 72% total solids in a single effect.

An entirely different type of evaporator, but also single-pass HTST in nature, has come into use in the food industry during the past several years. This is the mechanically-agitated film evaporator. The body is a cylinder which may be straight or tapered in either direction with respect to fluid flow, depending upon the flow characteristics of the material in process. The units may be mounted vertically for downflow or horizontally for cross flow of feed, again depending upon the nature of the feed material. The body of the evaporator is surrounded by a jacket for circulation of the heating medium.

In the straight body type, fixed clearance blades are mounted on a shaft passing centrally through the cylinder, constructed to clear the heat transfer surface by as little as $1/32$ in. In the tapered body type, adjustable blade clearance can be provided by longitudinal movement of the shaft. The rotor may be fitted with hinged wiper blades which contact the heat transfer surface, if required by the material in process. When the central shaft is driven, the rotor blades continually agitate and reform the film of product passing down the walls of the evaporator. Experience has shown that these evaporators are effective in making concentrates that become very viscous at high solids concentration, particularly when the material contains substantial amounts of pulp or fiber. Their general field of application in the food industries seems to be as an after-evaporator for further concentration of feeds that have been concentrated as far as practical in more conventional types of evaporator. One version of the wiped-film evaporator is shown in Fig. 5.31. The mechanically-driven wipers extend from the top of the heating jacket to the product outlet (bottom left) to assure discharge of even the most viscous materials. Feed enters near the top

Courtesy of
Rodney Hunt Machine Co.
FIG. 5.31. WIPED-FILM EVAPORATOR

(upper left) and passes downward over the swept heat transfer surfaces to the product outlet in a single pass. Evolved vapors flow upward through an entrainment separator to the vapor outlet (upper right). Two separate heating jackets can be provided so that different temperatures can be employed if required. The operating characteristics of a wiped-film evaporator on peach, pear, and apricot purées have been reported by Harper (1960). An unusual application of the wiped-film evaporator has been reported by Turkot et al. (1956). Preconcentrated juices of apple, grape, and cherry with added sucrose were fed to the evaporator for further concentration and were discharged as a molten product containing only 2–2.5% moisture. These products are further described in Chap. 12, Vol. 2.

It is clear from the developments outlined in preceding paragraphs that new demands are being imposed upon evaporators by the food industries, and that considerable effort is being made to meet these demands. It is unlikely that the common vacuum pan and the rising-film evaporator, the traditional workhorses of the industry, will be displaced. Instead, special types of evaporators will be used in conjunction with conventional types to produce the high-density food products demanded by prevailing conditions in the industry.

BIBLIOGRAPHY

ANON. 1942. Sardik cocktail. Western Canner Packer 34, No. 10, 43–44.
ANON. 1947. Process equipment cost estimation; estimating spray dryers. Chem. Eng. 54, No. 5, 125.
ANON. 1953. Modernize juice evaporator system. Food Process. 14, No. 2, 12–14, 17.
ANON. 1954. Speed-dries heat sensitive liquids. Food Eng. 26, No. 1, 36–37.
ANON. 1956. Versatile tomato juice line. Food Eng. 28, No. 1, 102–105.
ANON. 1957. Belt-trough dryers now in action on plant line. Food Eng. 29, No. 10, 77.
ANON. 1963. New concepts spark evaporation. Food Eng. 35, No. 2, 68–70, 75.
ANON. 1968. New process makes instant fruit sauce flakes. Can. Food Ind. 39, No. 12, 12.
ARNOLD, J. H. 1933. The theory of the psychrometer. I. The mechanism of evaporation. Physics 4, 255–262. II. The effect of velocity. Ibid. 4, 334–340.
ASHRAE. 1962. Fans. In Systems and Equipment. ASHRAE Guide and Data Book. Am. Soc. Heating, Refrig., Air Conditioning Engrs., New York.
ASHRAE. 1967. Applications. In Systems and Equipment. ASHRAE Guide and Data Book. Am. Soc. Heating, Refrig., Air Conditioning Engrs., New York.
BAKER, H. O., and RYDER, E. A. 1950. A method of measuring local internal temperatures in solids. Am. Soc. Mech. Engrs. New York Meeting, Nov. 26–Dec. 1. Paper 50-A-101.
BATES, R. P. 1964. Factors affecting foam production and stabilization of tropical fruit products. Food Technol. 18, 93–96.
BAUMEISTER, T., Jr. 1935. Fans. McGraw-Hill Book Co., New York.
BEAVENS, E. A. 1944. Cabinet dehydrators suited to small-scale operations. Food Ind. 16, No. 1, 70–72, 116; No. 2, 90–92, 134; No. 3, 75, 135–136.
BOUYOUCOS, G. J., and MARSHALL, R. E. 1945. How to control bin dryers. Food Ind. 17, No. 7, 96–98. Also Mich. Agr. Expt. Sta. Tech. Bull. 197.
BRADFORD, P., and BRIGGS, S. W. 1963. Equipment for the food industry. 3. Jet spray drying. Chem. Eng. Progr. 59, 76–80.
BREKKE, J. E., and TALBURT, W. F. 1950. Preparation of fig powder. USDA Bur. Agr. Ind. Chem. AIC-283. Albany, Calif.

BRITISH MINISTRY OF FOOD. 1946. Vegetable Dehydration. H.M. Stationery Office, London.

BROCKINGTON, S. F., DORIN, H. C., and HOWERTON, H. K. 1949. Hygroscopic equilibria of whole-kernel corn. Cereal Chem. 26, 166–173.

BROWN, A. H. et al. 1951. Rapid heat processing of fluid foods by steam injection. Ind. Eng. Chem. 43, 2949–2954.

BROWN, A. H., and VAN ARSDEL, W. B. 1944, 1951. Drying rate nomographs. III. White potato strips—vertical air flow. USDA Bur. Agr. Ind. Chem. AIC-31-III. Albany, Calif.

CARLSON, R. A., and MORGAN, A. I., Jr. 1962. Fouling inside verticle evaporator tubes. Food Technol. 16, 112–114.

CARRIER, W. H. 1938. Fan Engineering. Buffalo Forge Co., Buffalo, N.Y.

CHARLESWORTH, D. H., and MARSHALL, W. R., Jr. 1960. Evaporation from drops containing dissolved solids. AIChE J 6, 9–23.

CHARM, S. E. 1971. The Fundamentals of Food Engineering, 2nd Edition. Avi Publishing Co., Westport, Conn.

COOK, R. W. 1971. Evaporation in the Florida citrus industry. In Proc. 3rd Intern. Congr. Food Sci. Technol., Institute of Food Technologists, Chicago.

CORDING, J., Jr., WILLARD, M. J., Jr., ESKEW, R. K., and SULLIVAN, J. F. 1957. Advances in the dehydration of mashed potatoes. Food Technol. 11, 236–240.

DAVIDSON, W. F. et al. 1951. Engineering measurements. In Mechanical Engineers Handbook, 5th Edition. L. S. Marks (Editor). McGraw-Hill Book Co., New York.

DEDERT, W. G., and MOORE, J. G. 1963. New trends in evaporation. Ind. Eng. Chem. 55, 57–62.

DREW, T. B., DUNKLE, H. H., and GENERAUX, R. P. 1950. Flow of fluids. In Chemical Engineers Handbook. 3rd Edition. McGraw-Hill Book Co., New York.

DUFFIE, J. A., and MARSHALL, W. R., Jr. 1953. Factors influencing the properties of spray-dried materials. Chem. Eng. Prog. 49, 480–486.

DUNMORE, F. W. 1939. An improved electric hygrometer. J. Res. Natl. Bur. Std. 23, 701–714.

DURKEE, E. L., ELSKEN, R. H., and BARTA, E. J. 1961. Latest research boosts pallet-freezing efficiency. Food Eng. 33, No. 1, 84–86.

EDE, A. J., and HALES, K. C. 1948. The physics of drying in heated air, with special reference to fruits and vegetables. G. Brit. Dept. Sci. Ind. Res., Food Invest. Spec. Rept. 53.

ELSKEN, R. H. 1960. Temperature telemetry aids frozen food study. Eelectronics 33, 129–131.

FOGLER, B. B., and KLEINSCHMIDT, R. V. 1938. Spray drying. Ind. Eng. Chem. 30, 1372–1384.

FRIEDMAN, S. J., GLUCKERT, F. A., and MARSHALL, W. R., JR. 1952. Centrifugal disc atomization. Chem. Eng. Progr. 48, 181–191.

GINNETTE, L. F., GRAHAM, R. P., MIERS, J. C., and MORGAN, A. I., Jr. 1963. Tomato powder by foam-mat drying. Food Technol. 17, 811–813.

GOULD, H. P. 1907. Evaporation of apples. USDA Farmers' Bull. 291.

GRAHAM, R. P., HART, M. R., WILLIAMS, G. S., and MORGAN, A. I., Jr. 1965. Foam-mat-drying citrus juices. Food Technol. 19, 1273–1275.

HAGEN, H. F. 1951. Centrifugal and propeller fans. In Mechanical Engineers Handbook, 5th Edition. L. S. Marks (Editor). McGraw-Hill Book Co., New York.

HARPER, J. C. 1960. Viscometric behavior in relation to evaporation of fruit purées. Food Technol. 14, 557–561.

HARPER, J. C., and TAPPEL, A. L. 1957. Freeze-drying of food products. Advan. Food Res. 7, 172–234.

HART, M. R., GRAHAM, R. P., GINNETTE, L. F., and MORGAN, A. I., Jr. 1963. Foams for foam-mat drying. Food Technol. 17, 1302–1304.

HAVIGHORST, C. R. 1956. Mechanizing to top efficiency. Food Eng. 28, No. 1, 74–76.

HURXTHAL, A. O. 1938. Aeroform dryer. Ind. Eng. Chem. 30, 1004–1006.

HUSSMANN, P. 1963. Food dehydration by the BIRS process. In Lebensmitteltechnik,

158   FOOD DEHYDRATION

Dechema Monograph 46, 761–780. Verlag Chemie G.m.b.H., Weinheim-Bergstrasse. (German)

JASON, A. C. 1958. A study of evaporation and diffusion processes in the drying of fish muscle. *In* Fundamental Aspects of the Dehydration of Foodstuffs. Soc. Chem. Ind. (London) 103–135.

KERSHAW, F. 1938. Drying machinery. Ind. Eng. Chem. *30*, 1115–1118.

KILPATRICK, P. W., and BREITWIESER, E. 1961. Increasing evaporator capacity with polished tubes. Ind. Eng. Chem. *53*, 119–120.

KILPATRICK, P. W., LOWE, E., and VAN ARSDEL, W. B. 1955. Tunnel dehydrators for fruits and vegetables. Advan. Food Res. *6*, 314–369.

KLIS, J. B. 1963. Powdered molasses or honey solids. Food Process. *24*, No. 3, 100–101.

KNEULE, F. 1959. Drying. *In* Basics of Chemical Technology, Vol. 6. H. Mohler and O. Fuchs (Editors). R. H. Sauerländer & Co., Aarau and Frankfort a. M. (German)

KRISCHER, O. 1956. Drying Technology, Vol. 1, The Scientific Fundamentals of Drying Technology. Springer-Verlag, Berlin-Göttingen-Heidelberg. (German)

KRÖLL, K. 1959. Drying Technology, Vol. 2, Driers and Drying Processes. Springer-Verlag, Berlin-Göttingen-Heidelberg. (German)

KUPRIANOFF, J. 1962. Construction of food product driers and their operating characteristics. *In* Symp. Drying in the Food Industries. Springer-Verlag, Berlin-Göttingen-Heidelberg. (German)

LAPPLE, W. C., and CLARK, W. E. 1955. Drying methods and equipment. Chem. Eng. *62*, No. 10, 191–210.

LAPPLE, W. C., CLARK, W. E., and DYBDAL, E. C. 1955. Drying design and costs. Chem. Eng. *62*, No. 11, 177–200.

LASTER, R. 1953. Factors in the selection and design of a spray drier. Food Technol. *7*, 264–267.

LAWLER, F. K. 1960. Revolutionary plate evaporator concentrates orange juice. Food Eng. *32*, No. 3, 60–63.

LAWLER, F. K. 1962. Foam-mat-drying goes to work. Food Eng. *34*, No. 2, 68–69.

LAZAR, M. E. 1968. Modified drum dryer shows versatility. Food Eng. *40*, No. 12, 95–97.

LAZAR, M. E., and MORGAN, A. I. 1966. Instant applesauce. Food Technol. *20*, No. 4, 179–182.

LEGAULT, R. R., MAKOWER, B., and TALBURT, W. F. 1948. Apparatus for measurement of vapor pressure. Anal. Chem. *20*, 428–430.

LOWE, E., and DURKEE, E. L. 1959. Apparatus for treating particulate material with gaseous media. U.S. Pat. 2,876,558. Mar. 10.

LOWE, E., and HAWES, J. R. 1949. An improved heated-thermocouple anemometer for for use in air-blast freezers. Food Technol. *3*, 241–243.

LOWE, E., RAMAGE, W. D., DURKEE, E. L., and HAMILTON, W. E. 1955. Belt-trough, a new continuous dehydrator. Food Eng. *27*, No. 7, 43–44.

LOWE, E., and ROCKWELL, W. C. 1956. Continuous belt-trough drier. U.S. Pat. 2,745,194. May 15.

LYKOW, A. W. 1950, 1955. Experimental and Theoretical Fundamentals of Drying. Moscow, 1950 (Russian). Veb.-Verlag, Berlin, 1955 (German).

MCCORMICK, P. Y., LUCAS, R. L., and WELLS, D. F. 1963. Gas-solid systems. *In* Chemical Engineers Handbook, 4th Edition. McGraw-Hill Book Co., New York.

MAKOWER, B., and MYERS, S. 1943. A new method for the determination of moisture in dehydrated vegetables. Inst. Food Technologists. Proc. *1943*, 156–164.

MARKS, L. S. (Editor) 1951. Mechanical Engineers Handbook, 5th Edition. McGraw-Hill Book Co., New York.

MARSHALL, W. R., Jr. 1954. Atomization and Spray Drying. Chem. Eng. Progr. Monograph Ser. *2*, Vol. 50. Am. Inst. Chem. Eng.

MARSHALL, W. R., Jr., and FRIEDMAN, S. J. 1950. Drying. *In* Chemical Engineering Handbook, 3rd Edition. J. H. Perry (Editor). McGraw-Hill Book Co., New York.

MARSHALL, W. R., Jr., and HOUGEN, O. A. 1942. Drying of solids by through-circulation. Am. Inst. Chem. Eng. Trans. *38*, 91–121.

MARSHALL, W. R., Jr., and SELTZER, E. 1950. Principles of spray drying. I. Fundamentals of spray drier operation. Chem. Eng. Progr. *46*, 501–508.

MILLEVILLE, H. P. 1962. High-quality concentrates. Food Process. *23*, No. 10, 59–62.

MILLEVILLE, H. P., and ESKEW, R. K. 1946. Recovery of volatile apple flavors in essence form. Western Canner Packer *38*, No. 11, 51–54.

MOORE, J. G., and HESLER, W. E. 1963. Evaporation of heat sensitive materials. Chem. Eng. Progr. *59*, 87–92.

MORGAN, A. I., Jr. *et al.* 1960–1963. U.S. Pat. 2,934,441; 2,955,046; 2,955,943; 2,967,109; 2,976,158; 2,981,629; 3,031,313; 3,031,312; 3,064,722; 3,093,488 and patents in 18 other countries based on the above.

MORGAN, A. I., Jr., and CARLSON, R. A. 1960. Fouling inside heat exchanger tubes. Food Technol. *14*, 594–596.

MORGAN, A. I., Jr., GINNETTE, L. F., RANDALL, J. M., and GRAHAM, R. P. 1959. Technique for improving instants. Food Eng. *31*, No. 9, 86–87.

MORGAN, A. I., Jr., and WASSERMAN, T. 1959. Fouling of evaporator tubes by tomato. Food Technol. *13*, 691–693.

MORGAN, A. I., WASSERMAN, T., BROWN, A. H., and SMITH, G. S. 1959. Commercial-scale evaporation of tomato products in flash evaporators. Food Technol. *13*, 232–235.

MOSSEL, D. A. A., and VAN KUIJK, H. J. L. 1955. A new and simple technique for the direct determination of the equilibrium relative humidity of foods. Food Res. *20*, 415–423.

NAIR, J. H. 1963. Precooked sweet potato flakes go commercial. Food Eng. *35*, No. 7, 55–56.

NEEL, G. H. *et al.* 1954. Drying problems in the add-back process for production of potato granules. Food Technol. *13*, 230–234.

NOWLIN, R. L., and HENWOOD, C. I., Jr. 1955. Flash evaporation now applied to grape juice concentrate. Wines Vines *36*, No. 1, 25.

O'CONNELL, J. O., and NOWLIN, R. L. 1954. Instantaneous heating–flash evaporation. Food Process. *15*, No. 7, 14–15, 18.

PATSAVAS, A. G. 1963. Equipment for the food industry. 4. The spray dryer. Chem. Eng. Progr. *59*, 65–70.

PERRY, J. H. (Editor) 1950. Chemical Engineers Handbook, 3rd Edition. McGraw-Hill Book Co., New York.

PERRY, R. H., CHILTON, C. H., and KIRKPATRICK, S. D. (Editors) 1963. Chemical Engineers Handbook, 4th Edition. McGraw-Hill Book Co., New York.

PERRY, R. L. *et al.* 1946. Fruit dehydration. I. Principles and equipment. Calif. Agr. Expt. Sta. Bull. *698*.

PORTER, R. W., and CONSIDINE, D. M. 1950. Process control. *In* Chemical Engineers Handbook, 3rd Edition. J. H. Perry (Editor). McGraw-Hill Book Co., New York.

RHODES, T. J. 1941. Industrial Instruments for Measurement and Control. McGraw-Hill Book Co., New York.

ROCKWELL, W. C. *et al.* 1962. How foam-mat dryer is made. Food Eng. *34*, No. 8, 86–88.

SCHAFFNER, R. M., and HOEHLER, W. A. 1939. Determination of the performance and operating costs of a commercial dryer. Am. Inst. Chem. Eng. Trans. *35*, 303–322.

SCHANHALS, J., GARCIA, E., and ROBE, K. 1963. Waste heat in the flue gas dries tomato waste. Food Process. *24*, No. 8, 68–71.

SELTZER, E., and SETTELMEYER, J. T. 1949. Spray drying of foods. Advan. Food Res. *6*, 399–520.

SHERWOOD, T. K., and COMINGS, W. E. 1932. An experimental study of the wet-bulb hygrometer. Trans. Am. Inst. Chem. Eng. *28*, 88–117.

SMITH, D. A. 1949. Spray drying equipment–factors in design and operation. Chem. Eng. Progr. *45*, 703–707.

SPADARO, J. J., and PATTON, E. L. 1961. Continuous pilot plant process produces precooked dehydrated sweet potato flakes. Food Eng. *33*, No. 7, 46–48.

SPAUGH, O. H. 1948. Air flow through beds of dehydrated vegetables. Food Technol. *2*, 33–38.

TURKOT, V. A., ESKEW, R. K., and ACETO, N. C. 1956. A continuous process for dehydrating fruit juices. Food Technol. *10*, 604–606.

USDA. 1944. Vegetable and Fruit Dehydration—a Manual for Plant Operators. USDA Misc. Pub. *540*.

USDA. 1952. Drying shelled corn and small grain with heated air. USDA Leaflet *331*.

USDA. 1959. Management Handbook to Aid Emergency Expansion of Dehydration Facilities for Vegetables and Fruits. Western Util. Res. Develop. Div., Agr. Res. Serv., USDA, Albany, Calif.

VAN ARSDEL, W. B. 1951A. Principles of the drying process, with special reference to vegetable dehydration. USDA Bur. Agr. Ind. Chem. *AIC-300*.

VAN ARSDEL, W. B. 1951B. Tunnel-and-truck dehydrators, as used in vegetable dehydration. USDA Bur. Agr. Ind. Chem. *AIC-308*.

VAN ARSDEL, W. B. 1955. Simultaneous heat and mass transfer in a non-isothermal system: Through-flow drying in the low-moisture range. Am. Inst. Chem. Eng., Chem. Eng. Progr. Symp. Ser. *16*, 47–58.

VAN MARLE, D. J. 1938. Drum drying. Ind. Eng. Chem. *30*, 1006–1008.

WALKER, W. H., LEWIS, W. K., MCADAMS, W. H., and GILLILAND, E. R. 1937. Principles of Chemical Engineering, 3rd Edition. McGraw-Hill Book Co., New York.

WEBER, R. L. 1941. Temperature Measurement and Control. Blakiston Co., Philadelphia.

WEXLER, A., and BROMBACHER, W. G. 1951. Methods of measuring humidity and testing hygrometers. Natl. Bur. Std. Circ. *512*.

YARWOOD, J. 1961. High Vacuum Technique, 3rd Edition. John Wiley & Sons, New York.

ZIEMBA, J. V. 1962. Now—drying without heat. Food Eng. *34*, No. 7, 84–85.

CHAPTER 6

C. Judson King | # Freeze Drying

INTRODUCTION

Definition

Freeze drying is the removal of water from a substance by direct sublimation from the frozen state to the vapor state, without the water passing through an intermediate liquid state. For ice, direct sublimation is favored thermodynamically over melting and evaporation at conditions of temperature and water vapor partial pressure below the *triple point* of water.

Figure 6.1 shows a phase diagram for pure water. The triple point (0°C and 4.59 mm Hg, abs) is the one condition where three phases—solid ice, liquid water, and water vapor—coexist at equilibrium. Through the triple point pass three curves. These are the vapor pressure curve for liquid water, with a slope equal to $\Delta H_e/RT^2$, where ΔH_e is the latent heat of evaporation; the vapor pressure curve for ice, with a greater slope equal to $\Delta H_s/RT^2$, where ΔH_s is the latent heat of sublimation; and the curve for equilibrium between ice and liquid water. Below the triple point the vapor pressure of ice is less than that of liquid water, and as a result direct sublimation from ice to water vapor is favored by free energy considerations at temperatures and pressures below 0°C and 4.59 mm Hg.

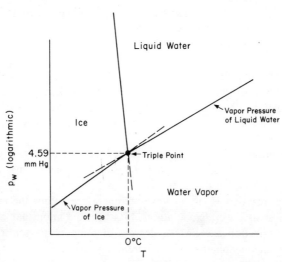

FIG. 6.1. VAPOR-LIQUID-SOLID PHASE DIAGRAM FOR PURE WATER; PARTIAL PRESSURE OF WATER VAPOR (p_W) VERSUS TEMPERATURE (T)

161

partial pressure below triple pt. & H₂O favours sublimation.

In any real food material the presence of dissolved substances and bound water will alter the triple point position for at least some of the water. These effects will be considered later.

Growth and Significance

Freeze drying has gained acceptance as the method of drying which will generally produce a product of the highest quality in comparison to other common methods of drying. Because of the need for preserving low temperature and low water vapor partial pressure, it is an expensive method of drying. Costs per pound of water removed were predicted by Bird (1964) to be in the range of 4–5¢ for sustained operation in large-scale plants. Costs experienced by processors today are usually considerably higher than this; costs in the range of 10–30¢ per lb have been cited.

By virtue of its position as a high-cost, high-quality drying method, freeze drying has found its application for specialty items where the quality gain offsets the costs. In the consumer market the largest application at present is for freeze-dried coffee, the growth of which in the period of 1967–1971 has been meteoric. Production of freeze-dried soluble coffee in 1970–1971 may be crudely estimated as 50 million pounds per year, and is in a period of rapid increase. Other freeze-dried products on the general consumer market include such items as chives, shallots, tea, meats for dried soups, entire soup mixes, and dinners and main dishes for campers and hikers. A considerable market has been developed for whole eggs for bakeries. A less successful effort was the inclusion of freeze-dried fruits in breakfast cereals.

In the United States the military accounts for a large portion of the production of freeze-dried foods. In particular, the Long Range Patrol Ration program generated by the U.S. Army Natick Laboratory represents another instance of production on a very large scale.

Benefits of Freeze Drying

Freeze drying is distinguished from other forms of drying by the presence of frozen water within the substance during drying. Another less-categorically distinguishing feature is the existence of relatively quite low temperatures during drying.

Low Temperature.—The low temperatures held during freeze drying result in a lesser occurrence of various degradative side-reactions during drying. This effect cannot be attributed simply to the fact that the rate of nearly any chemical or biochemical reaction is less at lower temperatures, since the rate of drying itself is also less at lower temperatures. Rather, the important comparison is between the activation energies, or degrees of temperature sensitivity, of the various competing phenomena. The apparent activation energy of water removal rates during the falling-rate period of drying corresponds closely to the latent heat of evaporation or sublimation of water, 9–12 kcal/gm mole (King, 1968). Most degradation reactions have a considerably higher apparent activation energy;

for example, 30 kcal/gm mole has been reported for nonenzymatic browning (Song *et al.* 1966; Kluge and Heiss 1967). The higher activation energy corresponds to a greater temperature sensitivity of the reaction rate, with the result that the higher activation energy of degradative reactions causes their rate to be less prominent in comparison with the drying rate at lower temperatures.

Temperatures of freeze drying are also usually below threshold temperatures for substantial protein denaturation (MacKenzie and Luyet 1967).

Frozen State.—The presence of a rigid ice structure at the location where sublimation occurs in freeze drying mechanically prevents shrinkage from occurring to any great extent during drying. As a result freeze drying is unique among drying methods by vitrue of giving practically no change in volume or physical arrangement of the solid material from that which existed in the frozen state before drying. The lack of shrinkage gives an internal porosity approaching the initial volume fraction of water or ice within the substance, with the result that under moderate conditions rapid and nearly complete rehydration of the product may be obtained. The absence of free liquid water during freeze drying gives other advantages as well, including no migration of dissolved solutes carried by capillary flow and no spattering or frothing from liquid water carried or entrained by the high-velocity escaping vapor.

Freeze drying occurs through the movement of a remarkably sharp boundary between fully hydrated and frozen material, on the one hand, and a nearly completely dry region, on the other hand. Consequently, there is a relatively rapid transition of any local region of the material being dried from the fully hydrated and frozen state to a nearly completely dehydrated state. This rapid transition minimizes those degradative reactions (e.g., nonenzymatic browning) which take place preferentially at intermediate moisture contents in the unfrozen state.

Finally, it has been established by Flink and Karel (1970A, B; Karel and Flink, 1969), and others that the excellent retention of volatile flavor and aroma species obtained during freeze drying is associated with low rates of diffusion of molecules of these substances in glassified microregions of the material being dried. This low diffusion rate is a direct result of low temperatures and drying from an adequately solidified state. Sauvageot *et al.* (1969) have shown that 80–90% of retention of naturally occurring volatile compounds is possible under well-chosen conditions of freezing and freeze drying for orange juice and raspberry juice.

Additional References

There have been several comprehensive reviews of freeze drying, which will be of use to the reader seeking more detailed information than is given in this discussion or in the other references at the end of this chapter.

An extensive review of research and development on freeze drying of foods, with emphasis upon the period 1964 to 1970, has been given by King (1970A). Previous reviews of this sort have been made by Burke and Decareau (1964) and by Harper and Tappel (1957). A list of 638 references on freeze drying prior to

1963 has been drawn up by the USDA (Corriden 1964). Two books edited by Rey (1964A, 1966) give a broad survey of freeze-drying research and practice up until the time of publication. Ginnette and Kaufman (1968) have reviewed product characteristics and requirements, along with conventional processing equipment used for freeze drying. Fulford (1969) has made a thorough review of Russian work in drying of solids in general, including a few references on freeze drying.

<h2 style="text-align:center">MORPHOLOGY OF FREEZING AND FREEZE DRYING</h2>

Freezing

As has been noted earlier, freeze drying causes little change in the solid structure of a food from that which existed before freeze drying. Freezing of foods necessarily causes changes in the microstructure, and, hence, the freezing step before drying is critical to the product characteristics which will exist after drying. By controlling freezing conditions it is possible to influence drying rates, rehydratability, product texture, retention of volatiles during drying, and product color.

Kuprianoff (1964) has surveyed the effect of freezing conditions on ice crystal size and shape in structured solid foods. Faster freezing rates lead to smaller ice crystals and, hence, smaller pores in the freeze-dried product, as reported also by Luyet (1962). King et al. (1968) used mercury intrusion porosimetry and measurements of nitrogen surface areas to determine pore size distributions for freeze-dried poultry meat as a function of the rate of freezing before drying, finding that the two methods checked well. Particularly interesting are the classical observations of Koonz and Ramsbottom (1939), who found that the location and number of ice crystals in frozen poultry meat changed from (a) numerous crystals distributed evenly within each fiber, to (b) several crystals located around the periphery of each fiber, to (c) single crystals extending along the center of each fiber, to (d) crystals formed outside the sarcolemma and in between adjacent fibers, as the freezing rate was decreased. The freezing rate also has a marked effect upon the ice crystal size and the resultant pore size of the freeze-dried product for food liquids, as has been shown by Kramers (1958) and Thijssen and Rulkens (1969), among others. The latter authors carried out unidirectional freezing of dextrin solutions at different rates, and found that the observed permeability after freeze drying checked well with the observed pore size.

The presence of dissolved solutes in foods can also have profound effects upon freezing characteristics. Spiess et al. (1969) and Kramers (1958) confirmed for various food liquids that an increasing dissolved solids content causes a lower porosity and lower pore size of the freeze-dried material under equivalent freezing conditions. Dissolved solutes also lower the freezing point of water. For foods such as meat and most vegetables the lowering of the freezing point is not great. Riedel (1969) summarizes extensive calorimetric data for beef which

he has obtained over the years. He concludes that the average freezing point of
the water present is about –5°C. Similarly, Sandall *et al.* (1967) found that –5°C
was the threshold temperature of the frozen zone for good product quality
during freeze drying of turkey meat.

Liquid foods which are predominantly carbohydrate solutions exhibit a much
greater depression of the freezing point.   Figure 6.2 shows the phase diagram
reported by Young *et al.* (1952) for the *d*-fructose-water system.   A eutectic of

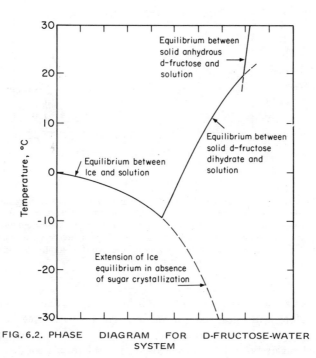

FIG. 6.2. PHASE   DIAGRAM   FOR   D-FRUCTOSE-WATER
SYSTEM

d-fructose dihydrate and ice is formed at – 10°C and 45 wt % fructose, anhydrous
basis. At sufficiently low temperatures between 0°C and – 10°C a mixture of less
than 45% fructose and water will form 2 phases at equilibrium—ice and a
saturated solution of fructose in water. A further complication for which systems containing fructose are notorious is impaired crystallization of the solid
sugar upon cooling. For such systems and for most forms of freezing the sugar
is prevented kinetically from crystallizing, and the freezing behavior will follow
the ice equilibrium curve—the dashed curve in Fig. 6.2. Consequently, even at
temperatures as low as – 30°C the mixture obtained in practice will be ice plus
a residual unfrozen highly viscous concentrate of about 68 wt % fructose in
water.   Figure 6.3 shows the experimental freezing curve reported by Riedel
(1949) for apple juice, along with predictions of the freezing curve made by

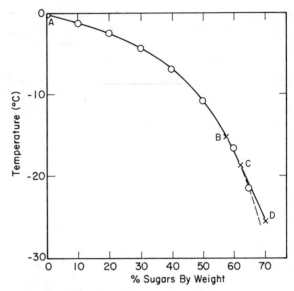

FIG. 6.3. FREEZING DIAGRAM FOR APPLE JUICE CON-
CENTRATE

O is data of Riedel (1949); ⸺ is prediction from binary data and
ideal solution theory; A–B is equilibrium with ice; B–C is equilibrium with ice and solid fructose dehydrate; C–D is equilibrium with
ice and solid fructose glucose hydrates; D is quaternary eutectic;
- - - - is extension of ice equilibrium curve for inhibited sugar
crystallization.

Chandrasekaran and King (1971A), utilizing available data for binary sugar
solutions, along with ideal solution theory. The predicted freezing curve considers apple juice to be a solution of d-fructose, d-glucose, and sucrose in water,
with the 3 sugars being in a typical ratio of 3:1:1 to one another. The solid
curve shows the prediction if the sugars are able to crystallize, and the dashed
curve shows the predicted extension of the ice equilibrium curve for inhibited
crystallization of sugar.

Impaired crystallization of dissolved solutes hampers freeze drying considerably. A fully solidified state is never achieved, and the microregions of unfrozen
concentrate may not be rigid enough to form a self-supporting porous structure
after the ice crystals are removed by freeze drying. This can lead to frothing and
spattering in a freeze drier and to *collapse* of the dried layer, which lowers the
rate of freeze drying considerably and leads to a poorly-dispersable product.
Limiting temperatures below which the frozen zone temperature must be held
during freeze drying in order to prevent collapse have been reported for a large
number of substances by MacKenzie (1965, 1966) and by Rey (1964B). Bellows
and King (1972) have found that tendencies of fruit juices, sugar solutions, and

other such solutions to collapse, melt, or become sticky during freeze drying can be analyzed quantitatively in terms of a force balance between surface tension and the viscosity of the unfrozen concentrate regions at the temperature of the sublimation front. Above a certain critical viscosity of the concentrate microregions collapse will not occur. Juices and solutions rich in fructose and, to a lesser extent, glucose are particularly subject to collapse or stickiness during freeze drying. The addition of substantial quantities of sucrose or lactose before freezing has been suggested as a way of overcoming the collapse problem for such substances (Stern and Storrs 1969; Moy 1970).

Under ordinary freezing conditions a number of liquid foods have been found to form a layer of relatively high solids content on the outer surface, which impairs water vapor removal during subsequent freeze drying (Lambert and Marshall 1962; Quast and Karel 1968). Granulation after freezing is one means of overcoming this problem, and another approach is "slush" freezing, in which the liquid is first partially frozen, with agitation, at an intermediate temperature, and the resultant slush is then fully frozen at a lower temperature (Quast and Karel 1968).

Color of the freeze-dried product is important in many cases. For coffee, it has been found (Cruz Picallo 1969; Petersen et al. 1970) that slow freezing before freeze drying gives a darker product color than does fast freezing. This is presumably the result of fewer reflective void-space surfaces in the product. Color is also influenced by the degree of melting during drying, corresponding to the condenser temperature. The condenser temperature also influences the product density, with a higher condenser temperature (more melting) giving a higher density and a darker color (Petersen et al. 1970). Several processing approaches for improving coffee product color have been suggested (Pintauro 1969).

Foaming of liquid foods before or during freezing prior to freeze drying has been recommended and used in several cases (Ginnette et al. 1967; Wertheim and Mishkin 1968; Pfluger et al. 1969; Stern and Storrs 1969). Foaming gives a means of influencing the density and vapor permeability of the dried product. Warman and Reichel (1970) and Poulsen (1970) describe equipment available for foaming and freezing.

Bound water is another form of water which will freeze at temperatures much lower than the freezing point of free water, and, in fact, may not freeze at all. Bound water is combined with the solid structure of a food such as by hydrogen bonding to polar groups of protein molecules. Riedel (1969) reports that 8–10% of the water present in beef is bound water which will not freeze even at temperatures as low as $-50°C$.

Freeze Drying

The simplest analysis of freeze drying postulates that drying occurs by means of uniform retreat of a sharp boundary between a fully frozen and fully hydrated region, on the one hand, and a fully dry region on the other hand. A schematic of this behavior for a two-dimensional geometry is shown in Fig. 6.4. A frozen core becomes smaller and smaller as freeze drying occurs, with drying from all four sides being postulated for the figure. There are three features of this model which are subject to question—the *sharpness* of the frozen front, the *uniformity of its retreat*, and the extent to which *complete drying* occurs as the front passes. We shall consider each of these points briefly; each is discussed in more detail elsewhere (King 1970A).

TIME

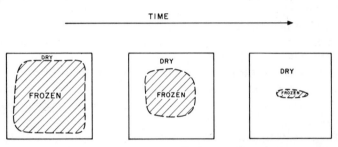

FIG. 6.4. RETREATING SHARP FROZEN FRONT

Sharpness.—From observations of the sublimation of ice spheres into vacuum, Luikov (1969) reports a number of phenomena which could cause the frozen front during freeze-drying processes to be indistinct. These include:

(a) The development of ice crystallites which have sizes ranging from a fraction of a millimeter to several millimeters and which oscillate rapidly and can be broken away by the high-velocity stream of escaping water vapor.

(b) The occurrence of desublimation of water vapor at some points of surface while sublimation occurs at other points, with the net rate of sublimation being the difference between the rate of sublimation and desublimation.

Measurements of moisture content and/or temperature profiles which suggest a diffuse spread of the frozen front during freeze drying have been reported by Brajnikov *et al.* (1969), Meffert (1963), and Luikov (1969). In each of these cases, however, it appears that the data may well reflect either an excessive amount of melting during the drying process, or else a nonuniform retreat of a still-sharp frozen front such that slices of the material contain the frozen zone at some points but not at other points (King 1970A).

Evidence supporting a quite sharp frozen front during freeze drying includes photographs of partially dried specimens reported by Clark and King (1971), King (1970A), and Beke (1969), as well as moisture profiles during freeze drying of beef slabs, obtained by gamma-ray attenuation measurements (Hatcher 1964). MacKenzie (1965, 1966) reports a number of interesting experiments in which freeze drying of thin slabs of various frozen aqueous solutions was observed in the field of a microscope. Extremely sharp vapor-ice interfaces were noted.

final moisture content ~ 3%

moisture remaining at end of process ≡ absorbed moisture

In some cases the solution composition and freezing technique combined to give $(v_p < v_{p\,ice}$ isolated ice crystals which did not form a continuous network. In such cases the *at T°c)* frozen front would still retreat sharply across each crystallite region, but it appeared that water vapor would have to redissolve and pass from one void space to another by a homogeneous diffusion mechanism.

It seems clear that there are factors such as structural irregularities and the crystallite phenomena observed by Luikov (1969) which can cause the sublimation front to be diffuse, but these effects operate over short distances in foods, usually less than 1 mm. For freeze-drying conditions which lead to desirable product quality the postulate of a sharp retreating frozen front is an excellent model.

Uniformity of Retreat.—Natural products have physical properties which will vary from one location in a substance to another. For foods, nonuniform physical properties can lead to nonuniform rates of retreat of the frozen zone during freeze drying. Two general effects can occur:

(a) If the permeability or effective diffusivity for water vapor varies from place to place within the dry layer, the rate of escape of water vapor under a given water vapor partial pressure difference driving force will also vary from place to place, causing the frozen front to retreat faster at some locations than at others. A nonuniform external mass transfer coefficient for water vapor at the outer surface of the material being dried can also have this same effect.

(b) A nonhomogeneous thermal conductivity of the dry layer, a nonuniform external heat transfer coefficient, and/or nonuniform heat supply to different points of the outer surface of the material being dried can cause tendencies for variations of temperature from one point to another along the sublimation front. If the thermal conductivity of the frozen region is not great enough to even out these inequalities, or if the frozen region is not contiguous, different temperatures at different points along the frozen front will cause different water vapor partial pressure driving forces for the mass transfer process and hence will cause nonuniform retreat of the frozen front.

Margaritis and King (1971) report measurements of the uniformity of retreat of the frozen front within slabs of turkey meat interrupted during freeze drying. The retreat of the frozen zone was found to be discernibly uneven although the front was sharp. Nonuniform retreat of the frozen front will be more noticeable and more important for slab piece geometries than for dice. Quast and Karel (1968) observed for freeze drying of coffee extract and model solutions that the frozen zone would become discontinuous during freeze drying, with islands of frozen substance remaining. The tendency for this behavior was dependent upon the way in which freezing was carried out before freeze drying, and apparently reflects different freezing rates at different locations within a specimen. Two-stage freezing, described above, virtually eliminated tendencies for the frozen zone to become discontinuous.

Completeness of Drying.—Some moisture should remain in the material being dried as the frozen front passes, at least an amount equal to the sorbed moisture which exerts a vapor pressure which is less than that of ice at any set temperature. For freeze drying carried out with heat supply to the outer dried surface, the amount of moisture left behind as the frozen front passes will not be great if local equilibrium is achieved between the dried substance and the vapor phase within pores of the "dry" layer. Sandall (1966) calculated the average moisture content of the dry layer, postulating local equilibrium for typical freeze-drying conditions for turkey meat, and found that the average moisture content should be 3%, dry basis. The rate at which equilibrium is reached between sorbed moisture and the vapor phase in the pores of the dry layer was investigated by Margaritis and King (1971), who found that the equilibration is substantially complete within 1 hr for freeze-dried turkey meat. Their experiment passed a gas stream through a slab of freeze-dried meat; they observed the transient change in pressure drop across the sample following a step change in the humidity of the permeating gas.

The low moisture content of the dry layer corresponding to local equilibrium with the pore vapor when heat is supplied by conduction across the dry layer results from the large temperature gradient across the dry layer. Other forms of heat input which avoid this thermal gradient—e.g., heat conduction across the frozen region from a contact heater, or microwave heat input—will give a much higher residual moisture content following the retreat of the frozen front. In those cases a more substantial amount of water will have to be removed by secondary drying after the passage of the sublimation front.

RATES OF FREEZE DRYING

Rates of freeze drying reflect four different rate-limiting processes which must occur in series with one another. Figure 6.5 shows a generalized schematic of freeze drying, in which the latent heat of sublimation must be transferred from a *heat source* to the sublimation fronts within pieces being dried, and the

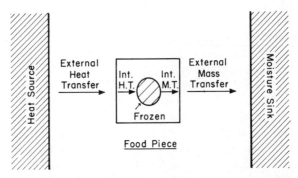

FIG. 6.5. RATE-LIMITING FACTORS IN FREEZE DRYING

water vapor generated must be transported from that point to a *moisture sink*, usually a refrigerated condenser. The potential rate-limiting factors are: (1) *External heat transfer*—from the heat source to the outer surface of each piece. (2) *Internal heat transfer*—from the outer surface of each piece to the sublimation front within, usually a conduction process. (3) *Internal mass transfer of water vapor*—from the sublimation front to the outer piece surface, a process of bulk diffusion, Knudsen diffusion, and/or viscous flow. (4) *External mass transfer of water vapor*—from the piece surface to the condenser or other moisture sink.

In conventional processing equipment, external heat transfer usually occurs principally by *radiation*, although conduction from contact plates is sometimes used and convective heating has been proposed and used on at least a pilot scale. External mass transfer reflects a *bulk flow* process in common low-pressure equipment, with pressure drops coming at points of constriction between the food and the condenser. In some instances, heat can be supplied to the sublimation front through the frozen region from a contact-heater; in that case internal heat transfer occurs by conduction through the frozen region. Penetrating radiation—e.g., microwaves or penetrating infrared radiation—will transfer heat from the source directly to the moisture, supplanting conduction as the internal heat transfer mechanism.

From our analyses we shall consider the form of heating and vapor removal corresponding to Fig. 6.5, which is by far the most common approach used in practice. In that case the rate of heat transfer during quasi-steady-state drying is given by

$$q = h_e(T_e - T_s) \tag{6.1}$$

$$= h_i(T_s - T_f) \tag{6.2}$$

$$= \left[\frac{1}{\dfrac{1}{h_e} + \dfrac{1}{h_i}}\right](T_e - T_f) \tag{6.3}$$

where

q = heat flux (Btu/hr-ft^2)
T_e = temperature of heat source ($^\circ$F)
T_s = temperature of outer piece surface ($^\circ$F)
T_f = temperature of sublimation front ($^\circ$F)
h_e = heat transfer coefficient external to piece (Btu/hr-ft^2-$^\circ$F)
h_i = heat transfer coefficient within the dry layer (Btu/hr-ft^2-$^\circ$F)

The mass flux of water vapor away from the sublimation front is given by

$$N_w = k_{gi}(p_{fw} - p_{sw}) \tag{6.4}$$

$$= k_{ge}(p_{sw} - p_{ew}) \tag{6.5}$$

$$= \left[\cfrac{1}{\cfrac{1}{k_{ge}} + \cfrac{1}{k_{gi}}} \right] (p_{fw} - p_{ew}) \qquad (6.6)$$

where

N_w = flux of water vapor (lb moles/hr–ft^2)

p_{ew} = partial pressure of water vapor in equilibrium with the moisture sink or condenser temperature (mm Hg)

p_{sw} = partial pressure of water vapor at the outer piece surface (mm Hg)

p_{fw} = partial pressure of water vapor in equilibrium with sublimation front (mm Hg)

k_{ge} = mass transfer coefficient external to piece (lb mole/hr-ft^2-mm Hg)

K_{gi} = mass transfer coefficient within the dry layer (lb mole/hr–ft^2-mm Hg)

The variables in these equations are related in two more ways:

$$q = (\Delta H_s) N_w \qquad (6.7)$$

where ΔH_s is the latent heat of sublimation of ice, and

$$p_{fw} = \text{function of } T_f \qquad (6.8)$$

which is the relationship for the equilibrium sublimation pressure of frozen water.

If h_e, h_i, k_{ge} and k_{gi} are established by the design of the drier and the properties of the substance being dried, and if T_e and p_{ew} are set by the temperature of the heat source and the condenser, Equations (6.3), (6.6), (6.7), and (6.8) are 4 independent equations in 4 unknowns (N_w, q, T_f, and p_{fw}), which uniquely fix N_w and hence the drying rate.

Constraints

Equations (6.3) and (6.6) take the form of a flux being equal to the product of a reciprocal resistance (a conductance) and a driving force. The driving forces, $T_e - T_f$ and $p_{fw} - p_{ew}$ will adjust so as to preserve Equations (6.7) and (6.8). The water flux and thereby the drying rate can, in principle, be increased by increasing the driving forces or by increasing the heat and mass transfer coefficients. The sizes of the driving forces which can be used are limited by two constraints, however:

(1) The frozen zone must not melt sufficiently to destroy the quality advantages of freeze drying. For meats this criterion means that T_f must not rise above about $-5°C$; whereas for materials such as fruit juices the limiting frozen zone temperature will be much lower, in the range of $-20°$ to $-35°C$.

(2) The outer surface temperature, T_s, should not become high enough to cause thermal damage, such as denaturation of proteins, to the dried product. For meats and a number of other foods the maximum value of T_s is found to be about $60°C$ ($140°F$).

These constraints indicate that the partial pressure driving force in Equation (6.6) can never be greater than p_{fw} at $-5°C$ (about 3 mm Hg), and that the temperature driving force in Equation (6.3) cannot be greater than $70°$-$85°F$; otherwise too low a value of p_{fw} would result from Equation (6.8).

It is these limits on the available driving forces for heat and mass transfer which necessitate that rates of freeze drying be so low in comparison with other forms of drying. Furthermore, the constraints on the driving forces indicate that gains in drying rates are to be made through alteration of the coefficients for heat and mass transfer, rather than the driving forces.

Controlling Resistance

As the heat source temperature is increased the heat transfer rate and hence the drying rate will increase, by Equations (6.3) and (6.7). The mass transfer rate must also increase, and therefore p_{fw} (and hence T_f) must increase, by Equation (6.6). One of the two constraints mentioned above will eventually enter to provide an upper limit on the drying rate which can be achieved while maintaining acceptable product quality. If the limiting value of the outer surface temperature, T_s, is reached first, the drying rate will be limited by Equation (6.2), and the drying rate can only be increased further by somehow increasing h_i, the internal heat transfer coefficient. The process is then considered to be *internal-heat-transfer limited*.

If, on the other hand, the limiting value of the sublimation front temperature, T_f, is reached first, the drying rate will be limited by Equation (6.6), and the drying rate can only be increased further by somehow increasing k_{ge} or k_{gi}, the mass transfer coefficients. The process is then considered to be *mass-transfer limited*. If k_{ge} is much larger than k_{gi}, then the term involving k_{gi} will dominate over the term involving k_{ge} in Equation (6.6), and the rate can only be increased by an increase in k_{gi}. Therefore for $k_{ge} \gg k_{gi}$ the process is rate-limited by the *internal mass transfer resistance*. Conversely, for $k_{gi} \gg k_{ge}$ the process is rate-limited by the *external mass transfer resistance*.

It is also possible to encounter the situation where the freeze-drying process is rate-limited by the *external heat transfer resistance*. This would occur when $h_e \ll h_i$ and the mass transfer coefficients are high enough so that p_{fw} is very close to p_{ew}. At the same time it must for some reason not be possible to raise the source temperature enough to encounter either of the constraints on T_s and T_f.

Most freeze-drying processes carried out on a commercial scale are internal-heat-transfer limited. Many laboratory experiments carried out in a vacuum flask with heat supply from the walls at ambient temperature are external-heat-transfer limited.

URIF Model

The model of a uniformly-retreating ice front (URIF) has been quite successful for the prediction and analysis of freeze-drying rates. As was established

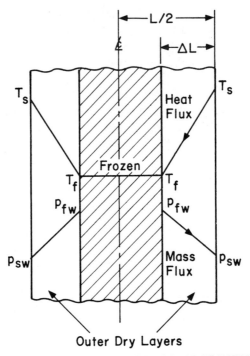

Outer Dry Layers

FIG. 6.6. URIF MODEL APPLIED TO SLAB GEOMETRY

earlier, the basic assumptions of this model are met surprisingly well in practice. Figure 6.6 shows the model as applied to slab geometry with drying from both sides. This configuration will be considered here; however analytical solutions are also available for spherical geometry (Clark and King 1971) and a cylindrical geometry (King 1970A), and computer solutions may be made for other geometries or for cases of nonhomogeneous or nonisotropic physical properties.

For the slab model, h_i and k_{gi} are given by

$$h_i = \frac{k}{\Delta L} \tag{6.9}$$

and

$$k_{gi} = \frac{D'}{RT\Delta L} \tag{6.10}$$

where

k = thermal conductivity of dry layer (Btu/hr-ft-°F)
ΔL = width of dry layer (ft) (see Fig. 6.6)
D' = effective diffusivity of water vapor within the dry layer (ft^2/hr)
R = gas constant = 555 mm Hg-ft^3/lb mole-°R
T = absolute temperature (°R)

Equations (6.9) and (6.10) ignore a number of secondary effects, including transient effects due to the heat capacity of the dry layer; influence of the vapor outflow upon the heat transfer rate; and thermal diffusion, surface diffusion, and simultaneous evaporation of residual water from the dry layer. These effects have all been examined either experimentally or theoretically for freeze drying of poultry meat (Sandall et al. 1967; Sandall 1966; Gunn 1967; Gunn and King 1971) and have been found to contribute effects of 4% or less. Solutions incorporating some or all of these effects have been published (Luikov 1966; Dyer and Sunderland 1967, 1968, 1969). The virtues of obtaining a simple, easily used model for freeze-drying rates by neglecting these effects altogether should, for most purposes, outweigh the gain in accuracy from the more complex solutions.

For the slab model, ΔL may be related to X, the fraction of initial moisture remaining, and L, the sample thickness, as follows

$$\frac{\Delta L}{L} = \frac{1 - X}{2} \tag{6.11}$$

under the assumption that all the moisture is removed locally as the sublimation front passes.

The rate of freeze drying is related to N_w by

$$-\frac{dX}{d\theta} = \frac{2 M_w N_w V_w}{L} \tag{6.12}$$

where

M_w = molecular weight of water = 18
V_w = volume occupied by unit weight of water in food initially (ft^3/lb)
θ = time since start of drying (hr)

Combinations of Equations (6.2), (6.3), (6.6), (6.7), (6.9), (6.10), (6.11), and (6.12) give the following equations relating drying rates to various driving forces:

$$-\frac{dX}{d\theta} = \frac{4kM_w V_w}{\Delta H_s L^2} \cdot \frac{(T_s - T_f)}{1 - X} \tag{6.13}$$

$$-\frac{dX}{d\theta} = \frac{4kM_w V_w}{\Delta H_s L^2} \cdot \left[\frac{T_e - T_f}{1 - X + \dfrac{2k}{Lh_e}} \right] \tag{6.14}$$

$$-\frac{dX}{d\theta} = \frac{4D'M_w V_w}{RTL^2} \cdot \left[\frac{p_{fw} - p_{ew}}{1 - X + \dfrac{2D'RT}{Lk_{ge}}} \right] \tag{6.15}$$

Values of T_f and p_{fw} for use in these equations come from a simultaneous solution of Equation (6.8) with Equation (6.15) and either Equation (6.13) or

Equation (6.14). Once the following conditions are achieved

$$1 - X \gg \frac{2k}{Lh_e} \tag{6.16}$$

$$1 - X \gg \frac{2D'RT}{Lk_{ge}} \tag{6.17}$$

the rate is governed entirely by the internal resistances to heat and mass transfer, and the driving forces in Equations (6.13) and (6.15) will bear a constant ratio to one another. Hence T_f and P_{fw} will be constant if T_e and p_{ew} are held constant during drying. Often, Equations (6.16) and (6.17) will be obeyed during such a large fraction of the drying time that T_f may be considered constant and h_e and k_{ge} may be ignored for the entire duration of drying; in fact, this is the desirable case for design of large-scale equipment, since it will correspond to the highest possible drying rates. Equation (6.16) may be ignored as one of the criteria if T_e is continually adjusted during drying to maintain T_s constant.

T_f and p_{fw} will also be constant if the inequalities of Equations (6.16) and (6.17) are reversed during the entire drying period; however, that case of external resistance control will correspond to very slow drying rates. In cases where both internal and external resistances are important, T_f will vary during drying and a numerical solution is necessary. This is also true if the heat is supplied through the frozen region rather than the dry region (Dyer and Sunderland 1968, 1969; Harper and Tappel 1957).

If $T_s - T_f$ is constant Equation (6.13) may be integrated to give the time required for complete drying, following the URIF model:

$$\theta = \frac{\Delta H_s L^2}{8kM_w V_w (T_s - T_f)} \tag{6.18}$$

Similarly for $p_{fw} - p_{ew}$ constant we have

$$\theta = \frac{RTL^2}{8D'M_w V_w (p_{fw} - p_{ew})} \left(1 + \frac{4D'RT}{Lk_{ge}} \right) \tag{6.19}$$

The predictions of Equations (6.13), (6.14), (6.15), (6.18), and (6.19) have been tested experimentally by numerous investigators for controlled freeze drying of slabs of a number of foods (Ginnette et al. 1958; Lusk et al. 1964; Sandall et al. 1967; Massey and Sunderland 1967; Bralsford 1967; Gunn and King 1971; Gaffney and Stephenson 1968; Magnussen 1969; Sharon and Berk 1969). Excellent agreement has been found, at least for the removal of the first 65-90% of the water present. In some cases where it has been possible to make a direct comparison, measured rates of freeze drying have been shown to agree well with independently measured values of k (Sandall et al. 1967; Bralsford 1967; Massey and Sunderland 1967) and D' (Gunn and King 1971) over a range of pressures when the URIF model is invoked.

Thermal Conductivity

Figure 6.7(a) shows the thermal conductivity of freeze-dried turkey breast meat as found experimentally by Triebes and King (1966). The thermal conductivity as a function of pressure undergoes a transition from a lower asymptote characteristic of the thermal conductivity of the porous solid matrix in a vacuum to an upper asymptote characteristic of the thermal conductivity of the heterogeneous medium formed when the pores are filled with a particular gas. The range of pressures over which the transition occurs is dependent upon the pore sizes within the freeze-dried substance and is therefore dependent upon the freezing rate before freeze drying. Because of the higher thermal conductivity of helium, the thermal conductivity in the presence of helium at higher pressures is greater than that in the presence of nitrogen. Thermal conductivities parallel to the direction of the meat fiber are larger than those normal to that direction. Thermal conductivities in the presence of water vapor are close to those in the presence of nitrogen (Triebes and King 1966).

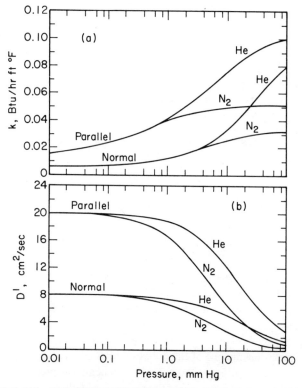

FIG. 6.7. TRANSPORT PROPERTIES OF FREEZE-DRIED TURKEY BREAST MEAT VERSUS PRESSURE, TYPE OF INERT GAS AND FIBER DIRECTION: (a) ABOVE—THERMAL CONDUCTIVITY; (b) BELOW—EFFECTIVE DIFFUSIVITY

Measurements of thermal conductivities have been made for numerous other freeze-dried foods and show the same general behavior. A tabulation of available data has been given by King (1970A).

Effective Diffusivity

Water vapor transport through the dry layer occurs by a combination of Knudsen diffusion, bulk diffusion, and viscous flow. The interaction of these phenomena is complex, the solution covering the full range of pressures and allowing for gradients in both total pressure and water vapor mole fraction has been given by Mason et al. (1967), Gunn (1967), Gunn and King (1969). For meats and a number of other substances the contribution of viscous flow is small under conditions where internal mass transfer contributes an appreciable resistance to the drying rate. To a good approximation for conditions where an inert gas is present and internal mass transfer is a significant resistance (Gunn and King 1971), D' is given by

$$D' = \frac{c_2 D^{\circ}{}_{AW} K_w}{c_2 D^{\circ}{}_{AW} + K_w P} \tag{6.20}$$

where

c_2 = dimensionless constant, dependent only on the geometry of the dry layer

$D^{\circ}{}_{AW}$ = the product of the total pressure and the bulk binary diffusivity for a gas mixture of water vapor and the ambient gas present in the drying chamber (mm Hg–ft^2/hr)

K_w = Knudsen diffusivity of water vapor in the dry layer (ft^2/hr)

P = Total pressure in drying chamber (mm Hg)

The Knudsen diffusivity is given, in turn, by

$$K_w = c_1 \sqrt{\frac{RT}{M_w}} \tag{6.21}$$

where

c_1 = a constant, dependent only on the geometry of the dry layer (ft)

R = gas constant = 6.44×10^{11} lb$_m$–ft^2/hr^2–lb mole–$^{\circ}R$

Figure 6.7(b) shows D' for turkey breast meat based upon typical values of c_1 and c_2 reported by Gunn and King (1971), in the presence of either nitrogen or helium. At low pressures the effective diffusivity reaches an upper, constant asymptote corresponding to the Knudsen diffusivity, which is independent of pressure. At higher pressure D' is inversely proportional to total pressure, reflecting the inverse dependence of the bulk binary diffusivity upon total pressure. The bulk binary diffusivity for water vapor and helium is greater than that for water vapor and nitrogen; hence D' in the presence of helium is greater, at higher pressures, than that in the presence of nitrogen. The effective diffusivity parallel to the fiber is greater than that normal to the fiber.

Values of c_2 for most freeze-dried materials should lie in the range 0.2-0.7. Values of c_1 will be greater for greater pore sizes, and will be dependent upon the freezing conditions before freeze drying.

When there is no substantial amount of inert gas in the drying chamber (e.g., when a vacuum pump holds the chamber pressure at the vapor pressure of ice in equilibrium with the condenser) and at sufficiently high condenser temperatures there will be a contribution of viscous flow to the mass transport in the dry layer, along with Knudsen diffusion. In the absence of gases other than water vapor D' is given by

$$D' = K_w + \frac{c_0 P_{av}}{\mu} \qquad (6.22)$$

where

P_{av} = arithmetic mean of the pressure at the outer surface and the pressure at the sublimation front (lb_f/ft^2) = 2.78 $\times$ P_{av} in mm Hg

μ = viscosity of water vapor (lb_f–hr/ft^2) = 2.09 $\times$ 10^{-5} $\times$ μ in cp.

c_0 = a constant, dependent only upon the geometry of the dry layer (ft^2)

In this case D' is greater at higher pressures, after being constant at an asymptotic value equal to the Knudsen diffusivity at lower pressures. Values of c_0 and c_1 for various freeze-dried materials may be obtained from data given by Gunn and King (1971), Harper (1962), El Sahrigi (1963), Thijssen and Rulkens (1969), and Kramers (1958).

Relative Rates of Freeze Drying

For a given material being freeze dried and a given drying chamber configuration, the drying rate as predicted by the URIF model [Equations (6.13)-(6.15) or (6.18) and (6.19)] is dependent upon (1) the piece size, L, (2) the temperature at which the outer surface is held, T_s, (3) the condenser temperature, T_c, (4) the type of inert gas, if any, present, and (5) the total pressure P. Because of the complex dependence of thermal conductivity and effective diffusivity upon pressure and type of inert gas, because of the nonlinear relationship between T_f and p_{fw} corresponding to the equilibrium sublimation pressure, and because of the constraints upon T_f and T_s for acceptable product quality, the dependence of drying rate upon these five factors is complex.

Table 6.1 shows the time required for freeze drying, as predicted by the URIF model for a slab, for various values of the independently adjustable parameters. The thermal conductivity and effective diffusivity are those of turkey breast meat parallel to the fiber (Fig. 6.7). External resistance to mass transfer is taken to be negligible ($k_{ge} \rightarrow \infty$). Other properties used for Table 6.1 are

ΔH_s = 1200 Btu/lb = 21,600 Btu/lb mole

V_w = 0.023 ft^3/lb (0.7 volume fraction water before freezing)

L = 0.50 in. (for drying from both sides)

= 0.25 in. (for drying from one side with the other side insulated)

TABLE 6.1

RELATIVE RATES OF FREEZE DRYING[1]

Chamber Pressure (mm Hg)	Temperature (°C)			Drying Time (Hr)	Control
	Condenser	Outer Surface	Frozen Zone		
I. No inert gas. $T_f \leqslant -5\,°C.$	$T_s \leqslant 60\,°C.$				
0.10	−40	60	−18	2.28	HT
0.29	−30	60	−17	2.26	HT
0.78	−20	60	−14	2.06	HT
1.95	−10	60	− 7	2.12	HT
II. No inert gas. $T_f \leqslant -25\,°C.$	$T_s \leqslant 60\,°C.$				
0.008	−60	28	−25	3.93	MT
0.030	−50	26	−25	4.10	MT
0.10	−40	18	−25	4.86	MT
0.29	−30	− 5	−25	9.63	MT
III. No inert gas. $p_{ew} = 0.10\,p_{fw}.$	$T_s \leqslant 60\,°C.$ Varying limiting T_f.				
0.003	−67	−45	−50	68.8	MT
0.010	−59	−26	−40	21.1	MT
0.029	−50	4	−30	7.1	MT
0.078	−42	52	−20	2.62	MT
0.10	−40	60	−18	2.28	HT
IV. Nitrogen added. $p_{ew} = 0.10\,p_{fw}.$	$T_s \leqslant 60\,°C.$ $T_f \leqslant -5\,°C.$				
0.10	−40	60	−18	2.28	HT
1.0	−38	60	−16	2.06	HT
3.0	−34	60	−11	1.91	HT
10.0	−30	60	− 5	1.92	HT&MT
20.0	−30	33	− 5	3.92	MT
760.0	−30	− 4	− 5	125.0	MT
V. Helium added. $p_{ew} = 0.10\,p_{fw}.$	$T_s \leqslant 60\,°C.$ $T_f \leqslant -5\,°C.$				
0.10	−40	60	−18	2.28	HT
1.0	−38	60	−16	1.96	HT
4.0	−34	60	−11	1.44	HT
12.0	−30	60	− 5	1.24	HT&MT
20.0	−30	44	− 5	1.48	MT
760.0	−30	− 4	− 5	56.3	MT
VI. Helium added. $p_{ew} = 0.10\,p_{fw}.$	$T_s \leqslant 60\,°C.$ $T_f \leqslant -25\,°C.$				
0.48	−46	27	−25	4.28	MT
1.0	−46	8	−25	4.50	MT
4.0	−46	− 6	−25	5.35	MT
20.0	−46	−18	−25	10.2	MT
760.0	−46	−25	−25	388.0	MT

[1] Basis: URIF Model; drying from both sides of slab; see text for physical properties.

The final column of Table 6.1 shows whether the drying rate is heat-transfer or mass-transfer controlled.

Section I of Table 6.1 shows drying times for no inert gas present, and for an upper limit of 60°C for T_s and an upper limit of -5°C for T_f, such as would correspond to freeze drying of meats. Compared to D', k is sufficiently low under these conditions so that the outer surface temperature limit is reached first rather than the limit on T_f. The drying rate is heat-transfer controlled, and the frozen zone assumes temperatures down to $-18°C$. As the condenser temperature is increased, p_{ew} increases and T_f must therefore increase in order to raise p_{fw} so as to maintain a sufficient driving force for mass transfer. Despite the reduction in $T_s - T_f$ as T_f increases, the increased pressure of water vapor in the dry layer increases k enough as the condenser temperature is raised so as to reduce the drying time slightly. The drying time will pass through a minimum and rise again toward infinity as the condenser temperature is raised toward $-5°C$. Since neither $T_s - T_f$ nor k changes greatly over the range of conditions covered in Section I, the drying time changes over only a narrow range, as required by Equation (6.18).

Section II of Table 6.1 covers the same situation as Section I except that now the upper limit on T_f is $-25°C$, as would correspond more closely to the freeze drying of coffee, juices, and other carbohydrate-rich food liquids. The lower value of T_f causes $p_{fw} - p_{ew}$ to be much lower, and thereby makes mass transfer a much more serious limit. Even for condenser temperatures as low as $-60°C$, the outer surface temperature cannot reach $60°C$ without causing T_f to exceed $-25°C$; consequently the process is always mass-transfer limited. The drying times are longer than for Section I because of the lower values of $p_{fw} - p_{ew}$, and the drying time increases sharply as the condenser temperature is raised, because increasing the condenser temperature increases p_{ew} markedly, and thereby decreases the driving force for mass transfer. The temperature which the outer surface can reach without T_f exceeding $-25°C$ decreases as the condenser temperature increases. This behavior follows from k and T_f not changing significantly while the drying rate decreases because of the lower mass transfer driving force. It is also important to notice that beyond a certain point lower condenser temperatures stop giving an increased rate. This is because p_{ew} has become quite small in comparison to p_{fw}, and hence further reductions in p_{ew} do not have much effect on the driving force, $p_{fw} - p_{ew}$. As a rule of thumb, the benefit of increasing the drying rate by decreasing the condenser temperature is offset by the increasing cost of the lower-temperature refrigeration medium required when p_{ew} becomes about 10% of p_{fw}.

Section III shows the effect of changes in the maximum allowable value of T_f, and is effectively a comparison of foods with different solidification temperatures. In all cases the condenser temperature is selected so as to give $p_{ew} = 0.10\ p_{fw}$, and T_s may not exceed $60°C$. For limiting values of T_f low enough so that the drying process is mass-transfer limited, the drying time increases greatly as the allowable T_f decreases. Very low condenser temperatures and very long drying times are required at low limiting values of T_f. Above a limiting T_f of $-18°C$, for the particular thermal conductivity and effective diffusivity properties considered, the process becomes heat-transfer limited as the value of T_s required for an equivalent amount of heat transfer reaches $60°C$, and the drying time becomes insensitive to the limiting T_f.

Section IV shows the behavior encountered for freeze drying in the presence of nitrogen, for the case where T_f may not exceed $-5°C$ and T_s may not exceed $60°C$. As was shown in Section I, the drying rate is heat-transfer limited at low pressures of inert gas. As is shown in Fig. 6.7, raising the pressure of the inert gas causes the thermal conductivity to increase but causes the effective diffusivity to decrease. Consequently, there is a tendency for a transition from heat-transfer control to mass-transfer control as the inert pressure is raised. As the pressure is raised to a few mm Hg, T_f increases until it reaches the limiting value of $-5°C$ at 10 mm Hg pressure. The process is mass-transfer controlled at higher pressures, and T_s must be reduced in order to keep T_f from rising above $-5°C$. Below the transition pressure the drying time decreases somewhat as pressure increases, because the increase in k with increasing pressure offsets the reduction in $T_s - T_f$. Above the transition pressure the drying time increases markedly as pressure increases, because D' falls in inverse proportion to pressure while $p_{fw} - p_{ew}$ is unchanged. A very long drying time is required in the presence of nitrogen at atmospheric pressure because of the very low value of D'.

Section V compares drying rates in the presence of helium with those in the presence of nitrogen which were shown in Section IV. Since both k and D' are higher in helium, the drying time is less than that in nitrogen at any pressure. The drying time falls much more sharply with increasing pressure in the heat-transfer limited regime below the transition pressure of 12 mm Hg, because the rise in thermal conductivity is so much greater in the presence of helium.

Section VI of Table 6.1 contrasts the behavior for freeze drying in helium when T_f may not rise above $-25°C$ with that shown in Section V where T_f could reach $-5°C$. The drying process is mass-transfer controlled at all helium pressures. As a result, $p_{fw} - p_{ew}$ does not change, and the drying time increases with increasing pressure at pressures large enough for bulk diffusion to be significant. At high enough pressures, the drying time becomes directly proportional to pressure. Because of the lower value of $p_{fw} - p_{ew}$ the drying times for a limiting T_f of $-25°C$ are longer than those for a limiting T_f of $-5°C$.

All the rates shown in Table 6.1 are for the transport properties of turkey breast meat in the direction of the fiber. If the properties normal to the fiber were used (i.e., drying perpendicular to the fiber direction), the drying times would be greater by factors of 1.5-3.

Thermal conductivities and effective diffusivities for other freeze-dried foods will be of similar orders of magnitude to those shown in Fig. 6.7. The particular values will vary from substance to substance, depending both upon the inherent structure of the substance and upon the freezing conditions. For liquid foods, which may be subjected to preconcentration before freeze drying, the porosity of the dry layer will decrease with increasing dissolved solids content before freezing and drying. Consequently the thermal conductivity will increase and the effective diffusivity will decrease as the initial dissolved solids content be- comes greater. At low enough solids contents the drying rate will be heat-transfer limited, and in that range the rate of freeze drying will increase as the solids content increases. Because of the changes in k and D', the frozen zone temperature, T_f, will increase with increasing solids content for a given surface temperature, T_s, and a given condenser temperature, T_c. This general behavior has been confirmed by Sharon and Berk (1969) for tomato juice, by Spiess et al. (1969) for maté extract, and by Monzini and Maltini (1969) for orange juice. Above some critical solids content the drying rate will become mass-transfer limited, and a lower value of T_s must be used if deleterious melting of the frozen core is to be avoided. Foaming of a liquid food before freezing is a way of increasing the porosity of the freeze-dried material and, hence, is a way of increasing the dissolved solids content at which the transition from heat-transfer to mass-transfer control occurs.

In Table 6.1 it is assumed that external resistance to mass transfer is not an important limit and that the external heat transfer coefficient is great enough so that the outer surface of the slab can indeed be held at the value of T_s indicated. If either or both of these conditions are not true, then the drying time predicted by the URIF model will be longer than shown. In particular, when significant pressures of an inert gas are used it is difficult to avoid having an important rate limit from external mass transfer.

The drying time will depend markedly upon piece size. For freeze drying controlled by internal resistances to heat and/or mass transfer, the predicted drying time is proportional to L^2, while for external resistances to heat and/or mass transfer controlling the drying time is proportional to L. Reducing the piece size is one way to achieving a higher rate to overcome the limit of a low maximum allowable T_f.

The drying times shown in Table 6.1 are for the slab geometry. Times predicted for the spherical or cylindrical geometry, or for a cubical shape, will be different. However the qualitative trends shown in the Table and the effect of piece size will be the same.

Terminal Drying Rates

In several cases where the predictions of the URIF model have been checked for the slab geometry it has been found that the last 10–35% of the water is removed at a slower rate than is predicted by the model (Kessler 1962; Lusk et al. 1964; Massey and Sunderland 1967; Sandall et al. 1967). Margaritis and King (1971) report experiments designed to reveal whether this slower rate is the result of uneven retreat of the frozen front or of slow removal of bound water remaining after the passage of the frozen front, or both. Nonuniform retreat of the frozen front was shown to occur in experiments of the type performed by Sandall et al. (1967), because of inhomogeneities in properties and because of variations of k_{ge} from point to point on the piece surface. Uneven heating can also cause nonuniform retreat of the frozen front. For poultry meat the rate of equilibration of bound water content of the fiber structure with respect to the prevailing humidity in the pore spaces was shown to be relatively fast compared to typical times required for freeze drying. This suggests, for meats at least, that slower removal of the last 10–35% of the water than predicted by the URIF model is principally the result of nonuniform movement of the sublimation front. This effect should be less pronounced for diced foods than for slabs, since drying in all directions will tend to minimize the effect of nonuniform frozen front retreat on the rate predicted by the URIF model for the particular shape in question.

RETENTION OF VOLATILE FLAVOR AND AROMA SPECIES

As was mentioned earlier, freeze drying usually gives particularly good retention of trace volatile flavor and aroma compounds present in the food. This strong retention of volatiles cannot be explained as adsorption onto dried material. As has been demonstrated quantitatively by Flink and Karel (1970A), volatile organic substances adsorbed onto freeze-dried carbohydrate substances after freeze drying are held much less tenaciously than are the same substances if present in homogeneous solution before freeze drying.

A more successful interpretation of volatiles retention comes through a diffusion concept, as originally suggested by Thijssen and Rulkens (1968, 1969). The relative volatilities of most volatile flavor substances in food solutions, such as fruit juices, are high enough so that virtually complete loss of these compounds would occur during an equilibrium vaporization or sublimation (Chandrasekaran and King 1971B, C). Much less loss of these substances occurs because of slow rates of diffusion to the evaporation or sublimation interface. Measurements of diffusion coefficients for various trace organic compounds in fruit juices and synthetic carbohydrate solutions (Menting *et al.* 1970; Chandrasekaran and King 1971B) show that the diffusion coefficients decrease markedly as the concentration of dissolved solids increases.

A simple diffusion model is not in itself sufficient, however. Karel and Flink (1969) have shown that volatile organic compounds retained by various sugars after freeze drying can be desorbed if the moisture content is brought back up to a high enough level. Over a certain range of moisture contents only a portion of the organic compound can be desorbed ultimately, and a new, lower asymptotic content of the organic substance is reached. This new asymptote is inconsistent with a simple diffusion model. Karel and Flink (1969) have demonstrated that rates of volatiles loss, and hence volatiles diffusivities, depend specifically upon the morphology of molecular aggregation and the degree of crystallinity in the material during freeze drying or subsequent treatment. The molecular morphology, in turn, is not a unique function of temperature and dissolved solids content, but, instead, reflects the entire processing history of the substance. Good retention is favored by a glassy, amorphous structure. Rewarming or rehumidifying to a recrystallization point causes a substantial volatile loss.

Figure 6.8 shows an idealization of the microstructure of a frozen liquid food (e.g., coffee extract or a juice concentrate) undergoing freeze drying. Interspersed

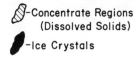

🖋-Concentrate Regions
(Dissolved Solids)

⬛-Ice Crystals

⬭-Interlinked Network of Voids,
from Sublimation of Ice
Crystals

FIG. 6.8. FREEZE DRYING OF FROZEN FOOD LIQUID

microregions of ice crystals and of residual concentrate or eutectic solid have formed upon freezing. Freeze drying consists of the retreat of a sublimation front, which removes the ice crystals through sublimation and dries the concentrate or eutectic regions by diffusion followed by evaporation, or by sublimation. The diffusion analysis may then be applied to each of the concentrate regions as the sublimation front passes. One advantage of freeze drying immediately apparent is the relatively short time during which the sharp sublimation front passes a given region and during which the concentrate in that region is exposed to a vapor interface while having a high enough moisture content and volatiles diffusivity to give an appreciable rate of volatiles loss.

TABLE 6.2

FACTORS FAVORING VOLATILES RETENTION DURING FREEZE DRYING

Factor	Effect
1. Greater velocity of sublimation front (faster freeze-drying rate)	Lower t
2. Greater thickness of concentrate microregions	Higher δ
3. Greater dissolved solids content of concentrate microregions, or lower temperature of concentrate microregions	Lower D

Discussions of the qualitative predictions of a diffusion model for the effects of freeze drying conditions on volatiles retention have been given by Thijssen and Rulkens (1968, 1969) and by King (1970B, 1971). One can picture volatiles retention as increasing with decreasing values of a diffusion Fourier group

$$Dt/\delta^2$$

where

D = diffusion coefficient of the volatile organic compound (ft^2/hr)

TABLE 6.3

EFFECTS OF PROCESSING PARAMETERS UPON VOLATILES RETENTION
DURING FREEZE DRYING

Prediction	Cause	Experimental Confirmation
Retention should increase with increasing dissolved solids content before freezing and drying.	Thicker concentrate microregions (in some cases can also be higher dissolved solids content of microregions).	Rey and Bastien (1962), Chandrasekaran and King (1969), Sauvageot et al. (1969),[1] Flink and Karel (1970B)
Retention should increase for slower rates of freezing.	Thicker concentrate microregions.	Sauvageot et al. (1969), Flink and Karel (1970B)
Retention should increase with decreasing piece size if internal resistances control, and should be independent of piece size if external resistances control.	Greater velocity of sublimation front if internal resistances control. No change in sublimation front velocity if external resistances control.	Sauvageot et al. (1969), Flink and Karel (1970B)
Complex effect of sublimation front temperature.	(a) Low T_f gives low D. (b) High T_f gives low t.	Sauvageot et al. (1969), Flink and Karel (1970B)
Retention should be similar for different species with quite different relative volatilities.	Diffusion coefficients do not vary widely from one trace organic compound to another.	Saravacos and Moyer (1968), Chandrasekaran and King (1969), Sauvageot et al. (1969), Flink and Karel (1970B)
Retention should be the same at different locations in the piece if external resistances control.	D, t and δ are the same throughout.	Flink and Karel (1970B)
Retention should be least in the vicinity of the last region to be vacated by frozen zone if internal resistances control.	Velocity of sublimation front is least for removal of last ice (higher t).	

[1] Denotes reference partly at variance with the prediction.

t = time during which diffusion can occur as sublimation front passes (hr)
δ = characteristic thickness of concentrate microregions (ft)

Table 6.2 shows three factors which should increase volatiles retention by decreasing the group Dt/δ^2. Table 6.3 shows various predictions about volatiles retention stemming from Table 6.2, and gives references to reported experimental confirmations of each prediction.

Chandrasekaran and King (1971B) have analyzed volatiles loss as an equivalent ternary diffusion process. The trace volatile component, water, and the dissolved solids are considered as three separate components, so as to allow for the very different fluxes of water and dissolved solids during drying, and so as to allow for the interactive effects between components and cross-diffusion coefficients.

PROCESSING EQUIPMENT

Freeze-drying equipment must provide a controllable heat source, some means of transporting the heat from the source to the food, a moisture sink (usually a condenser), a means of maintaining an appropriate level of vacuum, and the wherewithal of introducing and withdrawing food. Most freeze dryers are operated batchwise, although some continuous freeze dryers are coming into large-scale use.

Conventional Freeze Dryers

Figure 6.9 shows a schematic of a conventional batch tray freeze dryer. The operation is carried out in a cylindrical vacuum chamber, with a door at one end which may be removed for loading and unloading. The food to be dried is frozen before being loaded and is placed on flat trays, which are placed in numerous vertical layers supported on a movable platen truck. A heating medium—steam in Fig. 6.9—is supplied to the platen truck, and typically

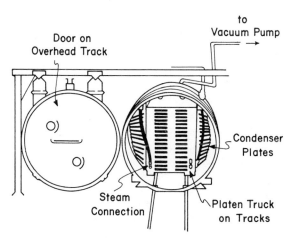

FIG. 6.9. CONVENTIONAL BATCH FREEZE DRYER

provides heat to the food material both by radiation from platens located above each tray and, to the extent that there is thermal contact between the food and the tray, by conduction from the tray itself. A circulating liquid, such as propylene glycol, can replace steam as the heat transfer medium. The desired level of vacuum in the chamber during drying is held by means of a mechanical vacuum pump in the process shown in Fig. 6.9.

Condenser and Vacuum Systems

Typically, between 55 and 90% of the weight of the food charged to a freeze dryer is water, which, because of the triple point partial pressure limitation, will expand by a factor of about 10^7 in volume upon sublimation. Consequently, very large volumes of vapor must be handled, and the condenser system is one of the most critical and expensive parts of a freeze dryer. The condenser heat transfer area must be of the same order of magnitude as the tray area.

In conventional plants a refrigerated, metal-surface condenser is commonly used. The water vapor desublimes as ice onto the condenser, and a thick layer of ice builds up. This layer of ice must eventually be removed somehow; typically, it is melted off by passing a heating medium through the refrigerant side of the condenser. As a result the condenser is inherently a batch operation.

In Fig. 6.9 the condenser is shown inside the drying chamber, as is typical of some of the more recent designs. Internal condenser elements may take the form of tubes or plates. Condenser units located external to the main drying chamber are also in common use. Some advantages and disadvantages of external condensers vs internal condensers are the following:

(A) External condensers may be supplied in parallel, allowing the operator to change condensers for regeneration at any time during the drying cycle. An internal condenser must be regenerated at the end of the drying cycle.

(B) An external condenser must be connected to the drying chamber by a large vapor transfer line, probably equipped with a valve to allow isolation of the condenser unit. The vapor transfer line provides additional pressure drop (external mass transfer resistance) and means that, for a given refrigerant temperature and for a given ice loading of the condenser before regeneration, the external condenser will probably require a greater heat transfer area than the internal condenser.

(C) For an internal condenser the design must guard against excessive heat loss by direct radiation from the heating elements to the condenser surface.

An internal condenser must be regenerated while the dryer is not in service; however, the time required for unloading and reloading the food is usually longer than the time required for ice melt-off. For both internal and external condensers it is important to ensure even access of the water vapor to all points of the condenser surface so as to guard against an uneven distribution of ice buildup.

Inert gases are usually removed by means of a mechanical vacuum pump; however, it is also possible to employ a steam jet ejector for this purpose. If a steam jet ejector is used, it is also possible to eliminate the condenser and remove both water vapor and inerts by way of the ejector. Barrett *et al.* (1964) have compared the economics and design of steam jet ejector systems as compared to refrigerated condenser-vacuum pump systems in various freeze-drying situations. To be efficient the steam jet ejector system requires a plenteous supply of cheap steam, since a multiple-stage unit is necessary.

Other methods for water vapor removal are possible. Rowe (1962A, B, 1964) has summarized other methods which have been used or tested; these include scraped surface condensers, liquid and solid desiccants, and cold, ice-immiscible liquids. Solid desiccants require a significant bed pressure drop, making access to all points of the desiccant bed difficult; also the desiccant must exert a low enough equilibrium water vapor pressure to permit attainment of the desired final food moisture content. This criterion points toward molecular sieve as the desiccant to be considered. Liquid absorbents, such as lithium or calcium chloride solution or ethylene glycol, offer the potential of a continuous condenser for freeze drying, but cannot provide the level of desiccation usually required for freeze drying without being refrigerated themselves. Absorption into these liquids can also be seriously rate-limited by liquid phase diffusion. Both liquid and solid desiccants require the addition of a substantial amount of latent heat and sensible heat for regeneration.

Condensation of water as ice onto the surface of a cold ice-immiscible liquid offers the possibility of a continuous condenser which does not require heat for regeneration. The ice can be separated by a simple process of filtration, settling, or the like. Thuse (1964) and Eolkin (1965) suggest using a spray of cold liquid for this purpose; whereas Shields (1952) and Kumar (1968) use cold liquid flowing downward along a refrigerated metal surface. The spray approach circumvents the need for refrigerated surfaces inside the chamber, but requires a very large liquid circulation rate because of temperature rise from the heat of condensation and also may give rise to food contamination. There are a number of restrictions on a liquid to be used for this purpose; for example, it must have a very low vapor pressure without at the same time having a high viscosity, and it must have a low freezing point. The liquid must also be cheap and/or highly insoluble in water so that liquid loss with the ice does not make the process uneconomic. Suitable liquids from the standpoint of freezing point, vapor pressure, and viscosity include low-molecular-weight silicone oil, certain Freons, and alkylated aromatic hydrocarbons (Kumar *et al.* 1970; Kumar 1968). Particularly attractive from the cost viewpoint are concentrated brines, such as aqueous solutions of calcium chloride or lithium chloride, which can be operated under saturated conditions of temperature and composition, such that ice is the equilibrium solid phase (Kumar *et al.* 1972).

Uniformity of Drying

When a large number of pieces of food material are being freeze dried together, it is desirable to achieve as uniform a final moisture content as possible, both to ensure complete dryness in the least amount of time and to avoid over-drying of fast-drying pieces. Clark (1968), King (1970A), and Kan and deWinter (1968), among others, have reported appreciable scatter in the final moisture content achieved by different pieces in a freeze dryer. Variations in terminal moisture content from piece to piece occur for a number of reasons, including (1) differences in piece size, reflected as differences in L in Equations (6.13) through (6.15), (2) uneven exposure to the heat source, (3) variations from piece to piece in thermal conductivity or effective diffusivity [see, e.g., Triebes and King (1966)], and (4) local buildups of water vapor partial pressure due to constrictions in the chamber.

The effects of these factors can be minimized by good equipment design, selection of food material, and preprocessing procedures.

Preconcentration

As was mentioned previously, freeze drying is inherently expensive in comparison to other common water-removal methods. Therefore, if any portion of the water present can be removed by any less expensive method, without losing the quality benefits of freeze drying, it will generally be desirable to do so. For liquid foods freeze-concentration is a means of removing some of the water, up to a solids content of perhaps 25–50%, without thermal treatment. Thus, there is little loss of volatile substances or other quality loss. A combination of freeze-concentration with freeze drying can thereby afford a less expensive process than freeze drying by itself, while still preserving the volatiles retention and ready reconstitution properties of freeze drying.

Another method of preconcentration of liquids which may be useful in connection with freeze drying is reverse osmosis.

Continuous Processes

The conventional freeze-drying plant depicted in Fig. 6.9 is operated on a batch basis. Continuous freeze drying is an attractive concept, for at least two reasons. First, there are inherent economies in labor and plant capacity to be derived from any continuous process in comparison with a batch process. Secondly, the condenser system in a batch freeze dryer must be sized to handle the large initial water vapor output at the beginning of a cycle; while in a continuous process the condenser must handle only a relatively constant water vapor load, corresponding to the average generation rate over the entire course of freeze drying. Countering these advantages of a continuous process are the difficulty of operating a continuous vacuum process where feed must be received and product must be discharged at atmospheric pressure, and the fact that many of the earlier freeze-drying plants have handled a multitude of different products, each requiring different operating conditions.

One approach to continuous freeze drying has been to modify the standard, batch tray-loaded freeze dryer into a process where carts loaded with trays pass continuously along a vacuum tunnel. The food enters on trays through a vacuum lock, freeze dries as the cart of trays passes along through the tunnel, and leaves the tunnel through another vacuum lock as product on trays (Dalgleish 1962; Oetjen 1966; Hackenberg 1966; Lorentzen 1970). Other approaches to continuous freeze drying have involved movement of particles along an inclined surface. One pilot unit for continuous freeze drying (Rockwell *et al.* 1965) allowed particulate food to tumble along a rotating, polygonal, heated tube; in a variant, heat is supplied through finned tubes which provide mixing action to the food pieces (Kaufman and Rockwell 1967). On a larger, industrial scale continuous freeze drying of particulate food matter has been carried out utilizing movement along inclined, vibrating beds (Togashi and Mercer 1966; Oetjen 1966; Oetjen and Eilenberg 1969). The vibrating action provides mixing of the particles with one another which can aid heat transfer through the layer of particles and which provides a more even exposure to the heat source. In some cases, however, vibration may cause particle attrition.

Other Processing Approaches

A summary of new processing approaches for freeze drying which have been disclosed through U.S. patents in the period 1960–1968 has been provided by Noyes (1968).

Most processing modifications have to do with supplying heat by some means other than radiation from a heated metallic surface. Possibilities include other forms of radiation, conduction and/or convection heat transfer from the heat source to the food surface.

Radiation.—Microwave heating has been considered seriously and tested on a developmental scale for freeze drying for some time. The attraction of microwave heating arises from the fact that microwave energy is dissipated selectively in substances of high dielectric constant, or, more correctly, high loss factor. In food materials, water has by far the highest loss factor; and so, with microwave heating, heat is delivered directly to the location of water in the food, obviating the need for heat conduction through the dry layer. If heat could be transmitted to the frozen core fast enough by microwave heating in freeze drying, it would be possible to maintain the frozen core temperature at the upper limiting value even at very low pressures of the drying chamber. Thus, the rate would be governed by the product of the maximum attainable driving force for mass transfer and the maximum attainable internal mass transfer coefficient (i.e., the Maximum D'). On the basis used for Section I of Table 6.1, the drying time would be 0.34 hr, 6 times faster than the rate achievable at low pressure with heat conduction across the dry layer, and almost 4 times faster than the maximum rate computed in Section V of Table 6.1 for drying in the presence of helium.

The theoretical aspects of microwave freeze drying and experimental findings have been summarized by several authors (Copson 1962; Parker 1968; Decareau 1970; King 1970A). Among the problems encountered have been the following:

(1) *Low Loss Factor for Ice:* Whereas liquid water has a very high loss factor, that of ice is quite low. Hence the microwave energy is dissipated largely to the bound, or unfreezable water in freeze drying.

(2) *Ionization:* Concentrated microwave energy can cause a glow discharge within the dry layer, causing discoloration and flavor damage.

(3) *Uneven Heating:* Larger food pieces contain a greater volume-to-surface ratio of water and hence will reach a higher core temperature during microwave heating. Also, loss factors increase at higher temperatures, causing locally hot spots to tend to melt.

Microwave heating provides the latent heat of sublimation through electrical energy, which is more expensive than steam or other heat sources. Economic analyses of microwave freeze drying (Hammond 1967) have shown that, although the operating costs are higher for this reason, capital costs can be lower because of the shorter drying cycle. Microwave energy may be most attractive economically when conventional freeze drying is used for the removal of the first 60–80% of the water, with microwave freeze drying used for the remainder.

Gouigo *et al.* (1969) report extremely short times for microwave freeze drying—1 hr for 1-in. thick beef slices and under 15 min for slices 2–3 mm thick. They attribute these rapid rates to a dynamic situation where a melted core exists within a frozen shell, as shown in Fig. 6.10. The microwave energy is taken up by the liquid water in the melted core at a rate fast enough to cause rapid enough drying to cause a substantial temperature gradient between the core and the sublimation front. The sublimation front is chilled by the latent heat of sublimation and thereby kept frozen. This concept is appealing as a route to a very fast drying rate, but it would seem difficult to achieve this behavior within some pieces without melting other pieces to an extent great enough to cause a poorer product. On the other hand, such a rapid freeze-drying

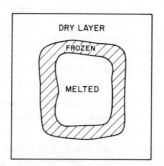

FIG. 6.10. MICROWAVE FREEZE DRYING WITH
A MELTED CORE

process may be able to stand lesser product quality and still be economically interesting.

Infrared radiation can also have the property of penetrating inward through the dry layer. Ginzburg and Lyakhovitsky (1969) report the use of 1.3 μ wavelength radiation for freeze drying, and indicate that it combines features of a high dry-layer permeability to radiation and a high frozen layer absorptivity.

Conduction.–Contact heating from a metallic surface supplies some of the heat in many conventional freeze dryers. There have also been units tested and built on a large scale which deliver most or all of the heat for freeze drying by conduction from contact heaters. One such process was the AFD (Accelerated Freeze Drying) process developed in Great Britain (Hanson 1961; Cotson and Smith 1962), in which heat was supplied from expanded metal inserts, which provided contact at some points for heat conduction while still providing a sufficiently open path for vapor escape from the outer food surfaces. Another such process is one described by Havighorst (1970), in which alternating layers of aluminum disks and food material are placed within long tubes, and heat is supplied by induction heating to the aluminum disks and by conduction from the disks to the food. This process must also encounter the problem of maintaining good contact and sufficient room for vapor escape at the same time, and does rely upon relatively expensive electrical energy as a heat source.

Convection.–Efforts to use convective heating for freeze drying have largely paralleled attempts to implement somehow the higher rates of drying predicted in the presence of helium or other light gases (refer to Table 6.1). This line of endeavor has been discussed in some detail elsewhere (King 1970A), and is summarized here.

Initial efforts were directed at freeze drying at atmospheric pressure so as to avoid the need for vacuum altogether (Meryman 1959, 1963). Experiments bore out the fact that drying rates are extremely slow at atmospheric pressure, in nearly all instances too slow to be practical (Lewin and Mateles 1962; Woodward 1963; Sandall et al. 1967; Sinnamon et al. 1968; Malecki et al. 1970).

Following the initial suggestions of Harper (1962, 1966), efforts were made to implement freeze drying in the presence of helium or other light gases at intermediate pressures where the drying rates should be highest, 7–30 mm Hg, as shown in Table 6.1. Kan and deWinter (1968) considered two methods for utilizing helium. Their first approach was to introduce helium into a conventional dryer. This produces a serious external mass-transfer limit on the drying rate and necessitates that the condenser surface be brought within a very few centimeters of the food surface at all points, requiring a complex design. Their second approach was to circulate the helium through the drying chamber and an external condenser. Heat would still be supplied by radiation. Because the partial pressure of water vapor in the gas stream must remain low in the drying chamber a very large gas circulation rate is required. At 10 mm Hg total pressure, a helium flow of about 40 cfm/ft^2 of tray area is required at system pressure if the drying rate is only 1 lb/hr ft^2 of tray area and if the gas leaving the drying chamber contains 1 mm Hg of water vapor. Because of the low volumetric heat capacity of a low pressure gas, much more helium circulation (about 2000 cfm/ft^2 at 10 mm Hg total pressure) is required if the heat of sublimation for the entire food charge is to be delivered by convection from the heat capacity of the entering gas stream, as has also been suggested (Tooby 1969).

A freeze-drying process which reduces the volumetric gas circulation requirements for convective heating utilizes a mixed bed of desiccant and food or alternating layers of food and desiccant, as shown in Fig. 6.11 (King and Clark 1968, 1969; Clark and King 1971). In passing through a food layer the gas loses heat to the food, causing sublimation, and at the same time picks up the generated water vapor. Then, in passing through the next layer of desiccant, the gas loses its water vapor to the desiccant and is heated by gain of the heat of sorption, readying it to encounter the next food layer. The preferred desiccant

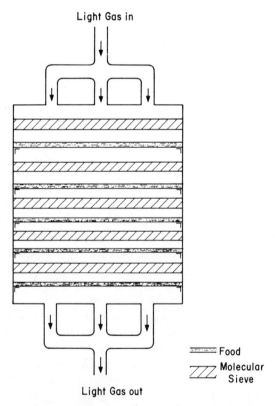

Light Gas in

Light Gas out

Food

Molecular Sieve

FIG. 6.11. FREEZE DRYING IN LAYERED BED

is molecular sieve because of its high moisture capacity at low partial pressures of water vapor. The heat of sorption is nearly equal and opposite to the heat of sublimation; thus the process requires no major external heat source during drying and no major amount of mechanical refrigeration. The desiccant is required in large quantity (on the order of 10 lb/lb of food) and must therefore be regenerated and reused many times. The food trays can be inserted and removed from the chamber, and the desiccant can be regenerated in place with hot gases. Molecular sieve particles are regenerated and reused 3000 times and more before replacement in most services.

Cycling of the drying chamber pressure between a higher and a lower limit has been suggested as a way of realizing the benefits of a high thermal conductivity and of a high effective diffusivity in one and the same process, but an analysis of the heat input integrated over a full pressure cycle shows that the benefit from this practice is quite small, or nonexistent (King 1970A).

Another approach toward reducing carrier gas compression requirements for water vapor removal in a convective process has been to employ a condensible carrier, immiscible with ice and water (Barth et al. 1965; Blake et al. 1968). Heptane and a moderately heavy Freon have been tested. Since the carrier gas is condensible in this case, it is possible to avoid the gas-compression step of other carrier-gas processes, but the circulation rate is still large, and the process may present phase separation problems and/or give odor contamination. Wistreich and Blake (1962) and Bohrer (1967) have suggested and tested freeze drying by direct immersion of the substance into a boiling liquid at the proper pressure to give a boiling temperature which will maintain freeze drying.

Freeze drying in fluidized beds has also been investigated. At lower system pressures, two difficulties have been encountered (Mink and Sachsel 1968); these are the tendency of the pressure drop through the bed to cause melting in the bottom of the bed and the effect of gas expansion, again due to the pressure drop, which results in only the top few inches being fluidized. As a result, low bed heights and consequent low food loadings are necessitated. At higher pressures, such as atmospheric pressure (Malecki et al. 1970), greater bed depths are possible, but the water vapor diffusivity becomes low enough to cause a very low rate of freeze drying, as indicated by the calculations reported in Table 6.1.

Compressed Freeze-Dried Foods

There has been recent renewed interest by the military in compressed foods. Freeze-dried foods have been found to provide a compressed food with good rehydration and textural properties, if they are rehumidified to provide adequate plasticity before compression (Brockmann 1970; MacKenzie and Luyet 1969). Freeze drying gives a major weight reduction without a significant concomitant volume reduction. Compression can give a high degree of volume reduction, allowing for more compact packaging and shipment.

BIBLIOGRAPHY

BARRETT, J. P., LAXON, R., and WEBSTER, P. H. N. 1964. Freeze-drying vacuum equipment—The economics of steam ejector and refrigerated condenser systems. Food Technol. *18*, 38–41.

BARTH, J. R., PELMULDER, J. P., and THUSE, E. 1965. Low pressure carrier gas sublimation. U.S. Pat. 3,218,728. Nov. 23.

BEKE, G. 1969. The effect of the sublimation temperature on the rate of the freeze-drying process and upon the volumetric change in meat muscle tissue. Proc. 12th Intern. Congr. Refrig., Madrid.

BELLOWS, R. J., and KING, C. J. 1972. Product collapse during freeze drying of liquid foods. Presented at Ann. Meeting, Am. Inst. Chem. Engrs., New York. (See also Cryobiology, in press.)

BIRD, K. 1964. Freeze drying of foods: cost projections. USDA Econ. Res. Serv., Marketing Res. Rept. *639*.

BLAKE, J. H., PELMULDER, J., and THUSE, E. 1968. Sublimation drying using a condensable heat carrier vapor. U. S. Pat. 3,382,584. May 14.

BOHRER, B. 1967. Azeotropic drying process. U.S. Pat. 3,298,109. Jan. 17.

BRAJNIKOV, A. M., VASSILIEV, V. A., VOSKOBOINIKOV, V. A., and KAUTCHECHVILI, E. I. 1969. Heat and mass transfer in porous materials during freeze drying under vacuum. *In* Symp. Thermodynamic Aspects of Freeze Drying, Intern. Inst. Refrig., Comm. X, Lausanne, Switzerland. (French)

BRALSFORD, R. 1967. Freeze drying of beef. J. Food Technol. (London) *2*, 339–352, 353–359.

BROCKMANN, M. C. 1970. Freeze drying. Chem. Eng. Progr. Symp. Ser. *66*, No. 100, 53–61.

BURKE, R. F., and DECAREAU, R. V. 1964. Recent advances in the freeze drying of food products. Advan. Food Res. *13*, 1–88.

CHANDRASEKARAN, S. K., and KING, C. J. 1971A. Solid-liquid phase equilibria in multicomponent aqueous sugar solutions. J. Food Sci. *36*, 699–704.

CHANDRASEKARAN, S. K., and KING, C. J. 1971B. Analysis of volatiles loss from food liquids during freeze drying and evaporative drying, as a ternary diffusion process. Presented at 13th Intern. Congr. Refrig., Washington, D.C. [See also AIChE J. *18*, 513–520, 520–526 (1972).]

CHANDRASEKARAN, S. K., and KING, C. J. 1971C. Retention of volatile flavor components during drying of fruit juices. Chem. Eng. Progr. Symp. Ser. *67*, No. 108, 122–130.

CLARK, J. P. 1968. Synthesis and evaluation of an improved freeze drying process. Ph.D. dissertation in chemical engineering, Univ. Calif., Berkeley.

CLARK, J. P., and KING, C. J. 1971. Convective freeze drying in mixed or layered beds. Chem. Eng. Progr. Symp. Ser. *67*, No. 108, 102–111.

COPSON, D. A. 1962. Microwave Heating in Freeze Drying, Electronic Ovens and other Applications. Avi Publishing Co., Westport, Conn.

CORRIDEN, G. A. 1964. Freeze Drying of Foods. A List of Selected References. USDA Natl. Agr. Library, List *77*.

COTSON, S., and SMITH, D. B. 1962. Freeze Drying of Foodstuffs. Columbine Press, Manchester, England.

CRUZ PICALLO, J. A. 1969. Freeze drying of coffee extracts. Proc. 12th Intern. Congr. Refrig., Madrid.

DALGLEISH, J. M. 1962. Leybold continuous plant equipment. *In* Freeze Drying of Foodstuffs. S. Cotson and D. B. Smith (Editors). Columbine Press, Manchester, England.

DECAREAU, R. V. 1970. Microwave energy in food processing applications. CRC Critical Rev. Food Technol. *1*, 199–224.

DYER, D. F., and SUNDERLAND, J. E. 1967. The transient temperature distribution during sublimation dehydration. J. Heat Transfer *89*, 109–110.

DYER, D. F., and SUNDERLAND, J. E. 1968. Heat and mass transfer mechanisms in sublimation dehydration. J. Heat Transfer *90*, 379–384.

DYER, D. F., and SUNDERLAND, J. E. 1969. The influence of varying interface temperature on freeze drying. *In* Symp. Thermodynamic Aspects of Freeze Drying. Intern. Inst. Refrig., Comm. X, Lausanne, Switzerland.

EL SAHRIGI, A. F. 1963. The permeability and thermal conductivity of gases in porous media. Ph.D. dissertation in agricultural engineering, Univ. Calif., Davis.

EOLKIN, D. 1965. Freeze drying. U.S. Pat. 3,210,861. Oct. 12.

FLINK, J., and KAREL, M. 1970A. Studies on mechanism of retention of organic volatiles in freeze-dried systems. J. Agr. Food Chem. *18*, 295-297.

FLINK, J., and KAREL, M. 1970B. Effects of process variables on retention of volatiles in freeze drying. J. Food Sci. *35*, 444-447.

FULFORD, G. D. 1969. A survey of recent Soviet research on the drying of solids. Can. J. Chem. Eng. *47*, 378-391.

GAFFNEY, J. J., and STEPHENSON, K. Q. 1968. Apparent thermal conductivity during freeze drying of a food model. Trans. Am. Soc. Agr. Eng. *11*, 874-880.

GINNETTE, L. F., GRAHAM, R. P., and MORGAN, A. I., Jr. 1958. Freeze drying rates. Natl. Symp. Vacuum Technology, Am. Vacuum Soc. Trans. *5*, Pergamon Press, New York.

GINNETTE, L. F., and KAUFMAN, V. F. 1968. Freeze drying of foods. *In* The Freezing Preservation of Foods, 4th Edition. D. K. Tressler, W. B. Van Arsdel, and M. J. Copley (Editors). Avi Publishing Co., Westport, Conn.

GINNETTE, L. F., LAMPI, R. A., and ABBOTT, J. A. 1967. Dehydration of solids-bearing liquids. U.S. Pat. 3,309,779. Mar. 21.

GINZBURG, A. S., and LYAKHOVITSKY, B. M. 1969. Using infrared radiation to intensify the freeze-drying process. Proc. 12th Intern. Congr. Refrig., Madrid.

GOUIGO, E. I., MALKOV, L. S., and KAOUKHTCHECHVILI, E. I. 1969. Certain peculiarities of heat and mass transfer during freeze drying of porous products in an ultra high frequency field. *In* Symp. Thermodynamic Aspects of Freeze Drying. Intern. Inst. Refrig., Comm. X, Lausanne, Switzerland. (French)

GUNN, R. D. 1967. Mass transport in porous media as applied to freeze drying. Ph.D. dissertation in chemical engineering. Univ. Calif., Berkeley.

GUNN, R. D., and KING, C. J. 1969. Mass transport in porous materials under combined gradients of composition and pressure. AIChE J. *15*, 507-514.

GUNN, R. D., and KING, C. J. 1971. Mass transfer characteristics of freeze-dried foods. Chem. Eng. Progr. Symp. Ser. *67*, No. 108, 94-101.

HACKENBERG, U. 1966. Freeze-drying apparatus. U.S. Pat. 3,273,259. Sept. 20.

HAMMOND, L. H. 1967. Economic evaluation of UHF dielectric vs. radiant heating for freeze drying. Food Technol. *21*, 735-742.

HANSON, S. W. F. 1961. The Accelerated Freeze-Drying (AFD) method of food preservation. Gr. Brit. Min. Agr. Fisheries Food. H.M. Stationery Office, London.

HARPER, J. C. 1962. Transport properties in gases in porous media at reduced pressures, with reference to freeze drying. AIChE J. *8*, 298-302.

HARPER, J. C. 1966. Method and apparatus for drying materials. U.S. Pat. 3,271,873. Sept. 13.

HARPER, J. C., and TAPPEL, E. L. 1957. Freeze drying of food products. Advan. Food Res. *7*, 171-234.

HATCHER, J. D. 1964. The use of gamma radiation to measure moisture distribution during drying processes. M.S. Thesis in mechanical engineering. Georgia Inst. Technol., Atlanta.

HAVIGHORST, C. R. 1970. Radical innovation in freeze drying. Food Eng. *42*, No. 6, 134-136.

KAN, B., and DEWINTER, F. 1968. The acceleration of the freeze-drying process through improved heat transfer. Food Technol. *22*, 1269-1278.

KAREL, M., and FLINK, J. 1969. Mechanism of volatile retention in freeze-dried carbohydrate solutions. Presented at Ann. Meeting Am. Inst. Chem. Eng., Washington, D.C. (Chem. Eng. Progr. Symp. Ser. in press.)

KAUFMAN, V. F., and ROCKWELL, W. C. 1967. Freeze-drying apparatus. U.S. Pat. 3,308,552. Mar. 14.

KESSLER, H. G. 1962. Heat and mass transfer in freeze drying of porous materials. Chem.-Ing.-Tech. *34*, 163. (German)

KING, C. J. 1968. Rates of moisture sorption and desorption in porous, dried foodstuffs. Food Technol. *22*, 509–515.

KING, C. J. 1970A. Freeze drying of foodstuffs. CRC Critical Rev. Food Technol. *1*, 359–451.

KING, C. J. 1970B. Recent developments in food dehydration technology. Presented at 3rd Intern. Congr. Food Sci. Technol., Washington, D.C.

KING, C. J. 1971. Freeze Drying of Foods. Chemical Rubber Publishing Co., Cleveland.

KING, C. J., and CLARK, J. P. 1968. Convective heat transfer for freeze drying of foods. Food Technol. *22*, 1235–1239.

KING, C. J., and CLARK, J. P. 1969. System for freeze drying. U.S. Pat. 3,453,741. July 8.

KING, C. J., LAM, W. K., and SANDALL, O. C. 1968. Physical properties important for freeze-drying poultry meat. Food Technol. *22*, 1302–1308.

KLUGE, G., and HEISS, R. 1967. Investigations on improving the quality control of dried foods in the particular case of freeze drying. Verfahrenstechnik *1*, 251. (German)

KOONZ, C. H., and RAMSBOTTOM, J. M. 1939. A method for studying the histological structure of frozen poultry. Food Res. *4*, 117–128.

KRAMERS, H. 1958. Rate-controlling factors in freeze drying. *In* Fundamental Aspects of the Dehydration of Foodstuffs. Macmillan Co., New York.

KUMAR, R. 1968. Development of a continuous condenser for the freeze-drying process. M.S. Thesis in chemical engineering. Univ. Calif., Berkeley.

KUMAR, R., KING, C. J., and LYNN, S. 1972. A continuous water vapor removal system for the freeze-drying process. ASHRAE J. *14*, No. 7, 38–45.

KUMAR, R., KING, C. J., and MORGAN, A. I., Jr. 1970. Apparatus for Vapor Condensation. U.S. Pat. 3,541,805. Nov. 24.

KUPRIANOFF, J. 1964. Fundamental and practical aspects of the freezing of foodstuffs. *In* Theoretical and Industrial Aspects of Lyophilization. L. Rey (Editor). Hermann, Paris.

LAMBERT, J. B., and MARSHALL, W. R., Jr. 1962. Heat and mass transfer in freeze drying. *In* Freeze Drying of Foods. F. R. Fisher (Editor). Natl. Acad. Sci.–Natl. Res. Council, Washington, D.C.

LEWIN, L. M., and MATELES, R. I. 1962. Freeze drying without vacuum: A preliminary investigation. Food Technol. *16*, 94–96.

LORENTZEN, J. 1970. Continuous freeze drying. CONRAD, the CONtinuous RADiation freeze drier. Presented at Intern. Freeze-Drying Symp., A/S Atlas, Copenhagen, Aug. 26–29.

LUIKOV, A. V. 1966. Heat and Mass Transfer in Capillary Porous Bodies. Pergamon Press, Oxford, England.

LUIKOV, A. V. 1969. Heat and mass transfer in freeze drying at high vacuum. *In* Symp. Thermodynamic Aspects of Freeze Drying. Intern. Inst. Refrig., Comm. X, Lausanne, Switzerland.

LUSK, G., KAREL, M., and GOLDBLITH, S. A. 1964. Thermal conductivity of some freeze-dried fish. Food Technol. *18*, 1625–1629.

LUYET, B. J. 1962. Effect of freezing rates on the structure of freeze-dried materials and the mechanism of rehydration. *In* Freeze-Drying of Foods. F. R. Fisher (Editor). Natl. Acad. Sci.–Natl. Res. Council, Washington, D.C.

MACKENZIE, A. P. 1965. Factors affecting the mechanism of transformation of ice into water vapor in the freeze-drying process. Ann. N.Y. Acad. Sci. *125*, 522–528.

MACKENZIE, A. P. 1966. Basic principles of freeze drying for pharmaceuticals. Parenteral Drug Assoc. Bull. *20*, 101–106.

MACKENZIE, A. P., and LUYET, B. J. 1967. Freeze drying and protein denaturation in muscle tissue. Nature *215*, No. 5096, 83–85.

MACKENZIE, A. P., and LUYET, B. J. 1969. Recovery of compressed dehydrated foods. U.S. Army Natick Lab., Natick, Mass. Tech. Rept. *70-16-FL*.

MAGNUSSEN, O. A. 1969. Measurements of heat and mass transfer coefficients during freeze drying. *In* Symp. on Thermodynamic Aspects of Freeze Drying. Intern. Inst. Refrig., Comm. X, Lausanne, Switzerland.

MALECKI, G. J., SHINDE, P., MORGAN, A. I., Jr., and FARKAS, D. 1970. Atmospheric fluidized bed freeze drying of apple juice. Food Technol. *24*, 601–603.

MARGARITIS, A., and KING, C. J. 1971. Factors governing terminal rates of freeze drying of poultry meat. Chem. Eng. Progr. Symp. Ser. *67*, No. 108, 112–121.

MASON, E. A., MALINAUSKAS, A. P., and EVANS, R. B. 1967. Flow and diffusion of gases in porous media. J. Chem. Phys. *46*, 3199–3216.

MASSEY, W. M., and SUNDERLAND, J. E. 1967. Measurement of thermal conductivity during freeze drying of beef. Food Technol. *21*, 408–412.

MEFFERT, H. F. Th. 1963. Heat transmission in freeze drying materials. Proc. 11th Intern. Congr. Refrig., Munich.

MENTING, L. C., HOOGSTAD, B., and THIJSSEN, H. A. C. 1970. Diffusion coefficients of water and organic volatiles in carbohydrate-water systems. J. Food Technol. (London). *5*, 111–126.

MERYMAN, H. T. 1959. Sublimation freeze drying without vacuum. Science *130*, 628–629.

MERYMAN, H. T. 1963. Apparatus for freeze drying at atmospheric pressure. U.S. Pat. 3,096,163. July 2.

MINK, W. H., and SACHSEL, G. F. 1968. Rapid freeze drying by the use of the fluidized bed. Chem. Eng. Progr. Symp. Ser. *64*, No. 86, 54–59.

MONZINI, A., and MALTINI, E. 1969. Studies on the freeze drying of frozen concentrated orange juice. *In* Symp. Thermodynamic Aspects of Freeze Drying, Intern. Inst. Refrig., Comm. X, Lausanne, Switzerland.

MOY, J. 1970. Vacuum puff-drying of tropical fruit juices. Presented at 30th Ann. Meeting Inst. Food Technologists, San Francisco.

NOYES, R. 1968. Freeze drying of foods and biologicals. Food Process. Rev. *1*. Noyes Development Corp., Park Ridge, N.J.

OETJEN, G. W. 1966. Freeze drying of food products. *In* Advances in Freeze Drying– Lyophilization, Research and New Applications. L. Rey (Editor). Hermann, Paris.

OETJEN, G. W., and EILENBERG, H. J. 1969. Heat transfer during freeze drying with moved particles. *In* Symp. Thermodynamic Aspects of Freeze Drying. Intern. Inst. Refrig., Comm. X, Lausanne, Switzerland.

PARKER, W. N. 1968. Freeze drying. *In* Microwave Power Engineering. E. C. Okress (Editor). Academic Press, New York.

PETERSEN, E. E., LORENTZEN, J., and FOSBØL, P. 1970. Colour and bulk density adjustments by freeze drying of coffee. Presented at Intern. Freeze-Drying Symp., A/S Atlas, Copenhagen, Aug. 26–29.

PFLUGER, R. A., SCHULMAN, M., and HETZENDORF, M. S. 1969. Freeze drying of foamed aromatic material. U.S. Pat. 3,482,990. Dec. 9.

PINTAURO, N. 1969. Soluble coffee manufacturing processes. Food Process. Rev. *8*. Noyes Development Corp., Park Ridge, N.J.

POULSEN, U. 1970. Frozen granules for industrial freeze drying. Presented at Intern. Freeze-Drying Symp., A/S Atlas, Copenhagen, Aug. 26–29.

QUAST, D. G., and KAREL, M. 1968. Dry layer permeability and freeze-drying rates in concentrated fluid systems. J. Food Sci. *33*, 170–175.

REY, L. (Editor) 1964A. Theoretical and Industrial Aspects of Lyophilization. Hermann, Paris.

REY, L. (Editor) 1964B. Fundamental aspects of lyophilization. *In* Theoretical and Industrial Aspects of Lyophilization. Hermann, Paris.

REY, L. (Editor) 1966. Advances in freeze drying. *In* Lyophilisation, Research and New Applications. Hermann, Paris.

REY, L., and BASTIEN, M.-C. 1962. Biophysical aspects of freeze drying. *In* Freeze Drying of Foods. F. R. Fisher (Editor). Natl. Acad. Sci.–Natl. Res. Council, Washington, D.C.

RIEDEL, L. 1949. Refractive index and freezing point of fruit juices as functions of concentration. Z. Lebensm. Untersuch. Forsch. *89*, 289–299. (German)

RIEDEL, L. 1969. Physical and physico-chemical changes during freeze drying of foods. Dechema Monograph. *63*, 115–125. (German)

ROCKWELL, W. C., KAUFMAN, V. F., LOWE, E., and MORGAN, A. I., Jr. 1965. Hextube freeze dryer permits continuous F-D. Food Eng. *37*, No. 4, 49–51.

ROWE, T. W. G. 1962A. Vacuum systems for freeze drying. *In* Freeze Drying of Foodstuffs. S. Cotson and D. B. Smith (Editors). Columbine Press, Manchester, England.

ROWE, T. W. G. 1962B. Water vapour removal in food freeze drying. Le Vide (Paris) *102*, 516.

ROWE, T. W. G. 1964. Recent advances in vacuum methods. *In* Theoretical and Industrial Aspects of Lyophilization. L. Rey (Editor). Hermann, Paris.

SANDALL, O. C. 1966. Interactions between heat and mass transfer in freeze drying. Ph.D. dissertation in chemical engineering, Univ. Calif., Berkeley.

SANDALL, O. C., KING, C. J., and WILKE, C. R. 1967. The relationship between transport properties and rates of freeze drying of poultry meat. AIChE J. *13*, 428–438. Reprinted in Chem. Eng. Progr. Symp. Ser. *64*, No. 86, 43–53 (1968).

SARAVACOS, G. D., and MOYER, J. C. 1968. Volatility of some flavor compounds during freeze drying of foods. Chem. Eng. Progr. Symp Ser. *64*, No. 86, 37–42.

SAUVAGEOT, F., BELEY, P., MARCHAND, A., and SIMATOS, D. 1969. Some experimental results on the behavior of volatile compounds of fruit juices during freeze drying. *In* Symp. Surface Reactions in Freeze-Dried Systems. Intern. Inst. Refrig., Comm. X, Paris. (French)

SHARON, Z., and BERK, Z. 1969. Freeze drying of tomato juice and concentrate: Studies on heat and mass transfer. *In* Symp. Thermodynamic Aspects of Freeze Drying. Intern. Inst. Refrig., Comm. X, Lausanne, Switzerland.

SHIELDS, J. R. 1952. Vapor condensing apparatus and method. U.S. Pat. 2,613,513. Oct. 14.

SINNAMON, H. I., KOMANOWSKY, M., and HEILAND, W. K. 1968. An experimental apparatus for drying particulate foods in air. Food Technol. *22*, 219–222.

SONG, P.-S., CHICHESTER, C. O., and STADTMAN, F. H. 1966. Kinetic behavior and mechanism of inhibition in the Maillard reaction. I. Kinetic behavior of the reaction between D-glucose and glycine, J. Food Sci. *31*, 906–913.

SPIESS, W. E. L., SEILER, R. S., and BRINKMANN, A. 1969. The influence of the dry substance content on the freeze-drying rate of Maté Extract (*Ilex Paraguay*). Proc. 12th Intern. Congr. Refrig., Madrid.

STERN, R. M., and STORRS, A. B. 1969. Method of drying sugar-containing materials. U.S. Pat. 3,483,032. Dec. 9.

THIJSSEN, H. A. C., and RULKENS, W. H. 1968. Retention of aromas in drying food liquids. Ingenieur *CH45*, Nov. 22.

THIJSSEN, H. A. C., and RULKENS, W. H. 1969. Effect of freezing rate on rate of sublimation and flavor retention in freeze drying. *In* Symp. Thermodynamic Aspects of Freeze Drying. Intern. Inst. Refrig., Comm. X, Lausanne, Switzerland.

THUSE, E. 1964. Apparatus for freeze drying. U.S. Pat. 3,132,929. May 12.

TOGASHI, H. J., and MERCER, J. L. 1966. Entrained particle removal method and apparatus. U.S. Pat. 3,276,139. Oct. 4.

TOOBY, G. 1969. Method for dehydrating materials. U.S. Pat. 3,466,756. Sept. 16.

TRIEBES, T. A., and KING, C. J. 1966. Factors influencing the rate of heat conduction in freeze drying. Ind. Eng. Chem. Process Design Develop. *5*, 430–435.

WARMAN, K. G., and REICHEL, A. J. 1970. Development of a freeze-drying process for foods. Chem. Engr. (London) *238*, CE 134–CE 139.

WERTHEIM, J., and MISHKIN, A. R. 1968. Powdered coffee extract. Brit. Pat. 1,102,587. Feb. 7. Freeze-drying apparatus. Brit. Pat. 1,102,588. Feb. 7.

WISTREICH, H. E., and BLAKE, J. A. 1962. Azeotropic freeze drying. Science *138*, 138.

WOODWARD, H. T. 1963. Freeze drying without vacuum. Food Eng. *35*, No. 6, 96–97.

YOUNG, F. E., JONES, F. T., and LEWIS, A. J. 1952. D-fructose-water phase diagram. J. Phys. Chem. *56*, 1093–1096.

CHAPTER 7

W. B. Van Arsdel
and
A. H. Brown

Drying Rates and Estimation of Drier Capacity

A datum which is essential to the successful designing of any drier or drying system, and almost as important for its satisfactory subsequent operation, is the drying rate for specified materials under specified conditions—that is, a quantitative statement of the rate at which water (or specified other liquid ingredient) can be removed from the initially moist or wet substance. In this book we shall be concerned only with foods and food substances.

Some of the earlier writers on the subject of drying, thinking only of the most familiar example, air drying, confined their analyses to the effects of air humidity, temperature, and velocity upon the rate of drying. This approach, it turned out, was little more than a useful introduction to a vast and complex field of knowledge that still remains to be more fully explored. All too often in the past the result has been a grossly underestimated degree of difficulty in accomplishing a particular task involving drying. Various techniques and procedures employed by designers and engineers are described in this chapter. Essentially, all such procedures include the equivalent of estimating a drying *rate* (or a specified succession of rates). Integration gives a drying *time*, and from this the drying *capacity* or *capability* of the drier in question follows immediately. A rather large degree of uncertainty is almost inevitable, so use of a generous margin or safety factor above the strict design estimate is advisable.

Long experience has shown that carefully planned and executed small-scale experimental drying tests can be used to simulate most types of full-scale drying quite well. Such tests are, in fact, relied upon by drier manufacturers to guide the construction of equipment to accomplish commercial drying tasks.

The air drying of wet pieces has complexities of its own, as will become apparent in the following discussion, but it does lend itself to relatively simple physical and mathematical analysis. For that reason the classic early analyses of the drying operation (Lewis 1921; Sherwood 1929, 1930, 1931, 1932, 1936; Sherwood and Comings 1932, 1933) were directed primarily to the tray drying of pieces, and much of the later theoretical development has continued in that line.

Experimental study of piece drying should employ a carefully designed drier equipped for precise control of the temperature, humidity, and velocity of the air stream in which the wet body is supported. Figure 7.1 is a diagrammatic sketch of such a drier, designed specifically for study of the air drying of cut pieces of fruits or vegetables, uniformly spread on shallow mesh-bottom trays. Fresh air drawn in past the adjustable recirculation damper *B* is pulled through

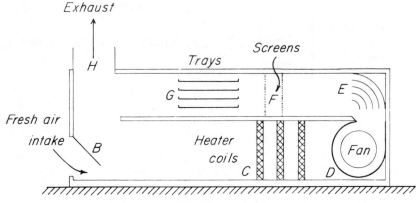

FIG. 7.1. DIAGRAM OF EXPERIMENTAL TRAY DRIER (ELEVATION)

multiple fin-coil steam heaters C by the centrifugal fan D. The fan discharges through a set of turning vanes E and perforated screens F intended to straighten out and equilize the air flow through the tray section G. Exhaust air leaves the drier at H. In some designs the entire tray section is supported on a balance arm so that its gross weight can be followed continuously during the drying. Usually, however, individual trays are easily removable for quick weighing on separate scales.

Sketches of a pilot-scale cabinet drier which has given satisfactory service have been published by the USDA Western Regional Research Laboratory, Agricultural Research Service, Albany, Calif. (drawings C-112 and C-113, 1943). The drier is designed to take trays 3 ft sq and is constructed mainly of plywood, with mineral wool insulation. It is steam heated by finned coils capable of transferring 1,100,000 Btu per hr to air at 60°F. The centrifugal circulating fan delivers 9000 cu ft of air per minute at a static pressure of $1\frac{1}{2}$ in. of water.

Only a few investigators have reported studies of the air drying of isolated pieces of wet food material, experiments being planned and executed in such a way as to separate the effects of all the important variables. One of the most significant is Jason (1958), who has described his specially designed equipment for studying the mechanism of drying of lean fish flesh, cut into carefully measured parallelopipeds of appreciable size. The drying apparatus automatically recorded drying conditions and sample weight, and was operated continuously over long periods of time. The frequent measurements made it possible to analyze drying rates in great detail.

Ede and Hales (1948) used a cabinet-type experimental drier of fairly conventional design in their study of the drying of potato and carrot strips. They first tried a procedure in which the individually weighed pieces were carried on small hooks suspended by threads in the air stream, but abandoned it in favor of a method utilizing 24 measured pieces at once on a wire-bottom tray, with air flowing down through the almost unobstructed tray; the results agreed well with those obtained by the more arduous thread-suspension method.

Krischer (1956, 1963) describes an experimental drier intended to isolate the individual variables as completely as possible. A steady stream of air of known temperature, humidity, and velocity is passed through a rectangular duct, 800 mm long, 80 mm wide, and 50 mm high; at intervals in the bottom of this duct are 4 circular openings 37.5 mm in diameter. One test sample, carried on a sensitive balance, is supported at each of these openings with its upper face flush with the duct opening. One sample is water jacketed so that its internal temperature can be maintained at the wet-bulb temperature of the air; another sample is controllably heated at its lower face; a third sample is heated by radiation from an infrared heater positioned over a window in the duct; and the fourth sample is left to find its own equilibrium temperature.

FACTORS INFLUENCING THE RATE OF AIR-DRYING OF PIECE-FORM WET SOLIDS

Controllable physical conditions in an air-drying experiment will usually include the dry-bulb and wet-bulb air temperatures, the atmospheric pressure, and the air velocity past the wet body. A basic condition is, of course, the chemical and physical nature and structure of the material being dried, which will be defined as closely as is feasible. If the body being dried consists of an assemblage of smaller pieces (for example, kernels of blanched sweet corn, or a quantity of diced, blanched, carrots or potato), some definition of the physical dimensions and arrangement will be used to describe it for this purpose. A common situation has been the drying of a prepared vegetable, cut in half-dice, a thin layer of which is spread evenly on trays or screens and supported in the air stream; the exact arrangement and exposure of the wet pieces cannot be described in detail, but some related measurable factor can be given. For example, a $1/2$-in. thick layer of dice evenly spread on a tray can be weighed and characterized as a load of X pounds per square foot of that commodity.

Very few reports of careful drying experiments were available before the publication by Culpepper and Moon (1937) on the drying of Kieffer pears cut into pieces of various sizes. Activity picked up sharply with the coming of World War II. Drying rates of cut vegetables were studied extensively (Van Arsdel 1942, 1943A, B; Brown and Kilpatrick 1943; USDA 1944; British Ministry of Food 1946; Ede and Hales 1948). Studies on meat were reported by Ede and Partridge (1943) and on fruits by Perry (1944) and Perry et al. (1946). Van Arsdel (1951) later described and discussed more completely the experiments on vegetables.

Of all the conditions which affect the rate at which a wet or moist material can be dried, the most fundamental are the physical structure and chemical makeup of the material itself. In part, the result is obvious and predictable. For example, there is only about $1/2$ as much dry solid in a piece of carrot flesh as there is in a piece of potato of exactly the same dimensions and therefore the same surface area. Under drying conditions the two pieces will initially lose moisture at just about the same rate, expressed in pounds per hour, because their surfaces are completely wet. But if we express moisture content on the dry basis, the initial drying rate of the carrot piece will be about twice as great as that of the potato piece, in pounds of water per pound of dry solids per hour. However, other effects of composition and structure, especially in the later stages of drying, will be just as diverse as the food materials themselves, and as impossible to predict or compute as their aroma or texture. We can characterize them by various significant measurements of such properties as the water vapor of the wet or moist material at a specified temperature.

The Sorption Isotherm

A moist organic material, held at constant temperature in a small evacuated chamber connected to a sensitive manometer, displays a vapor pressure which approaches a steady equilibrium value characteristic of the material, its moisture content, and the temperature. The experimentally determined relation between water vapor pressure and moisture content at equilibrium is sometimes known as equilibrium relative humidity or more often as equilibrium moisture content. The quantitative relation between vapor pressure and moisture content at constant temperature is a vapor pressure isotherm.

The water content of practically all fresh foods is so high that the vapor pressure at equilibrium is substantially the same as that of pure water. As water is removed by concentrating or drying, the vapor pressure falls, at first only very slightly but then more and more steeply. Figure 7.2, based on the data of Gane (1943), illustrates this behavior in the case of carrots. The scale of moisture content in this diagram reads from right to left in order to let the direction of change correspond with decreasing moisture content, as in drying.

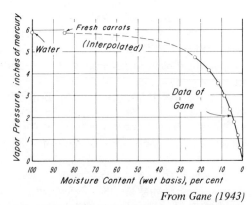

From Gane (1943)

FIG. 7.2. WATER VAPOR PRESSURE OF CARROT AT 140°F
AS A FUNCTION OF MOISTURE CONTENT

The relationship between the amount of volatile component (such as water) in a solution or mixture and the equilibrium pressure of that component in the surrounding vapor, as expressed in a sorption isotherm, has been the subject of extensive research. It has important theoretical implications (see Heiss 1968).

Free Moisture

The term "free moisture" is sometimes used to mean the amount of moisture in a body that is in excess of the amount which would be in equilibrium with air at the given temperature and humidity. It is also sometimes used in distinction to "bound moisture," which has no well-defined meaning but connotes water held within a substance by relatively strong forces so that it is difficult to re-move. Other terms can generally be used which have more clearly defined meaning.

Definition of Moisture Content

This term is one of those that always should be defined operationally—that is, by stating the exact procedure used to determine the value. The meaning of the term is seriously ambiguous unless the method used is clearly understood.

Reports of research on drying are frequently open to criticism on this account. Significant differences in the apparent meaning of results are possible, especially in the low-moisture region which also is very important for food dehydration. Stitt (1958) reviewed this entire question and made a critical evaluation of eight methods. The one generally used by workers in the USDA Western Regional Research Laboratory for referee determinations is the vacuum oven method of Makower et al. (1946), calling for 40 hr of drying at 158°F for potatoes and carrots, 30 hr at 140°F for cabbage and onions. The loss in weight is reported as "moisture." Many purchase specifications are written in terms of a 6-hr vacuum oven method; in dehydrated potatoes this gives a result about 2% lower than the method of Makower et al.—for example, it might give 6% weight loss, reported as moisture, instead of the 8% loss that would have been found after 40 hr of drying. For routine control determinations of moisture content, the various rapid empirical methods or instruments are often used. Some of these employ the rapid heating of a small weighed sample for a specified arbitrary length of time; others indicate the electrical resistance of a sample or its dielectric constant as that affects the tuning of a resonant circuit. All such methods are calibrated by use of one of the standard moisture determination methods.

The group of curves which follow in this chapter show the change of moisture content with time in the course of air-drying cut pieces of certain vegetables. Moisture content is expressed on the dry basis, and the curves show it on a logarithmic scale so as to open them out in the region of low-moisture content, where further drying is always slow.

Figure 7.3 compares the drying behavior of potato pieces and carrot pieces of nearly the same size, under the same external conditions. The carrot pieces were $1/4$-in. thick, the potatoes $3/16$-in.; both were $3/8$-in. square. Drying was on metal

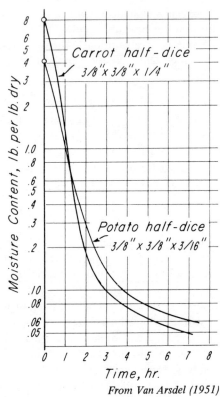

From Van Arsdel (1951)

FIG. 7.3. DRYING CURVES FOR CARROT AND POTATO
HALF-DICE

mesh-bottom trays in air at 160°F, wet-bulb temperature 100°F, tray loading
1.5 lb per sq ft, air velocity 800 fpm. The carrot pieces reached a final moisture
content of 0.06 in 5 hr, as against 7 hr for the potato pieces.

Differences in the composition of the material are known to have an effect on
the drying rate. Blanched (scalded) material dries more rapidly than unblanched,
at least in the high-moisture range, probably because the scalding kills the tissue
and makes cell membranes more freely permeable to water. A. H. Brown (unpublished report, Nov. 10, 1943) and his associates at USDA Western Regional
Research Laboratory compared the drying rates of potato pieces varying widely
in sugar content (the difference was produced by varying the temperature at
which the potatoes were stored) and found that while the drying rate was unaffected by sugar content down to a moisture content of about 0.30 lb moisture
per pound dry solids, the drying time from $W = 0.30$ to $W = 0.075$ was longer
the higher the sugar content. For the material he was using, Brown determined
that the drying time in this low-moisture range was approximately proportional
to either one of the following two expressions: [1 + 0.059 (percentage total

sugar)] or [1 + 0.12 (percentage reducing sugar)]. The sugar content is expressed as percentage of the weight of dry solids. The experimental data were not extensive enough to determine which of these expressions is the more accurate.

SHAPE, SIZE, AND ARRANGEMENT OF THE MATERIAL PIECES

Classical drying theory (Lewis 1921) predicts that if the surface film resistance to moisture transfer away from the wet piece is negligible in comparison with internal diffusional resistance, the drying rate will vary inversely as the square of the piece thickness. Van Arsdel (1947) showed that this relation should remain true even if the internal diffusional resistance is not constant, but a function of moisture content.

The influence of piece size on the course of drying is illustrated by the data of Ede and Hales (1948). Figure 7.4, taken from their bulletin, shows drying curves for julienne strips of potato of three different sizes. The drying was carried out on large trays, the back edges of which dried materially slower than the front edges; the curves are for the material near the front edges of the trays.

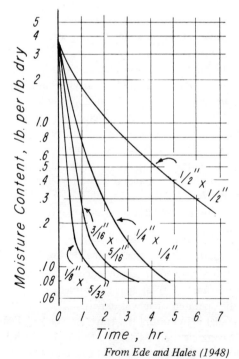

From Ede and Hales (1948)

FIG. 7.4. EFFECT OF PIECE SIZE ON COURSE OF DRYING OF POTATO STRIPS

Trays were loaded at 1.5 lb per sq ft, air velocity was 960 fpm, the temperature was 158°F, and the wet-bulb temperature 95°F.

From this illustration it is plain that a small difference in the thickness of vegetable pieces can cause an altogether disproportionate change in the drying time. A difference is evident at all stages of drying, but is far more marked in the low-moisture range than near the beginning. This is what would be expected. During the initial phases the rate of evaporation per unit of surface changes but little. Now suppose that we compare a single cube with two half-cubes cut from a similar cube. The weight of dry solids in the 2 halves will be the same as in the whole cube, but their combined surface will be 33% greater. Their initial gross drying rate should be greater than that of the cube in about the same proportion. Next, assume that we compare 6 separate cubes with 6 similar cubes put together to form a strip 6 times as long as it is thick. By the same kind of reasoning we can infer that the initial drying rate of the cubes will be some 38% greater than that of the strip.

In the later phases of drying the thickness of solid substance through which water must diffuse will become the controlling factor. If the rate varies inversely as the square of the thickness, 9 times as long will be required for a given amount of drying if the piece is 3 times as thick.

Drying times may actually be reduced to the order of a second if the piece size is reduced far enough. This is the secret of the great success of spray drying, in which the individual particles may be only a few microns in diameter and their time of contact with the hot air only a few seconds.

In the opposite direction, the reason why whole carrots or quartered potatoes are not commercially dehydrated is that the drying time would be so long as to be completely impractical, even if a reasonably good final product could be made, which is doubtful. The sizes into which vegetables are cut for commercial dehydration represent a compromise between the need for rapid drying and the desire to serve the consumer large pieces of the products. Dehydrated whole fruits, such as prunes, represent a special case in that dehydration is continued only to about 22% moisture, thus avoiding the low-moisture phase completely, and the quality of the fruit remains acceptable even with so long a drying time as 24–36 hr and a material temperature which may rise as high as 165°F for a period of many hours.

Disposition of the Material with Respect to the Drying Air

The traditional tray drying arrangement successfully exposes a very large area of drying surface per unit of total space occupied, but must be carefully designed and properly operated or it will experience serious trouble with uneven drying. In commercial dehydrators the trays are stacked 1 above another to a height of 6–7 ft, leaving clear air passages a few inches high between successive trays (Van Arsdel 1951; Kilpatrick et al. 1955). Tray bottoms are perforated or slotted in various ways. The main air stream, passing horizontally between trays

at a velocity of up to 1000–1200 fpms is intensely turbulent and creates local-
ized pressure differences which, in turn, produce more or less flow of air *through*
the layer of wet material. Special tray designs are sometimes employed deliber-
ately in order to increase the amount of through-flow; an increase in the drying
rate, especially for heavily loaded trays, would be expected (Eidt 1938). Irregularities in loading the material on the trays may have the doubly evil effect of
locally increasing the thickness of the wet layer and diminishing the free space
left open for air flow. The quantitative effect of all these variables is a highly individual consequence of the dehydrator design and operating conditions.

Load of Wet Material Per Unit Tray Area

Cut vegetable pieces are commonly loaded on trays in a reasonably uniform
layer from less than $1/2$ in. to more than 1 in. deep; whole prunes may form
roughly a double layer, approximately 2 in. deep. Loading per square foot of
tray area is commonly from something less than 1 lb to as much as 3 lb or more.
In a well-conducted operation careful attention is given to maintaining a very
uniform spread of the cut material on the trays and very uniform and predetermined total weight on each tray.

Figure 7.5 illustrates the effect of varying the weight of potato half-dice
spread on a metal-mesh tray at the unit rates of 1.0, 1.5, 2.0, and 3.0 lb per sq ft
of tray surface. Constant drying conditions of 160°F temperature, 100°F wet-
bulb temperature, and an air velocity of 800 fpm were assumed.

Increasing the tray loading reduces the rate of drying materially during the
early stages, but as the drying progresses the rates become more and more nearly
equal; at a final moisture content of $W = 0.06$ in these potato pieces there was
only 17% difference in drying times between the 2 extreme loadings which differ
in a ratio of 3:1. After the moisture content falls to about 0.20 no further effect of the initial loading density can be seen. In the low-moisture range shrinkage of the pieces has reduced even a 3-lb layer to a very open structure, through
which the air can circulate almost as freely as it does through the still lighter
layer remaining from a 1-lb initial loading. If the original load had been much
heavier than 3 lb we can surmise that an effect on drying rate would be seen
even at the lowest moisture level. A reduction in final rate would be especially
likely to occur if the material were cut into thin slices instead of dice, because
the slices would tend to stick together, making, in effect, a much thicker body
of material through which the moisture must diffuse. A similar adverse effect on
rate would occur if the prepared material were so soft that pieces would mash
together during the spreading operation or that the bottom layers would crush
together under their own weight.

M. E. Lazar, of USDA Western Regional Research Laboratory, showed in an
unpublished report dated June 9, 1945 (Van Arsdel 1951) that the initial rate of
drying of a trayload of $3/8 \times 3/8 \times 3/16$ in. carrot half-dice corresponds approximately with the rate of evaporation from 3–4 sq ft of free water surface per

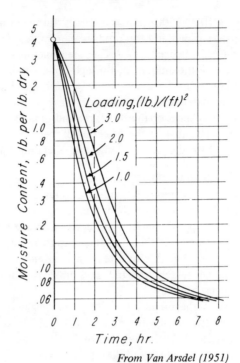

From Van Arsdel (1951)

FIG. 7.5. EFFECT OF TRAY LOADING ON COURSE OF
POTATO HALF-DICE

square foot of tray surface. The evaporation takes place almost exclusively from the top layer of pieces, so that the initial rate of loss of weight from a heavily loaded tray is little, if any, greater than from a lightly loaded tray. So long as the tray surface is at least completely covered with pieces, the initial drying rate determined by weighing the whole trayload must therefore be approximately inversely proportional to the initial loading per square foot of tray.

TEMPERATURE, HUMIDITY, AND VELOCITY OF AIR OVER THE MATERIAL BEING DRIED

Wet-Bulb Depression

The most important single factor correlated with drying rate is the wet-bulb depression of the air flowing past the wet body—that is, $t - t_w$, the difference between dry-bulb and wet-bulb air temperatures. If this difference is zero the air is saturated and no drying takes place (Carrier 1921).

Figure 7.6, adapted from Ede and Hales (1948) and Ede (1958), shows gross drying rate of single potato strips, $5/16 \times 5/16 \times 2\frac{1}{2}$ in., in air at 70°C (158°F), flowing at 10 ft per sec, and with wet-bulb depressions ranging from less than 10°C to almost 40°C. The 3 curves show that during the early phases of drying

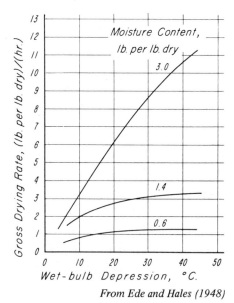

Wet-bulb Depression, °C.

From Ede and Hales (1948)

FIG. 7.6. EFFECT OF WET-BULB DEPRESSION ON DRYING
RATE OF POTATO STRIPS

(W = 3.0 lb water per pound dry solids) the drying rate is very nearly proportional to the wet-bulb depression; at an intermediate phase (W = 1.4) increasing wet-bulb depression from 20° to 30°C increases the rate only a little, and increasing the depression further would have even less effect; in the fairly dry strips (W = 0.6) increasing the depression to more than about 20°C has little or no effect on rate. In all cases, of course, the rate drops off sharply when the wet-bulb depression falls further and approaches zero.

These relationships reflect the drastic change in the permeability of potato tissue to water as the moisture content is reduced. In the early stages of drying internal transfer of water takes place readily and drying rate is controlled almost exclusively by the surface resistances to evaporation, while in later stages the rate is mainly controlled by the internal resistances to moisture flow, so that an increase in the external drying potential (by increasing the wet-bulb depression) has little effect.

Ede and Hales (1948) reported that the drying rates of carrot strips and shredded cabbage are, like the drying rate of potato strips, approximately proportional to wet-bulb depression at the higher levels of moisture content. Guillou (1942) and Perry (1944), on the other hand, showed that the drying rate of whole prunes is substantially independent of wet-bulb depression so long as the relative humidity of the air is less than about 40%; in this case the main resistance to be overcome is evidently always the internal resistance to moisture movement.

The proportionality of drying rate to wet-bulb depression, and to vapor pressure difference during the constant-rate phase of drying (Carrier 1921), leads to the following widely used expression:

$$\left(\frac{dW}{d\theta}\right)_e = aG^{0.8}(t_a - t_w) \qquad (7.1)$$

where

W	= moisture content, lb water per lb dry solids
θ	= time, hr
a	= proportionality factor
G	= mass-velocity of air stream, lb/hr sq ft cross-section area of air passage
$(t_a - t_w)$	= wet-bulb depression, °F

Air Temperature (Dry-Bulb)

The effect of changing the air temperature at constant wet-bulb depression is illustrated by the curves in Fig. 7.7, computed for the drying of potato half-dice

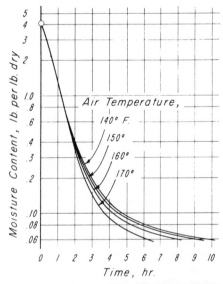

From Van Arsdel (1951)

FIG. 7.7. EFFECT OF AIR TEMPERATURE ON COURSE OF DRYING POTATO HALF-DICE AT CONSTANT WET-BULB DEPRESSION

on metal-mesh trays at temperatures of 140°, 150°, 160°, and 170°F, and a wet-bulb depression of 50°F in every case. The trays were loaded at 1.5 lb per sq ft, air velocity was 800 fpm.

The initial rate of drying, down to a moisture content of about 1.0, is sub-

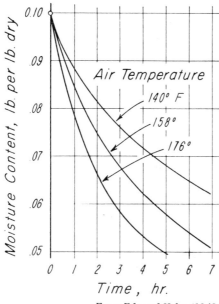

Time , hr.

From Ede and Hales (1948)

FIG. 7.8. EFFECT OF AIR TEMPERATURE ON COURSE OF DRYING POTATO STRIPS IN THE LOW-MOISTURE RANGE

stantially identical in all four curves, but in the low-moisture range the drying rate is substantially greater at the higher temperatures. Figure 7.8, adapted from Ede and Hales (1948), shows the course of final drying of potato strips below a moisture content of 0.10 at temperatures of 60°, 70°, and 80°C; neither wet-bulb depression nor air velocity has any further appreciable effect on the drying time, but the air temperature does. In this low-moisture range the drying is so slow that the cooling effect of evaporation is inappreciable and the pieces of material assume very nearly the dry-bulb temperature of the air. The internal redistribution of moisture, which is the rate-determining factor in this phase, is accelerated by this rise of the material temperature.

Air Velocity

Figure 7.9 illustrates the course of drying as computed for four conditions in which the air velocity across the tray of potato half-dice is the only variable. Tray loading is 1.5 lb per sq ft, air temperature is 160°F, and wet-bulb depression is 60°F. Air velocities are 400, 600, 800, and 1000 fpm across the tray surface. The curves for velocities of 800 and 1000 fpm are virtually identical, and only the curve for the lowest velocity is significantly different; the differences are all at the high-moisture end of the curves, and below a moisture content of about 0.50 the drying rate appears to be substantially independent of air velocity. Other comparisons made in the USDA Western Regional Re-

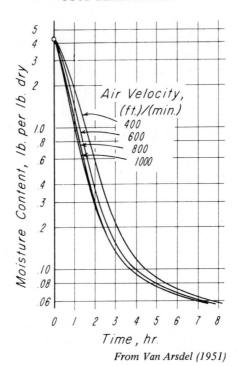

From Van Arsdel (1951)

FIG. 7.9. EFFECT OF AIR VELOCITY ON COURSE OF DRYING
POTATO HALF-DICE

search Laboratory showed, however, that a change in air velocity exerts a more pronounced effect if the trays are more heavily loaded than 1.5 lb per sq ft. Apparently an increase in air velocity, and the accompanying increase in the turbulence of the air stream passing between trays, produces a greater proportion of through-circulation in the heavier layers.

According to Ede and Hales (1948), the initial rate of drying of small trays of potato strips is proportional to about the 0.7 or 0.8 power of the air velocity. This corresponds with the velocity exponent for the rate of evaporation from a free water surface.

Barometric Pressure

The experiments upon which published drying rates are based were all conducted in locations not far above sea level, and hence at a barometric pressure not far different from the "normal," 1.00 standard atmosphere, 29.92 in. of mercury. The effect of a substantially lower pressure, such as will prevail in a mountainous area, can, however, be predicted with some assurance from general physical principles. It is not a very marked effect in any air-convection type of dehydrator.

Regardless of the barometric pressure, the temperature of moist material in the dehydrator will at first quite closely approximate the wet-bulb temperature of the air and will gradually rise closer and closer to the dry-bulb temperature of the air. During the early stages the rate of drying will be approximately proportional to the difference between the vapor pressure of water at the wet-bulb temperature and the partial pressure of water vapor in the air. This difference will be less if the barometric pressure is low.

Important in determining the effect on total drying time is the influence the barometric pressure may have on drying rates in the low-moisture range. The main rate-determining factor there, namely the internal resistance to transloca-tion of moisture, should be nearly unaffected by barometric pressure; the diffusivity of water in the partly dry material is controlled by the moisture content and temperature of the piece, and the latter will be substantially the same as the dry-bulb temperature of the air.

Summing up, the effect of a lower barometric pressure is to require a some-what greater wet-bulb depression to produce the same drying rate, but the difference will be appreciable only in the early phases of the drying. This result may be set against the fallacious belief of some dehydrator designers and operators that more rapid drying can be realized if the air circulation fan and dampers are placed so that the drying compartment will be under "suction" —that is, below the outside atmospheric pressure rather than above it. The arrangement may have its advantages for other reasons, but not for that one. In the first place, the "suction" produced by the types of circulating fan used in dehydrators is negligible in comparison with the atmospheric pressure; the pressure in the dehydrator would be reduced at most only a few tenths of an inch of mercury. The effect on drying rate, however slight, is in the opposite direction—that is, the rate is reduced—if the dehydrator temperatures are maintained unchanged.

CONDUCTIVE AND RADIATIVE SOURCES OF ADDITIONAL HEAT SUPPLY TO MATERIAL BEING DRIED

The drying experiments conducted at USDA Western Regional Research Laboratory and those described by Ede and Hales (1948) show that even minor differences in tray design and construction and drier arrangement will produce substantial differences in drying rate. No complete theoretical analysis of the effective factors is available. Results of operation in full-size driers have, however, been in reasonably good accord with design prediction based on small-scale experiments, especially if certain rather obvious factors are taken into account. Among these factors are the conductive and radiative heat sources over and above the main heat supply carried as sensible heat in the main air stream; the magnitude and arrangement of these supplementary heat sources will affect particularly the equilibrium temperature of wet material on the trays.

In the experiments at the Western Regional Research Laboratory, drying of vegetable pieces was found to be as much as 20% faster during the early drying stages on trays whose bottoms were made by rolling "expanded metal" into a fairly heavy diamond-mesh sheet than on trays with bottoms of thin wood slats spaced about $1/8$ in. apart. Some of the increased rate on the metal mesh bottoms may have been a consequence of the higher proportion of opening, but the greater effect was probably a rise in temperature of the wet material to several degrees above the wet-bulb temperature of the air, because of the high heat conductivity of the metal mesh. The metal itself would assume a temperature somewhere between the dry-bulb temperature of the air, to which it would be exposed on one side, and the temperature of the wet material in contact with its other side.

The wet-bulb temperature itself is the result of a heat balance between evaporative cooling and convective and radiative transfer of heat from the hotter surroundings. In the standard case all of these surroundings are at the dry-bulb temperature. This will also be approximately true for all of the closely stacked trays in a dehydrator; the wet material on a tray will "see" only the bottom surface of the tray above. On the other hand, if a body at higher temperature, such as an infrared radiator, is introduced into the drier the heat balance will be shifted and the material on the tray will assume a temperature higher than the wet-bulb temperature of the air. In vacuum drying, heat transfer by convection being greatly reduced, infrared radiation is often used to supplement what heat can be conducted to the wet material from a heated supporting shelf or conveyor belt. When the drying rate decreases as the material approaches dryness, the energy input to the radiators must be reduced or the temperature of the material will exceed the allowable maximum.

In preceding pages, the effects of various external conditions upon the course of drying have been discussed, in each case assuming that all variables except the one under discussion are held constant. In many important kinds of dehydrator, however, the principle of the operation imposes an inherent and determinate kind of variation on the drying conditions. A quantitative description of the operation then requires determination of the course of drying, and especially the total drying time, under a particular set of these variable conditions. For a specific example, in a quasi-continuous (or "progressive") tunnel-and-truck dehydrator a single piece of the product experiences a marked change in the temperature and humidity of the air flowing over it during the residence time of the piece of material. The air velocity will also change somewhat as a consequence of these temperature and humidity changes and the gradual volume-shrinkage of the product. Both the drying time (and hence the daily output capacity of the dehydrator) and the quality of the product are affected by the manner in which these changes occur.

APPROXIMATION TO ADIABATIC CONDITIONS IN TUNNELS

The kind of food dehydrator called a "tunnel" (see Van Arsdel 1951; Kilpatrick *et al.* 1955) is operated as a quasi-continuous steady-state system in which the wet material is introduced at one end of the drier, is moved progressively in a number of steps through the long enclosure, or tunnel, in which the hot air stream is flowing, and is removed at the other end of the drier. For purposes of analysis and preliminary design we can usefully regard an ideal tunnel operation as truly continuous and truly steady-state.

A further great simplification is accomplished by regarding the drying section of the tunnel as adiabatic in operation. This can be no better than an approximation. Adiabatic operation of a tunnel would be a condition in which the trucks, trays, and other equipment, and the dry substance of the material, all have negligible heat capacity, that heat losses through the walls of the tunnel are negligible, and that the temperature of the wet product is, and remains at, the thermo-dynamic wet-bulb temperature of the air flowing in the tunnel; all of the heat absorbed through the evaporation of water would then be accounted for by the decrease in dry-bulb air temperature. Brown (1943) and Lazar (1944) examined this approximation critically and concluded that for the range of conditions encountered in tunnel dehydrators for vegetables the errors resulting from its use are smaller than the other inherent uncertainties of such systems. This is mainly a consequence of the high initial moisture content of these materials and resulting overwhelming importance of the heat of evaporation in comparison with the sensible heat lost in the outgoing trays, trucks, and dry product. The wet-bulb temperature of air in practical tunnels will usually fall less than 1°F between the "hot end" and the "cool end" of the tunnel. The British Ministry of Food (1946) in its bulletin *Vegetable Dehydration* described the performance of two-stage tunnels in potato dehydration; the fall in wet-bulb temperature through the tunnel was somewhat less than 0.5°F.

APPROXIMATE PROPORTIONALITY BETWEEN AIR TEMPERATURE CHANGE AND CHANGE OF MOISTURE CONTENT

Besides the approximate constancy of wet-bulb temperature, adiabatic conditions imply that the change in temperature of the air between any 2 points along the tunnel is approximately proportional to the change in mean moisture content of the material between the same 2 points. This follows from a simple mass balance on the water transferred from material to air between the two points and the fact, apparent upon inspection of the psychrometric chart, that an adiabatic cooling line—that is, a line of constant (thermodynamic) wet-bulb temperature—is very nearly straight. We can write the following expression for the resulting relation:

$$\Delta t = -1,000 \, z \, \Delta H \qquad (7.2)$$

where

Δt = change in air temperature between two points on an adiabatic cooling line (°F)

ΔH = change in absolute humidity between the same two points (lb)/(lb dry air)

z = nearly constant slope of the lines, and the multiplier 1000 is used to give z a convenient magnitude

Thus z is the decrease in air temperature for an increase of 0.001 in absolute humidity. The negative sign signifies that temperature decreases as humidity increases.

The slope of adiabatic cooling lines changes slightly from point to point on the psychrometric chart. Values of z at four widely separated points are as follows:

Wet-bulb temperature $90°F$
Air temperature $120°$, $z = 4.28°F$
$180°$, $z = 4.35°F$
Wet-bulb temperature $120°F$
Air temperature $140°$, $z = 3.81°F$
$200°$, $z = 3.96°F$

Losses of sensible heat in practical equipment always result in a somewhat greater fall in air temperature than this for a rise of 0.001 in absolute humidity. Many approximate drier calculations are, in fact, made on the assumption that $z = 5°F$.

As stated above, a mass balance on the water in the moist material and in the air at any 2 points along the continuous tunnel equates the amount of water vapor added to the air between those 2 points in a given length of time such as 1 hr with the fall in water content of the material passing through that section of the tunnel in the same length of time:

$$AG(H_2 - H_1) = \text{water vapor added to the air flowing in 1 hr between points}$$
$$\text{1 and 2} \qquad (7.3)$$

where

A	= cross-section area of the tunnel (sq ft)
G	= mass velocity of the air (lb dry air)/(hr) (sq ft cross-section)
H_2 and H_1	= absolute humidities of the air at the two points (lb water vapor)/(lb dry air)

$$\frac{L_0 Sl(W_1 - W_2)}{\theta_R(W_0 + 1)} = \text{weight of water evaporated per hour in section of tunnel between points 1 and 2} \qquad (7.4)$$

where

L_0	= initial load of wet material per square foot of tray surface (lb)/(sq ft)
S	= area of tray surface per foot of tunnel length (sq ft)/(ft)
l	= total length of the tunnel (ft)
W_1 and W_2	= mean moisture contents of material in the tunnel at points 1 and 2 (lb)/(lb dry solids)
θ_R	= total residence time of material in the tunnel (hr)
W_0	= initial moisture content of the material as it is loaded into the tunnel (lb)/(lb dry solids)

Equating the two expressions and rearranging, we have,

$$H_2 - H_1 = \pm \frac{L_0 Sl}{A G \theta_R (W_0 + 1)} (W_1 - W_2) \qquad (7.5)$$

and if we replace $H_2 - H_1$ by its value as given by Equation (7.2) we obtain,

$$t_2 - t_1 = \pm \frac{1,000 z L_0 Sl}{A G \theta_R (W_0 + 1)} (W_1 - W_2) \qquad (7.6)$$

This we might call the "tunnel equation." The plus sign applies before the second member if the tunnel is in counterflow operation (that is, loading at the "cool end" of the tunnel, discharging at the "hot end"), while the minus sign applies if the tunnel is in parallel or concurrent flow operation ("hot end" loading). If we are satisfied to use the approximate value $z = 5$ for the relation between temperature fall and humidity rise the equation becomes:

$$t_2 - t_1 = \pm \frac{5,000 L_0 Sl}{A G \theta_R (W_0 + 1)} (W_1 - W_2) \qquad (7.7)$$

The coefficient of $W_1 - W_2$ in the right-hand member is constant under this assumption, and we can collect all the terms into a single constant, the "tunnel constant,"

$$t_2 - t_1 = \pm b(W_1 - W_2) \qquad (7.8)$$

where
$$b = \frac{5,000 L_0 Sl}{A G \theta_R (W_0 + 1)}$$

Equations (7.2) through (7.8) can easily be transformed so as to express the approximate proportionality between rise in air humidity and fall in air temperature in terms of the rate of supply of wet material to the tunnel or the rate of output of dry material from it, instead of the total residence time of material in the tunnel, θ_R. Also by slight modification of some of the terms in these equations they can be made to apply directly to continuous conveyor dehydrators.

ESTIMATION OF THE DRYING CAPACITY OR CAPABILITY OF A DRIER

Estimation of the output of dry product that can be obtained from a drier, expressed in terms of pounds per hour, tons per 24-hr day, or the like, involves essentially the integration of a drying rate varying with respect to time, between the limits of an initial high ingoing moisture content and a lower outgoing moisture content. Of course the design and construction of the drier itself and the operation of its auxiliary equipment will fix an upper limit to the total amount of evaporation it can accomplish in a given period of time. Within that limitation, the drier's capability will be set by the drying rates obtainable from the specified wet material between the specified moisture levels.

A theoretical maximum evaporative capacity of an air drier is reached when the cooling of the air stream due to the evaporation reduces its temperature to the wet-bulb temperature so that the air is saturated. In practice substantially less evaporation will ever be permitted, so that the exit air can still produce a reasonably good drying rate by evaporation of additional moisture. If this precaution is not taken and the drier is allowed to be overloaded with wet incoming material, the drying it will accomplish drops almost to zero, the time of exposure becomes very long, and the quality of the outgoing product may be ruined; the warm, moist material may then even mold. It must also be remembered that under normal conditions the material in an air drier will be heavily contaminated with air-borne bacteria, yeasts, and molds, not to mention dust, soot, or other atmospheric pollutants.

Now if the mean moisture content of the wet material entering the drier is W_0 lb moisture per pound dry solids, and that of the "dried" material leaving the drier is W_f lb per pound dry solids, then the amount of evaporation performed in this drier is $W_0 - W_f$ lb per lb dry solids handled. The carrier of wet material (trays or belt or mesh conveyor) enters the drier with a load of L lb dry solids per hour. If conditions are such that solids are neither added nor lost in the drier (so that the "accumulation" is equal to zero), the "dried" material leaves the drier at the same rate, L lb dry solids per hour. Then the total rate of evaporation in this drier is $L (W_0 - W_f)$ lb per hr, and this is the "capacity" of the drier under these conditions. It can also be expressed in terms of weight of wet ingoing material handled per hour, tons of wet material per 24-hr day, pounds of "dried" material per day, or other appropriate unit, as desired.

DRYING TIME BY ANALOGUE EXPERIMENTATION

Analogue experimentation simply consists in setting up small-scale controllable drying equipment in which all the circumstances of a practical drying operation are duplicated, insofar as possible, in everything but scale; drying time is then determined directly from the results of that operation. In other words, this is a pilot-scale simulation of practical conditions. The method could conceivably be applied to investigations of any type of drying whatever, and, in fact, it is the only satisfactory way to test systems which, although simple enough to operate, are hopelessly complicated in theory. This is the case, for example, with continuous conveyor-type through-flow dehydrators and belt-trough driers. On the other hand, small-scale simulation of spray drying is not fully satisfactory because the operation can only be duplicated in a full-scale drying chamber.

Analogue simulation of tunnel dehydration, particularly of vegetables, has been studied more extensively than most other design procedures. A well-designed experimental "cabinet" drier (i.e., a drier in which a suitable sample of the wet material is disposed as it would be in the full-scale drier, but is dried as a stationary batch under controlled conditions of air temperature, humidity, and velocity) is required for this purpose.

Broughton and Mickley (1953) describe an especially thorough study of the analogue procedure, illustrated by the experimental drying of soap and wet insulating board. The drier is specially equipped with thermocouples embedded in the stock being dried, so that material temperature, as well as air temperature, can be monitored continuously, along with the net weight of material on the tray. In advance of the experiment general heat- and mass-balance equations are set up, incorporating the specified conditions of air temperature, humidity, and mass velocity so as to relate the change of moisture content of the sample at any time to the corresponding change of air temperature in the hypothetical tunnel drier. Equation (7.6), it will be remembered, is a somewhat simplified form of a similar balance. Now a short time after the beginning of the experiment the weight and temperature of the sample are measured. Air temperature is immediately changed by the amount prescribed by the balance equation. Drying is continued in this way, temperature of the air being changed in increments as required by the change in weight of the sample. Then the drying time for that material under the combination of conditions prescribed is given directly by the time required in the experimental drier for the sample to reach the specified final moisture content (or sample weight).

A somewhat simpler procedure, involving no attempt to include control of stock temperature in the analogue setup, and probably suffering somewhat in faithfulness of reproduction of full-scale conditions on that account, has been described by Van Arsdel (1951). The procedure can be described most clearly by means of an example. Suppose that carrot dice are to be dehydrated in a counterflow truck-and-tray tunnel (assumed continuous in operation) which will hold 10 truckloads, each with a tray area of 540 sq ft. The prepared carrot dice, with an initial moisture content of $W_0 = 8.40$, are to be spread on metal-mesh trays at a loading of 2 lb per sq ft. The circulating fan is to supply 40,000 cfm of air at 160°F and a wet-bulb temperature of 95°F to the hot end of this tunnel. The product is to be dried to a final moisture content of 5%, moist basis ($W_f = 0.053$). We wish to carry out the drying experiments that will be needed to determine drying time under these conditions and hence the output capacity and other performance characteristics of the tunnel.

First we need to know what air velocity to use in the drying tests; a fairly rough approximation will suffice. The temperature at the cool, or loading, end of the tunnel may be expected to be perhaps 110°F; air flow at that temperature should be 37,000 cfm (application of Charles' law). Now if the free cross-section area around the trucks and between loaded trays is, say, 33 sq ft, the mean air velocity over the trays in the cool end of the tunnel should be 1,120 fpm.

Next, we find from the psychrometric chart that the absolute humidity of air at 160° and wet-bulb temperature 95° is 0.0210 and its humid volume is

16.2 cu ft per lb of dry air. Then the mass air flow through the tunnel is 2465 lb of dry air per minute.

Our immediate object is to lay out a schedule of change for the air temperature in the test run that will simulate the temperature change in the tunnel. However, we do not yet know what retention time in the tunnel will suffice to bring mean moisture content of the product down to 5%. We can find out by making a minimum of 2, and preferably 3, test drying experiments which will bracket the true unknown figure. This can be accomplished as follows:

We know from the form of Equation (7.6) or (7.8) that if the air temperature at points along the tunnel is plotted on coordinate paper against the mean moisture content of the product at the same points a straight line will result, within the accuracy of the simplifying assumptions made in the preceding section. We shall therefore set up a diagram like Fig. 7.10, in which air tempera-

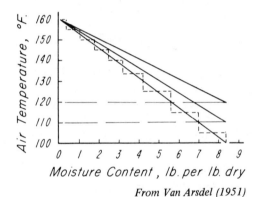

From Van Arsdel (1951)

FIG. 7.10. DIAGRAM USED FOR SCHEDULING EXPERIMEN-
TAL DRYING RUN

ture is the ordinate, mean moisture content the abscissa. We know the coordinates at one end of the line—temperature 160°F, moisture content 0.053—and the moisture content, 8.40, but not the temperature at the other end. We assume 3 different temperatures, say 100°, 110°, and 120°F, in the expected range of this unknown temperature, and draw the 3 corresponding straight lines. Each of these lines maps a schedule for carrying out 1 of the 3 test runs; the temperature in the experimental cabinet will start at, say, 100°, and will be raised in small increments in accordance with the mean moisture content of the material on the tray, as estimated from frequent weighings of the tray. The wet-bulb temperature of the air in the test drier will be maintained unchanged at 95°F during the entire experiment (for a closer approximation, wet-bulb temperature can also be changed from time to time to correspond to known heat losses rather than adiabatic operation). Practically, it is unnecessary to make the weighings and adjustments of temperature continuously; the desired straight-line relationship can be closely approximated in a series of small steps, as shown in one of the lines in Fig. 7.10.

The 3 test runs will give us 3 different values of the time required to dry the product to a moisture content of 5%. The lower the wet-end temperature we have chosen, the longer this time will be. Now the three drying times will be plotted, as in Fig. 7.11, against the wet-end air temperature. On the same

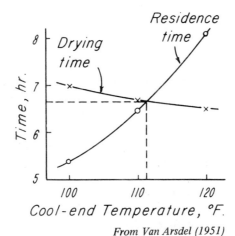

From Van Arsdel (1951)

FIG. 7.11. ESTIMATION OF DRYING TIME FOR SPECIFIED
TUNNEL CONDITIONS

diagram we shall plot another curve which we take from the tunnel equation, Equation (7.6), to show the relation of residence time to wet-end air temperature in this tunnel:

$$t' - t'' = \frac{1,000zL_0Sl}{AG\theta_R(W_0 + 1)} (W_0 - W_f) \tag{7.9}$$

If we insert the numerical values of our example this reduces to:

$$160 - t'' = \frac{1,000 \times 5 \times 2 \times 5,400}{2,465 \times 60 \times 9.40\theta_R} (8.40 - 0.053)$$

$$= \frac{323}{\theta_R}$$

For a wet-end air temperature of $100°$ this gives a residence time of 5.38 hr; for $110°$, 6.46 hr; and for $120°$, 8.07 hr. These are the points which determine the residence-time curve on Fig. 7.11.

Now the point at which the drying-time and residence-time curves intersect gives us the values we have been seeking, namely, a cool-end temperature of $112°F$ and a time of 6.65 hr. Retention of the material in the tunnel for that length of time (that is, inserting a freshly loaded truck about every 40 min and withdrawing a dry one at the same time) will, we are predicting, just dry it to a mean moisture content of 5%. The 24-hr output of dry product should be

$$\frac{5400 \times 2 \times 1.053 \times 24}{9.40 \times 6.65} = 4375 \text{ lb}$$

The same kind of procedure can be used to predict the behavior of a two-stage tunnel, such as the widely used combination of a parallel flow first stage and a counterflow finishing stage. A more elaborate series of test runs must be made, however, because the moisture content of the product at the point of change-over from first to second stage will not be known in advance. In practice, because of the inevitable variability of experimental raw materials and conditions in predrying steps, it may be necessary to replicate experimental runs and apply the *mean* results to the graphical determination of drying time. In addition, of course, results should be discounted enough to allow for the expected imperfections of design and operation of practical dehydrators. Only experience can give any guidance in this. The usual causes of poorer performance than expected are uneven distribution of hot air flowing through the tunnel, careless loading and careless stacking of trays, and major air leaks at the high-pressure end of the tunnel.

The experimental procedure used to secure an analogue prediction of drying time in a continuous conveyor-type through-flow dehydrator must, of course, be quite different from the method just described. A through-flow experimental drier will be used. The perforated support will be similar to the perforated conveyor. The volume of air flow per square foot of supporting surface will be made equal to that expected in the full-scale drier; the direction of air flow must be reversible, and the temperature and humidity of the air be controllable by the operator. Temperature and humidity conditions must be chosen in advance for each of 3 or 4 segments of a single test, corresponding to the 3 or 4 separately controllable sections of the conveyor dehydrator. These drying conditions will be kept constant during each segment. The time of exposure in each segment will be made equal to the length of time the product will remain in that section of the continuous conveyor for some one chosen value of the rate of travel of the conveyor. If, as is sometimes done, the product is to be dumped from one conveyor onto a slower moving one, a similar mixing and respreading will be done in the experimental unit. Ordinarily 3 such runs will be required, corresponding to 3 different rates of conveyor travel. When the moisture contents of the products of the experimental runs have been determined, the proper conveyor speed (and therefore drying time and evaporative capacity) can be estimated by a graphical interpolation process. Obviously a considerable number of test runs must be made if various combinations of temperature and humidity in the different sections of the drier are to be tried; for example, to find the combination which gives the highest production of acceptable dry product.

DRYING TIME FROM DRYING RATES DETERMINED
UNDER CONSTANT CONDITIONS

The "Point-Condition" Method

The classical method of estimating drying time, as described by Lewis (1921) and Walker *et al.* (1937), assumes that drying rates determined by means of a series of experiments at a number of different constant drying conditions can simply be integrated over the specified sequence of changing conditions.

$$\theta = \frac{1}{A_0} \int_{W_1}^{W_2} \frac{-dW}{(dW/A\,d\theta)} \qquad (7.10)$$

This has been known as the "point-condition" method of solution. It has been shown to give satisfactory agreement with experience in the drying of many nonhygroscopic materials. Broughton and Mickley (1953) comment, however, that the conditions for its applicability are so stringent that it has not been very widely useful.

Integration of Drying Rate Data

Direct integration of drying rates, as in Equation (7.10), is theoretically allowable only if the rate of drying of a moist body is strictly determined by the value of its mean moisture content at any instant, and not at all by the previous drying history. This can never be exactly true in any actual case; the drying rate of a moist body at any instant is determined by the surrounding air conditions and the temperature and moisture content at the *surface* of the body, not the mean. In turn, the surface moisture content and temperature reflect the internal gradients which have become established in the course of all that has gone before. Extensive studies of the drying rates of several vegetables have shown that this effect of previous drying history is substantial and must be taken into account. It is automatically eliminated as a factor, of course, in the analogue procedures described above.

Development of the "point-condition" method for taking account of the change in drying conditions encountered by a piece of wet material in its progress through a tunnel is simple and straightforward if the drying rate is a linear or other simple function of mean moisture content and air temperature and humidity. Badger and McCabe (1936) and Walker *et al.* (1937) gave the integrated forms of Equation (7.10) for adiabatic counterflow and parallel-flow driers, based on the assumptions, first that in the initial constant-rate phase the rate is proportional to $H_s - H$ (the difference between the air humidity and saturation humidity at the same wet-bulb temperature), and second, that in the entire falling-rate phase the resistance to surface evaporation is the controlling factor and the rate is proportional to the remaining "free" moisture content, $W - W_e$. However, the actual drying behavior of important food materials is so far from conformance with these or any other very simple relationships that the analytical integration of Equation (7.10) has little practical interest.

Nomographic Estimation of Drying Time

If a material whose drying characteristics are not very completely known is to be dried, use of one of the analogue experimental procedures described above is the only satisfactory recourse, laborious though it may be. However, there is a large and important class of drying problems in which the specific behavior of a particular raw material is relatively unimportant; this includes such questions as determining the preferable arrangement of a dehydrator (counterflow, parallel-flow, or multiple-stage), the optimum proportion of air recirculation in a tunnel, the relation between tray loading and tunnel drying capacity, and the optimum proportion between lengths of primary and secondary stages of a two-stage tunnel. Solution of such problems as these is best attacked through application of generalized drying rate relations which can typify the drying behavior of broad classes of materials.

Guillou (1942) showed that the drying rate of prunes in a tunnel dehydrator, down to the usual "dried fruit" moisture level of about 17%, is proportional at all times to the "free" moisture content; the empirically determined constant contains the factors of air temperature, humidity, and velocity, and the size of the fruit. He, and later Perry (1944) and Perry *et al.* (1946) applied the generalized relation to the design of a dehydrator in which an optimum balance is found between heat costs and combined power, labor, and capital costs.

A group of investigators at the USDA Western Regional Research Laboratory (Brown and Kilpatrick 1943; Van Arsdel 1942, 1943B, 1951; Brown 1943, 1951; Brown and Van Arsdel 1944, 1951; Brown and Lazar 1944, 1951; Lazar *et al.* 1944, 1951; Lazar and Brown 1945, 1947, 1951; and Van Arsdel *et al.*, 1947, 1951), analyzed various ways of correlating and reporting their extensive studies of the drying rates of white potato in riced, strip, and half-dice forms, carrot pieces, shredded cabbage, onion slices, sweet corn, and sweet potato strips. Empirical equations proved to be impractical. The results were eventually published by USDA as a series of nomographic charts under the designation, *Drying Rate Nomograph–AIC-31.* They were numbered I through VIII.

In each case at least two separate charts were drawn for each material—one giving the time required to dry from the initial moisture content, W_0, down to an intermediate value ranging from $W = 0.10$ to 0.25, and the other giving the additional time required to bring the moisture content from that intermediate level to a final level ranging from 0.02 for cabbage to 0.06 for corn and sweet potatoes. The charts are thus designed to read in drying times directly, instead of proceeding by way of integration of drying rates; in fact, the authors counsel caution in the use of the charts to compute drying rates. For example, the nomographic solution exhibits a perceptible discontinuity of drying *rate* at the point marking passage from the high-moisture chart to the low-moisture chart, but the slight discontinuity in the slope of the drying curve is negligible in the estimation of total drying time.

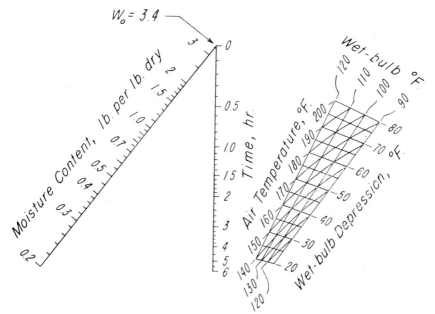

FIG. 7.12. NOMOGRAPH FOR ESTIMATING DRYING TIME OF POTATO HALF-DICE—
HIGH MOISTURE SEGMENT

Figure 7.12 illustrates the type of chart used in these nomographs. The one shown here on a reduced scale gives an estimate of the drying time of potato half-dice from an initial moisture content of $W_0 = 3.4$ to a moisture content of 0.20 at the end of the high-moisture segment of the estimate. The other conditions are a tray-loading of 1.5 lb per sq ft (metal-grid trays), and air velocity of 800 fpm temperatures in the range of 110°-200°F, and wet-bulb temperature depressions in the range of 20°-80°F. Alignment of a point in the temperature network on the right of the chart with any point on the left-hand scale of moisture contents gives a time, in hours, at the intersection with the center scale. A second alignment chart then provides the value of a multiplying factor, which converts the time required under the conditions specified above to the time required at some other air velocity in the range of 400-1200 fpm, and some other tray loading in the range of 0.5-2.5 lb per sq ft. A third chart supplies a drying time from $W = 0.20$ to the final moisture content, W_f, for temperatures from 100° to 170°F and wet-bulb temperatures from 80° to to 110°F. A final nomograph supplies a value for the length of time required to dry to the "reference value" of W_0, namely 3.4, from any higher initial value that may have been found in a different raw material.

A partial test of the validity of the procedure was made by P. W. Kilpatrick, of the USDA Western Regional Research Laboratory, by conducting a long series of experimental runs with shredded cabbage as the raw material, simulating a wide range of counterflow tunnel operating conditions. Results summarized in an unpublished report dated Jan. 21, 1946, indicated that nomographic predictions of drying time are adequately conservative. For example, when the tray-loading was 1.5 lb per sq ft the experimental drying time down to a final moisture content of 0.05 under counterflow temperature conditions was 7.7 ± 0.2 hr, whereas the nomographic solution gave a time of 7.9 hr.

The nomographic charts of the *AIC-31* series, being based upon tray drying experiments, are much more helpful in the design and operation of practical dehydrators than in throwing light on the theory of drying. They lend themselves readily to investigation of the effects of any of the operating conditions upon the performance of a tunnel dehydrator. The typical procedure is closely similar to that described above for analogue simulation of tunnel drying. A set of tunnel operating conditions (tunnel arrangement, total tray surface, unit tray-loading, total air flow, hot-end air temperature, and wet-bulb temperature) and initial material moisture content are combined with 3 values of cool-end air temperature to give 3 straight lines relating air temperature to mean moisture content, as in Fig. 7.10. Each of these lines is replaced by a series of small steps (for example, 5° change in air temperature), as suggested in the Figure. The nomograph is then applied to obtain the successive small segments of drying time, which are summed to give three values of total drying time. The latter are plotted against cool-end air temperature, as in Fig. 7.11. A plot of residence time versus cool-end temperature on the same chart then intersects with the drying-time curve at a point which gives the required solution to the problem.

One serious drawback exists in applying the *AIC-31* nomographs to practical equipment design. Seemingly minor differences in the pretreatment or physical condition of the wet material may have entirely disproportionate effects on drying rates. There has been no tested way to allow for these effects or to estimate their amount.

BIBLIOGRAPHY

BADGER, W. L., and MCCABE, W. L. 1936. Elements of Chemical Engineering, 2nd Edition. McGraw-Hill Book Co., New York.
BRITISH MINISTRY of FOOD. 1946. Vegetable Dehydration. H.M. Stationery Office, London.
BROUGHTON, D. B., and MICKLEY, H. S. 1953. Design of full-scale continuous tunnel driers. Chem. Eng. Progr. *49*, 319–324.
BROWN, A. H. 1943, 1951. Drying rate nomographs. II. Blanched sweet corn. USDA Bur. Circ. *AIC-31-II.*
BROWN, A. H. 1944, 1951. Drying rate nomographs. IV. Shredded cabbage. USDA Bur. Circ. *AIC-31-IV.*
BROWN, A. H., and KILPATRICK, P. W. 1943. Drying characteristics of vegetables— riced potatoes. Trans. Am. Soc. Mech. Engrs. *65*, 837–842.
BROWN, A. H., and LAZAR, M. E. 1944, 1951. Drying rate nomographs. V. Onion slices. USDA Bur. Circ. *AIC-31-V.*
BROWN, A. H., and VAN ARSDEL, W. B. 1944, 1951. Drying rate nomographs. III. White potato strips—vertical air flow. USDA Bur. Circ. *AIC-31-III.*

CARRIER, W. H. 1921. The theory of atmospheric evaporation, with special reference to compartment driers. Ind. Eng. Chem. *18*, 432–438.

CHANCE, E. M., NOEL, W. A., and PEASE, V. A. 1951. Preservation of fruits and vegetables by commercial dehydration. USDA Circ. *619*.

CULPEPPER, C. W., and MOON, W. H. 1937. Factors affecting the rate of drying of Kieffer pears. USDA Tech. Bull. *592*.

EDE, A. J. 1958. Some physical data concerning the drying potato strips. *In* Fundamental Aspects of the Dehydration of Foodstuffs. Soc. Chem. Ind. (London) 136–142.

EDE, A. J., and HALES, K. C. 1948. The physics of drying in heated air, with special reference to fruit and vegetables. G. Brit. Dept. Sci. Ind. Res., Food Invest. Spec. Rept. *53*.

EDE, A. J., and PARTRIDGE, S. M. 1943. Dried meat. IV. The effect of some physical factors on the rate of drying of minced meat in heated air. J. Soc. Chem. Ind. *62*, 194–200.

EIDT, C. C. 1938. Principles and methods involved in dehydration of apples. Can. Dept. Agr. Tech. Bull. *18*.

GANE, R. 1943. The activity of water in dried foodstuffs; water content as a function of humidity and temperature. *In* Dehydration. U.K. Progr. Rept. (London) Sec. X, Part 1.

GOUILLOU, R. 1942. Development of a fruit dehydration design. Agr. Eng. *23*, 313–316.

HEISS, R. 1968. Stability and Sorption Behavior of Low-moisture Foods. Springer-Verlag, Berling. (German)

JASON, A. C. 1958. A study of evaporation and diffusion processes in the drying of fish muscle. *In* Fundamental Aspects of the Dehydration of Foodstuffs. Soc. Chem. Ind. (London) 103–125.

KILPATRICK, P. W., LOWE, E., and VAN ARSDEL, W. B. 1955. Tunnel dehydrators for fruits and vegetables. Advan. Food Res. *6*, 314–369. Academic Press, New York.

KRISCHER, O. 1956. The Scientific Fundamentals of Drying Technology, 1st Edition. Springer-Verlag, Berlin-Göttingen-Heidelberg. (German)

KRISCHER, O. 1963. Drying Technology, 2nd Edition, Vol. 1, The Scientific Fundamentals of Drying Technology. Springer-Verlag, Berling-Göttingen-Heidelberg. (German)

KRISCHER, O., and KRÖLL, K. 1956, 1959. Drying Technology, Vol. 1, The Scientific Fundamentals of Drying Technology (Krischer, 1956). Drying Technology, Vol. 2, Driers and Drying Processes (Kroll, 1959). Springer-Verlag, Berlin-Göttingen-Heidelberg. (German)

LAZAR, M. E. 1944. Deviations from adiabaticity in tunnel dehydrators. USDA Western Regional Res. Lab. Unpublished Rept.

LAZAR, M. E., and BROWN, A. H. 1945, 1947, 1951. Drying rate nomographs. VII. White potato half-cubes. USDA Bur. Circ. *AIC-31-VII*.

LAZAR, M. E., and BROWN, A. H. 1947, 1951. Drying rate nomographs. VIII. Carrot pieces. USDA Bur. Circ. *AIC-31-VIII*.

LAZAR, M. E., KILPATRICK, P. W., and BROWN, A. H. 1944, 1951. Drying rate nomographs. VI. Sweet potato strips. USDA Bur. Circ. *AIC-31-VI*.

LEWIS, W. K. 1921. The rate of drying of solid materials. Ind. Eng. Chem. *13*, 427–432.

MAKOWER, B., CHASTAIN, S. M., and NIELSEN, E. 1946. Moisture determination in dehydrated vegetables. Vacuum oven method. Ind. Eng. Chem. *38*, 725–731.

PERRY, R. L. 1944. Heat and vapor transfer in the dehydration of prunes. Trans. Am. Soc. Mech. Engrs. *66*, 447–456.

PERRY, R. L. et al. 1946. Fruit dehydration. I. Principles and equipment. Calif. Agr. Expt. Sta. Bull. *698*.

SHERWOOD, T. K. 1929. The drying of solids. Ind. Eng. Chem. *21*, I, 12–16; II, 976–980.

SHERWOOD, T. K. 1930. The drying of solids. III. Mechanism of the drying of pulp and paper. Ind. Eng. Chem. *22*, 132–136.

SHERWOOD, T. K. 1931. Application of theoretical diffusion equations to the drying of solids. Trans. Am. Inst. Chem. Engrs. *27*, 190–200.

SHERWOOD, T. K. 1932. The drying of solids. IV. Application of diffusion equations. Ind. Eng. Chem. *24*, 307–310.

SHERWOOD, T. K. 1936. The air drying of solids. Trans. Am. Inst. Chem. Engrs. *32*, 150–168.

SHERWOOD, T. K., and COMINGS, E. W. 1932. The drying of solids. Trans. Am. Inst. Chem. Engrs. *28*, 118–133.

SHERWOOD, T. K., and COMINGS, E. W. 1933. The drying of solids. V. Mechanism of drying of clays. Ind. Eng. Chem. *25*, 311–316.

STITT, F. 1958. Moisture equilibrium and the determination of water content of dehydrated foods. *In* Fundamental Aspects of the Dehydration of Foodstuffs. Soc. Chem. Ind. (London) 67–88.

USDA. 1944. Vegetable and Fruit Dehydration–A Manual for Plant Operators. USDA Misc. Publ. *540.*

VAN ARSDEL, W. B. 1942. Tunnel dehydrators and their use in vegetable dehydration. I. Factors governing the choice of a dehydrator, and types of tunnels. Food Inds. *14*, No. 10, 43–46, 106; II. Physical laws of dehydrator operation. *Ibid. 14*, No. 11, 47–50, 103; III. Operating characteristics of tunnels. *Ibid. 14*, No. 12, 47–50, 108–109.

VAN ARSDEL, W. B. 1943A. Tray and tunnel drying methods and equipment. Proc. Inst. Food Technologists *1943*, 45–51.

VAN ARSDEL, W. B. 1943B. Some engineering problems of the new vegetable dehydration industry. Heating, Piping, Air Conditioning, ASHVE Sec. *15*, No. 3, 157–160.

VAN ARSDEL, W. B. 1947. Approximate diffusion calculations for the falling-rate phase of drying. Chem. Eng. Progr. *43*, 13–24. Also USDA Bur. Circ. *AIC-152.*

VAN ARSDEL, W. B. 1951. Principles of the drying process, with special reference to vegetable dehydration. USDA Bur. Circ. *AIC-300.*

VAN ARSDEL, W. B., BROWN, A. H., and LAZAR, M. E. 1947, 1951. Drying rate nomographs. I. Riced white potatoes. USDA Bur. Circ. *AIC-31-I.*

WALKER, W. H., LEWIS, W. K., MCADAMS, W. H., and GILLILAND, E. R. 1937. Principles of Chemical Engineering, 3rd Edition. McGraw-Hill Book Co., New York.

CHAPTER 8

Edward J. Barta
M. E. Lazar
C. L. Rasmussen

Dehydration Plant Operations

INTRODUCTION

The successful dehydration of any food commodity is the ultimate result of the consistent consideration of many cumulative factors. After the initial basic conception it is necessary to investigate, solve and evaluate all technological, economical, and environmental aspects essential to the commercial production of the final product. Subsequently it is mandatory to continuously review, refine, and, if necessary, change plant operations in conformity with advancing technology.

This chapter is concerned primarily with a consideration of dehydration plant operations, although matters that apply generally to all food manufacturing are included. Operations which characterize specific food commodities are presented in the corresponding chapters in Vol. 2—e.g., onions, potatoes, tea, coffee, soups, etc.

Appropriate sections of this chapter discuss the subjects of raw materials; plant location; plant layout and construction; preparation, drying, and post-drying operations; raw material, in-plant, and product quality control; plant sanitation; economic considerations; and waste and pollution control. The drying steps are outlined more specifically in the chapters pertaining to the various commodities in Vol. 2, since a total consideration of all facets of the above is beyond the intended purpose of this chapter. For more detailed information attention is invited to the chapter Bibliography.

RAW MATERIAL SUPPLY

Raw Material Requirements

In a successful dehydration operation, the prime importance of an adequate supply of raw material permits no alternatives to proper plant location. The plant must be located where suitable raw material can be made available. Too often this factor has not been given proper attention in the establishment of a dehydration plant, and the result has been failure. Among the factors that can be cited as contributing to such failures are unsuitability of raw material for dehydration, poor production and harvesting practices, insufficient or irregular supply of raw material delivered to the dehydration plant, excessive costs of hauling and handling, high prices often resulting from fresh market competition, high raw material production costs, disagreement between growers and plant operators about terms of sales, and poor procurement practices of the operators.

The quality of raw material determines or limits the quality of the end product; affects to a large extent the costs of peeling, trimming, and inspecting; and greatly influences the yield of product from a given input of raw material, and, in turn, product cost. Quality and price must be considered together in raw material procurement. Even though one lot of raw material may cost more per pound than another, because of its better quality the costlier lot may require less processing and provide greater yield so that the total production cost per pound of finished product may actually be less than that for the other lot. Thus, the buyer must carefully evaluate both price and quality and determine which combination of the two will give the best final product at lowest cost.

The suitability of a potential raw material supply should be judged in light of the following factors:

Variety.—A variety or grade of raw material must be used that will yield a dehydrated product having the necessary quality characteristics after reconstitution. Some varieties are better than others in this respect, and one variety may grow better in one location than in another. Generally, dehydration plants are located where raw material is best for dehydration and available at the lowest possible price. Thus, Idaho has many potato plants and California many onion plants. The prospective dehydrator must ascertain if raw material available in a proposed area is of a proved variety for dehydration and grown under conditions proper for that variety.

Overall Shrinkage Ratios, Yields, and Costs.—The ratio of the weight of incoming raw material to the weight of finished product ready for packaging is called the overall shrinkage ratio. Typical values of this ratio for a number of important vegetables are listed in Appendix C, Tables A.2 and A.3. The higher the ratio for a given product, the greater will be the unit cost of the dried product. Naturally, low shrinkage ratios are to be desired, consonant with the limitations of the particular vegetable or fruit. Factors important in determining overall shrinkage ratios include: (1) moisture content of raw material; (2) peel, cores, rots, bruises, deep eyes, outer leaves, and other undesirable material that must be removed and discarded; (3) size and shape of raw material (small or irregular shapes have greater peeling, trimming, sizing, and inspection losses); (4) rejects for poor color, odor, and composition; and (5) rejects of dried material smaller than acceptable minimum screen size—fines, for example.

The overall raw material yield is simply expressed as the ratio of output to input (Rasmussen 1967). Evaluation of the ratio is useful for (1) obtaining a measure of the operating efficiency by relating actual operations to the theoretical, (2) considering the influence of new or modified procedures, or the substitution of other raw material sources, on the product yield and the raw material cost.

The mathematics involved are not complex. However, difficulty may be encountered in making yield and other calculations due to change in the moisture level. In dehydration and other food concentration processes, the water component is removed but the solids component remains essentially the same. The solids content should therefore be the basis of calculations. Complications arise due to losses encountered in preparation (peeling, etc.), in processing (leaching, spillage, etc.), and in product improvement (rejects, fines, etc.); all of these can be accounted for by a loss factor. What remains is the actual recovery. The yield of finished product as a percentage of entering raw material is expressed by the following equations:

$$Y_f = \frac{Y_p S_r}{S_f} \tag{8.1}$$

$$Y_f = \frac{Y_p S_r R}{S_f \, 100} \tag{8.2}$$

$$R = \frac{Y_f S_f \, 100}{Y_p S_r} \tag{8.3}$$

where

Y_f = yield finished product, % (quantity actually packaged)
Y_p = yield prepared raw material, % (after peeling, blanching, etc.)
R = recovery of solids, % (accounts for spillage, leaching, product rejects)
S_r = solid content of original raw material, %
S_f = solid content of product, %

The raw material cost per pound of finished product involves a consideration of the price of the raw material as delivered to the preparation line, the raw material yield, the solid contents of the raw material, the solids content of the finished product and the recovery factor. The cost may be calculated from the following expressions:

$$C = \frac{100 \, P}{Y_f} \tag{8.4}$$

$$C = \frac{100 \, P \, S_f}{Y_p S_r} \tag{8.5}$$

$$C = \frac{10000 \, P \, S_f}{Y_p S_r R} \tag{8.6}$$

where

C = raw material cost per pound finished product, cents or dollars
P = price raw material delivered to preparation line, cents or dollars

Maturity and Freshness.—Raw material must be of the proper maturity for dehydration. Immature vegetables and fruits are generally unsatisfactory in size, type, and amount of solids content, flavor, and texture. Overmature materials may be woody, fibrous, overly soft, or decayed. It is often impractical or uneconomical to harvest only raw material having the desired maturity, so a sizing and grading operation is sometimes necessary. Often this grading is done in the field so that unwanted material is not hauled into the plant.

Cultural and Harvesting Practices.—To achieve the desired quality for dehydration, raw material must be grown, harvested, and handled under proper conditions. Judicious use of irrigation water, fertilizer, and pesticides, as well as careful harvesting, curing, storing, and hauling procedures are essential. Excessive irrigation just before harvest may increase water content of the raw material and adversely affect overall shrinkage ratio. Improper use of pesticides may impart residues that are not sufficiently removed in processing (Hard and Ross 1959; Joslyn and Heid 1963); flavor may be affected; but more important, the residue may be harmful to consumers and may render the product liable to seizure by health authorities. Furthermore, residue tolerances as established by Federal Food and Drug regulations are becoming even more restrictive as to both type and allowable concentration. Quality is preserved by keeping fruits and vegetables dry after harvest, avoiding mechanical injury, and holding at proper temperature and humidity. Storing the raw commodity is discussed later in this chapter.

Harvest Season.—A growing area with a long harvest season is to be preferred to extend processing season and minimize necessity for prolonged raw material storage. Fruits and vegetables, such as apples, potatoes, sweet potatoes, and onions can be held in storage for several months if necessary, and varieties that store well are required. To ensure continuous plant operation, storage for only moderate periods, a few days to several weeks, is necessary for most raw materials.

To extend the period of raw material availability, two or more different varieties of vegetables can be planted with differing growing seasons and maturity dates. Staggering planting dates over the total allowable planting time also extends the processing season. In areas where the topography permits, vegetables can be planted at different elevations so as to mature over a longer period of time.

Raw Material Handling and Storage.—Sacks, crates, baskets, and barrels previously used for hauling produce to plants or storage are being replaced in many areas by bulk handling in large tote boxes, trailers, or trucks. While use of bulk containers greatly reduces handling costs, more bruising may occur. In most cases, however, careful bulk handling has proved economical.

Handling and storing must be done under conditions that preserve the fresh quality of raw material. Several basic precautions should be observed: (1) contamination from dirt and other debris, insects, rodents, microorganisms, and moisture must be avoided; (2) damage to tissue by bruising, cutting, and abrasion must be prevented; and (3) proper storage temperatures, humidity, air circulation, and light exposure must be provided; physical appearance and moisture content are affected by the storage conditions and important changes can occur in chemical composition and nutritive value.

Importance of Raw Material with Respect to Plant Location.—The general area of plant location is usually determined by raw material availability. Quality of the dehydrated product and unit costs of operation are largely dependent upon the quality, grade, solids content, and cost of raw material. These quality and cost aspects of raw material apply not only to its condition at time of harvest, but also to its condition as it is fed to the preparation line. The requirements for a good location include:

(1) Shipping distances for raw material should be at a minimum. Not only will this help reduce damage during shipment, but it will reduce costs. Dehydrated products from most fruits and vegetables weigh only $1/20$ to $1/3$ as much as the raw material received. Location of plant near raw material supply, therefore, effects minimum overall cost of hauling the commodity from farm to ultimate user. Furthermore, the dehydrated product needs no refrigeration or special handling as do most of the raw materials.

(2) The area under consideration must be able to produce sufficient quantities of raw material so that the usual relationships between supply and demand will not be adversely affected by the requirements of a new processing plant. Areas close to large metropolitan markets should be avoided because their production-distribution setup is usually geared to fresh-market demands.

Techniques of Raw Material Procurement

Two basic methods of raw material procurement are generally used: contracting for future supply, and buying on the open market. Although variations of each are employed, only the two basic types of procurement are discussed below.

Contracting for Future Supply.—Before a crop is planted or harvested, the dehydrator contracts with the grower to accept delivery of all or a specified part of the crop at predetermined prices and under a delivery schedule usually determined by the processor. This method of buying has both advantages and disadvantages, but it is generally considered the most satisfactory way of obtaining raw material for processing. Its success depends upon the integrity of both grower and processor, the skill of the grower in producing raw material of the desired quality, and the financial resources of both parties to the contract. Hence, only growers with established reputations are relied upon to furnish raw material to a processing plant.

A typical grower-processor contract has these advantages to the grower: (1) a sure market or outlet for the crop; (2) a specified price which should yield a satisfactory profit; (3) assistance from the dehydrator in obtaining desired seed, fertilizer, and equipment; (4) assistance in harvesting, if the contract so provides—the dehydrator may arrange for the complete harvest; (5) aid in financing the crop—banks and other credit associations usually welcome reasonable applications for loans from farmers with contracts; and (6) the benefits of processor's research projects on cultural practices and improved varieties or strains.

The dehydrator also benefits from the grower-processor contracts. He is assured of: (1) a raw material supply of desired variety, quality, and quantity delivered according to a schedule designed to meet requirements of the dehydration operation; (2) a fixed price for raw material unaffected by fluctuations of market prices at time of harvest; and (3) a sound basis for planning operations, deliveries of finished products, and financing requirements.

The contract may stipulate that the processor provides necessary seed. The processor then has immediate control of the seed for desired quality and better control of planting schedules to help assure a steady flow of raw material into the dehydration plant.

Grower-processor contracts have some disadvantages, however. In spite of all possible precautions regarding planting time, seed used, and cultural practices, crop yields may vary considerably from those anticipated. Thus, problems may arise as to what disposition is to be made of any excess of crop, or where necessary additional raw material can be obtained if yields are low.

Some growers may be tempted to break their contract, or they may attempt to deliver more or less raw material than is actually grown on land covered by the contract, depending upon whether the contract price is above or below market price at harvest time. The processor should not allow such practices. Careful wording of the contract is necessary to help avoid misunderstandings and to provide means for settling disputes and assessing penalties for failure to comply with terms of the contract.

The following specific points should be covered in a grower-processor contract in addition to the general requirements of valid contracts (USDA 1959):

(1) Variety and source of seed; if seed is furnished by processor, state price charged to grower and terms of payment.

(2) Map showing location of field, with a legal description of property and statement of total number of acres involved.

(3) Date of planting, with or without definite substitute dates, based upon desired harvesting and delivery dates.

(4) Statement setting forth any limitations of amount and time of irrigations, use of fertilizer, and other cultural practices that may affect solids content, quality, and value of crop.

(5) Statement announcing right of processor to inspect fields and sample the commodity.

(6) Establishment of right of processor to finish cultivation, harvest, and delivery, in the event the grower is unable for any reason to do so.

(7) Standards of maturity used to determine harvest time; specify who decides when crop is to be harvested; the grower wants maximum tonnage, which usually means over-maturity; the processor wants top-grade dehydration quality, which usually means harvesting in earlier stages; and to assure proper quality, contracts should be written so that processor, through the field agent, is sole judge as to time and rate of harvest.

(8) Specify who decides method of harvest—in case there are alternate methods.

(9) Statement of weighing procedures, whether to be done by public weighmaster, or to be done at plant.

(10) Point of delivery, whether roadside, field, shipping point, or dehydration plant.

(11) Statement of how inspection and grading are to be done and by whom.

(12) Quality standards (minimum or grades) and allowances or tolerances for dirt, injury to commodity, small sizes, off-grade material, etc.

(13) Minimum and maximum rate of quantities to be delivered to plant.

(14) Price per unit, according to grade, with or without premiums for low-shrinkage commodities, or on average solids content of the fresh commodity; high-solids material, which is preferred for dehydration, should command premium prices.

(15) Responsibility in case of delay and subsequent deterioration of commodities in transit from farm to plant.

(16) Adjustment in case harvest yield greatly exceeds that normally expected or that specified in contract; processor may agree to take all the commodity delivered, but all in excess of a specified amount to be at a reduced price.

(17) Transferability of contract.

(18) Methods for handling disputes.

(19) Penalties for inadequate or nonperformance.

Specimen contracts can be obtained from various associations of growers, canners, and freezers. Some state agricultural colleges and experiment stations can also help with matters of contracting between growers and processors.

Open-Market Purchases.—Open-market purchases may be used to supply all raw material needs of a dehydration plant or to supplement purchases made under contract. This method of procurement probably works best in areas where extremely large quantities of raw commodities are grown. For example, a nearby processor may quite satisfactorily procure his potatoes on the open market in Idaho or Maine after they are harvested, because quantities needed would be only a small fraction of the total supply available in those areas. He can then carefully select his requirements from potatoes in storage, based upon their quality for dehydration. The purchase would, of course, be subject to prevailing market prices.

Except in special cases, open-market purchases may have more disadvantages than advantages. The processor stands to lose more in paying the high prices associated with a small crop than he can possibly gain in paying the lower prices accompanying a large crop. A contract will protect a processor from excessive prices, yet he will doubtless be able to operate satisfactorily if raw material prices drop below contract price at time of harvest.

Another satisfactory source of raw material is the sort-outs from packing house operations. Such raw material may be perfectly sound but be rejected because size, shape, and appearance may not be suitable for fresh market requirements. The quantity required by the processing plant, however, must be small compared with the total supply of raw material if the plant is to depend upon this source for a major portion of its needs. Otherwise, the processor may find that insufficient supplies are available at the desired price if market or supply conditions change.

Sometimes a processor may buy an entire lot of raw material, but use only a portion of it for processing. The lot is graded and the portion grading high in appearance and size is sold at premium prices to the fresh market.

Licensed Inspections

An optional nonregulatory federal-state inspection service is available in nearly all districts which commercially grow fruits and vegetables. This is known as the "Shipping Point Inspection Service." The service of a trained and licensed government inspector can be obtained for a fee for continuous inspection of all raw material coming into the plant. He will inspect according to U.S. standards for grade and size and other specifications in the grower-processor contract. Information about such inspection service and the U.S. standards for fresh fruits and vegetables can be obtained from the Fresh Products Standardization and Inspection Branch, Fruit and Vegetable Division, Consumer and Marketing Service, USDA, Washington, D.C., or a local office of the Agricultural Marketing Service.

PLANT LOCATION

General Requirements

A properly selected plant site must consider all of the cost and revenue factors that relate to the production of the product or products involved. A satisfactory plant location is established by a monetary appraisal of the raw material and market locales; the direct and indirect labor costs; the necessary transportation and storage facilities; all services such as water, power, and sewage; the industrial tax structure; adequate waste disposal; and numerous other considerations of variable significance. Maximum profit over a prolonged period of time is the ultimate goal. Much has been written in trade journals, textbooks, and various governmental and scientific publications about plant location. A thorough search of the literature is well worth the time and effort of the management of any prospective dehydrator (von Allman 1960; Anon. 1956, 1960, 1962B, 1967B; Bierwert and Krone 1955; Burton 1943; Fulton 1964; Gray 1960; Mohlman 1950; Riches and Forbes 1958; Tomb 1952; Torrey 1965; USDA 1959). Points of special importance in dehydration plant location include the following:

(1) Availability of an adequate supply of raw materials; this has already been covered in the preceding section.
(2) Adequate facilities for disposing of solid and liquid wastes and for prevention of nuisance odors.
(3) Ample supply of pure water.
(4) Suitable fuel for operation of the drier, boilers, and heating system; and sufficient electric power for operating blowers, motors, and lighting equipment.
(5) Sufficient and suitable labor for processing, including supervisory staff.
(6) Surroundings free from contamination of all kinds.
(7) Adequate transportation facilities.
(8) Adequate area at plant site for initial needs and for possible future expansion.
(9) Proper climate for proposed dehydration operation.
(10) Proper industrial environment.

(11) State and local ordinances, regulations and restrictions.
(12) Appropriate physical characteristics of the site relative to the proposed operations.
(13) Proximity to similar or related plants.
(14) Community attitude and relationship towards industry.
(15) Industrial and personal tax structure.
(16) Relative cost and profit ranking of potential sites.
(17) Fiscal responsibility of local governments.

The following discussion is not an exhaustive treatment of the factors involved in plant location; mainly, the points of particular concern to dehydration are considered. Dehydrators should make comprehensive surveys of several potential plant locations before final decisions are made.

Waste Disposal

Waste disposal is a problem of major importance; it must be fully solved when considering a new plant and requires continuing consideration in all food-producing facilities. Next to inadequate raw material supply, no other problem can become so serious especially in view of increasing restrictions on all forms of pollution as imposed by federal, state and local regulations. A dehydration plant processing 100 or more tons per day of fruits, vegetables or other raw foods will produce up to 30% of that weight in the form of solid waste from peeling, trimming, coring, sorting, or boning operations, as well as other plant refuse (Anon. 1969A; O'Connell 1957; Hart and McGauhey 1964; Samuel 1965; Ziemba 1960).

Solid Waste Disposal.—In the past it was common practice to haul the accumulated solid waste to land fill and garbage dumps or back to the farms for mulch and fertilizer value. Such practices are no longer considered appropriate because of nuisance and pollution factors. Instead, solid wastes, wherever possible, should be converted to salable products. Some types can be disposed of directly as animal feed; other types may be utilized for the production of yeast, alcohol, starch, pectin, dry feed, and other useful by-products (Jackson 1962). These and other outlets do not necessarily return a profit to the parent plant but they do offer a means of disposal at a lower cost than other methods. The low value of the waste necessitates minimum transportation and handling costs. The by-products recovery plant must be located at or near the dehydration facility. Frequently, several neighboring processing plants can use the same recovery plant with mutual advantage.

Process modification offers a promising approach to the suitable disposal of solid wastes. A task force, organized at the USDA Western Utilization Research and Development Division, working on agricultural pollution evolved plans of action and suggested specific research areas pertaining to the handling of several food processing wastes (Clark 1970; Kohler 1970). "In-field" processing of certain fruits and vegetables has been studied and applied successfully to tomatoes. Advantages of this technological change include (1) the immediate return of the solid waste to the fields, (2) reduction of the quantity of waste, (3) increase in the yield of product, and (4) utilization of wash waters from the field processing system for irrigation purposes.

A mobile pilot plant for the field processing of tomatoes successfully handled mechanically-harvested tomatoes on a continuous basis almost immediately after the harvest. In comparison with normal cannery procedures there was a significant increase in the volume of single strength juice. The product was suitable for transport to a cannery for storage, further concentration, drying, or formulation into sauces, catsup, and other tomato products (Wagner 1970; Schultz et al. 1971; Miers et al. 1971).

Certain solid materials, such as soiled paper, water-soaked cardboard, plastic bags, and the like, do not lend themselves to recovery and cannot be converted into useful products. Then, incineration may be the only economical method of disposal. Burning in open pits and poorly designed incinerators can no longer be tolerated because of pollution by smoke, odors, and fly ash. Today there are available incinerator systems which can be operated efficiently, economically, and without any adverse effect on the environment (Anon. 1969A; Taggart 1967B).

Under certain conditions it may be expedient and most desirable to disintegrate high-moisture fruit and vegetable waste to finely divided pulps and to dispose of the resulting slurry by transfer to the liquid waste system for biological degradation.

Liquid Waste Disposal.—During the preparation of fruits and vegetables for dehydration there are also produced enormous volumes of liquid wastes, frequently to the extent of a million gallons per day. Such wastes are produced in varying proportions at each of the several preparation stages. Their general characteristics vary widely with regard to the nature of the substances in suspension or solution as well as with their concentration as shown by Table 8.1. Specific characteristics are dependent upon the commodity being processed.

TABLE 8.1

CHARACTERIZATION OF LIQUID WASTES FROM A DEHYDRATION PLANT

Source	Quantity	Polluting Nature[1]
Washing or fluming incoming raw material	Large	Low[2]
Peeling and washing	Moderate to large	High[3]
Washing or fluming prepared material	Small to moderate	Very high
Blanching (water)	Small to moderate	Very high
Cleanup wash water	Variable	Variable[3]

[1] Usually measured by BOD (biological oxygen demand) or COD (chemical oxygen demand).
[2] Contains large amounts of soil, other natural contaminants.
[3] May contain chemicals, detergents or bactericides that are harmful to aquatic plant or animal life.

The concentration, while seemingly low, can represent a significant portion of the incoming raw material due to the enormous volumes involved; and, because of the high biological oxygen demand (BOD), can influence subsequent treatment procedures. Waste waters produced by washing or fluming to remove field dirt usually have high inert solids in suspension and low BOD values, while wash and blanch waters from processing are high in organic solids and possess correspondingly high BOD values. Obviously, optimum treatment for removal of the pollutants would differ. For this reason, it is now recommended that the several waste water streams produced in food processing be segregated and held separate for (1) possible multiple usage before treatment, and (2) recombination of the treated effluent streams from the separate intermediate treatment systems for final polishing and ultimate disposition. Several basic methods with numerous variations, improvements, and modifications to meet specific requirements are employed for the treatment and disposal of liquid wastes (Alikonis and Ziemba 1967; Anon. 1969A; Baxter 1962; Bonem 1962; Gill 1963; Samuel 1965; Swanson 1962; Van Heuvelen 1962; Warrick et al. 1959; Rose et al. 1970).

Depending upon its initial characteristics, the waste stream is subjected to a logical sequence of treatments, each of which produces effluents suitable for further improvement or disposal. The stages involved are (1) pretreatment, (2) primary-, (3) secondary-, and (4) tertiary-treatments (Dlouhy and Dahlstrom 1969; Willoughby 1969). The function(s) of each stage are as follows:

Pretreatment.—The purpose of this treatment is to remove from the waste water stream all of the larger sized matter such as leaves, stems, scraps, culls, etc. Usually, such material is larger than 10 mesh and too large for rapid biological oxidation. Removal is readily accomplished by means of continuous self-cleaning screens. Liquid effluent from the screening processes may be suitable for discharge to a municipal sewage system but in many cases must be subjected to further treatment steps. The screenings can be converted to animal feed, fertilizers, etc., and in some cases are ground to fine pulp and reintroduced into the waste stream for subsequent biological degradation.

Primary Treatment.—Municipal sewer codes frequently limit the dissolved and suspended solids load that industry can pump into the sewage disposal system. Then it becomes necessary to employ further treatment to reduce the load to acceptable limits. Primary treatment is the second stage and is ordinarily accomplished by two controlled sedimentation steps. First, the heavy inorganic matter (sands, grits, etc.) is removed by short time detention of the waste water in a detention chamber. The time required is about 2–3 min. In the case of large volume flows the settlings are removed continuously by mechanical means and disposed of by burial or land fill. Simple means such as shovels and buckets may be quite adequate for intermittent removal in the case of small-scale operations.

The overflow stream, free of the bulk of inert substances but still loaded with finely divided organics and solubles, now enters the second sedimentation step. The solids in suspension settle much more slowly and hence retention tanks of larger size must be used so as to allow retention periods in the order of ½–3 hr. The desired action is purely mechanical, so that retention times are no longer than necessary for the intended purpose. The time must not be so long as to allow septic conditions to develop within the sludge blanket when gasification will occur and the sludge will begin to float. Retention times may often be reduced by controlled addition of certain coagulants or flocculants.

The accumulated solids are removed by rotating plows and pumped to centrifuges or filters. The recovered sludge can be reclaimed for feed or fertilizer use or transferred to anaerobic digesters for complete decomposition. The suspended solids in the influent waste may be reduced by as much as 65% and the BOD by 35–40%. The liquid effluent from primary treatment, now much lower in suspended solids but still loaded with solubles should be subjected to secondary treatment.

Secondary Treatment.—Influent to this treatment stage carries a low suspended solids (colloids) load and all the soluble organic solids present in the original liquid wastes. Effective removal of these solids to acceptable levels is accomplished by biological oxidation involving the growth of microorganisms under aerobic conditions. For this purpose two separate means may be employed; namely, (a) trickling filter systems and (b) activated sludge digestion.

(A) Trickling filters: The partially treated waste is distributed by rotating nozzles or sprays over the top of a bed of coarse stone or slag. Recently a plastic material has been developed as a filling for the filter bed (Rose *et al.* 1970). Degradation of the organic solids takes place as the waste trickles over the filling. This action is accomplished by a film of live microorganisms that grow on the surface of the stone or slag. To support the activity, free circulation of air through the voids of the bed is necessary, essentially counter-current to the direction of waste flow. The process is actually an oxidation of the organic matter.

Effluent from the filter must be subjected to clarification, since the liquid carries varying amounts of sloughed-off biological film. Large open settling ponds are used for this purpose. The sludge is directed to anaerobic digesters; the pond effluent is discharged to a waterway since the BOD has been reduced by as much as 99% of the initial value. Or, as will be discussed later, the effluent may be subjected to a final treatment stage where phosphorous and nitrogen compounds are removed.

It should be noted that the term "trickling filter" is a misnomer. There is no filtering action per se. The system does have the advantages of simplicity and the ability to operate effectively under various hydraulic loadings and over wide ranges of the organic composition and concentration.

(B) Activated sludge system: In place of the filters discussed above, the degradation of organic solids may be effected by the activity of aerobic organisms within retention tanks. Under optimum environmental conditions, including good food supply, adequate air for respiration, and the proper microfauna, the organisms develop rapidly and the rate of biological oxidation is accelerated. Normally, the time required is in the region of several hours. The bacteria settle to and collect at the bottom of the retention tank and in part are recycled for addition to the fresh influent. The remaining sludge is withdrawn and along with other sludges pumped to digesters where complete decomposition of organic matter takes place under anaerobic conditions. This final anaerobic digestion takes place in tanks under warm conditions but even then the reactions require long retention times in order to reduce sludge volume to the maximum degree.

The final digester sludge is dewatered on sand beds or by suitable filters, dried, and disposed of as a high humus product suitable for agricultural purposes. Final disposal may also be by land fill or by incineration.

The activated sludge process is characterized by relatively high area requirements and high capital expenditures. Considerable power is necessary to operate pumps, air compressors, filters, aerators, and other mechanical equipment. An adequate supply of dissolved oxygen in the waste undergoing treatment is vital to successful operation. The necessary oxygen level is maintained by the bubbling of compressed air through diffusers located at an appropriate distance from the waste liquid surface. More rapid solution of the air can be obtained by the use of mechanically-operated surface aerators. Recent investigations show that the use of compressed oxygen speeds up the treatment of liquid wastes and may be commercially feasible (Anon. 1969B). The acceleration is a result of higher mass transfer rate of the pure oxygen and the higher settling rates of the bacterial sludge.

The effluent from the activated sludge system is relatively clear and has a low BOD. Generally, it can be discharged directly into the waterways. However, to guard against accidental carry-over of suspended solids the effluent should, as in the case of trickling filters, pass to retention ponds.

Tertiary Treatment.—After food plant liquid wastes have been rid of their suspended and dissolved organic loads, the effluents from secondary treatment systems still carry in solution certain nutrient compounds containing nitrogen and phosphorous. In the future, federal, state and local regulations may require that these elements be removed in order to reduce or eliminate the undesirable development of algae and other plant growth in the nation's streams and lakes. Considerable investigations of the problem are under way. Present methods of removal are expensive and not realistic from a cost-versus-benefit aspect.

The phosphorous can be precipitated in the form of insoluble compounds. Both nitrogen and phosphorous can be removed by growing algae. The latter method would require extensive pond areas and harvesting of the algae growth to remove the assimilated nutrients. The harvested growth might lend itself to by-product recovery, conversion to soil conditioners and fertilizers, or, for use as a feed supplement.

Other Methods.—Variations and improvements of the above systems are numerous. Lagooning under anaerobic as well as aerobic conditions is practiced extensively and is a suitable disposal method. Odors may be a problem but may be controlled by proper operations. Appreciable areas are needed for the lagoons (Bonem 1962; Gould 1962; McIntosh and McGeorge 1964; Gilde 1969). Spray irrigation and surface flow treatment involve the spraying of processing water waste over land areas whereby filtration plus biological activity on land surface, with or without a crop cover, are responsible for waste removal. Such systems are less extensive than conventional secondary treatment facilities (Dunstan and Lunsford 1955; Sanborn 1953; Gilde 1969).

Costs.—The cost of liquid waste treatment will vary widely because of the nature and concentration of the pollutants, the required effluent characteristics, the process selected, and the costs of construction and supervision. The maximum expected cost will be in the region of 1-2% of finished product cost and equivalent to about 0.7¢ per lb of BOD removed. The figures cited include operating costs and interest on investment but should serve only as a rough guide to probably costs. The final cost, whatever it may be, will be added to cost of product produced and in the end be paid for by the ultimate consumer. It must again be emphasized that more than one option is capable of purifying waste waters; consequently, a thorough analysis of actual conditions must be undertaken by a qualified team under supervision of management or by a competent consulting agency.

Utilities

Water.—Water is used in a dehydration plant for many reasons: washing the commodity at various stages of preparation, steam generation, plant cleanup and sanitation, fluming both raw and partially prepared material, cooling, and other purposes. It is obvious that because much water comes into contact directly with the commodity, steam made from the water also comes into contact with the commodity, and the product comes into contact with equipment cleaned with water, so the water used must be pure and contain no off-odors or contaminants. Water used in processing operations must conform to the standard of potability in *Drinking Water Standards* issued by the U.S. Public Health Service (U.S. Dept. Health, Education, Welfare 1949).

The quantity of water used may be as much as 5000-10,000 gal. per ton of raw material processed. Obviously, a plant must be located where large quantities of pure water are available continuously throughout the processing season.

A dehydration plant's water supply may come from its own wells a municipal water system, or a river, canal, or lake (Thomas 1966). If plant water supply is not obtained from an approved municipal system or from pure well water, some type of purifying treatment (such as filtration, aeration, and/or chlorination) will probably be required (Joslyn and Heid 1963). For certain processing needs it may be necessary to treat the available water so as to remove the trace elements which have a deleterious effect on appearance, taste, color, or texture of the finished product. It is well known that iron and manganese must be held to very low levels because of adverse influence on color and appearance. On the other hand, calcium and magnesium are removed completely from waters used for processing peas, beans, and legumes (Brody 1970) but may be added to tomatoes to improve firmness. Steam used for blanching or any other operation where it comes into direct contact with the product must be clean and free from odors or contaminants. If the main steam supply contains entrained oil, boiler compound or pipe scale, it will be necessary to install a separate reboiler, supplied with clean water, to generate the process steam. A sample of condensate from the steam line should be completely odorless and free of any turbidity.

The consumption of water for personal and industrial uses is at an unprecedental high level and shows no sign of reduction. In the very near future the available surface and underground sources will not be able to meet the demand (Ratzesberger 1964; Eliasen 1963). Processors may find that highly mineralized waters, brackish and sea, can be employed if subjected to efficient continuous ion exchange treatment (Higgins 1969). Water conservation is mandatory at all stages of processing. Significant savings can be made by any of the following: (1) the reuse of process waters (Clarke 1962; Denman 1961; McIlheny 1967; Leavitt and Ziemba 1969); (2) the judicious use of water at all times by regulation of requirements essential to the operation; (3) the renovation of used water by mechanical and/or chemical treatment with subsequent recycling to the system (Stepan 1963; Morris 1963); (4) the design of equipment for more effective water utilization; (5) the elimination of water in certain operations, for example, the substitution of mechanical conveyors for fluming systems; (6) the employment of "dry washing" of dirty raw materials prior to conventional wet washing; and (7) the substitution of radically new processing procedures which require less or no water (Graham *et al.* 1969A).

In addition to conserving water, logical restrictions on excessive washing and fluming reduce leaching losses from peeled and cut raw material. The quantity of waste water, and consequently the magnitude of the disposal problem, is reduced. In all food processing plants there should be a water management program with the objective of determining not only the overall but also the specific processing requirements. This can be accomplished by carefully considered analysis. Control of the water consumed by departments and processing stages can be established by the installation of meters, the routine readings of such devices, and the frequent scrutiny of the amounts consumed. Management must set up and rigorously support a clear channel of responsibility and authority over water usage and supply adequate funds for the initiation and maintenance of the water conservation program. Employees must be informed of the nature and scope of the program, their responsibilities with respect to undesirable practices and the need to use water and steam most effectively. The water conservation program must remain active at all times in order to attain maximum success (Scheel 1968).

Fuel.—Fuel requirements depend upon the dehydration method used and the preparation treatment required. Major demands for heat are for blanching and drying. Heat for drying may be obtained from several sources, but blanching requires steam or boiling water. Theoretically, blanching requires about 8 boiler horsepower (bhp) per ton of material blanched per hour, but because of heat and steam losses, actually about 16 bhp is required in an average blancher. Other demands for steam are shown in Table 8.2 for a potato plant, given as an example.

TABLE 8.2

AVERAGE STEAM REQUIREMENTS IN A DEHYDRATION
PLANT
(Basis: Five Tons of Potatoes per Hour)

Operation[2]	Steam (Bhp[1])
Preheating	35
Peeling (steam)	30
Peeling (lye)	20
Blanching	80
Drying (steam-heated)	700
Bin drying	30
Cleanup	180[3]

[1] One boiler horsepower = evaporation of 34.5 lb of water per hour.
[2] Does not include building heat.
[3] Intermittent duty only.

Heat for drying in air-convection driers may range from 1300 Btu per lb of water evaporated to several times that much, depending upon the type of drier and operating conditions. Efficiency of heat use will be greatest if direct firing is used. Direct firing is the combustion of the fuel (gas or other clean, low-sulfur fuel) in the air stream so that the products of combustion mix with the air used for dehydration. This method is widely used in the United States.

If the heat must be supplied primarily from coal, wood, or low-grade fuel oil, it must be transferred indirectly to the air stream. Many of the dehydration plants in the Pacific Northwest were equipped to burn fuel oil and transfer the heat to the air by means of an extensive set of sheet-iron flues. Most modern dehydration plants where gas is not economically available use high-pressure automatically fired steam boilers; the heat is transferred by means of finned or other extended-surface pipe coils.

Power.—Electric power requirements depend largely upon the type of dehydration system used. In a plant processing about 100 tons of vegetables per day, 200–400 kw of connected load is common. The major demand for power is for operating blowers in convection-type driers, but a dehydration plant uses electrical energy in practically every step in the process (Joslyn and Heid 1963).

Energy consumption for plant lighting and for powering water pumps, conveyors, and other equipment will be relatively small. Electricity cannot economically supply heat for evaporation of water except under conditions that make radiant heat transfer the method of choice—for example, in vacuum puff drying and freeze drying. Here the energy cost will not be an important consideration in the overall economics of the process.

Labor.—Labor requirements in dehydration plants are continually being reduced as technologic developments are introduced into the industry. Statements of specific labor needs in the following paragraphs must be judged in light of recent advances and be adjusted accordingly. Inasmuch as most labor needed in a dehydration plant can be readily trained for the job, location of the plant in an area of skilled workers is not essential. Both on-the-job training and training schools should be used to make most effective use of available labor. Typical process labor requirements per shift in a plant processing 100 tons per day of vegetables in piece form are shown below;

Superintendent			
or foreman	1	Quality control technicians	1–2
Floor ladies	2	Women—trimming, inspect-	
Boilerman	1	ing, and packaging	20–50
Mechanics	1–2	Men—common labor and	
		machine operators	5–10

The exact labor requirements vary greatly depending upon kind, size, and grade of raw material processed; care used in peeling, trimming, and inspecting; type of drier used; extent of automation; and kind of packaging. The labor breakdown given above shows the relatively large demand for women in operations that require hand trimming after peeling, inspecting, and packaging in comparatively small-size packages.

Typical operations for male employees include feeding to the preparation line; handling raw material and finished product manually or with trucks; and operating machines such as peelers, blanchers, slicers, driers, automatic inspection equipment, and packaging machinery. The mechanics lubricate and maintain the equipment, make repairs and adjustments, sharpen cutting knives, and may construct some items of equipment.

An area considered for a plant site must have available, either locally or within reasonable commuting distance, a supply of capable labor that may amount to 200 or more for a 3-shift operation. Smaller towns in farming areas have been found to be good sources of a reasonable amount of labor in food processing plants. Labor supply is quite stable in the smaller communities because many of the people are involved in farming operations and are not as likely to move away as itinerants. The labor force is drawn mainly from housewives, farmers and helpers in off-season, and students.

A survey of the labor supply of an area should include a study of local labor-management relations, responsibilities and requirements shown by labor union groups, and general attitude of the community with respect to labor and industry.

Noncontaminating Surroundings.—A plant processing food products must be constructed and operated in a sanitary manner, so it must be located where local conditions are conducive to a sanitary operation. Location would not be advisable in an area known to be highly infested with insects, rodents, and other sources of contamination. Their presence indicates a generally low level of sanitation unacceptable for food processing purposes, and the cost of making and maintaining sanitary conditions within a plant in such an area may be prohibitive.

Areas experiencing high concentrations of air-borne pollutants are also to be avoided. In most dehydration operations, large volumes of air are blown across or through the product. Odors, dust particles, or other foreign materials that may be carried by the air are deleterious to the product and may make it unacceptable for food uses. No food dehydration plant should be located where noxious contaminants are chronically present. Among the chief offenders in imparting objectionable contaminants to the air are paper pulp mills, chemical plants, sewage treatment plants, city dumps, incinerators, oil refineries, and rendering plants. Wastes and water disposal methods of nearby plants may also adversely affect water supply.

Transportation.—Many dehydration plants are adequately serviced entirely by trucks, although having rail service also available might be necessary in some situations to ensure prompt movement of goods. Good, well-maintained roads leading to the plant site are prime requisite of any plant location. The roads must be usable and passable in all kinds of weather.

Area at Plant Site.—Plant site requirements fall into several classes: (1) area for processing plant and other structures; (2) space for maneuvering, loading, and unloading trucks and for freight cars (including truck-trailer combinations); (3) parking area for employees' and visitors' cars and for trucks; and (4) space for future plant expansion. Many new food processing plants are being located in rural areas, away from the congestion and competition for space. The current trend from multiple-story plants to one-story plants, and the vastly increased demand for automobile parking space, have considerably raised the requirements for land. Even esthetic considerations are more important now than they were some years ago; these also may increase the need for land.

The present tendency in the dehydration industry, as in all other industry, is toward the construction of sophisticated complexes rather than just plants. Special emphasis and consideration are being given toward the adaptation of new as well as older, redesigned facilities to the surrounding environment. Modern plant areas offer many extra features pertaining to sanitation, employee comfort and recreation facilities, and including separate plant services for power, maintenance, and repair. All contribute to the need for more land area (Anon. 1968B; Ziemba 1967).

The dehydration building alone may occupy 2–3 acres of land. In addition, space should be provided for storage of surplus equipment. In some areas, a large raw material storage area may be necessary. For ordinary situations, 5-10 acres of land may be minimal. Some new plants have hundreds of acres of land available at the plant site. Such acreages are an absolute necessity if lagooning or spray irrigation is used for waste water disposal. These areas should be located some distance from the processing plant.

Climate.—Weather conditions that prevail during harvesting and processing operations are important in plant location. Some commodities are usually processed immediately after harvest, and weather that seriously disrupts harvesting will also affect plant operation. This is one reason why irrigated areas of the West are preferred for dehydration plants; rainfall in these areas is usually quite low during harvest periods, and application of water to the crops through irrigation gives better control of growing conditions. These affect both the quality and the moisture content of the commodity at time of harvest.

Weather may interfere directly with dehydration operations. On days of high absolute humidity, it may be impossible to produce a satisfactory dried product. Plants located where humidities are high may require dehumidification of air used in the final drying stages and in packaging rooms.

Heat requirements for drying are greatly affected by outside air temperatures. For a drying temperature of $175°F$, outside air at $75°F$ must be raised $100°$; If, however, the outside temperature is $0°F$, the air temperature must be raised $175°$. With the greater heat losses that also will occur at the lower temperature, fuel cost may easily be doubled. Drying facilities must be designed for the complete range of weather conditions that will be experienced, or the plant capacity will either be unsatisfactory at times or the operating costs will be unduly high.

Industrial Environment.—This is an intangible element which can be assessed only from a study at the proposed plant location. It includes many factors, among which are the following: present and future taxation patterns, trends in land use, employee attitudes, labor-union activity, economic growth rate, and attitude of community with respect to new plants in its area.

Good public relations are essential to the successful operation of all commercial enterprises. The dehydration plant is no exception. Every company must initiate such relationships prior to the selection of a specific plant site. Failure to do so may produce an unfavorable climate for many years thereafter. There is no fast-bound procedure for the generation of favorable relationships; and the mechanics for the development therefore vary between companies and within a company from one site to another. The objective is always the same: namely, to furnish correct, pertinent information to the public, and beginning at the time that options are taken on potential sites. Initial information need be only general in nature.

Upon the selection of a specific site, public announcement should be made through all news media giving details on the exact location, magnitude of the project, products to be produced, type and amount of employment, and, perhaps most important, the company background. Such information should be directed towards those segments of society concerned with educational, financial, transportation, real estate, and environmental interests as well as the average individual citizen. Contacts should be made by meetings of high level company personnel with municipal, school, professional, business, and civic groups. The burden of public relations falls upon the field project manager who must know and be able to discuss company policies with respect to labor relations, wages, pollution control, supply procurement, and processing operations as well as requirements for power, labor, water, and other services. A strong healthy community-company relationship will be developed by recognizing and satisfying the need for mutual information during the introductory phases of a project and throughout the entire period of productive operation (Day 1960).

PLANT LAYOUT AND CONSTRUCTION

Plant Layout

The success of a dehydration plant, from the standpoint of both cost and product quality, may well depend upon the way in which it is built and the processing steps laid out. The following section discusses the main points to be considered in plant layout and thus indicates those topics which bear thorough investigation. While each plant differs in many respects from others, there are certain basic features of layout that should be followed by all plants to achieve satisfactory and efficient operations (Jensteat and Ziemba 1969):

(1) Driveways and parking areas for trucks, busses, and cars should be adequate in size and be dust free (preferably covered with concrete or asphalt), well drained, and readily accessible.

(2) Loading and unloading docks or areas should be suitably covered, have sufficient clearance, depending upon handling equipment and methods used, and be located so that trucks standing alongside will not block driveways or access areas or be blocked as trucks arrive or leave.

(3) The premises of the processing plant should be free from conditions objectionable to food processing operations. There should be no poorly drained areas in the immediate vicinity of the plant. Bins or tanks for holding waste material should be constructed and located so that they present no objectionable odors or appearances to the main processing areas and grounds.

(4) Building layout should permit future expansions without necessitating major revisions of existing layout. Expansion of a particular operation, drying, for example, should be possible without major rearrangement of other functions. Locating the important functions on the perimeter of the building is an effective way of providing for this requirement.

(5) Various processing areas should be completely separated from one another so as to prevent moisture, odors, dust, and noise from traveling between other areas. The wet and dry ends of the process must be separate, because the moisture from the washers and blanchers cannot be tolerated where the dried product is being handled.

(6) Both hot and cold water should be available at appropriate places to facilitate equipment hook-up and plant cleanup, and to obviate need for long water hoses being run throughout the plant.

(7) All tanks and other equipment holding water or solutions should be equipped to prevent back-siphonage of liquids into potable water lines.

(8) Sufficient space must be provided for each person so he can function freely without being hampered by lack of space. Efficient use of trimming and inspection personnel is aided by proper design and operation of the trimming tables or belts. Ample space, at least 30–36 in., must be allowed for each worker to avoid crowding. Reaching distances must be minimized to reduce strain and fatigue.

(9) It is important to provide accessibility and sufficient space to repair, replace, and maintain operating equipment.

(10) Straight-through flow of materials is preferred, and cross-flow should be avoided wherever possible. Movement of workers and trucks should be organized so as to permit a well-regulated flow without delays from cross-traffic or bottlenecks. Walkways and truckways should be wide enough to permit movement in both directions. If employees must cross the preparation line in going to or from their work stations, adequate passageways must be provided. Two methods commonly used are passageways under elevators or elevated equipment, and bridges or stairs over conveyor belts or other low machines. Safety regulations must be carefully observed where people move through the plant (Joslyn and Heid 1963).

(11) Various functions and facilities should be located conveniently to related functions. The steam boiler should be located as near as feasible to the point of greatest steam use. Drinking fountains and refreshment bars should be convenient to the greatest concentration of workers. Packaging supplies should be stored adjacent to the packaging room, and raw commodity should be stored near the point where it is fed to the preparation line.

(12) Adequate lighting, heating, and ventilation should be provided in all parts of the plant (Anon. 1950; Joslyn and Heid 1963; Kahler 1951; Lamb 1954).

Good nonglare lighting is required, especially for operations involving inspecting and trimming. In the general areas of the plant, from 20–25 foot-candles of illumination are advisable. Somewhat less may be needed in storage areas and in corridors. Supplemental lighting is necessary for trimming, inspecting, and record-keeping areas, with at least 50 foot-candles being advisable. The fixtures should be constructed and located so that they properly light the desired areas or objects without causing glare, eyestrain, or annoyance to the employees in both the immediate and the adjacent areas (Epstein 1965).

The type of lighting used will depend upon requirements in each installation. Generally, more illumination can be obtained from a given power input to fluorescent than to incandescent lights. With fluorescent equipment, 4 watts per square foot of floor area give 50–60 foot-candles; with incandescent equipment, the same wattage gives 25–30 foot-candles (Kahler 1951).

Ceilings and walls affect lighting and should preferably be painted light colors. Windows should be covered with glass or plastic having high light transmissibility. Where workers are exposed to the sun's rays or heat through windows or skylights, suitable coverings of light-diffusing and/or heat-absorbing materials should be installed.

Today much more consideration is given to the external illumination of processing plants and adjacent service areas. This is accomplished by flood lighting which serves as an architectural tool to enhance the personality and attractiveness of the plant, and to improve the security within the confines of the plant area. Indirectly, the improved illumination benefits employee morale. Many techniques are available to produce the desired as well as special effects by the use of incandescent, fluorescent, and colored lamps. Control of external illumination should be automatic and based on photoelectric or elapsed time. The services of an illumination expert are recommended in order to ensure that the desired results are obtained at the least expenditure for equipment, maintenance, and power (Heck 1964).

(13) Plants that process foods by dehydration should be designed to operate continuously and efficiently even though raw material supply may vary in quantity or in grade. Capacities of the various processing steps should be balanced so that piling-up or restriction of partially-processed material does not occur.

(14) Sanitary facilities and personal hygiene. Unfortunately, sanitary facilities are badly neglected in some plants. The importance of installing and maintaining proper facilities cannot be overemphasized. Clean, well-ventilated, well-lighted, screened, and ample rest rooms with adequate toilet facilities are essential for the health, comfort, and morale of the employees. Facilities should be conveniently located so that no employee must travel more than 150–200 ft, nor more than 1 flight of stairs. Rest rooms should be plainly labeled, and should have accommodations based on the maximum number of each sex employed on the premises at one time. Recommendations have been set forth by the American Standards Association (1935).

Washing facilities must be provided close to the toilet rooms. Employees must be instructed to wash their hands before beginning work and after visiting the toilets. Prominent signs to this effect should be posted in the toilet rooms. Dressing rooms and lockers should be provided, particularly if special uniforms are required to be worn in the plant. Head coverings must be worn by both men and women to prevent hair from falling into the food.

First-aid rooms and supplies should be provided for treating minor illnesses or injuries, and should be maintained under the supervision of a capable nurse. When a plant does not have a nurse in attendance, at least two individuals on each shift should have training in simple first aid to meet emergencies until the doctor arrives. Names and telephone numbers of nearest doctors, ambulances, and hospitals should be posted.

Typical Layouts.—Suggested plant layouts for daily capacity of about 100 tons of raw material are shown in Fig. 8.1, 8.2, and 8.3, in which combinations of various processing techniques are illustrated. The layout shown in Fig. 8.1, is for a plant dehydrating root-type vegetables, using lye peeling, one-stage counterflow dehydrators, and bin finishing. The large storage cellar in lower right-hand corner is used in a potato plant.

The next layout, Fig. 8.2, is for dehydrating root-type vegetables, such as sweet potatoes. In this illustration, dehydration is done with continuous belt-conveyor driers, peeling is done by steam, and finish-drying is accomplished in bins. Space required for the drying operation is much reduced by the use of conveyor driers, labor requirements are lower, and maintenance is reduced to a minimum.

The third layout, Fig. 8.3, is for dehydrating vegetables which do not require blanching. Two-stage driers are illustrated, in which the first stage provides parallel flow and the second, counterflow. Other types of driers can also be used

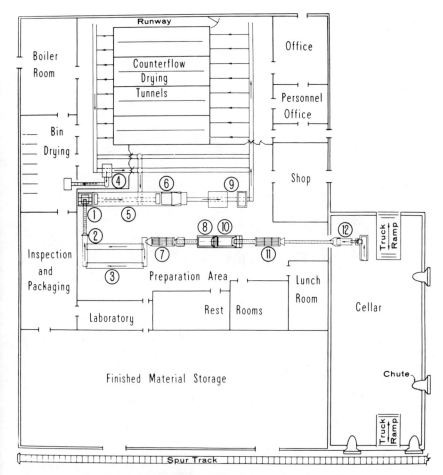

FIG. 8.1. PLANT LAYOUT FOR DEHYDRATING ROOT-TYPE VEGETABLES THAT REQUIRE BLANCHING

Illustrated are facilities for lye peeling and one-stage counter-flow dehydration. (1) dicers, (2) inspection belts, (3) trimming lines, (4) tray unloader, (5) blancher, (6) sulfite spray, (7) washer, (8) peeler, (9) tray stacker and scales, (10) preheaters, (11) washer, and (12) inspection belt.

on vegetables not blanched. Conveyor-belt driers are finding increasing popularity in drying onions and garlic. The layout shown indicates expansion possibilities.

No scale of size is indicated on these layouts, as each installation should be tailored to the specific requirements of the plant. Some of the newer dehydration plants have been built with very generous allowances for space—both in the building and in the total plant site. This is a very desirable trend and contrasts

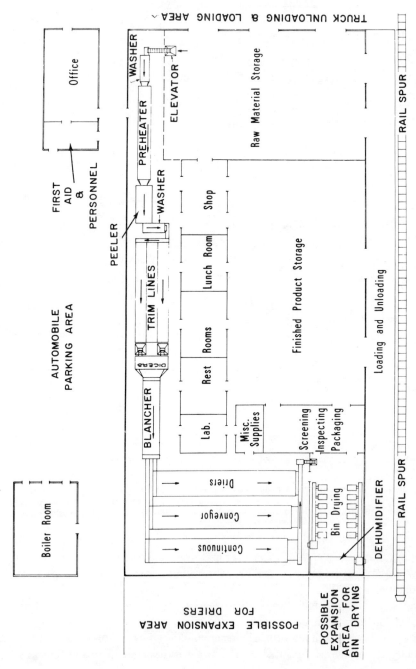

FIG. 8.2. PLANT LAYOUT FOR DEHYDRATING ROOT-TYPE VEGETABLES IN WHICH STEAM PEELING AND BELT-CONVEYOR DRYING ARE ILLUSTRATED

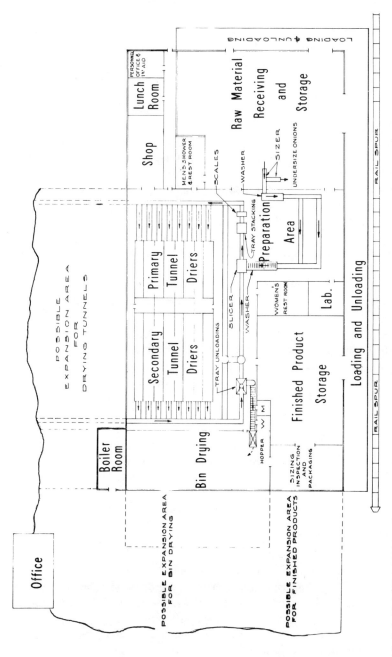

FIG. 8.3. PLANT LAYOUT FOR DEHYDRATING VEGETABLES THAT DO NOT REQUIRE BLANCHING AND ILLUSTRATING TWO-STAGE DRYING

greatly with some plants, particularly a few built during World War II, in which inadequate space was allowed for normal operation, let alone often-needed re-arrangements and expansion.

Standby Services and Equipment

Delays caused by the stoppage of power, fuel, or water, or by the breakdown of equipment can be extremely costly. In addition to the payment of wages for employees who are idled by such delays, and the loss of output of finished product, partially processed material may be lost if it is held for any extended length of time. It is advisable, therefore, to provide standby services to at least permit completion of the processing of goods in progress and to have on hand sufficient spare parts or machines to permit rapid repair or replacement of defective equipment.

Plants remotely located and depending upon a single transmission line for power may very well decide that standby generator facilities are justifiable. Even if not large enough to run the complete plant, the generator should at least provide sufficient power to operate the driers, so as to complete the dehydration of all material already started through. For plants depending upon outside sources of water, a standby water well would provide ensurance for finishing operations or for operating at reduced capacity. The well would also provide water for additional fire protection and may make possible lower fire insurance rates.

A reserve supply of liquid fuel in tanks will provide ensurance against interruptions in the delivery of natural gas, oil, or other fuels used. To obtain natural gas at the lowest possible rates, a plant may contract to take delivery on an interruptable schedule. If a shortage of gas occurs, the utility company can restrict or stop the flow of gas to the processing plant. For such contingencies, a reserve supply of tank gas would keep the plant operating.

An adequate supply of spare parts is needed in any processing plant. Standby items of equipment may also be advisable, particularly if the plant is located some distance from the suppliers of equipment. One means of obtaining better flexibility in operation, while at the same time ensuring against losses caused by equipment breakdown or adjustment, is to provide two or more units to perform certain functions. If a processing line requires 2 or more machines, such as cutters, to handle the rated capacity, installation of 1 extra cutter is advisable. This will permit replacement of parts and knife-sharpening on a rotational basis without interfering with product throughput.

A properly equipped machine shop is essential to good operation. Parts and supplies to be kept on hand should include electric motors, pumps, conveyor belts, switches, welding equipment, pipes of various sizes, other plumbing supplies and equipment, electrical wire, conduits, lumber, paint, equipment maintenance supplies, and various other equipment and supplies for plant and grounds maintenance and cleanup.

Some of the foregoing standby services and equipment may have the appearance of costly and dispensable luxuries, but the case for thorough preparation for the unexpected should not be lightly brushed aside. Additional capital expenditures for these purposes add comparatively little to the cost burden on a pound of finished product. It must not be forgotten that in many food dehydration plants that operate over a long season, the raw material and operating expenditures can, within a couple of months, exceed the entire cost of constructing the plant in the first place. Loss of income on account of a few weeks shutdown (perhaps caused by equipment breakdown) may prove financially fatal.

Building Requirements

Traditional approach has been the construction of a structure followed by selection, receipt, and placement of equipment; and finally, the connection of the necessary services. This type of procedure is time-consuming and of questionable efficiency. Modern process and production requirements are more complex and demanding; and for that reason food processors are enlisting the coordinate advice and services of engineers and consultants. Their approach follows the policy of studying the process and production line in complete detail and then designing and constructing the required structure. Thus, a step-wise progressive procedure results which (1) defines the process requirements; (2) produces specifications and bids for equipment; (3) establishes layouts based on actual dimensions of equipment complete with piping, instrumentation, and electrical needs; and (4) finally, designs the building to meet architectural, structural and service requirements to best fit the processing scheme. Good engineering allows for ample flexibility, growth, and maximum utility (Anon. 1968C; Armstrong 1965; Epstein 1965; Camp and Mason 1968).

The climate of the areas where plants are to be located will impose certain building requirements, as will the local building codes and the physical characteristics of the plant site. Certain basic points, however, apply to all buildings, wherever located:

(1) Good typical wall construction includes concrete, bricks or blocks, tile, or wooden frame covered with sheet-metal, asbestos board, or plaster. Both fire resistance and serviceability are desirable. The materials should be impervious, easily cleanable, and resistant to wear and corrosion. Wood, plasterboard, porous acoustical materials, and other absorbent materials should be avoided. Fire walls, fire doors, and emergency exits should be provided at appropriate places.

(2) Floors should be made of dense, water-resistant concrete free from crevices. A nonskid finish should be added to tile or vitrified brick to prevent slipping.

(3) Ceilings should be of sufficient height for good working conditions and for necessary clearance. Usually a height of 14 ft is sufficient except in product storage areas which may have higher clearances. Nonporous, easily-cleaned materials should be used for the ceilings.

(4) Adequate floor drainage must be provided in all areas where water is used, either in processing or cleanup. Floors to be flushed should have a slope of $^1/_8$ to $^1/_4$ in. per ft to provide adequate drainage. Insufficient slope results in wet floors that promote unsanitary situations as well as creating unsafe conditions for workers. Too much slope permits wash water to run off too fast to float away food particles. Drains should be covered with gratings that will withstand the heaviest anticipated loads, stationary or moving. Drain troughs should have smooth vertical sides, rounded bottoms, and be sloped $^1/_{16}$ to $^1/_8$ in. per ft to maintain sufficient water velocity. Floor-to-wall junctions should be coved to prevent harboring of food residues that will attract animal or insect pests and develop mold growths.

(5) Processing equipment should be elevated to allow access underneath for cleaning. Surrounding catwalks should be made of open steel grating to allow for proper washing.

(6) One of the serious problems in food plant sanitation is the large amount of steam escaping from process operations and the resulting condensate which forms on all cool surfaces, particularly metal. Overhead water pipes should be insulated to prevent dripping from condensate. Adequate ventilation is needed to prevent clouds of steam from forming under the roof. Wherever possible, the load on the ventilating system must be relieved by exhaust systems or hoods directly over the steam contributing equipment. Hoods and ducts must be designed to trap dust and draining of condensate and to allow for cleanout.

(7) Good plant construction will promote good sanitation (Potter 1966). Ledges or other areas that tend to collect dirt, debris, and miscellaneous items should be avoided. Inside window sills may be constructed at a $45°$ angle. Also to be avoided are inaccessible areas in corners, behind or over equipment, overhead construction that permits the collection of dust and dirt that may drop into the product, and uncovered tanks, vats, and storage bins. Plant sanitation will be improved, and maintenance and cleanup cost reduced by proper attention to these and other construction details. Design of food plants for maintaining sanitation is of great enough importance to require consultation with specialists in this field before final plans are formulated.

Agencies concerned with the sanitary construction and operation of food plants include the Food and Drug Administration, U.S. Department of Health, Education, and Welfare; the U.S. Department of Agriculture (both in Washington, D.C.); and similarly named departments in the various states. Specifications and standards for food plants have been developed by various agencies, both governmental and trade. The National Sanitation Foundation, School of Public Health, University of Michigan, Ann Arbor, has published standards for food preparation and service equipment. "3A Standards" were promulgated jointly by the International Association of Milk and Food Sanitarians, Inc., Shelbyville, Ind.; the U.S. Public Health Service, Department of Health, Education, and Welfare, Washington, D.C.; and the Dairy Industry Committee, 1012–14th St., Washington, D.C. The Baking Industry Sanitation Standards Committee, 511 Fifth Ave., New York, N.Y., has issued "BISSC Sanitation Standards."

(8) Nontoxic paint should be used in all plants where food products are processed, stored, and handled. Noncorroding and nontoxic metals are preferred wherever they come into contact with the product. Stainless steel is generally preferred when the requirements of an operation justify the cost.

(9) Buildings should be constructed to protect against extremes in weather, contamination from windblown dust and bacteria, and infestation by insects and

rodents. Screens, self-closing outside doors, and generally tight construction are advisable.

ECONOMIC CONSIDERATIONS

Size of Plant

The sizing of a dehydration plant is often based on the simple conception of the immediate demand for the product. Such a plant will be grossly undersized in the event of heavier than anticipated demands and the profit potential will never be fully realized. On the other hand, it is also possible to err by oversizing by too great a margin with attendant higher costs of construction and idle plant capacity. Accurate data are needed to optimize capacity and profitability for which purpose Hess and Weaver (1961) recommended the use of algebraic models. Growing markets for any product show four distinct stages, namely: an incubation period, relatively short, and lasting from 2 to 5 yr; a long growth period characterized by rapid increase in demand, lasting 5–20 yr; then, a leveling-off period with stabilized market demand and with vulnerability to substitution by newly developed products, time ranging from 5 to 30 yr; and finally, a decline period which may be extremely fast, even as short as 2 yr. The design capacity of plants to be constructed during the growth and leveling-off stages must necessarily be based upon an accurate estimate of the growth and ultimate demand level, respectively. Certainly, a knowledge of the competition in the given field is of vital importance (Coleman and York 1964).

Since World War II, there has been a pronounced upward trend in the size of vegetable dehydration plants. Formerly, plants processing 50 tons of raw material per day were considered to be a desirable size. Even though cost and operational data for a 100-tons per day plant are given herein, this may be considered too small in some areas for some products. Some of the present vegetable dehydration plants have capacities of several hundred tons of raw material per day, and it is not unrealistic to predict that plants of the future will process a thousand tons per day.

It is difficult, if not impossible, to estimate what a dehydration plant will cost without having detailed information on all important factors of construction. But if the cost of one size of plant is known, it is possible to estimate, at least roughly, the costs of other sizes. Chilton (1950) showed that for process plants, the cost of a plant increases as the six-tenths power of the plant processing capacity, as illustrated in this formula:

$$\frac{\text{Cost of plant (Size A)}}{\text{Cost of plant (Size B)}} = \left(\frac{\text{Capacity of Size A}}{\text{Capacity of Size B}}\right)^{0.6}$$

This particular formula may not apply very closely to all dehydration plants, because many items of equipment used are furnished in multiples. For example, doubling dehydration capacity may require 2 identical driers, instead of just 1 drier of larger size. For dehydration plants an exponent of eight-tenths may be closer than six-tenths. On this basis, if a 100-ton-a-day plant costs $1,000,000, the costs of other sizes would be:

Ratios of Plant Sizes	Estimated Ratio of Plant Costs	Plant Size (Tons per Day)	Estimated Construction Cost ($)	Cost per Ton of Capacity ($)
0.50	0.6	50	600,000	12,000
1.00	1.0	100	1,000,000	10,000
1.5	1.4	150	1,400,000	9,300
2.0	1.7	200	1,700,000	8,500
3.0	2.4	300	2,400,000	8,000

Another aspect of plant size which has an important influence upon successful operation is the matter of product quality. The larger the plant, the better able it is to provide a good program of quality control. During World War II, many small plants were not able to maintain the necessary quality of dried products as well as large plants; the resulting difficulties with procurement agencies led to the elimination of some plants so that the bulk of production was eventually done by a few large plants.

Even with these and the other advantages and economies of size, the large plants are not necessarily the only successful dehydrators. The great importance of raw material costs and quality in a dehydration operation suggests that one enjoying a particular advantage in raw material procurement, either cost- or quality-wise, may still be able to compete effectively, even if his plant is smaller than others. Likewise, the disadvantages of small size may be partially or fully offset by an excellent low-cost labor supply. Other offsetting advantages of the small plant may be (1) the possibility of operating over a very long season because of favorable conditions and (2) the desire to produce a product of such outstanding quality that a select market is willing to pay a premium price.

Capital Requirements

The capital required to establish a successful dehydration plant is well in excess of the amount needed solely to build and equip the plant. Not all of the capital need be in cash, however, because assured credit is equally effective. In addition to plant cost, capital requirements must include such items as prepayments to growers and other costs associated with the preliminary phases of raw material procurement; costs of supplies, including packaging materials, chemicals, and maintenance items; get-ready costs such as salaries and expenses of key personnel during survey, construction, and plant break-in periods; prepayments for insurance and utilities; and sufficient resources to pay all operational costs until a steady flow of cash is received from sale of finished products.

It may take a rather long time before a new plant is able to produce an acceptable product on a continuous basis. New plants will be subject to many shutdowns and delays as equipment is adjusted and new employees learn their duties. The start-up of a new plant is the culmination of much effort based on careful execution of research, evaluation, design, and construction. A smooth start-up is obviously the desired objective but may be delayed by equipment and personnel problems whereupon costs mount rapidly because of no return on the investment, wasted raw materials, utilities, manpower, contract difficulties, and loss of market. A carefully planned start-up is essential and must provide for a well selected organization team consisting of (1) a specially chosen technically qualified operating group; (2) a plant production group for supervision and line control (this group later assumes full plant control); (3) a maintenance group composed of the regular plant staff with additional technical advisers; and (4) a laboratory group composed of the normal technical staff reinforced with highly trained technicians if necessary. All groups must work as a coordinated team with adequate, clearly defined channels of communication, responsibility, and authority. An information center with a readily available filing system is vital to effective start-up operations. The files must contain all information relative to the project design, process volume, engineering data, plant layout, operating instructions, analytical procedures, and pertinent calculations (Finlayson and Gans 1967).

Total financial requirements may well be several times greater than the basic plant, equipment, and grounds costs.

Multipurpose Plants

It is recognized that an idle plant is a costly one, and that year-around operation is desirable. For some commodities, such as potatoes, under the improved storage conditions that are being used, a plant may operate most of the year if it is located in the right area. In some sections of the country, a few commodities are available much of the year, for example carrots and greens in California. Some plants process several different vegetables or fruits. The combinations that might be feasible will depend on the processing requirements and equipment used as well as upon what fruits and vegetables are available. Root vegetables such as potatoes, carrots, and beets, in piece form, can be advantageously processed in the same plant because of the similarity in their operations for peeling, cutting, blanching, and drying. Onions, garlic, and peppers, none of which requires blanching, make a good combination. If the fruits and vegetables to be processed in the same plant are quite different in their requirements, then the plant setup must be flexible to allow readily for the changes needed for the various raw materials. An integrated complex composed of canning, freezing, and dehydration activities would significantly increase the effective utilization of equipment, facilities, and trained personnel over longer periods of time; and reduce overall capital requirements.

Principal Personnel Needs

Three special types of know-how are needed in a dehydration operation: raw material procurement, plant management and personnel handling, and dehydration technology. Generally, the key men in these positions are hired on an annual basis. Some supervisors, however, are hired on an hourly basis when the plant is operating. It is important that a plant make every effort to retain key personnel in off-seasons so as to keep a nucleus of skilled help and supervisors to start each season and carry on effectively. Off-season work that can be used profitably to keep the best employees on the staff include plant repair and improvement, process modification, warehousing and shipping finished product, and planning and getting ready for the next operating season.

The field agent must be well-versed in all phases of raw material production and harvesting procedures and storage characteristics of the raw material. Education in agricultural sciences, experience in raw material procurement, and a personal knowledge of the growing areas are essential.

To assure the continuous production of a product that meets the requirements of the buyer, the plant should have a well-qualified quality control department (Brown 1960; Livingston 1955). The head of the department might be a chemist, chemical engineer, or food technologist. The laboratory technicians should preferably have some technical training, but a substantial part of their work can be done by intelligent persons with only on-the-job training by the quality control supervisor.

Ordinary production line personnel can usually be recruited from the local labor pool, trained to attain the required level of performance, and retained for many relatively short processing seasons. A high turn-over rate is costly since replacements require additional training and may be difficult to acquire because of labor unrest or gossip and speculation relative to company policies. Production line personnel may be retained by pay inducements and fringe benefits which are abreast of industry.

The procurement of higher level key personnel for supervision, engineering, sanitation, waste disposal, managerial, and control functions is more difficult and requires far greater consideration. Large organizations employ active recruitment programs which offer employment to qualified graduates of technical schools, colleges, and universities. The graduates may be from institutions offering short two-year training programs to those with bachelor's and higher degrees. In most cases the graduates require further on-the-job training involving conferences, seminars, and classes. Personnel with specific talents may also be obtained through listing of the available positions in newspapers, technical journals, trade publications, and employment agencies.

The retention of key personnel depends entirely on company policies, which must offer opportunity for advanced responsibility, professional advancement, and recognition of good performance (Anon. 1963; Sharpe 1970).

Figure 8.4 presents an organization chart that might serve as a model for a dehydration plant (USDA 1959). In smaller plants, some functions may be combined under one person. But whether they are handled singly or combined, these functions must be provided in some manner in each plant for successful

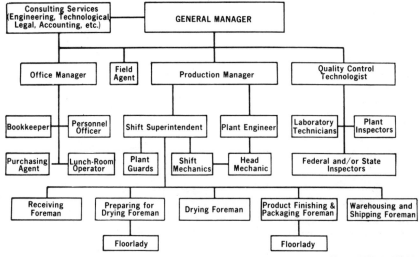

From USDA (1959)

FIG. 8.4. ORGANIZATION CHART FOR A VEGETABLE OR FRUIT DEHYDRATION PLANT

operation. Joslyn and Heid (1963) present a comprehensive discussion of staff organization, functions, and techniques in food processing plants.

In addition to plant personnel, there will be need for services from outside organizations and consultants. Both state and federal government inspection services are available to processors on a fee basis. They may inspect and certify as to the quality of raw material, and they may provide continuous inspection of the processing operations and of the finished products. The specific state agencies involved will vary with each state. Generally, they would be under the State Department of Agriculture. For the federal government, the following two branches are involved: Fresh Products Standardization and Inspection Branch, and the Processed Products Standardization and Inspection Branch, Fruit and Vegetable Division, Consumer and Marketing Service, USDA, Washington, D.C. Both branches have regional offices in selected areas throughout the country.

The plant will probably have periodic need for outside consulting services, particularly in the planning stages and during initial operation. Possible needs include legal, fiscal and accounting, engineering, process, and management counseling. Money spent in getting appropriate advice from those who are experts in their fields will often be returned manyfold in better operation and avoidance of trouble (Anderson 1969; Van Meter 1962).

PREDRYING OPERATIONS

For most fruits and vegetables, the preparation procedures that precede dehydration have many common features (see Fig. 8.5, 8.6, and 8.7). In general, the

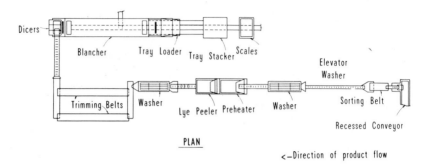

PLAN

<—Direction of product flow

ELEVATION

FIG. 8.5. L-ARRANGEMENT ILLUSTRATING PREDRYING STEPS FOR PREHEATING AND LYE PEELING POTATOES

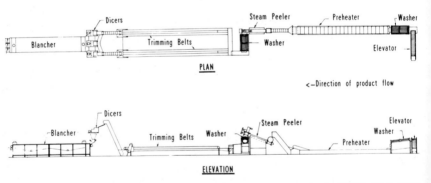

PLAN

<—Direction of product flow

ELEVATION

FIG. 8.6. IN-LINE ARRANGEMENT ILLUSTRATING PREDRYING STEPS FOR PRE-HEATING AND STEAM PEELING SWEET POTATOES

sequence of operations that follows receiving and storing at the plant includes feeding to line, grading, washing, inspecting, peeling, postpeeling washing, trimming, cutting, blanching, and cooling. Some commodities require pre- or posttreatment in connection with peeling or with blanching. Washing, inspecting, and grading are sometimes repeated at intermediate stages. It is possible, even probable, that one plant will be able to process many different vegetables, with only minor modifications. In this chapter, the specific examples given of procedures in the preparation for drying apply in general to most fruits and vegetables that are dehydrated and illustrate principles and techniques.

The engineers and food technologists on the plant staff are responsible for

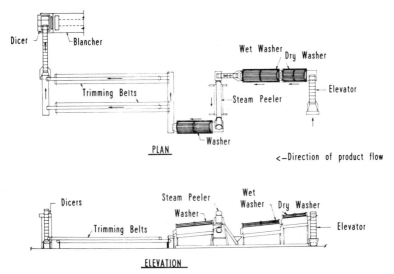

FIG. 8.7. L-ARRANGEMENT ILLUSTRATING PREDRYING STEPS FOR STEAM PEELING CARROTS

carefully planning predrying operations and for training operating personnel in the performance of their duties in each operation. All personnel involved in handling tender fresh foodstuffs should be made aware of the undesirable consequences that can be triggered by physical damage to the commodity, leading to an inferior final product. Training of personnel must include education on the effects of deteriorative enzyme action, growth of molds and yeasts, and infestation by animal pests, which lead to unnecessary losses in quality and nutritive value in foodstuffs that have been mishandled during processing (Harris and von Loesecke 1971; Makower et al. 1952; Makower and Ward 1950; Talburt and Legault 1950).

Receiving the Commodity

Selection of procedures for handling raw commodity shipments arriving at a dehydration plant depends on several factors: (1) form of the food (preprocessed or in its harvest state); (2) type and variety of commodity; (3) harvesting methods, containers used, and field grading and cleaning already performed; (4) hauling methods; (5) weighing, sampling, grading, and lot control required; and (6) holding, storing, and conditioning required before feeding to the processing line.

Inadequate material handling can reduce the capacity of otherwise good processing plants. Transportation and labor costs are increasing sharply. This situation is forcing present and potential processors to study their material handling setup with respect to bulk handling, efficient design, and automation. There is a strong trend towards the purchase and installation of complete systems. Thus, a single supplier coordinates, furnishes, installs, and automates all material handling components to provide push-button control of the flow of material from the point of reception to the point of final product disposal (Leinen 1966; MacDonald and Leopold 1968).

Preprocessed foods that are used as starting material for dehydration may be in one of many forms or states: fluid or solid; single-strength or concentrated; frozen or canned; sterilized or pasteurized; bulk or packaged. Each form will usually be best handled by established procedures or by simple, obvious methods. New and improved materials-handling techniques are continually sought by progressive plant operators. As an example, liquid tomato concentrates are packed aseptically in 55-gal. drums for reprocessing, in place of packing in No. 10 tin cans (Robe 1958; Anon. 1958). The drums are specially constructed, with tin electrolytically applied to the interior after the side seam is welded. Quality advantages of aseptic canning are combined with bulk-handling benefits of drum shipments. In another example, 4000-gal. rubberized nylon-fabric tanks were developed for use in shipment of orange juice (Anon. 1961B). This is a 453-lb tank, 30 ft long, equipped with stainless steel fittings and a throw-away plastic liner, and can be rolled up compactly for return. In still other examples, citrus concentrates are shipped in steel drums lined with polyethylene; and frozen peas and string beans are packed in fiberboard boxes with liners, in multi-wall paper bags, and multiwall boxes.

Should the field processing of fruits and vegetables be widely accepted, there would necessarily be radical changes in the transportation of the preprocessed commodities to the canneries. Likewise, the storage and handling of such products would require major modifications (Clark 1970; Schultz et al. 1971; Miers et al. 1971).

Raw commodities for processing are handled by methods considerably different than commodities for fresh market. Hauling is done in pallet boxes, lugs (see Fig. 8.8), crates, baskets, or sacks, but bulk hauling in large trucks and trailers is often used if the food is not susceptible to mechanical damage. The truck or trailer is lifted or tilted for unloading (see Fig. 8.9). Some trucks are equipped with bottom-discharge doors or with powered discharge conveyors built lengthwise into the bed of the truck.

Commonly-used portable types of materials-handling equipment (Parker et al. 1954) needed in a dehydration plant include: (1) pallets (for boxes, crates, barrels, drums, bags, and cartons) constructed mainly of wood, but sometimes of metal or plastic; (2) pallet boxes; (3) dead skids (solid feet); and (4) semilive skids (1 pair solid feet, 1 pair casters). Other types include hand transporters (manual or powered) used for light loads, and lift-trucks (gasoline or electric powered) used for loads up to 5000 lb or more. Lift-trucks are marketed with a wide variety of attachments such as clamp arms for bales, barrels, drums, etc., and scoops for shoveling and dumping free-flowing materials. Semiportable and fixed materials-handling equipment include chutes and slides, flumes and sluices,

Courtesy of Western Canner and Packer

FIG. 8.8. HANDLING OF FIELD LUG-BOXES

Courtesy of Western Canner and Packer

FIG. 8.9. TILT-TRUCK METHOD OF UNLOADING AT PLANT

screw conveyors, flight conveyors, belt conveyors, drag chains, bucket or cleated-belt elevators, roller conveyors, vibrating conveyors, and pneumatic conveyors.

Raw material received at the dehydration plant is usually weighed (a large scale that will weigh truck-trailer combinations is required), sampled, and labeled for lot control. Sometimes it is graded at this time, by government inspectors or by plant personnel. Provision must be made for determining the amount of extraneous matter in the incoming fresh commodity, if purchase contracts specify price adjustments for net weight. The extraneous material should be eliminated either in dry washer or in grading machines, similar to those described in later sections of this chapter.

Storing the Raw Commodity

Storage is usually required for the following purposes: (1) to ensure continuous supply of raw material to the processing line; (2) to extend the length of processing season; (3) to condition certain commodities such as sweet potatoes, potatoes, and onions; (4) to ripen certain fruits, e.g., pears; or (5) to hold raw material obtained during favorable price situations.

Storage facilities, adequate to ensure a continuous supply of raw material to the processing line, should be provided at or near the plant. Space is required for quantities needed to operate the plant for at least ten days.

Temperature and humidity conditions required in storage areas depend upon the raw material and the purpose served by storage. Plants processing citrus juices or concentrates, green peas, green beans, or other frozen preprocessed items, require frozen storage space, usually 0°F. Most fresh fruits and vegetables store best at about 32°F, as shown in Tables 8.3 and 8.4. For commodities such as bananas, potatoes, sweet potatoes, green peppers, and cranberries, storage temperatures as low as 32°F are not only unnecessary but are often detrimental. Potatoes that have been held at recommended cold storage temperatures of 38–40°F are more suitable for dehydration if they are conditioned by holding at 65–70°F for 1–3 weeks. This treatment allows the sugar, which has accumulated in the living tuber at the lower temperatures, to be reduced by natural

TABLE 8.3

STORAGE CONDITIONS FOR FRUITS

Commodity	Storage Temp (°F)	Relative Humidity (%)	Approx Storage Life	Avg Freezing Temp (°F)
Apples	30–31	85–90	[1]	28.4
Apricots	31–32	85–90	1–2 weeks	28.1
Berries (common types)	31–32	85–90	7–10 days[2]	29–30
Cherries, sweet	31–32	85–90	10–14 days	24.5
sour	31–32	85–90	10–14 days	28.0
Cranberries	36–40	85–90	1–3 months	27.3
Peaches	31–32	85–90	2–4 weeks	29.4
Pears, Anjou	29–31	88–92	2–7 months	26.9
Bartlett	29–31	88–92	2–7 months	28.5

Source: Selected data from Wright *et al.* (1954), Desrosier (1970), Anon. (1962A).
[1] Several weeks to 12 months.
[2] Gooseberries, 3–4 weeks.

TABLE 8.4

STORAGE CONDITIONS FOR VEGETABLES

Commodity	Storage Temp (°F)	Relative Humidity (%)	Approx Storage Life	Avg Freezing Temp (°F)
Beans, green	45	85–90	8–10 days	29.7
Beets, topped	32	90–95	1–3 months	26.9
Cabbage	32	90–95	3–4 months	31.2
Carrots, topped	32	90–95	4–5 months	29.6
Garlic	32	70–75	6–8 months	25.4
Onions	32	70–75	6–8 months	30.1
Peas, green	32	85–90	1–2 weeks	30.0
Peppers, green	45	85–90	8–10 days	30.1
Potatoes	38–40	85–90	6–9 months	28.9
Sweet potatoes	55–60	80–85	4–6 months	28.5
Tomatoes, ripe	40–50	85–90	7–10 days	30.4
Tomatoes, mature green	55–70	80–85	3–5 weeks	30.4

Source: Selected data from Wright *et al.* (1954), Desrosier (1970), Anon. (1962A).

respiration. High-sugar potatoes are susceptible to discoloration during dehydration and subsequent storage. Onions and garlic, which store well when held in common storage (room temperature) in many areas, must be allowed to dry out after harvest to facilitate peel removal during processing.

Sweet potatoes require special treatment quite different from other vegetable crops. Freshly-dug sweet potatoes should be given a preliminary curing treatment to permit healing of wounds and abrasions incident to harvesting and handling and to prevent entrance of decay organisms. The curing treatment consists of storage at 85°F and 90% RH (or higher) for a period of about 10 days. After this treatment, the commodity is stored at about 55°F and 75–85% RH, where it will remain in good condition for periods up to 4–5 months. Sweet potatoes stored at lower temperatures will soften and rot.

To maintain optimum relative humidity in storage areas, some form of humidity control must be provided. Reliable automatic humidity controllers are now available. For most fruits and vegetables that are to be dehydrated, storage at 85–90% RH is optimum (see Tables 8.3 and 8.4). For commodities that require rapid air circulation, relative humidity in the storage area must be high to prevent wilting of the commodity. Allen and Pentzer (1935) reported that doubling the rate of air movement in storage areas increased moisture loss by about $\frac{1}{3}$, equivalent to the effect of a 5% drop in relative humidity.

Fresh fruits and vegetables remain "alive" after harvest. Living plant tissues resist spoilage organisms; therefore, storage conditions must not cause death of the fruit or vegetable. When living plant tissues respire, they consume oxygen and natural sugars, and release carbon dioxide, moisture, and energy in the form of heat. The heat released is an important factor in determining the refrigeration load during storage (see Table 8.5). Metabolic rate, or respiration, increases with temperature, and reaches a maximum at about 100°F.

A special type of storage known as "controlled atmosphere" (CA) in the United States, is used to prolong the storage life of apples. In the United Kingdom, this type of storage is known as "gas storage" (Kidd and West 1950). The fruit is held in good condition for periods up to 8–12 months, by a combination

TABLE 8.5

APPROXIMATE RATES OF EVOLUTION OF HEAT BY CERTAIN FRESH FRUITS AND VEGETABLES

Commodity	Storage Temp (°F)	Heat Evolved per Ton of Commodity per 24 Hr (Btu)
Apples		
Yellow Transparent	32	1,500
	40	2,660
	60	7,880
	70	12,380
Jonathan	32	700–800
	40	820–840
	60	2,610–3,470
Winesap	32	300–320
	40	590–600
	60	2,270–2,350
Beans, lima, Fordhook	32	2,330
	40	4,300
	60	21,990
	70	29,220
Beans, snap, stringless green pod	32	6,160
	40	10,600
	60	40,850
	70	49,590
Beets, topped	32	2,650
	40	4,060
	60	7,240
Cabbage, Globe	32	1,200
	40	1,670
	60	4,080
	70	6,120
Carrots, topped	32	2,310
	40	3,470
	60	8,080
Onions, dry, Yellow Globe	32	660–1,100
	50	1,760–1,980
	70	3,080–4,180
Potatoes, Irish Cobbler	32	440–880
	40	1,110–1,760
	70	2,200–3,520
Sweet potatoes, Nancy Hall, cured	60	4,280

Source: Wright *et al.* (1954).

of 3 effects which reduce the natural respiration rate: (1) low temperature—the basic principle of cold storage; (2) reduced oxygen content in the storage atmosphere—oxygen is required for respiration; and (3) increased carbon dioxide content in the storage atmosphere—carbon dioxide slows chemical reactions involved in respiration. The apples are stored in gastight refrigerated rooms; after several days the natural respiration of the fruit reduces oxygen content and increases carbon dioxide content of the gas in the storage space. The desired ratio of carbon dioxide, oxygen, and nitrogen is maintained by admitting small amounts of air into the room, or by scrubbing out part of the carbon dioxide by circulating the air through a tower with sprays of caustic soda solution. Supplemental methods are used to shorten the period required to adjust the composition of the atmosphere in the apple-filled CA room to retain more of the fresh quality of the fruit. For example, nitrogen is used to sweep the oxygen from the room packed with containers of apples. Bottled nitrogen may be used or the nitrogen may be generated by combustion of atmospheric air with a suitable fuel and scrubbing the carbon dioxide out of the combustion gases before the latter are passed into the CA room. Cost of CA storage for apples has been estimated to be 10–50¢ per bu for each storage season, depending upon the period of storage and the method used. The atmosphere and conditions in storage must not cause the fruit to "die." Details of CA storage for Starking Delicious variety of apples have been investigated by Schomer and Sainsbury (1957), and for several other varieties by Smock (1949, 1950). It was found that different varieties of apples should not be stored in the same CA room, because "scald" and other storage disorders tend to develop in the fruit. Besides, each variety responds best to one characteristic set of storage conditions that may not be best for another variety. Recently, CA storage has been found experimentally to be beneficial for use with several other fruits and vegetables.

Strongly scented fruits and vegetables such as apples, celery, cabbage, potatoes, onions, and garlic, must not be stored together because transfer of odors and flavors may occur. Some commercial storage houses circulate the air from the storage room through beds of adsorbent (activated carbon) to remove volatiles or off-odors (Wright *et al.* 1954; Smock and Southwick 1948), but this practice has been justified only in some cases (Schomer and Sainsbury 1957).

Sanitary conditions in storage rooms must be maintained through a program of regular inspections and immediate implementation of corrective measures. All decaying material must be removed from the storage area, followed by a thorough cleaning of the affected area. Chemicals applied to the food to control ripening, sprouting, molding, or pests, must be approved by FDA. According to the Food Additive Amendment of 1958, the applicant for approval of a new additive must furnish proof that the chemical used is harmless to humans in the amounts used. Lists of additives that have already been approved are published periodically.

A problem associated with storage is the condensation of moisture on the surface of the commodity after it has been removed from the cold room. If processing is started as soon as possible after removal, and the commodity is not subjected to extended holding periods under conditions that will cause decay, condensation will not be a serious problem.

Feeding the Commodity to the Processing Line

At the head of the processing line, a steady and continuous flow of raw commodity must be provided. Often, the rate of production is controlled at this point in the plant. Usually the simplest method to feed the commodity is to dump the contents of the sack, box, crate, or other container directly into the hopper of the first stage of the process (Fig. 8.10 and 8.11). Bulk shipments that are fed directly to the line can be dumped directly into the feed hopper. Conveyors and elevators are commonly used to transfer commodities from the receiving or storage area to the processing area. Powered scoops, sometimes in combination with portable conveyors, are used to move material from bulk storage piles to flumes, conveyors, or trucks. Some root vegetables are conveyed by fluming, sometimes for considerable distances. This method is inexpensive, decreases bruising, serves as a prewashing step, and reduces airborne dust in the area. Combination washer-elevators provide means for washing or softening the soil adhering to the commodity. Water-filled feed hoppers reduce bruising of the commodity being charged.

Provision should be made for blending of lots of raw commodity to maintain efficient plant operation. Blending is done when one lot of raw commodity is exceptionally free of defects and another is below standard in this respect. If used without blending the latter will require many more trimmers. A proper blend of the two lots allows a reasonable and steady rate of product flow and efficient utilization of labor.

Courtesy of Veg-A-Peel Co., Inc.

FIG. 8.10. FEED HOPPER AND ELEVATOR COMBINATION

Courtesy of Basic Vegetable Products, Inc.
FIG. 8.11. FEEDING SACKED ONIONS TO LINE

The empty containers can be transported back to the field on the trucks that are returning for another load. Frequently, empty boxes, pallets, sacks, etc., must be stored at the plant from one season to the next. The containers required to supply a dehydration plant represent a major investment,[1] and they must be stored with care to obtain maximum useful life. Boxes, crates, and pallets may be stacked outdoors if necessary (Fig. 8.8), but sacks must be stored indoors and kept dry to prolong their life.

Grading

Grading may be performed at the time the commodity is received at the plant, but is sometimes done after washing when the physical characteristics of the commodity are better exposed. Factors that may be considered in grading are size and shape, color, texture, density, chemical composition, blemishes, and insect infestation. Grading is sometimes used in conjunction with a side operation of packing for the fresh market. In the dehydration plant, sizing and grading of fruits and vegetables serve not only to determine the value of the commodity for processing but assist in several ways in making the operation profitable. Maturity, color, flavor, and defects largely determine the quality of the finished product; usually sale contracts define and specify the grading requirements of the finished product as well as the raw commodity. Food grading

---

[1]For example, the 200,000 burlap sacks needed in a 100-ton-a-day onion dehydration plant would cost about $40,000. Bushel crates for a 100-ton-a-day sweet potato plant would cost about $150,000.

that is required to protect the public health and to prevent fraud in the sale of off-grade or adulterated products, is controlled by governmental agencies at federal, state, or local levels, and is supplemented by actions of trade organizations.

Grading is often manual but for some commodities, mechanical grading devices have been developed (see Fig. 8.12). Peas are graded for maturity by brine

Courtesy of Lockwood Grader Corp.

FIG. 8.12. SIZE GRADER AND DEBRIS ELIMINATOR

flotation after being graded for size and blanched. "Fancy" quality peas will float in a brine of 1.04 sp gr whereas "standards" will float in a brine of 1.07 sp gr. Peas which sink in the heavier brine are designed as "substandards" or "seconds."

Potatoes are also graded by brine flotation when total solids content is a factor in the quality of the dehydrated product; total solids content and specific gravity are related factors.

An ingenious method of continuously grading cranberries is used in which the berries are bounced on step-like boards; the unsound berries do not bounce and are eliminated.

Dry raw materials, such as beans and peas, can be made free of stones, discolored berries, and other objectionable matter by being subjected to the scrutiny of an electric eye. As the raw material flows at a controlled rate over the inner surface of a rapidly spinning cone a change in light reflection actuates an air jet which blows out the individual pieces of offensive material. It should be feasible to apply this principle for the grading of almost any fruit or vegetable at some stage of preparation for dehydration or to the dehydrated product prior to packaging.

Sizing

The terms sizing and grading are synonymous in some operations, particularly if the dehydration plant also packs the commodity for the fresh market. Sound, high quality raw material which does not meet fresh market requirements, is perfectly suitable for dehydration in most cases. Sizing, or the separation of field-run raw material into lots according to size or shape, can benefit the dehydration operation in several ways: (1) maximum performance and yields are obtained in the peeling and cutting machines that are correspondingly adjusted for size of material; (2) blanching and drying operations are better controlled; (3) finished products have greater uniformity; and (4) lots of commodity of special size can be diverted into operations producing different types of product. Sizing is performed manually, or with one or more of many different types of mechanical equipment:

Screens.—Flat—shaking, vibrating, or tapping; with hole sizes and shapes as required for the particular commodity; or cylindrical—rotating screen, perforated sheet metal, rods, or slats in the outer shell.

Rolls, Belts, or Slats.—Fixed or travelling; with tapered, graduated, or diverging spacings (see Fig. 8.12).

Weighing Machines.—Continuous; automatically weigh and channel each unit into different lines (used primarily for fresh market pack).

Inspecting

A preliminary hand-sorting of the raw material is performed at the beginning of the line or receiving point. Sometimes it is advantageous to inspect the commodity after it has been cleaned. Inspectors remove: (1) stones, twigs, and other foreign matter that may damage machines; (2) defective raw material that would increase trimming labor after peeling and inspection difficulties after dehydration; and (3) rotten material that would foul processing equipment and adversely affect product quality.

One or two inspectors stationed alongside conveyors carrying the raw foodstuff are often sufficient at this stage in the preparation of many commodities.

Cleaning

In the dehydration plant, cleaning is the first treatment that alters the physical condition of the foodstuff, and may therefore be considered the first true processing step. Cleaning serves to remove dirt, leaves, twigs, rocks, insects, insecticidal residues, and other contaminants. Tramp metals are removed by magnetic separators or other metal detectors. Cleaning is required under statutes that protect public health; however, other important advantages accrue, since removal of contaminants reduces spoilage rates, protects machines against damage from foreign materials, and improves the efficiency of the peeling equipment and other preparation machines (Manock *et al.* 1964).

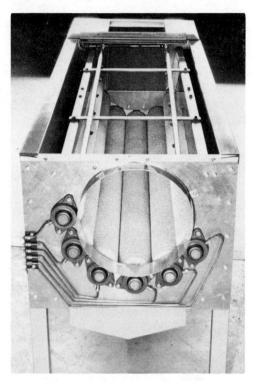

Courtesy of Veg-A-Peel Co., Inc.

FIG. 8.13. BRUSH-TYPE WASHER

Cleaning is performed by either dry or wet methods, or combinations of both. Dry methods involve continuously tumbling the commodity on vibrating screens or other units equipped with parallel rolls, discs, or brushes (Fig. 8.13), or in rotating horizontal drums constructed of bars, rods, slats, or coarse screen (Fig. 8.14). The dry cleaning units resemble equipment described under "Sizing" or "Washing." The tumbling action loosens adhering soil, which falls through the openings, along with other debris. Removal of loose soil and debris in the dry washer reduces water requirements in the wet washer, reduces the load on the sewage system, and provides a means for adjustment of purchase price of the commodity on a net basis. The need for dry washing at this stage will depend on the commodity and its condition. However, the equipment required is not costly and is usually justified, even if only for standby operation for severe cases.

Wet washers are similar in size and form to the dry washers described previously except that sprays of water are installed and directed on the tumbling foodstuff (see Fig. 8.14). For maximum effectiveness, the spray nozzles must be supplied with high-pressure water, at least 50–80 lb per sq in. The nozzles must

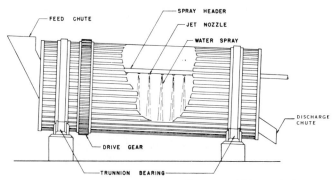

Courtesy of Diamond Alkali Co.

FIG. 8.14. ROTARY-TYPE WASHER

be designed for the pressure and volume to be used, fineness of spray, distance from product, and angle of impingement. All parts of each tumbling fruit or vegetable must be exposed to the full force of the sprays, but without injury to the product. Sometimes the wet washers are preceded by soaking troughs or tanks in which commodities are conveyed by means of belts, drag chains, or screws. Long periods of immersion are sometimes needed to loosen or soften caked or sticky soils. Wet washers must not be used on commodities such as onions that are to be flame peeled.

Preparing for Drying

The cleaned raw foodstuff, whole and intact except where pretrimming may have been required, must now be converted into the form in which it will be dehydrated. Depending upon the commodity and the dehydration method used, various operations will be required, for example, peeling, coring, trimming, cutting, slitting, pulping, juicing, blending, etc. With only a few exceptions, such as onions and garlic, the raw prepared solid foods will be blanched or cooked; liquid food will be homogenized, blended, heated, evaporated or concentrated; and finally, the desired additives will be incorporated or applied. The operations and sequences will vary for different types and forms of commodity—a great many combinations are possible. The discussion that follows treats the general practices used in preparation operations. It is impossible within the scope of this chapter to present all variations. The managing and technical staff of a plant must select the procedures and the sequences to be used with specific commodities.

Preconditioning.—Heating in water is a procedure sometimes used with potatoes and sweet potatoes to precondition them before the peeling operation. Potatoes are heated for about 4–7 min at 135°–160°F, and sweet potatoes are heated for about 30 min at 125°–140°F. Preheating serves several purposes; (1) it improves the uniformity of peel removal; (2) it reduces discolorations after peeling and during drying; (3) it minimizes trimming and inspection labor; (4) it increases yield of product; and (5) it increases the capacity of lye and steam peelers by reducing heat load and by making control easier. Scott *et al.* (1945) demonstrated the advantage of preheating before lye peeling with three varieties of sweet potatoes (Table 8.6). Discoloration in sweet potatoes after lye peeling

TABLE 8.6

EFFECT OF PREHEATING BEFORE LYE PEELING SWEET POTATOES

		Loss in Percentage of Fresh Weight		
Variety	Preheated[1]	Peel Loss[2]	Trim Loss	Total Loss
Big Stem Jersey	Yes	17.0	4.0	21.0
	No	16.2	29.2	45.4
Maryland Golden	Yes	17.5	3.5	21.0
	No	16.5	9.0	25.5
Porto Rico	Yes	15.5	3.0	18.5
	No	14.0	13.0	27.0

[1] Preheated 30 min in water at 125°F.
[2] Lye-peeled 5 min in 10% lye at 217°F.

was claimed by Scott to be due to "the activation of oxidase and reaction with catechol tannins in the cambium area." When sweet potatoes were preheated for 30 min at 125°F before lye peeling, a temperature of 205°F was attained in the cambium area during lye peeling, high enough to inactivate the catechol oxidase.

Preheaters, some of which are similar in design to the soakers already described, include rotary, screw, drag chain, belt, etc., types. Unlike the soakers, however, the water is heated, usually by direct injection of steam. Screw-type preheaters are similar in design to screw-type water blanchers, but the former are operated at lower temperatures.

Peeling

Almost all fruits and vegetables that are dehydrated in piece or fluid form must be peeled. Many variables are involved in the peeling operation, and some of them are beyond the control of the operator. The crop itself may vary from day to day and from grower to grower. Freshness is important—sometimes shriveled or corky skins develop and require special peeling treatment. Bruised or blemished crops require special peeling conditions. Type of storage treatment also changes peeling characteristics. Some commodities require treatment with wetting agents for effective peeling by immersion methods. It is a challenge to the skill and ingenuity of the operator to evaluate all significant variables and adjust the process for maximum efficiency. The margin of profit in a dehydration plant often depends upon the effectiveness of the peeling operation, which, in turn, determines product yield and expenditure of trimming labor. Through continued study and improvement of techniques, development of ingenious peeling devices and auxiliaries, and exercise of careful control of the peeling operation, peeling and trimming losses can be minimized, trimming labor can be reduced, and attractive products can be produced.

Peeling methods currently used may be classified into three general types: mechanical, chemical, and thermal. Each type has characteristic advantages.

Mechanical Peelers.—Mechanical devices are used for peeling apples (see Fig. 8.15). In one machine, an operator takes two apples, one in each hand, and places them simultaneously into feed cups on the machine. The following opera-

Courtesy of Western Canner and Packer

FIG. 8.15. MECHANICAL APPLE PEELER

tions then proceed automatically. The fruit is grasped firmly by centering jaws and moved into position where it is impaled on a hollow coring spindle; the apple rotates with the coring spindle while a swiveled paring blade contacts the surface and follows the contour of the fruit, removing a thin uniform peel; the coring spindle is withdrawn and the cored and pared apple is transferred to a second set of centering jaws; a curved, finger-like blade enters the core cavity from above, and with a rotating cut frees the remaining internal seed cell portions. Small fragments are removed, after the apples are sliced, by washing and screening in rotary or vibrating devices. A radial-knife attachment for the machine can be used to cut the prepared fruit into pie-type wedges in the same operation. The fruit can also be cut as desired in a separate machine. Lopez *et al.* (1958) studied yield factors and trim times in several plants peeling apples by this method and correlated the results with variety, size, and grade of the fruit processed.

Another type of mechanical peeler removes the peel from root-type vegeta-

Courtesy of Veg-A-Peel Co., Inc.

FIG. 8.16. CONTINUOUS ROTARY-TYPE ABRASIVE PEELER

bles by abrasion (Fig. 8.16). The foodstuff is tumbled and thrown against surfaces coated with abrasive, while a spray of water washes away the loosened
skins. Abrasion peeling may be used to good advantage in some cases, but must
be properly operated for best results. Gooding *et al.* (1960) found that average
peeling losses in abrasion peeling of carrots were reduced from 19.9 to 16.4% by
reducing the machine speed and by making other adjustments. Early-crop, thin-
skinned potatoes peel well by abrasion with a minimum of weight loss. "Rus-
setted" varieties and those with deep eyes or very irregular and nonspherical
shape usually lose 25–50% more weight with abrasion peeling and may require
20–40% more trimming labor to produce an acceptable product, in comparison
with chemical peeling methods (see below). Abrasion peelers usually have a
lower water consumption than other peeling methods. Abrasion peelers are also
very effective as a means of removing peel previously loosened by chemical or
heat pretreatment, and are frequently installed in lines following flame, steam,
or lye peelers.

Chemical Peeling.—Chemical peeling and treating of certain foods have been
used in this country since colonial days. Bitting (1917) presented an historical

review of lye peeling and described 6 lye-peeling devices patented in the United States during the first 15 yr of the 20th Century. Many different types of chemical peeling methods have been investigated, but only those methods employing hot lye solutions have survived and have become firmly established in commercial operations. The emergency expansion of the dehydration industry during World War II provided a great impetus to the development of lye peelers.

In peeling methods involving the use of hot lye solutions, the following factors must be considered: (1) control of lye penetration for proper peel removal; (2) provision against safety hazards; (3) protection against corrosion; (4) disposal of spent lye; (5) removal of all traces of lye from the peeled product (trimmings must be equally well washed if they are to be used for stock feed); (6) treatment of some commodities with dilute acid after lye peeling, to prevent discoloration; and (7) provision for lye storage and makeup facilities.

The principle variables involved in lye peeling are: (1) the time of immersion in the lye bath; (2) the temperature and concentration of the lye solution; and (3) the commodity characteristics (type, variety, maturity, and storage history). Peeling with hot lye combines chemical attack with thermal shock; the tissue just under the skin is disintegrated, the skin is loosened and scrubbed off.

Lye-peeling methods as originally developed used boiling or near-boiling lye solutions in concentrations just high enough to be effective. A typical curve showing the approximate retention time for potatoes in near-boiling lye at various concentrations is shown in Fig. 8.17 (USDA 1944). The boiling point of lye at various concentrations is shown in Fig. 8.18. Modern practices tend toward use of higher concentrations and sub-boiling temperatures; immersion time is adjusted as required. Advantages of lower treatment temperatures are: (1) deep cooking of the outer tissues is reduced or eliminated, yields are higher, and "heat rings" are avoided; (2) heat losses and evaporation from the lye bath are reduced; and (3) hazards of boiling, splashing, leaking, overflowing, or dripping are reduced. Harrington et al. (1956) studied peeling of potatoes with lye at temperatures from $130°$ to $160°F$ and concentrations in the range of 10–25% and concluded that low-temperature peeling of potatoes is a feasible commercial operation that may result in reduction in peeling loss and trimming labor. Where the presence of a thin cooked surface layer is not objectionable, use of higher temperatures results in faster peeling.

A major improvement in the process for the caustic peeling of potatoes has been developed recently at the USDA Western Regional Research Laboratory. The process has been successfully operated on a commercial scale and offers several highly significant advantages, namely: an 80% reduction in caustic usage; a 95% reduction in water consumption in the peeling process; almost total recovery of waste peel solids; and, the elimination of large volumes of liquid waste with high BOD.

In the commercial application of the development, washed potatoes are contacted for 3 min with 12–14% lye solution; then held at ambient temperature for about 5 min. This retention time allows the lye to penetrate, act upon the

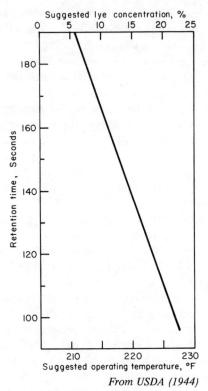

From USDA (1944)

FIG. 8.17. SUGGESTED CONDITIONS FOR LYE PEELING POTATOES

skin, and the temperature to equalize. The potatoes are now surface heated for 2–3 min under gas-fired infrared heaters at 1600°F and are then ejected into a mechanical peeler. This device consists of multiple rollers covered with flexible rubber projections and revolving at differential speeds. The projections rapidly abrade the softened peel from the surface within a few seconds to the extent of 95%. All the removed peel is thrown off by the projections and removed as a residue with 20–25% solids content. The peeled potatoes drop directly into water to remove small amounts of residual peel and to cool the product. The quality of peeling is excellent and equal to or better than conventional. The improvement can be readily introduced into existing potato processing plants (Anon. 1970B; Graham *et al.* 1969B; Graham 1970; Smith 1970; Cyr 1971).

Woodroof *et al.* (1948) studied the peeling of peaches with lye concentrations varying from 2.6 to 39.6% and temperatures from 140° to 200°F, and the peeling of sweet potatoes with 10% lye at 210°F. The authors concluded that for sweet potatoes the best peeling conditions were 5–10% lye solutions at boiling temperatures (212°–220°F), but for peaches, 150°–160°F was maximum to avoid objectionable "heat rings" in the fruit. Total alkali consumed was about

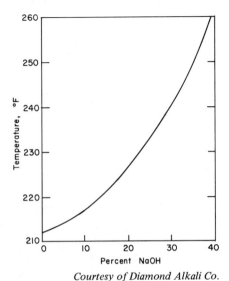

Courtesy of Diamond Alkali Co.

FIG. 8.18. BOILING POINT OF LYE SOLUTIONS AT ATMO-
SPHERIC PRESSURE

8–13 lb per ton of peaches and 28–40 lb per ton of cured sweet potatoes. Detergents added to the lye solution improved the yield of product only slightly; consumption of caustic was increased in half the tests and decreased in the rest.

Morgan *et al.* (1966) investigated the removal of bran from wheat and several other cereal grains by chemical peeling. The product retains all of the endosperm, including the highly nutritious aleurone layer, and loses most or all of the bran layers. The grain is first soaked in water and completely cooked by steam. Then the bran layer is loosened by the action of strong, hot caustic and removed by vigorous washing with water. Warm dilute acid restores surface whiteness and neutralizes residual caustic. The debranned grain is then dried by warm air.

Any of the various wheat varieties can be subjected to the caustic peeling process to produce a final bran-free product which, in reality, is an improved form of bulgur. Bulgur, as such, is an ancient food commodity prepared and used extensively by the people of the mid-eastern and asiatic countries. If the cooking step is omitted, an uncooked bran-free product is easily obtained.

Lankler and Morgan (1943) also studied the use of wetting agents in lye peeling and concluded that "successful chemical peeling depends upon the ability of the agent to attack the skin before the temperature at which it is used cooks the outer layer of flesh." Elberta peaches, Bartlett pears, MacIntosh apples, quinces, beets, turnips, parsnips, celeryroot, potatoes, and carrots were experimentally peeled in lye by Lankler and Morgan with and without added alkyl aryl sulfonate (0.5%). When the wetting agent was used, peeling time, lye concentration, and bath temperature could be reduced for optimum peel. The maximum effect of the added wetting agent was obtained at lye concentrations between 5 and 20%, with optimum at 10%.

Olsen (1941) found that lye peeling and acid peeling were equally effective in the peeling of 3 varieties of peaches when 0.5% wetting agent was added to the peeling bath, providing the fruit was evenly and thoroughly ripened, either on the tree or in storage.

Mazzola (1946) compared nine methods of peeling potatoes and concluded in favor of lye peeling, basing his conclusion on the superior adjustability of the lye method for variation in the size, shape, variety, and storage history of the raw material.

Arthur and McLemore (1955) investigated the peeling of sweet potatoes in a pilot-plant rotary lye peeler using a retention time of 6 min in 20% lye at 220°F, and found that peeling losses varied between 20 and 35%, depending on variety, size, and storage history of the sweet potatoes, and on the preheating conditions used on the root before peeling.

Dunlap (1944) reported a 65% increase in yield of dehydrated potatoes in a commercial operation, when the peeling method was changed from abrasion to lye. This result probably demonstrates the logical conclusion that lye peeling has greater advantage over abrasive peeling when the product to be peeled is irregularly shaped or has bumps, crevices, or pits.

Caldwell (1943) summarized the peel and trim losses of 19 varieties of potatoes when peeled with 10–12% lye for 7½ to 10 min at 190°F.

Raisins ("soda dipped") and prunes are sometimes treated with lye before dehydration. The purpose is not to "peel" in these instances, but merely to "check" the skins to allow more rapid rehydration rates as well as faster dehydration. A hot solution of 0.6% lye or sodium carbonate is used for raisins, and 0.6–1.8% lye is used for prunes.

A summary of ranges of conditions used in lye-peeling some commodities is shown in Table 8.7. Commodity characteristics are very important and exact operating conditions to be used in each case must be determined by trial. Peel losses per se do not necessarily indicate degree of efficiency, since an inefficient peeling method will give a low peel loss, but large trim losses will more than eat up the apparent saving.

Lye peeling is suitable for almost all root vegetables and some fruits, and is performed either in batch-type or continuous operations. Batch peeling is used in relatively small-scale operations and is usually performed by dipping baskets of commodity in a hot lye bath for a predetermined time and then washing off the loosened peel and residual lye. Continuous lye peelers can be used with any scale of operation. The rotary, or wheel-type peeler (see Fig. 8.19) consists of a perforated steel drum with internal vanes that form pockets, rotating partially submerged in hot caustic solution. The drum is enclosed within a concentric shell to keep the commodity confined while the drum rotates. The commodity enters the drum pockets from an overhead or side chute, moves around with the

TABLE 8.7

LYE PEELING OF FRUITS AND VEGETABLES

Commodity and Variety	Caustic Solution (°F)	% Lye	Dip Time (Min)	Lye Used[1] (Lb/Ton)	Peel Loss (%)	Ref
Potatoes						
(Irish Cobbler)	220	12	2.5	30	22	(a)
(Irish Cobbler)	220–250	13–35	0.8–2.8	–	15	(d)
(Irish Cobbler)	155–160	25	5	–	20	(d)
(Irish Cobbler)	190–210	14–20	2–3	40–80	–	(e)
(Russet Burbank)	150	15–25	4	–	14–25	(b)
(Russet Burbank)	218–219	20	2.2	25	23	(f)
(Irish Cobbler)	240	18	3	30	–	(f)
(Katahdin)	217–220	25	2.5	25	–	(f)
(Chippewa)	200	30	2.0	16–32	–	(f)
Carrots						
(Unknown)	212	5	2.7	–	–	(g)
(Unknown)	218–220	6–8	1	8.6	–	(f)
	214–218	5–10	1–2	–	–	(e)
	214–218	5–6	0.5–1.5	–	14	(a)
Sweet potatoes	220	20	6	–	20–35	(h)
	218	12	4	30	25	(a)
	218	12	1–2	–	–	(e)
	218	15–18	4.3	–	–	(f)
	210	10	6	35	12.9	(c)
Peaches						
(Elberta)	155	6	1–3	12	5–17	(c)
(Unknown)	140 max.	10[2]	0.3–0.7	–	–	(e)

[1] These values are from limited observations. See text for variables.
[2] Follow with acid dip to prevent darkening.

(a) Diamond Alkali Co. (1956).   (e) Pennsalt Chemicals Corp. (1965).
(b) Harrington et al. (1956).   (f) Combined Food Board (1944).
(c) Woodroof et al. (1948).   (g) Havighorst (1943).
(d) Mazzola (1946).   (h) Arthur and McLemore (1955).

drum through the lye solution, and is carried upward to the discharge chute. A steam coil is provided in the tank to keep the lye solution hot, or the lye solution is circulated through an external heat exchanger.

The draper-type continuous lye peeler consists of a long, narrow tank equipped with a metal wire-mesh belt for conveying the food-stuff through the bath. The belt is equipped with advancing flights or lugs to ensure uniform movement of material through the tank. If the commodity floats, an overhead belt is provided to submerge the product as it advances through the tank. Means are provided for draining excess lye solution from treated material leaving the peeler. In some variations, the conveyor belt is entirely confined within the tank to avoid excessive loss of heat and prevent dripping of caustic outside of the tank. The bottom of the tank should be sloped to a sump to assure good drainage of the sludge that collects from reaction of the lye with the product.

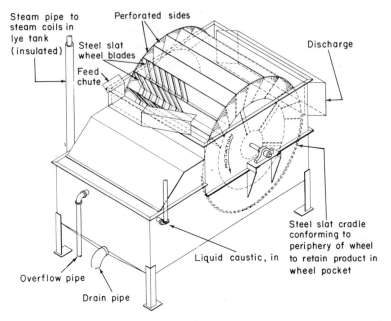

FIG. 8.19. A ROTARY-TYPE LYE PEELER WHICH MAY ALSO BE USED AS
A PREHEATER OR BLANCHER

The heating coil should be of adequate size to heat the caustic solution rapidly to the desired temperature. If the coil is located inside the tank it should be remote from the sludge sump to avoid continuous thermal agitation of the suspended solids. If an external heat exchanger is used, provision should be made to remove suspended peel fragments and sludge from the circulated lye solution by a strainer or other means. Automatic controls should be provided to maintain the proper temperature during operation. Direct steam injection heating must not be used because of dilution of the lye solution.

The spray-type lye peeler (Dunkley 1921) is similar to the draper type, except that the conveyor runs above the level of the lye solution. Hot lye is sprayed onto the commodity on the conveyor and drains back into the tank for recirculation.

Lye peelers, in common with other types of peelers utilizing heated media, require $1\frac{1}{2}$ to 8 bhp of steam per ton per hour of capacity. Steam demand will rise with higher peeling temperatures and with longer retention times.

Copper, bronze, brass, aluminum, lead, zinc, cadmium, and tin should not be used in construction of a lye peeler because these metals are attacked by caustic soda.

Washing must always follow immediately after lye peeling to remove the caustic. A simple test for detecting the presence of residual caustic on the peeled product coming from the washer, is to place a drop of an alcoholic solution of phenolphthalein on the surface. The appearance of a pink stain shows excessive residual lye and indicates that additional washing is needed.

Lye (commercial caustic soda) is obtained in cake (700 lb in steel drums), flake (400 lb in steel drums), or liquid form (8000-10,000-gal. tank cars or 3200-4000-gal. tank trucks). Cake is cheaper than flake but must first be broken up or be melted with a steam lance. Use of these forms of lye requires makeup tanks and circulating pumps. Liquid lye (50% solution) is the cheapest form of caustic soda. Tank cars for liquid lye must be provided with internal heating coils, since the solution solidifies at about 53°F. Sometimes tank cars of lye are shipped hot, and the heat is retained long enough to prevent solidification of the lye before the car is emptied. Prospective users of lye should consult commercial manufacturers of this chemical to determine the form of lye that might best suit their purpose, the auxiliary equipment required, the techniques used, and the safety precautions necessary. Informative bulletins are published by chemical companies (Diamond Alkali Co., 1962) and are usually available on request.

All personnel who are to handle solid or liquid forms of caustic soda, or who are likely to be exposed to this chemical should be carefully instructed as to the hazards of lye. A small particle or droplet of solution will cause painful injury to the eyes with possible loss or impairment of vision. Painful, slow-healing burns are caused by contact of caustic with the skin. Wearing apparel made of wool, silk or leather is rapidly destroyed by caustic soda, but cotton clothing is more resistant. Goggles and rubber protective clothing should be worn during handling of caustic soda. A safety shower and an eye fountain should be provided nearby in case of accident, and personnel should be thoroughly instructed in emergency first aid information. In case of accident, medical attention should be obtained at once, even for burns that do not appear serious.

An experimental chemical peeling method (Anon. 1957) employed a solution of sodium hexametaphosphate, a water-soluble phosphate glass. Peaches immersed in a hot 1% solution peeled readily. Although the peeling solution was slightly alkaline (pH 8.2), the mechanism of peeling was reported to be unlike that with lye in that "the phosphate combines with the calcium of the protopectin in the middle lamella of the cells; the protopectin solubilizes and the outer skin layer separates readily from the flesh of the peach." It was claimed that more ascorbic acid was retained in the product peeled by this method than by other chemical methods for peeling peaches.

Acid peeling (Olsen 1941) is a chemical method that has limited application only in the peeling of peaches and has not been successful commercially.

Peeling with a boiling saturated salt brine (USDA 1944; Mazzola 1946; Eidt and MacArthur 1944) can be classed as a chemical method but would more properly fall into the category of *thermal shock*. The sodium chloride probably acts only to elevate the boiling point of the bath into the range 226°-228°F. However, it is believed that the residual salt on the surface of the peeled product retards discoloration. Peeling with brine has not enjoyed commercial success. One application is reported (Mazzola 1946) in which the brine treatment was followed by passage through an abrasion-type peeling unit.

Thermal Shock.—This type of peeling method can be divided into two sub-types. In the first subtype, direct exposure to flame at about 1000°F or higher first dries the outer surface of the commodity and then burns it to a char (Hemmeter 1946). The commodity to be peeled is conveyed and tumbled through an oven fired by either liquid or gaseous fuel. The carbonaceous layer is removed by vigorous scrubbing in a washer. This method, which has undergone many years of development, is used on onions, beets, and potatoes (Eidt and MacArthur 1944; USDA 1961). Fuel and maintenance costs are likely to be high in this peeling method. Asselbergs and Pavrie (1956, 1961) peeled apples experimentally by exposure to an infrared source at 1520°F, for 9 to 30 sec and reported a peeling loss of only 2.5% (as compared with the usual 15–18% loss by mechanical peeling).

In the second subtype of thermal-shock peeling method, the commodity is treated with a hot medium (water, brine, oil, steam, or air) and the flesh immediately under the skin is cooked to the softening point. The peel is then removed in jet-spray or abrasion washers. Pilorz (1955) described a commercial continuous peeling operation for tomatoes in which the fruit was gently tumbled in a blast of air at 700°F, the skins were split and blown away. It was claimed that higher yields were obtained by this method, and at low cost compared with conventional water-scalding methods used previously. In addition, it was pointed out that the layer of flesh directly under the skin, rich in ascorbic acid and in red pigment, was not lost in the new method.

Steam peeling has become increasingly popular in dehydration plants. Peeling with steam can be done batchwise or continuously. In the batch steam method (Mazzola 1946; Anon. 1944) for potatoes, the washed tubers were preheated 3 min in water at 170°F, then charged into retorts (Fig. 8.20) in lots of about 200 lb. The retorts, with 80 lb per sq in. internal steam pressure, rotated slowly for 1½–2 min. The steamed potatoes were discharged into a washer equipped with rough rubber-covered rolls, and the potatoes were tumbled under sprays supplied with water at 80 lb per sq in. Peel and trim losses were reported to average 26%.

Continuous steam peeling (Anon. 1945) is performed in a machine consisting of a screw conveyor in a cylindrical tube inclined upward toward the direction of flow (see Fig. 8.21). Rotary valves seal the screw conveyor at both ends for operation at 80–100 lb per sq in. steam pressure. The product enters the rotary feed valve and is carried in the inclined screw to the discharge valve. The steamed product is discharged into the washer and skin eliminator that follows. Steam pressure and retention time are automatically controlled in the peeler so that depth of penetration is just sufficient to completely and uniformly loosen the skin. Continuous steam peelers now in use can process 3–5 tons per hr of apples,

Courtesy of Idaho Potato Growers, Inc.

FIG. 8.20. OPERATOR IS LOADING ONE OF THE TWO PEELERS IN THIS BATCH-TYPE STEAM PEELER

Courtesy of Western Canner and Packer

FIG. 8.21. CONTINUOUS-TYPE STEAM PEELER

$3^1/_2$–6 tons per hr of potatoes, and 5–8 tons per hr of carrots or sweet potatoes. Steam demand is 775–1000 lb per hr, or 23–30 bhp. Variations in peeling capacity may be anticipated paralleling variations in previous history of the commodity to be peeled.

Some units have been developed to employ a combination of steam and lye (Adams *et al.* 1960). Eidt and MacArthur (1944) peeled onions by exposure to steam at 212°F for a short period, followed by light abrasion peeling. Hemmeter (1948) devised a machine to peel onions with a blast of steam after the ends of the bulbs were sawed or sliced off.

A novel method of peeling tomatoes was described by Straniero (1956) in which the fruit was immersed in saturated salt brine (NaCl) at 5°F for 30–40 sec, to form ice crystals and rupture the flesh cells immediately under the skin. The tomatoes were then plunged into water at 86°F and in 8–10 min, it was claimed, "enzymes released from the broken cells acted on the pectins that normally hold the skin on the tomato, leaving it free in a skin sac." The skin was then removed in conventional washers.

A summary of the peeling methods that are commonly used for fruits and vegetables is shown in Table 8.8. These methods are frequently used to advantage in combinations; for example, light abrasion peeling can be used following lye or steam peeling.

TABLE 8.8

SUMMARY OF COMMONLY USED PEELING METHODS

Apples	Mechanical, lye, steam
Beets	Lye, steam, flame, abrasion, combination[1]
Cabbage	Manual (with mechanical aids)
Carrots	Lye, steam, flame, abrasion, combination[1]
Onions	Flame, steam, abrasion
Peaches	Lye, steam, acid
Peppers, pimiento	Flame, hot oil, mechanical (corers)
Potatoes	Lye, steam, infrared heat, abrasion, combination[1]
Sweet potatoes	Lye, steam, abrasion, combination[1]
Tomatoes	Steam, hot water, hot air

[1] "Combination" refers to arrangements using two or more of the methods listed.

The washing operation that follows peeling is basically a part of the peeling operation. Loosened peel must be removed. Rotary washers (see Fig. 8.13 and 8.14) are effective if well-designed nozzles are used and supplied with water at 80–100 lb per sq in. pressure. Vigorous tumbling abrades the product, and exposes all surfaces. Tenacious peels, or portions that are only softened, require more vigorous scrubbing. Abrasive peelers are sometimes used for this purpose. The brush washer (Fig. 8.13) consists of a series of parallel rotating brushes over which the product tumbles and is scrubbed while being sprayed with water from overhead.

When lye is used in peeling, sufficient water and adequate exposure time must be allowed in the washer to eliminate the last traces of lye. Some products require a dilute acid dip following washing to prevent later discoloration.

Topping, Rooting, and Coring

Special procedures are required for some commodities. For example, carrots, onions, and other root-type vegetables are topped and rooted; cabbage is cored and the outer leaves are removed; and bell peppers are cored and seeded.

Carrots are topped to remove stem ends and "green crown," and the thin, woody, root ends are cut off. Normally these portions remain after peeling, and therefore a heavy load is imposed on the postpeeling trimming personnel. Mechanized units are available for topping and rooting carrots before peeling.

Onions are topped and rooted also, an operation that facilitates the removal of the thin "paper shell" outer skin. In one mechanical method, size-graded onions are individually positioned by hand on a rotating turret; the onions are conveyed between two circular saws, which cut off the top and root ends. High pressure water sprays or steam jets are then used to remove the loosened skins. In another type of operation, operators manually hold each size-graded onion against a special water-driven rotary knife, removing first one end and then the other end of the bulb. The outer skin can then be removed by conventional methods. Residual paper shell skin can be removed by an air classification method, after onions are dried.

Cabbage is cored, and any damaged outer leaves are removed by hand labor before the heads are shredded. Coring is done manually but with the aid of special equipment. One method consists of cutting the cabbage head in two with a long knife, which is hinged at one end and counterbalanced so that the knife will return to the elevated position when released by the operator. Each half is then held flat side down and pushed over a sharpened ring set in the table top, and the core is scooped out. A rotary device used for coring cabbage is similar to that described for use with onions. With this device it is advantageous to presize the cabbage heads, to avoid unnecessary waste.

Courtesy of Diamond Manufacturing Corp.
FIG. 8.22. CORING MACHINE FOR BELL PEPPERS

Bell peppers are cored with water-driven rotary corers as above. A recently developed machine is also used, in which the operation is entirely automatic after an operator places the individual peppers in the feed cups (Fig. 8.22).

Trimming and Inspecting

Following peeling, a final hand trimming is required to remove residual skin, eyes, roots, discolored areas, cuts or bruises, diseased or insect-damaged portions, and other defects. Most of the hand labor that is expended on the commodity in a dehydration plant is utilized in this operation. It is at this point that the cost benefits of an efficient peeling operation become apparent.

The size of the trimming line and the number of operators required vary widely, depending upon the commodity, its variety, grade, and storage history, and the type of product to be made. If a large fraction of the peeled commodity must be trimmed, the throughput will be reduced per trimmer. If, on the other hand, a good grade of commodity is peeled by an efficient method, and only a small fraction of the peeled commodity must be handled for trimming, the throughput per trimmer will be increased. For some products, for example, potato granules or potato flakes, less trimming of the peeled commodity is required, since residual peel and some blemished portions of the potato are eliminated during processing. In a well-planned operation, provision must be made for sufficient space along the trimming belt to accommodate the maximum number of trimmers that will be necessary under the worst conditions anticipated. For the average plant, the amount of material that can be inspected and trimmed per person is shown in Table 8.9 for seven selected commodities. Estimates of yields are shown in Table 8.10. See also Appendix C, Table A.2.

To make efficient use of trimming personnel, material for trimming must flow through the line without interruption and at the proper rate. Many types of trimming belt arrangements have been devised. One circulating type, called "merry-go-round" for obvious reasons, is used to advantage (see Fig. 8.23). In

TABLE 8.9

OUTPUT OF TRIMMED MATERIAL PER WORKER

Commodity	Trim Operations	Lb/Hr Raw Basis
Apples	Peeling, coring, trimming	150–300
Cabbage	Coring, quartering, trimming	500–750
Carrots	Topping, rooting, trimming	200–300[1]
Beets	Topping, rooting, trimming	200–300
Onions	Topping, rooting, trimming	150–300[2]
Potatoes	Trimming	150–300[3]
Sweet potatoes	Trimming	120–200

[1] 500 lb/hr with automatic topping machine in line.
[2] 700 lb/hr with mechanical aids.
[3] 1000 lb/hr when potatoes are for flakes or granules (see text).

TABLE 8.10

APPROXIMATE YIELDS OF SEVEN COMMODITIES
COMMONLY DEHYDRATED
(Basis: 1,000 Lb Raw Commodity)

Commodity	Prepared (Lb)[1]	Finished (Lb)[2]	Moisture (%)
Apples	650–800	120–145	23
Cabbage	650–750	47– 55	4
Carrots	750–850	90–100	4
Beets	700–800	80– 90	4
Onions	850–900	95–100	4
Potatoes	750–800[3]	150–160[3]	6
Sweet Potatoes	700–900	200–250	5

[1] Ready for dehydration.
[2] Will be reduced slightly by final inspection.
[3] For piece-form potato products.

this design, three parallel belt conveyors are arranged side-by-side, except that the center belt assembly is elevated so that the lower or return portion is at the same level as the top sides of each flanking belt. The top sides of all three belts travel in the same direction. The trimmers, stationed on both sides of the three-belt assembly, pick up each piece, trim it if necessary, and place it on the top side of the center belt to continue on in the process. Material that escapes trimming and reaches the end of the outer belts is diverted by a diagonal bar to

Courtesy of FMC Corp.

FIG. 8.23. PREPARATION AREA IN DEHYDRATION PLANT

A merry-go-round type trimming belt is in foreground. A belt-type
steam blancher is in background.

the bottom side of the center belt, and is returned to the beginning of the trimming line. Trimming wastes are handled by either of 2 methods: (1) each of the outer belts is divided into 2 lanes by a steel strip over the belt; the inner of the 2 lanes carries untrimmed material, the outer carries off the trimmings; or (2) chutes placed beside each worker convey the trimmings to the lower or return side of the outer belts, or directly to flumes or conveyors in the floor.

Trimming belts that do not circulate the foodstuff are used if darkening or other problems are caused by delay after peeling (see Fig. 8.24). These single-

Courtesy of Western Canner and Packer

FIG. 8.24. NONCIRCULATING-TYPE TRIM LINES

pass conveyors are usually controlled by starting and stopping, or by varying speed, as required to match the load and the trimming labor. Single-pass conveyors can be classified according to the number of channels used on each belt (see Table 8.11).

Washing is sometimes used after trimming to clean the product or to retard development of discoloration in the subsequent travel of the peeled and trimmed

TABLE 8.11

NONCIRCULATING TRIMMING SYSTEMS

Number of Channels	Distribution of Flows[1]
1	U and T on top belt, W in pails, chutes, flumes
2	U and W on return belt, T on top
2	U on return, T on top, W in pails, chutes, flumes
3	U and W on side belts, T in middle channel
3	U and T in middle channel, W on side belts
3	T in middle channel, U on sides, W in pails, chutes, flumes
5	W, T, U, T, W in order across the belts

[1] Symbols: U = untrimmed, T = trimmed, and W = waste.

product. Various types of washing devices are used, but often only water sprays are installed over conveyors, elevators, or chutes carrying the trimmed food to the next operation. In some instances, flumes are used to carry the commodity after trimming.

Cutting or Subdividing

The prepared food at this stage might be cut into cubes, chunks, slices, strips, rings, shreds, wedges, etc., or it might be pulped, juiced, or homogenized. For some operations, the prepared foodstuff is first blanched or cooked before it is subdivided (beets, for example). The foodstuff is commonly prepared in various sizes and shapes. The size and shape of pieces are governed primarily by the market requirements for dehydrated products; however, two important purposes are also served by the cutting: (1) blanching and drying are facilitated; and (2) rate and completeness of rehydration of the dried product is improved. Table 8.12 indicates some of the common forms and sizes of some dehydrated foods.

TABLE 8.12

COMMON FORMS OF DEHYDRATED VEGETABLES

Commodity	Size or Form	Market Use
Potatoes	$3/8 \times 3/8 \times 3/8$ in.	Soups, salads
	$3/8 \times 3/8 \times 3/16$ in.	Soups, salads
	$1/4 \times 1/4 \times 1/4$ in.	Soups, salads
	$1/2 \times 1/2 \times 1$ in.	Stew chunks
	$1/8 \times 1 \times 1$ in.	Hash brown, au gratin, salads
	$1/8$ in. slices	Hash brown, au gratin, salads
	$3/16 \times 3/16$ in. strip	Soups and casseroles
	$5/16 \times 5/16$ in. strip	Soups and casseroles
	Flakes	Instant mashed, general cooking
	40–80 mesh granules	Instant mashed, general cooking, pancakes, soups
Carrots	$3/8 \times 3/8 \times 3/16$ in.	Soups, vegetable dishes
	$3/8 \times 3/8 \times 3/32$ in.	Soups, vegetable dishes
	$3/16 \times 5/16$ in. strip	Soups, vegetable dishes
	$3/16, 1/8, 3/32$ slices	Soups, vegetable dishes
Cabbage	$1/8$ in. shreds, $3/8$ in. dice	Soups, vegetable dishes
Onions	$1/8$–$1/4$ in. slices (rings)	Soups, seasoning
Tomato	Flakes	Soups, seasoning, gravies
	Powder	Soups, seasoning, gravies, juice

Several types of machines are manufactured for cutting foodstuffs. One type (Fig. 8.25) may be adjusted for cutting slices, strips, or cubes and other "chunks," in many sizes. Figure 8.26 illustrates the operating principle of the machine shown in Fig. 8.25, for cutting cubes or other rectilinear cuts. The prepared commodity is fed into the rotating slicing shell and is forced against

Courtesy of Urschel Laboratories, Inc.

FIG. 8.25. CUTTING MACHINE FOR SLICES, STRIPS, CUBES,
OR CHUNKS

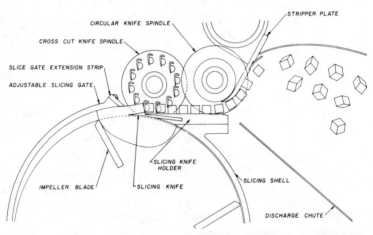

Courtesy of Urschel Laboratories, Inc.

FIG. 8.26. OPERATING PRINCIPLE OF CUTTER SHOWN IN FIG. 8.25

the slicing knife by centrifugal force. In one pass, the commodity is cut into slices (thickness determined by the adjustable slicing gate), then strips (cross-cut knife spindle), and finally cubes (circular knife spindle).

Cabbage is cut into shreds of various thicknesses in machines commonly used in sauerkraut manufacture. Sometimes devices for orienting the commodity are used in conjunction with cutters to obtain a desired type or direction of cut. For example, potatoes for producing dried slices are cut normal to the long axis, onions for rings are cut normal to the stem-root axis, cabbage is cut into shreds across the leaf structure. In the latter two examples, "slabs" (pieces cut parallel instead of normal to the indicated direction) must be minimized, because these cuts dry more slowly than the bulk of the material and usually must be sorted out after drying because they are still too damp.

Although each cutting machine has a very large capacity, up to 5000–10,000 lb per hr, multiple cutting-machine lines are desirable to allow maintenance and repair without disrupting continuous production. The knives on the cutting machinery should be kept sharp by conscientious, regular maintenance. Dull knives cut irregular shapes and bruise the tissues, causing deterioration of nutritive factors and general quality. Cutting machines must be safe-guarded against damage from foreign objects such as rocks, wood, and metal that might be present in the raw material stream. Sometimes a vibrating screen with strong water sprays is used just ahead of the cutters. Magnetic detectors and eliminators are used to remove iron. Detectors based on the use of radiofrequency fields are used for detection of nonferrous contaminants. This type of protection for cutting machines can save much trouble and avoid lost time.

Other types of equipment are used for comminuting foodstuffs for certain dehydration operations. Riced or extruded shreds are produced from cooked potatoes or sweet potatoes by roll or screw-type action that presses the product through suitable perforations, usually $3/8$-in. diameter or smaller. For production of granules or flakes, potatoes are commonly mashed in a screw-type unit which presses them through a grid of $1/2$-in. diameter parallel rods spaced $3/8$–$1/2$ in. apart. In a recently-developed unit for mashing or ricing potatoes experimentally the cooked sliced potatoes are pressed through the outer perforated drum by two solid rolls. It is important to avoid fracturing large numbers of potato cells when mashing, to reduce the pastiness of the mashed potatoes made from the final dried powder or flakes.

Potatoes are again washed after they are cut into pieces to remove free surface starch, to help obtain a uniform spread on the drying surfaces, and to produce a loose, nonclumped, free-flowing dried product. Some cut commodities such as potato and carrot dice are flumed from the cutter to the next operation. Fluming of small or thinly-cut pieces of foodstuff usually causes losses of soluble nutrients, although the leaching effect is reduced by allowing a buildup of soluble solids in the flume water. Caution must be exercised to prevent buildup of microbiological activity at the same time. Leaching and consequent removal of sugars is beneficial in preparation of certain potato products because it reduces some types of darkening in drying and in storage. Sulfite or other additives can be applied to the cut commodity during fluming if it is desired to do so before the blanching operation, or if blanching is not used.

Blanching, Scalding, or Cooking

Preservation of foods by canning, freezing, or dehydrating requires control or prevention of the actions of enzymes and of microorganisms. These agents, both

Courtesy of USDA Western Regional Res. Lab.

FIG. 8.27. PILOT-SCALE DRAPER-TYPE ATMOSPHERIC
STEAM BLANCHER

of which are responsible for undesirable changes in food materials, are usually completely inactivated during the heat processing involved in commercial canning procedures. However, in freezing and in dehydrating, the products are rarely, if ever, sterile. Blanching, scalding, and cooking are terms often used interchangeably in reference to the practice of heating raw foods for short times at boiling or near-boiling temperatures. During blanching, the microorganism count in foodstuffs is substantially reduced (Weiser *et al.* 1971); sometimes the foods become practically sterile (Hucker *et al.* 1943). However, during exposure to the nonsterile conditions that exist in the processing, dehydrating, and packaging operations that follow blanching, the dried food product is recontaminated with microorganisms. Recontamination is held to a minimum by sanitation measures in most plants. Control of subsequent microbial action in the product is effected by dehydration to low moisture levels.

   In dehydration, blanching serves not only to inactivate enzymes and prevent or retard development of undesirable odors, flavors,[2] and colors during dehydration and storage, but also to partially cook the tissues and render the cell membranes more permeable to moisture transfer. The drying rate is increased, more rapid and complete dehydration is obtained, and texture is improved when the blanched product is prepared for the table.

   Enzyme systems in foodstuffs are extremely complex and vary with different commodities (Weiser *et al.* 1971). Usually both oxidizing and hydrolyzing enzymes are present. Most of these deterioration catalysts are inactivated at temperatures of 160°F and up, but usually 190°F is considered minimum for safety.

---

[2]The role of enzymes in food flavors has been studied by Hewitt *et al.* (1956), Koenigsbacher *et al.* (1959), and Mackay and Hewitt (1959).

Sometimes only a minute or two of exposure in the blancher is required, but longer times are used in most cases to ensure complete inactivation. Tests for ∕ peroxidase, one of the most heat-resistant enzymes, are commonly used to determine adequacy of blanch (Hucker *et al.* 1943; Cruess 1947; Moyer *et al.* 1952; Masure and Campbell 1944). Morris (1958) devised a rapid method for testing for the presence of residual peroxidase after blanching, using a specially prepared test paper. Moyer *et al.* (1952), Woodroof *et al.* (1946), and Pinsent (1962) observed apparent regeneration of peroxidase in vegetables that had been found free of peroxidase activity after blanching. Balls (1962) theorized that many oxidative enzymes, being proteins with metal-containing groups, are inactivated by denaturing the protein and splitting off the metal group; however, the enzyme is reactivated if the protein reverts to its original state and the metal group is reattached. Jansen *et al.* (1960A, B) and Jansen (1961) found that enzymes that were "bound" to cell walls were more stable to heat and other treatments, as well as more resistant to detection.

Practically all major food commodities that are preserved by dehydration are blanched or otherwise heat-treated during processing. Notable exceptions are onions, garlic, and other seasoning materials, and fruits that are sulfured[3] before drying. As a general rule, when the products of enzyme-catalyzed reaction in foodstuffs are undesirable, blanching is used to eliminate enzymes; when the products of enzyme-catalyzed reaction are desirable, as in onions and garlic, blanching is not used before dehydration.

In the "dry-blanch-dry" (DBD) process (Lazar and Powers 1959; Lazar *et al.* 1961), and the dehydrocanning or dehydrofreezing processes (Powers and Lazar 1959; Lazar *et al.* 1961), the blanching treatment is delayed until after the commodity is partially dehydrated; the desired tissue structure can thereby be better controlled in the final product. Enzymatic action that might otherwise occur before blanching is retarded by temporary expedients such as treatments with small amounts of sulfur dioxide, citric acid, or salt.

During blanching, the time of exposure to the heating medium required for a given commodity is a function of several factors:

(1) Piece size—To obtain effective enzyme inactivation, all parts of the product should reach at least 190°F. It is obvious that longer exposure is required for larger pieces, to allow penetration of heat to the centers (see Fig. 8.28).

(2) Temperature—Suitable temperatures must be maintained throughout the blancher. In mountainous regions (lower barometric pressure), exposure times must be increased to compensate for the lower temperature of the condensing steam.

---

[3] Sulfur dioxide treatment, traditional for some sun-dried fruits and also adopted in some vegetable dehydration operations, prevents the catalytic action of enzymes; protection lasts only as long as adequate concentrations of sulfur dioxide remain. Frequently, sulfur dioxide is used in addition to the blanching treatment (Schultz 1960).

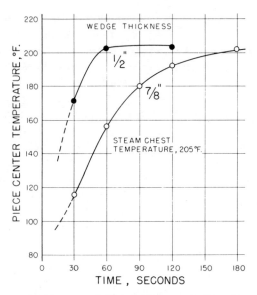

FIG. 8.28. EFFECT OF PIECE SIZE ON CENTER TEMPERA-
TURE DURING BLANCHING OF APPLE WEDGES

(3) Depth of load—Heat must penetrate into the center of the bed of material so that all pieces will reach the desired temperature.

(4) Blanching medium—Blanching in water usually requires less time than blanching in steam at the same temperature, because of the rapid application of heat to each piece in the liquid medium, as against the relatively slow penetration of steam into the bed of pieces.

Because operating conditions for blanchers are highly dependent on many variables, only a general statement can be made regarding blanching conditions for different cases. Root-type vegetables usually require about 2–4 min of blanching in an atmosphere of steam at 210°–212°F, when cut into small dice, thin slices, or thin strips; about 5–15 min retention time for larger chunks, slices, or strips. About 15–20 min are required for cooking quarters or slabs of potatoes for production of flakes, granules, or shreds. Leafy vegetables required only ½–2 min exposure, and must be loaded lightly into the blancher to avoid matting.

At the present time (1971) all commercial blanchers operate with either hot water or steam, although other methods have been investigated experimentally (Moyer and Stotz 1945; 1947; Asselbergs and Pavrie 1961). For a time, blanching with hot water predominated in Great Britain and steam blanching was preferred in the United States. Today, however, the blanching operation is better understood and each method is used where advantageous for specific commodities and products. With steam it is sometimes more difficult to obtain a uniformly-blanched product when deep beds or large pieces are blanched. The outside surfaces or layers of commodity are sometimes overcooked before the interior material is adequately heated. However, by avoiding overloading of blanchers and by use of properly designed steam nozzle arrangements, this difficulty has been minimized. Excellent results have been obtained experimentally when controlled amounts of air are introduced into the steam chest of the blancher to reduce the blanching temperature to as low as 190°F (Lazar et al. 1963; Hendel et al. 1960, 1961). Previously, entrance of air into the steam chest was considered undesirable and blanchers were designed with "humps" in the center to trap a pure steam atmosphere. Of course, if the commodity is sensitive to exposure to oxygen during heating, air must be excluded from the blancher.

A new concept in blanching—Individual Quick Blanch (IQB)—has been extensively investigated in the laboratory and under pilot-plant conditions (Lazar et al. 1971A, B; Bomben et al. 1972; Lund et al. 1972).

In the IQB system, pieces of fruits or vegetables are spread in a single layer on a mesh belt moving rapidly through the steam chest of the blancher. Maximum heating rates result because of the complete exposure of each individual piece to the live steam. After relatively short exposure to the steam, and before the exterior portions of the fruit or vegetable become overcooked, the heated product is transferred onto another belt to produce a deep bed which then moves slowly through an insulated chamber. The heat added plus the holding time under essentially adiabatic conditions result in an equilibration of the product temperature to a mass average temperature necessary for inactivation of the enzymes. All investigations demonstrate that the IQB process completely inactivates the enzymes without overcooking of the product tissue. Thus, the final finished products possess materially improved texture.

The IQB process offers a further advantage because of a reduction in the loss of juices (BOD solids) to the blancher effluent. The juice volume as well as its concentration are significantly reduced in comparison to conventional blanching. If the initial fruit or vegetable surface is preconditioned (predried or prewarmed) an additional reduction in the loss of soluble solids is attained since the preconditioned surface absorbs most, if not all, of the steam condensed thereon. Obviously the product quality is improved, and the pollution, due to aqueous effluents from the dehydration plant, is materially reduced.

Water blanchers can be operated conveniently at any desired temperature up to boiling. It is generally conceded that water blanching results in greater losses of soluble nutrients. Lee (1958) reviewed the blanching process for peas, snap beans, lima beans, carrots, potatoes, and spinach, and determined the effects on the sugars, proteins, carotene, thiamine, riboflavin, niacin, ascorbic acid, and mineral substances. Losses of nutrients by leaching were higher during blanching in water than during blanching in steam, consistent with findings of other investigators (USDA 1944; Melnick et al. 1944; Woodroof et al. 1946; Gooding et al. 1960; Ministry of Agriculture, Fisheries, and Food 1958). In some products made from potatoes, leaching of sugars is desirable to reduce the nonenzymatic browning that occurs during drying or storage. Goodling et al. (1960) found that water-blanched carrots lost up to 30% of the dry solids by leaching. Losses by leaching were reduced to 15% if the concentration of solids in the blanch liquor was built up to 2.5%, and reduced even further to only 10–11% at 4–5% solids in the blanch water. However, only 8% of dry matter was lost with steam blanching. Gooding also found that dried carrots that had been water-scalded had a shorter storage life (at 98°F) than those that had been steam-scalded, and theorized that precursers of browning reactions are formed in the scald liquor, and the carrots become impregnated with these products. In other studies of water blanching (Ministry of Agriculture, Fisheries, and Food 1958), buildup of solids in the blanch liquor ("serial blanching") was found to be limited to a maximum of 1% for potatoes, 1.5% for cabbage, and 2.5–3% for carrots, before initial off-flavor developed and storage stability of the dried product was impaired.

Sulfite compounds are sometimes added to the scald liquors in water blanchers. The value of the addition of other chemical agents such as phosphates or carbonates has not been substantiated, except with cabbage shreds, where a small amount of sodium carbonate added to the scald liquor has improved color retention in the product.

Blanchers are often custom-made according to individual requirements and preferences; however, a great variety of types and sizes are available · from manufacturers of food processing equipment. Blanchers may be batch or continuous—batch type are inexpensive and convenient for small operations. In simple batch-type blanchers, baskets of prepared commodity are immersed in vats of hot or boiling water, or placed into steam retorts. Some leafy foods such as cabbage cannot withstand transfer from the blancher and spreading on the drying surfaces because these commodities become soft and mash or mat excessively if they are transferred after they are blanched—these materials are blanched directly on the trays on which they will also be dried. Trays of prepared food may be blanched batchwise in drying-car lots in steam cabinets, or continuously on belt or chain conveyors that carry the trays through steam chests.

Continuous blanchers used in dehydration plants are of two basic types, belt and rotary. Belt types are very common (see Fig. 8.23) and are used primarily with steam blanching. Usually the commodity is loaded directly onto the wire mesh belt and is spread evenly to the proper depth (usually 1 in. to as much as 6 in. deep) by means of mechanical devices such as vibrating feeders, cross-belts, plows, revolving rakes, or brushes. If the cut vegetables are flumed to the blancher, they can flow directly onto the belt; the water drains through the wire-mesh belt into a sump. The belt, driven by a variable speed drive (to allow adjustment of blanch time) carries the product through a steam chest, where nozzles installed above and below the belt provide an atmosphere of steam, usually controlled automatically at some value between 200° and 212°F. In the front portion of the steam chest, the nozzles must be closely spaced to provide for the greater heat load at the entrance, where the product must be quickly heated to blanching temperature. The jets of steam must not impinge directly on the bed of product, to avoid damaging the product or disturbing the uniformity of the bed. Heavy canvas curtains or other air locks are provided at both ends of the steam chest to prevent excessive losses of steam and also to prevent uncontrolled drafts of air from entering and reducing operating temperatures. Forced cooling of the product after blanching (as is used in freezing plants) is not necessary. The steam chest should be provided with quick-opening lids to allow access for cleaning. If necessary, water sprays and brushes may be installed on the return section of the belt for either continuous or intermittent cleaning. Belt blanchers usually range from 2 to 6 ft in width and 30 to 60 ft in length. When long cooking times are required, the blancher length might be 100 ft or more.

Sanitation is a requirement of mounting importance during the blanching phase of fruit and vegetable processing. Equipment manufacturers and plant managements must carefully evaluate design features and materials of construction of the moving as well as the stationary elements of the blancher system. Sanitary, corrosion-free construction with effective, easy cleaning is mandatory. All surfaces contacting the food as well as those contaminated by liquid drippage or solids accumulation must be readily cleanable. Automatic cleaning-in-place (CIP) systems, through the judicious use of water and detergents, can effectively remove and dispose of scale, burn-on, and other residues resulting from the blanching operation. The CIP system offers the advantage of lower labor and materials costs as compared to the old manual type system (Swayne and Robe 1969; Milleville and Gerber 1964; Gerber 1966).

Capacity of a belt steam blancher may be determined from the following formula:

$$C = \frac{0.03wlL}{\theta} \tag{8.7}$$

Steam requirements may be estimated as follows:

$$S = \frac{5.5C(t_2 - t_1)}{E} \tag{8.8}$$

where

C = capacity, tons per hr
S = steam requirements, boiler horsepower (bhp)
E = efficiency of blancher, %
L = load on the belt, lb/sq ft
θ = time of blanch, min
w = width of belt, ft
l = length of steam chest, ft
t_2 = blanching temperature, °F
t_1 = temperature of incoming material, °F

To illustrate the use of this formula, assume a blancher with the following characteristics: belt width, 5 ft; steam chest, 50 ft; load on belt, 4 lb per sq ft;

blanch time, 4 min; blanch temperature, 212°F; incoming material temperature, 62°F; and blancher efficiency 60%. Capacity is then calculated as follows:

$$C = \frac{0.03 \times 5 \times 50 \times 4}{4} = 7.5 \text{ tons per hr}$$

Steam requirements are:

$$S = \frac{5.5 \times 7.5 \times (212 - 62)}{60} = 103 \text{ bhp}$$

Efficiencies of blanchers depend upon steam leakage and vent losses, as well as upon heat loss through the blancher walls. Efficiencies usually range from 33% in poorly designed and operated units, to as high as 90% in well-designed and properly operated units. Steam economy is usually better in water blanchers than in steam blanchers.

Belt units are occasionally used for water blanching. A wire-mesh belt, usually fitted with flights, conveys the product through a tank of heated water. Where needed, a second belt is provided over the first belt to submerge products that float.

Rotary-type continuous units are used for either steam or hot water blanching. One type commonly used (see Fig. 8.29) is similar to an ordinary screw conveyor;

Courtesy of Rietz Manufacturing Co.

FIG. 8.29. ROTARY SCREW-TYPE BLANCHER

steam is injected at regular intervals directly into the trough conveying the product. Sometimes the trough is jacketed and heated with steam; in one model, a hollow screw is used and steam is passed through the screw to supplement the action of the jacket. Screw blanchers using hot water as the blanching medium operate with internal water levels at about center shaft height, to provide positive movement forward and avoid back-flow eddies of product. When steam is used, screw blanchers are loaded with product almost to the top of the screw; they then have almost twice as great a volumetric capacity as when water is used. However, water blanching does not require quite so long a retention time, and this partially compensates for the shallower fill. Screw blanchers are available in a variety of sizes from about 9 in. diameter by 10 ft long, to about 25 in. diameter by 30 ft long, for steam use; for water use, sizes range from 2-ft diameter by 15 ft long, to 4-ft diameter by 20 ft long. Screw blanchers are readily cleaned and sanitized, have low maintenance costs, and occupy relatively little floor space.

Another common type of rotary blancher consists of a perforated drum, mounted on trunnions, in a covered tank containing heated water (see Fig. 8.30).

Courtesy of Western Canner and Packer

FIG. 8.30. ROTARY DRUM-TYPE WATER BLANCHER

The product is fed into the blancher at one end and is conveyed to the discharge end through the hot water by a spiral flight inside the blanching drum. At the discharge end, the liquid is drained from the product back into the tank. Another type of continuous rotary blancher was described by Hemmeter (1951) and is similar to the rotary lye peeler (see Fig. 8.19). Products that are too tender to withstand the abrading, compressing, tumbling actions of the various types of rotary blanchers are handled better in belt-type units.

Blancher parts that come into contact with foodstuffs should be made of stainless steel. Black iron and galvanized iron units were common for many years. The additional cost of building units of stainless steel has been found to be well justified, since the reduced corrosion will result in fewer breakdowns, smoother and more continuous operation, and longer equipment life, and will eliminate metallic contamination of the product. Use of stainless steel is mandatory where sulfiting solutions are applied before blanching, or are sprayed onto the product in the blancher.

Additives

Under the provisions of the Food Additives Amendment of 1958 and the Color Additives Amendment of 1960 to the Federal Food, Drugs and Cosmetic Act, before an additive may be used, the proponent of the additive must establish its safety in the intended use, and must obtain a favorable decision from the Food and Drug Administration permitting that use. An additive must perform the function claimed for it, and the amount to be used must not be greater than is reasonably required to achieve the desired effect. Restrictions and definitions under the Amendments have been the subject of much discussion within the food industry. Initial approved usage does not guarantee permitted use in the future; consequently, processors must keep abreast of developments and, at least periodically, review the status of the type and amount of additives permitted in foods for human or animal consumption. Committees, both governmental and private enterprise (National Canners Assoc. 1968) continue to study the problems involved in the administration and enforcement of the Amendments. Actions and recommendations are then published in appropriate trade and food journals (Lawler 1959; Ives and Nagler 1960; Baier 1961). Textbooks on the manufacture and preservation of foods devote entire chapters to the subject of food additives (Graham 1968; Potter 1968; National Canners Assoc. 1968).

An extensive index of food and color additives, for which proposals have been made or petitions filed to establish a legal position, and for which regulations have been issued under the Additive Amendments of 1958 and 1960, is published yearly. The compilation is prepared from official actions as published in the Federal Register; and includes reference to the U.S. Code of Federal Regulations and the Food and Color Additives Directory (Hazelton Laboratories 1970). The use of the Index and reference to regulation numbers should be made in conjunction with the Food and Color Additives Directory or other reliable source of information governing the subject items. Decisions regarding the legality of the use of additives should be made with reference to an up-to-date source of Federal Regulations and, in some cases, consultation with competent experts in the field of food and color additives.

For a great many years, sulfur dioxide has been used as an additive to preserve dried foods. Originally, foods were exposed to the fumes of burning elemental sulfur, before being put out to dry in the sun. This practice is still used in the preparation of sun-dried apricots, peaches, pears, nectarines, and the like (Phaff and Mrak 1948; Fisher et al. 1942). For over 20 yr, treatment with solutions of sulfite prior to dehydration has been practiced on such foods as apples, snap beans, cabbage, carrots, potatoes, and sweet potatoes. In the United Kingdom, where blanching by immersion in hot water has been popular, it was found convenient to '"sulfur" by adding sulfite salts to the blanching bath. Application of sulfite by an immersion technique adds another operation to steam-blanching processing sequences, and might nullify one advantage of this method of blanching, namely, low leaching losses. Therefore, the sulfite solution is sprayed on the commodity in the blancher or at the discharge from the steam chest. Penetration into the interior of the pieces of product is required (Duckworth and Tobasnick 1960). Solutions used range from 0.2–0.5% (as SO_2), and are made up of sodium sulfite and sodium bisulfite in approximately equal proportions. If a greater proportion of sodium sulfite is used, the pH is too high, activity of sulfur dioxide is low, and penetration into the flesh is decreased. If a greater proportion of sodium bisulfite is used, problems of corrosion of equipment are increased. Solutions are usually applied in the proportion of 1 gal. to 10 to 50 lb of product, although the quantity used will depend upon factors such as: (1) product specifications for SO_2 content, (2) variety of commodity, (3) piece size, (4) drying method and conditions used, and (5) location of the sulfite sprays. In some instances, addition of small amounts of soda ash (sodium carbonate) to the sulfite liquor has improved the color retention of cabbage shreds. Sulfur-bearing oils have been used commercially in direct-fired dehydrators and found effective, although control of product sulfur content by this method is not reliable. Vacuum-chamber sulfiting to shorten sulfuring time and increase SO_2 takeup, has been investigated experimentally (Anon. 1961A).

Sulfiting helps to protect carotene and ascorbic acid in foods during dehydration and storage, but causes large losses of thiamine. However, most fruits and vegetables that are sulfited are not the ones relied upon to be major sources of thiamine; they do contain substantial amounts of carotene and ascorbic acid.

Close control of the sulfiting procedures must be exercised to maintain sulfur dioxide content within the desired limits in the dehydrated product. In the past, some European countries have not allowed sale of sulfited products, or have limited the allowable sulfur content.

Other additives such as ascorbic acid, citric acid, and sodium chloride, have been used to retard enzymatic browning or oxidation during processing. Jansen (1958A, B) proposed the use of sulfhydryl compounds to inhibit plant enzymes. Bedrosian et al. (1959) investigated the use of borates to inhibit oxidative enzymes in apple tissue. Makower (1960) and Makower and Boggs (1960) investigated the chemical inactivation of enzymes in vegetables before dehydration.

Starch coating of carrots before dehydration has been recommended (Masure et al. 1950) for improving the storage characteristics of the dried product. A hot solution of starch may be sprayed onto the carrots as they leave the blancher.

DRYING OPERATIONS

After the predrying operations have been completed the product is dried. While predrying, drying, and postdrying operations are discussed separately, they are in fact strongly interdependent. Types and forms of product desired determine what predrying operations are necessary, restrict or define the type of drying techniques that must be used, and indicate the required types of post-drying steps. Examples can be cited to show how procedures in one part of the process affect what can be done in other parts. Overblanching shredded cabbage may convert it to a soggy, slow-drying mush. Sulfiting somewhat more heavily than normal may permit higher drying temperatures to be used, resulting in shorter drying times. The excess sulfur dioxide is usually driven off in such a drying operation, leaving an acceptable sulfur content in the product. In another example, excessive production of fines in the cutting of piece-form products, or in other handling or drying operations, increases the need for screening and inspecting in postdrying operations, and decreases final product yield. Fines will be overdried and perhaps even scorched. These, and other examples that could be cited to demonstrate the interdependency of the three major processing subdivisions, indicate that no one phase can be planned without consideration of its overall effect.

Since the first edition of this text, there have been many advances in drying technology; this is indicative of the fluidity of the operations. In addition to the old tried and proved systems, the modern processor must consider the feasibility of employing new concepts in drying operations which may involve the application of osmosis, dispersion, microwaves, fluidized beds, centrifugal beds, and superheated vapors. Any of the above, if employed, would necessitate the use of different conditions with respect to the physical nature of the substance undergoing dehydration (foam, liquid, concentrate, solid) and certainly the product to be produced. The equipment necessary to accomplish the desired results must necessarily be designed and operated to make optimum use of the myriad variations that are possible (Van Arsdel 1965; Rolfe 1965; Anon. 1966A; Tucker 1968; Huxoll and Morgan 1968; Lance and Lang 1970).

POSTDRYING OPERATIONS

Screening

Most purchase contracts for dehydrated foods specify the screen size range desired. During production of dehydrated cut foodstuffs, "fines" are formed in the cutting operation and in the normal movement of the product through the processing line. Screening is therefore required to remove the unwanted fine material, which sometimes represents a financial loss to the operation. Care should be exercised in the handling and packaging of the dried product to minimize production of fines. Some dehydrated products, especially onions and cabbage, are kept warm to minimize brittleness during handling after drying.

Removal of fines (size-classification) is usually accomplished by passing the dry product over vibrating wire cloth or perforated metal screens and collecting the fractions separately. The acceptable fraction passes on to the final inspection operation. Some products, such as onions, garlic, celery, etc., are ground fine when prepared for use as a seasoning powder. Obviously, fines would be included in the usable fraction in this instance. The coarse fraction, which may still be damp, is recycled for further processing.

Inspecting

After the finished product has been screened, it is inspected to remove discolored pieces or other imperfections and foreign materials such as wood, metal, and other contaminants. The product is inspected while it moves along on a continuous belt (see Fig. 8.31). The belt is usually white and strong light

Courtesy of Basic Vegetable Products, Inc.

FIG. 8.31. INSPECTING DRIED PRODUCT—ONION FLAKES

is provided. The material must not be spread too thickly on the belt and the travel must not be too rapid. Each inspector picks out the imperfect material by hand, or by using a flexible tube connected to the source of suction. Magnetic or other metal detection devices should be installed to guarantee removal of stray metal.

Electronic sorting machines are being used on some small piece-form products. In these high-speed machines, each piece is picked up from a spinning bowl by suction ports at the periphery of a revolving vertical disc, and passes before an electric eye which scans each piece for color. Off-colored pieces trigger a jet of compressed air which knocks them off the disc into a reject line. The pieces that pass continue on to a short inspection belt where final inspection is used to check the operation of the machines.

Samples of the finished product are taken at this stage for laboratory analyses that are required for control.

Packaging

The terms packaging and packing are often used synonymously. Packing usually denotes the act of filling containers for shipment of the finished plant products; packaging has the same meaning in the general sense, but includes the broader aspects—the design features of the package or container, as well as the engineering features of the operation. Packaging is now considered as a unit operation by chemical engineers, and packaging engineering has become an important science.

Packagiṇg units and materials must satisfy a number of general requirements: (1) complete protection of the dehydrated product against moisture, light, air, dust and microflora, foreign odors, animal pests, and corrosion; (2) strength and stability to maintain original container properties through storage, handling, and marketing; (3) size, shape, and appearance to promote salability of the product and convenience in use; (4) materials composition approved for use in contact with foods; and (5) cost compatible with the value of the contents and the degree of protection needed (Sacharow 1970).

Dehydrated products are packed for institutional and remanufacturing trade in large units such as sacks, bags, drums, bins, cartons, and cans. Smaller containers are used for retail market packs. Special liners of plastic are sometimes used. Barail (1954) lists the properties of twelve plastic materials used in packaging engineering. Considerable research effort continues to be expended on the development of new packaging materials (Shockley 1962; Farrell 1962).

As the variety of dehydrated foods increases, the industry is faced with the need for new techniques and materials for the packaging of its products whether intended for home, institutional, or further processing uses. Guidelines to meet the requirements of nutritionists, economists, engineers, packaging consultants, and governmental regulations must consider the influence of such factors as weight, cost, size, economy, durability, disposability, permeability, shelf-life, and even the possible interactions between the food and the packaging materials. Food processors, especially those with smaller scale operations, must depend to an increasing degree upon the services of suppliers to furnish the necessary expertise and to meet competition. Future packaging materials will be ecologically oriented with the objectives of direct reuse, reclamation, and biodegradable disposal (Ball 1970; Baker 1967; Anon. 1966B). The significance of the above objectives becomes even more impressive when one considers that, in the United States, 15% of the sales dollar is regarded as an average cost of the packaging (Anon. 1966C).

Trends in food are in the direction of functional innovations which often involve the use of composite containers which may consist of plastics, papers, and metals. The field of plastics ranges from clear film to opaque rigid containers which may be fabricated from acrylic, styrene, polyethylene, cellophane, polypropylene, vinyl, and many others (Hannigan 1969).

In the developing countries proper packaging contributes to a greater food supply. There the package must withstand severe handling and adverse climatic conditions; and resist the destruction of food by mold, insects, and rodents. Losses attributable to insect damage are estimated to be as high as 40% in some situations because of inadequate packaging material, lack of proper equipment, and poor handling systems. In many cases the employment of insect and rodent barriers would offer a great improvement but no single type of package would offer a perfect solution. Most of the common types of packaging are susceptible to entry by insects, although laminae film in conjunction with aluminum foil, offers effective resistance provided that closures and seams are properly sealed. Unfortunately, the availability of raw packaging material is extremely limited; advanced type plastic film is unavailable because of economic and trade reasons; and, machinery is often obsolete as well as severely limited in scope.

The economic level of developing nations is subminimal and for that reason reusable packaging is most desirable. The empty bag or container can become a useful household item (Sacharow 1970).

Some dehydrated commodities must be packed in inert gas—nitrogen is usually used. The gassing operation may be done on specially equipped semi-automatic can-closing machines, with large vacuum pump connected to give rapid pull-down of pressure. The vacuum is relieved with nitrogen. Oxygen levels of 1–2% can be routinely attained. Gas packing of special containers such as foil pouches requires very special filling and handling equipment. Great care must be exercised to avoid any leaks whatever in the container seams, because even a minute pinhole can lead to eventual equilibration of oxygen content inside and out, due to the pumping action of barometric pressure changes.

Vacuum packing also has been used for dehydrated products, but the container must withstand the pressure differential without leaking under all conditions of handling and storing. The vacuum needed to be effective is difficult to attain in commercial practice.

Dehydrated products that must have very low moisture contents to withstand storage are sometimes packed with a small envelope of desiccant included in the container. The envelope, called "in-package desiccant" or "IPD," is permeable to moisture but does not allow contamination of the product with the desiccant. Moisture is transferred slowly from the product to the desiccant during storage.

Compressing of Dehydrated Foods

The ratio of the fresh prepared weight of a food to the final weight after dehydration varies from 3:1 or less (for high-solids commodities such as sweet potatoes) to 12:1 or greater (for low-solids commodities such as cabbage, celery, or tomatoes). Volume reduction is always much less than weight reduction. Therefore, savings in shipping space, storage space, and container materials, as well as cost of handling, would be effected if dehydrated products were compressed without damage into units of higher bulk density.

The need for development of compact rations for overseas shipment was indicated by logistics studies during World War II, and a study of the techniques required and factors involved in compression of dehydrated foods was made by the USDA Western Regional Research Laboratory (USDA 1948). Some of the

TABLE 8.13

COMPRESSION OF DEHYDRATED FOODS—CONDITIONS USED AND
RESULTS OBTAINED

Food	Form	Moisture Content (%)	Temp (°F)	Max Pressure (Lb per Sq In)	Dwell (Sec)	Density Uncompressed (Lb per Cu Ft)	Density Compressed (Lb per Cu Ft)	Volume Reduction (%)
Beets	Diced	4.6	150	1200	0	25.0	65	62
Cabbage	Shredded	3.5	150	2250	3	10.5	60	83
Carrots	Diced	4.5	150	4000	3	18.7	65	71
Onions	Flaked	4.0	130	700	0	11.9	50	76
Potatoes	Diced	14.0[1]	150	800	3	23.0	50	54
Rutabagas	Diced	5.6	150	5500	0	28.0	65	57
Sweet potatoes	Diced	6.1	150	3500	10	27.0	65	58
Apples	Nuggets	1.8	130	1200	0	20.0	65	61
Apricots	Halves	13.2	75	300	15	35.0	75	53
Cranberries	Whole	5.5	150	2000	5	12.7	55	77
Peaches	Halves	10.7	75	300	30	36.0	73	51
Prunes	Whole	12.4	75	300	30	43.0	73	41
Egg powder	Spray dried	5	75	850	1	26.0	50	48
		2	75	1000	30(max)	26.0	46	43

Source: Abstracted and condensed from USDA (1948).
[1] Dried to 7% after compression.

general problems investigated included breakage and production of fines; size, shape, density, and coherence of food blocks; and storage life, rehydration, and organoleptic quality of the compressed products. The study was terminated with some problems still unsolved. A summary of some of the conditions found applicable in compressing specific foods was made (see Table 8.13). An example of the economy of space obtained in compression of dehydrated carrots is shown in Fig. 8.32.

Courtesy of Western Canner and Packer

FIG. 8.32. COMPRESSED BLOCKS OF DEHYDRATED DICED
CARROTS

QUALITY CONTROL

We have emphasized throughout this chapter that it is important to start with a good quality raw material and protect its quality through all of the processing steps. Quality is, of course, the general concern of all employees in a dehydration plant, but responsibility for the evaluation and control of quality factors is best assigned to a special quality control department. When uniformly-good products are made, with a minimum of rejects, not only will the operation be more profitable, but the reputation of the company will be enhanced in the dehydrated food market.

In a small organization, quality control tests may be performed by a single individual who may be capable of making only a limited number of a few types of control tests. However, in a large organization, a complete, well-organized quality control department is essential. Joslyn and Heid (1963) list five functions of the quality control department: (1) establishment of specifications for raw products, supplies, processes, and packages for finished products (water and steam used in the plant must be also classed as "supplies"); (2) development of test procedures for measuring quality levels—some test procedures have already been established by federal or state regulations, and inspection services are available for a fee; (3) development of procedures for sampling product (at various stages of preparation); (4) recording and reporting production data; and (5) training production personnel in control methods.

To the above list must be added the indirect function of control of process variables, because the yield and quality of product usually depend upon temperatures, pressures, retention times, concentrations, humidities, etc., used in the processing operations. In this function, close collaboration is needed between quality control and production departments.

In common with other types of food processing organizations, a dehydration plant requires research and development to improve its present operations and to ensure its future. The quality control laboratory may perform this function or a separate department may be set up for this purpose. The quality control department must obviously collaborate closely with all major departments in the organization, such as purchasing, sales, production, research and development, and general management.

Joslyn and Heid (1963) define the factors involved in evaluating quality: appearance (eye appeal, judged by sense of sight), kinesthetic (hand and mouth feel, judged by sense of touch), and flavor (judged by sense of taste and smell). These authors also present a comprehensive discussion of the quality factors and methods for their evaluation. Kramer and Twigg (1970, 1973) present the fundamentals of food quality control.

Quality control measures and techniques are essentially the same for all foods. When employed under close supervision and performed by trained personnel, the measures do reflect the stability of the food during processing and drying. Chemical, physical, organoleptic, and microbiological assays are used extensively to control processes and to protect the processor as well as the consumer.

Chemical analyses are employed to detect changes in solids, ash, pH, carbohydrates, fats, nitrogen, and vitamins as the raw material progresses through the various stages to the final product. They are necessary for maintaining and substantiating the level of additives and nutrients as shown on package labels. The time for and complexity of chemical analyses can range from a few minutes with simple equipment to many hours, requiring the use of complicated and expensive apparatus (Cox and Pearson 1962).

Physical and organoleptic examinations are relatively easy quality control tests; many of which are also applied by the consumer. The most important of these tests are the measurement of color, odor, taste, texture, and appearance. Color and texture are evaluated by electronic and mechanical equipment which measure forces and electric currents related to those properties. All of the physical properties mentioned can also be evaluated by well-trained panels of judges. The organoleptic assays usually correlate very closely with the chemical and physical tests.

Microbiological assays generally require appreciable time to produce and to correlate the results. They are most important for the detection of microorganic contamination which may produce undesirable effects due to bacterial metabolism during processing, storage, and subsequent rehydration of the food. The assays should differentiate between the nonpathogenic and pathogenic flora. The nonpathogenics, while present in enormous numbers, may be of no significance and may be tolerated in the final product. However, it must be emphasized that an abnormally high level of certain specific nonpathogenic organisms is often an index of plant sanitation. Control agencies employ this index to establish, modify, or completely change sanitation as well as operational procedures within the processing facility. On the other hand, the pathogens require complete destruction in order to ensure safety to the consumer (Liuzzo 1966).

Quality control measures require modern facilities and techniques. Properly trained personnel are essential to conduct the assays and must be under such technical supervision as is capable of interpreting the results. The size and composition of the quality control group will necessarily vary with the nature of the processing operations. In all cases the investment in personnel and equipment is fully justified (Anon. 1967A; Kramer and Twigg 1970, 1973).

PLANT SANITATION

Organizing a Sanitation Program

The management of a dehydration plant must focus considerable attention on sanitation as an essential part of good plant operation, and must train personnel to apply the principles of sanitation properly in all phases of operation. Because consumers are not in a position to know the sanitary quality of the dehydrated food offered for sale, they must rely upon various governmental agencies (federal, state, and local) to inspect sanitation practices in the plants that process the foods, and to enforce minimum legal standards. Although management should fulfill its moral obligations to consumers, real economic benefits also accrue to the plant operator from good sanitation practices. They include: more efficient operation, good personnel relations, reduced safety hazards, and product quality improvement. Doyle and Stark (1961) list ten essentials for organization of a complete sanitation program in a food processing plant:

(1) Management must be thoroughly convinced of the value of sanitation, and must give the program wholehearted support.

(2) The building layout and construction must exemplify the best in modern sanitation design and practice.

(3) Equipment and facilities must be built and installed to create the minimum of sanitation problems and the maximum of ease in cleanup, resulting in the ultimate in economy.

(4) There must be a sanitarian on the job—properly trained, dedicated to his work, and endowed with adequate authority to carry out his responsibility.

(5) Other supervisory personnel must be educated as to the importance of sanitation, and must cooperate in seeing that it becomes the law of the plant.

(6) Employees must find in the plant examples of good housekeeping, safety practices, and individual hygiene.

(7) The sanitarian must have adequate sanitation tools and supplies.

(8) There must be a carefully worked out, written set of sanitation procedures.

(9) The sanitarian must keep fully informed on governmental, industrial, and other scientific sanitation developments.

(10) Management, the sanitarian, and other supervisory personnel should regularly audit or evaluate conditions and review sanitation procedures and practices.

Microbiological Control

Perhaps the most important index of the effectiveness of sanitation practices used in a dehydration plant is the concentration of microorganisms in the product. Some purchase contracts specify the limits of microbiological population. However, even if high counts of viable organisms are not found in the dehydrated products, the presence of microbiological activity during intermediate processing steps might have already damaged flavor, color, or other quality factors of the food. Even fresh, sound food crops are contaminated, at least on the surface, with bacteria, yeasts, and molds (Hucker *et al.* 1943; Weiser *et al.* 1971). It is therefore not surprising that physical damage to fruits and vegetables promotes spoilage, since it provides entry for microorganisms and food for their development. The plant equipment is continually being contaminated by the very food being handled, even with the most thorough washing. Many of the operations required in the preparation of various dehydrated foods have a marked effect on the survival of microorganisms in the finished products; dehydration does not necessarily destroy microbial life. Critical factors are: (a) pretreatment and handling before dehydration; (b) time required for dehydration; (c) maximum temperature reached by the product during processing; (d) amount of residual moisture; and (e) preservatives used.

Federal and state regulatory agencies are imposing strict tolerances on the bacterial and mold counts in all foods. Real and potential hazards exist in products containing eggs, milk, cereals, and meats during preparation, storage, and reconstitution under conditions favorable to microbiological growth. The processing plant has the responsibility of eliminating all risk due to pathogens, preventing contamination and maintaining quality during reasonable shelf-life. Management must establish and strictly enforce (1) specifications for raw materials and finished products; (2) sanitary practices for plant and personnel; (3) processing, storage, and distribution procedures; and (4) education of all personnel on the importance of microbiological control (Anon. 1968A; Van Meter and Egan 1966; Taggart 1967A).

Cleanup Practices

Effective, economical sanitation is required in all phases of food processing and distribution; and can be attained by the concerted use of proper equipment, supplies, labor, and supervision. The maintenance of the desired level of cleanliness involves costs which are added to the other production costs. Such expenditures may be minimized by the employment of properly designed and operated cleaning-in-place (CIP) automated systems. The concepts of sanitation must include such differing considerations as physical, chemical, and microbiological cleanliness (Semling 1967).

Physical cleanliness alludes to the absence of visible dirt or soil on equipment and surroundings as determined by visual examination of exposed surfaces. In the past, this method of plant inspection was the basis of evaluating cleanliness. It is completely inadequate; and, furthermore, useless for CIP systems; for these, other approaches are necessary, including the removal of small vulnerable parts such as gaskets, seals, valves, and gages.

Chemical cleanliness refers to the removal of food residues which collect on processing surfaces due to interactions, decompositions, and depositions. The deposits can seriously interfere with heat transfer efficiency, quality of the food, and accentuate microbial activity. The removal of these deposits is accomplished by the use of chemical agents or detergents; these can be so effective as to remove all traces of the residues. Proper equipment, detergent, and knowledge of cleaning systems are essential for each specific application.

Microbiological cleanliness requires that microorganisms which originate from the raw material or that may be introduced during processing from the surroundings be removed by the cleaning procedure. Modern cleaning procedures employing high temperatures, alkaline conditions, and adequate contact time destroy nearly all organisms except a few spore formers. The last may be eliminated by further use of sanitizing agents.

A good sanitation program results from the use of technological developments, the employment of new and improved chemical agents, and modern procedures and equipment (Maxcy 1968; Hlavacek 1968). Today, the trends are away from manual, time-consuming procedures to completely automated central systems which control the amount and type of detergent; the amount and type of sterilizing agent; the time of contact, temperature, and alkalinity; and the sequence of rinsing, cleaning, and sanitizing phases (DeLuchi and Robe 1966; Dimarco 1964; Bartlett 1966; Holler and McCollough 1969; Scholle 1969; Rohrer and Robe 1970).

Cleanup procedures in a food preparation plant should be carefully organized and executed. Consideration must be given to three types of problems: (a) visible product waste, foreign matter, and slimes; (b) microorganisms; and (c) residual chemical contamination from washing compounds. To initiate a cleanup program, a survey of the entire plant must be made to determine the requirements to reach a state of acceptable cleanliness, to estimate the time and procedures necessary, and to fit the cleanup program smoothly into routine plant operations. Cleanup procedures, to have maximum effectiveness, should be divided into two types, continuous and periodic. Diligent observance of continuous cleanup reduces the load on the periodic cleanup crews. Continuous cleanup consists, for example, of application of sprays of water to the return side of belts, or of immersion and brushing of belts in a sanitizing solution. Equipment that is used intermittently, such as holding tanks, cutters, auxiliary belts, and drying equipment, should be cleaned between uses. Responsibility must be assigned for immediate cleanup of spillage before it can be tracked over a larger area.

Use of sanitizing agents in the washing operations eliminates slimes and controls microbial population. Sanitizing agents should be: (a) nontoxic and not obnoxious to humans; (b) tasteless, odorless, and colorless in their effect on food products; (c) highly efficient as germicides, especially against heat-resistant strains; and (d) noncorrosive to equipment. Liquid chlorine and certain chlorine-liberating compounds, when properly used, possess these characteristics and are inexpensive. It is quite practical, particularly in larger plants, to introduce chlorine-type sanitizing agents into the water system, for continuous and automatic control of microorganisms. This practice is known as "in-plant chlorination." Information on chlorination practices is given by Joslyn and Heid (1963).

Periodic cleanups are performed at regular intervals, such as coffee-breaks or rest periods, end-of-shift, or daily plant shutdown. Regularly assigned personnel should be used for cleanup to allow them to become thoroughly familiar with their duties. Sequences of cleanup operations should be indicated, and a supervisor should be responsible for filling out a checklist form. Types of cleaning operations and sequences will vary from plant to plant, but for a typical plant handling fresh commodities, the following sequence is suggested (Assoc. of Food Industry Sanitarians 1952; Parker and Litchfield 1962):

(1) Dismantle equipment as far as necessary or practical.

(2) Do not allow waste from equipment to spill onto the floors or contaminate other lines.

(3) Wash equipment with low-pressure water to remove gross debris. Care should be taken to avoid contaminating other equipment in the area.

(4) Remove waste or gross debris from the floor either by hauling it away or by flushing it into the gutters.

(5) Remove slime or other deposits with detergents, high-pressure water or steam, or other effective means.

(6) Apply a germicidal agent where necessary.

(7) Wash all equipment with potable water to remove residual detergents or germicides. Allow equipment to cool after cleaning.

Pest Control

Pests that may infest a food processing plant include rodents, birds, and insects. Rodents carry diseases such as bubonic plague, endemic typhus, infectious jaundice, trichinosis, Salmonella food poisoning, and others. Most of these are transmitted from rodent to man by fleas, lice, or mites, or by contamination of food with rodent excreta and urine. Birds are a nuisance in a plant because they may contaminate food with feathers and excrement. Insects damage foods by deposits of eggs or larvae, by body parts, by excreta, and by damaging containers.

Rats and mice are rodents of primary concern to food processors. The rat, because of its size, is more obnoxious and is the greater menace; ranges over a greater area within the plant; and even a single individual can produce enormous damage in very short time. The annual rat damage bill amounts to several billion dollars with about $5.00 attributed to the food consumed per animal, $50.00 to product contamination, and $2.00 to property damage. Mice are small but far more prolific than rats; they tend to stay within small areas and always close to their food supply. A single pair of mice can produce 60 offspring per year, and, each pair will consume up to 8 lb of production per year and damage far greater amounts. The total cost is again enormous.

Evidence of rodent infestation is not difficult to detect. Within the infected areas will be the characteristic droppings, damaged bags and containers, urine stains, tracks, smudge marks, nesting material, and musty odors.

Rodent control is based on preventive actions which involve measures that should be taken during the design and construction phases of the plant buildings and continued vigilance thereafter. Rodent proofing necessitates the installation and maintenance of barriers capable of preventing entry of the pests. Doors must be quick, self closing, and properly fitted. Windows must be screened with hardware cloth and openings around all service facilities such as pipes, conduits, and drains barred by flashings. Ordinary materials of construction suffice as barriers against mice but metals are required against rat entry because of their strong gnawing ability. It is essential to eliminate all external harborage, such as old lumber, equipment, and weeds from the plant premises as well as potential food supplies.

Extermination becomes necessary when infestation occurs in spite of preventive measures. Trapping and baiting procedures are available; only trapping methods can be allowed in processing areas but both methods are permitted in all other plant areas. Rodenticide baits may be liquid or solid and are available in many types of specific ingredients as well as the more convenient prepared mixtures. Selection of the best rodenticide depends upon environmental factors. There are many tricks that can be employed to ensure success of both trapping and baiting procedures. In exceptional cases when infestation is extremely severe fumigation of the premises must be resorted to. Whatever method of rodent extermination is employed provisions must be made for the recovery and disposal of the destroyed pests (Hugé 1961; Anon. 1964).

Insect problems are caused by two types generally characterized as (1) the fliers and (2) the crawlers. Thus, gnats and bees are representative of the flying class and are especially attracted to products during raw material storage and subsequent processing by the evolved odors. The crawling types are represented by the many varieties of ants and beetles. Ants can pose a problem in almost any stage of storage or processing while beetles are encountered most often in relatively dry storage areas. The flying insects can be controlled with insecticide sprays, air curtains and black light units with electrified grids, preferably outside the processing area. Control of the ant or beetle type pest can be attained by the use of suitable baits, aerosol type insecticides and, again, in extreme cases, closed room fumigation.

The bird problem is generally confined to open, exposed areas; and can be eliminated from processing or storage areas by careful screening of all ports of entry. Some control in exposed areas can be attained by the use of ultrasonics, harassing lights, and the application of repellent agents on roosting areas.

Control and extermination of pests is a highly specialized field and must not be practiced by amateurs, particularly where poisonous baits or sprays are involved in the proximity of foods. Assistance must be obtained from qualified public or private pest control agencies.

AIR PURIFICATION AND AIR POLLUTION CONTROL

Contaminated air and its control must be considered from two viewpoints; first the removal and control of contaminants to adequately purify the air entering the process system; and second, the removal of objectionable pollutants from the air stream leaving the processing plant. The mode of operation, in some respects, is similar in both cases; but the objectives are sufficiently different to warrant separate consideration.

Air Purification

Air entering the processing plant may require purification for two main reasons; namely, (1) to improve production and (2) eliminate contamination caused by air-borne bacteria, odors, and other matter. The treatments will vary from those requiring only simple air-conditioning to complex systems involving multiple filtration, washing, heating, humidity, and temperature control. Requirements establish the specific treatment or treatments. Thus, milk powder and fruit juice powders require the use of low humidity air in the agglomerating, redrying, cooling, and packaging of the products; whereas, simply conditioned air suffices for warehouses, many preparation steps, and employee comfort in offices, lunch, and rest rooms. For the production of many dehydrated products, e.g., eggs, milk, etc., bacteria-free air is a basic requirement.

The selection of an air purification system must be based on a detailed study of the needs, efficiency and costs. In some cases, separate clean air sources to meet different conditions are recommended and installed. For example, for the production of milk powders, (Olson and Mistelske 1968) six separate systems were installed to supply purified air for the following purposes: (1) filtered air to ventilate the warehouse area; (2) filtered, conditioned air for comfort in the locker-lunch room complex; (3) multiple-filtered, conditioned air to blending and packaging rooms; (4) absolute-filtered and cooled air for cooling the agglomerated dry powdered product; (5) roughly-filtered and medium-filtered air for the agglomerating room and base powder storage; and (6) multiple-filtered (rough, medium, and absolute) air for agglomerating the final product.

Many air cleaning techniques are available. For most purposes filtration is the best; but others may include washing, scrubbing, electrostatic precipitation, incineration, and ultraviolet sterilization, alone and in various combinations. Filtration alone can provide for any level of solid contamination reduction, ranging from removal of only the gross sized particles down to and including submicron size particulates and bacteria. Thus, it is feasible to obtain a super clean air with solids removed to the extent of 99.97% and down to 0.3μ in size. To maintain low level air contamination, the ventilating system must provide efficient filtration, distribution, scavenging, and air change with a positive pressure inside the processing area. Such a system will be capable of reducing contamination generated within the room, due to processing activity and to personnel, by employing streamline flow across or by turbulent mixing. Streamline flow is rather difficult to attain and turbulent mixing requires up to 18 changes per hour. Return flow of the room-contaminated air to the purification system is desirable (Food Engineering Staff 1967).

Air cleaning equipment, using techniques mentioned above, will now be considered:

Filters.—Filters employ fibers upon the surfaces of which the particles are retained. The fiber diameter should be less than that of the smallest particle to be removed in order to maximize the deposition area and to keep the free space as high as possible and thereby reduce the resistance to air flow. Filters are designed to provide several degrees of particle removal.

Roughing Filters.—These remove large quantities (10–60%) of particles down to the $1-5\mu$ size and even some bacteria. Two types are used; (1) the coated fiber and metal screen type which can be cleaned, retreated, and used repeatedly; and (2) the packed loose fiber types which are nonreusable.

Medium Filters.—These further clean the air leaving the roughing filter, remove up to 90% of matter in the $1-5\mu$ range and are constructed of compressed fibers of cellulose or glass. They offer higher resistance to air flow and when loaded with contaminants are replaced. They produce relatively clean air without material reduction in flow rate and are employed as prefilters for higher efficiency units.

High Efficiency Filters.—These are essentially biological filters capable of removing up to 99% of microorganisms, including the 1μ level. They are constructed of fine glass, cellulose, or asbestos fibers. Resistance to air flow is high and increases as the filter picks up the solid particles. Filters are replaced when the air flow resistance becomes excessive.

Ultra High Efficiency Filters.—These can further purify the air if introduced into the air system. They can remove up to 99.97% of bacteria in the 0.3μ range. Cellulose, glass, and ceramic fibers are again employed; they are packed to such a degree that initial resistance is around 1 in. of water and the face air velocity reduced to 5-7 fpm. After continued use resistance builds up to 4-5 in. of water; then the filters must be replaced. These filters are always preceded by suitable prefilter units.

Air Washers.—These include spray towers, water screens, and baffles wherein the air-borne particles impinge on a wetted surface and are carried away by the liquid stream. They are useful for fairly good removal of dust particles (to $1-5\mu$ range) but not recommended for bacteria removal, especially when the water is so recirculated that it becomes heavily contaminated with matter removed from the air.

Air Scrubbers.—Scrubbers are generally more effective than washers and can remove up to 90% of particulate matter in the low micron range. The air stream again contacts the liquid, which usually is hygroscopic and bacteriostatic in nature. The organisms are destroyed when the scrubbing liquid is heated to remove water absorbed from the air stream. High efficiency filters are installed downstream to improve the total particle removal.

Electrostatic Precipitators.—These can remove up to 90% of smoke and dust, and a high proportion of bacteria when air is caused to flow through a high voltage field. The charged particles collect on the electrode of opposite charge, from which they may be removed periodically by mechanical means. Under optimum conditions the electrostatic precipitator can be useful as a filter of medium efficiency.

Air Incineration.—This has the highest reliability for the complete removal of organisms; and, if the temperature is sufficiently high, for the elimination of odors. For the destruction of bacteria, temperatures of around $625°F$ are adequate; for odor elimination the temperatures increase to the $1200°F$ range. In either case, the air must be forced through a heated zone and subsequently cooled by regenerators or heat exchangers before introduction into the processing system. Inorganic dust particles originally present or produced by the incineration must be removed by subsequent treatment.

Ultraviolet Air Sterilization.—This is effective against air-borne bacteria except when the organisms are protected by dusts. The ultraviolet rays have only limited penetration ability and the lamps require frequent maintenance and testing.

Air Pollution Control

The gaseous effluents from food processing plants, discharged into the atmosphere by fans, blowers, incinerators, ventilating systems, power plants, and waste disposal systems and dumps, do contribute to air pollution. The air streams may carry dusts, vapors, and odors as are often produced in preparation and processing operations, in the recovery of by-products from wastes, and in the disposal of useless materials. In the past, dehydration plants, because of their generally isolated locations, have not been subject to excessive restrictions for the control of gaseous plant effluents. As the population density increases and the plants become surrounded by homes and businesses the emissions come under greater scrutiny. This may ultimately result in a clamp-down on the offender by federal, state, and local agencies. Odors from the drying of onions, garlic, fish meal, poultry wastes, the recovery of citrus peel for animal feed, and the production of oils and fats by rendering plants can become extremely offensive, even at a considerable distance from the source of origin. Dusts from the drying, roasting, milling, and conveying operations of such products as milk, tea, coffee, spices, sugars, and cereals likewise create nuisance and hazardous problems which must be solved. Smokes from food plant driers, incinerators, and power plants are obvious pollutants consisting of carbon particles, fly ash, oils, and grease; and, in addition, carry the invisible oxides of carbon, nitrogen, sulphur, and organic solvent vapors. The visible constituents of emitted smokes draw first attention and become the initial target of regulations (Alikonis and Ziemba 1968).

Serious problems are encountered in adopting and enforcing air quality standards which best meet the requirements of individual communities because of the variation in the nature of the pollutants, the degree of removal to be effected, and the location of the plant. In some states air pollution legislation has received a high order of priority; in many states essentially none. Some progress had been made in establishing guidelines which define the degree of control, the method of control, and the place at which control is most effective. All too often subordinate agencies tend to impose unduly restrictive regulations which lead to excessive costs. Satisfactory solutions require close cooperation between industry, the community, and the regulating agency. Consideration must be given to the cost versus benefit relationship. In no case can the protection of health become an issue of compromise (Alikonis and Ziemba 1968; Anthony 1970).

At any plant where there exists the possibility of air pollution subject to regulations, its management must take such actions as will establish the nature of the emissions, their amount, and their frequency, in order to establish the relative degree of pollution. Smoke, dusts, and odors are difficult to evaluate in exact values but an estimate can be made by conducting and observing simple tests and by the magnitude of community complaints. A check on local ordinances, if any, or information from communities with established control will help to establish a working base for the specific plant. Trained pollution control personnel or outside experts can evaluate the seriousness of the problem and recommend the course of future action.

Reduction, or preferably elimination, of the pollution will again follow practices that often are employed in other industries. Also, it is advisable to consider other approaches such as the use of alternate methods of production, the introduction of improved equipment, the creation of fewer or lesser amounts of wastes; or, the development of procedures to profitably recover the pollutants. If, after the above studies, the problems of smoke, dust, odors, and other contaminants still persist, then measures for their control must be undertaken, generally in accordance with the following (Anon. 1965, 1970A; Cross and Ross 1967; Alikonis and Ziemba 1968).

Odors and Vapors.—These may be controlled by: (1) The use of packed scrubbers and water sprays which will dissolve up to 90% of the odor or vapor. If necessary, the remainder can be removed by catalytic incineration. (2) An incineration system, which when operated at temperatures ranging from $1000°$-$1500°F$, is very effective; especially if employed in conjunction with heat recovery components to generate process steam. The initial costs are high, as is the cost of operation, but heat recuperation techniques can reduce operating cost by as much as 90%. (3) The injection of oxidizing agents such as chlorine, ozone, and permanganate into the scrubber or spray tower system. The oxidizing agents improve effectiveness of odor removal and only slightly increase the operating cost.

Dusts and Fumes.—These are controlled by the installation of some suitable type of collector. Effective operation of such devices depends on particle size, desired collection efficiency, and available operating pressure. Particle size is probably the most critical factor and for that reason fume removal is ordinarily difficult. Equipment and limitations are as follows:

(1) Standard dry and wet type cyclones which remove particles down to 25μ.

(2) Improved cyclone collectors, operating singly or in series, with efficiencies up to 90% for dusts in the $5-10\mu$ range.

(3) Bag filters consisting of a battery of individual cloth bags, wherein the dust is filtered out of the contaminated air as it flows through the cloth. The initial dust deposit serves as a highly efficient filter medium. Dust removal may be by the action of reverse jet rings or be periodic automatic shaking whereby the dust layer falls into hoppers beneath the bags. Bag filters have high dust removal efficiency, usually above 90% even for particles in the submicron range.

(4) Wet scrubbers effective for the removal of $1-5\mu$ particulates at efficiencies which depend upon the nature of the dust and the operating conditions. The particles are transferred from the air to the scrubbing liquid, from which they may be removed by centrifuging, filtration, or simple overflow to the liquid waste system.

(5) Electrostatic precipitators which have been considered under the subject of air purification for processing purposes.

Dust must be controlled in the plant area and environs by surfacing roads and dirt areas used for temporary storage, or by treating with oil or water sprays. When the plant is operating, dry dusty nearby fields must not be worked if the prevailing wind is likely to carry dense dust clouds into the plant area.

BIBLIOGRAPHY

ADAMS, H. W., HICKEY, F. D., and WILLARD, M. J., Jr. 1960. Lye-pressure steam peeling of potatoes. Food Technol. *14*, 1-3.

ALIKONIS, J. V., and ZIEMBA, J. V. 1967. Waste treatment. Food Eng. *39*, No. 7, 89-97.

ALIKONIS, J. V., and ZIEMBA, J. V. 1968. Air pollution—clean it up. Food Eng. *40*, No. 7, 71-76.

ALLEN, F. W., and PENTZER, W. T. 1935. Studies on the effect of humidity in the cold storage of fruit. Proc. Am. Soc. Hort. Sci. *33*, 215, 223.

AMERICAN STANDARDS ASSOC. 1935. American Safety Code of Industrial Sanitation for Manufacturing Establishments. Z4. 1-1935. Am. Stds. Assoc., New York.

ANDERSON, J. B. 1969. How outside consultants ease way to plant construction. Food Eng. *41*, No. 9, 94-96; *41*, No. 10, 135-144.

ANON. 1944. Dehydrated food production stepped up with new peeling process. Fruit Prod. J. *23*, 302-304.

ANON. 1945. Continuous steam peeler. Food Ind. *17*, 561.

ANON. 1950. Lighting for canneries. Illum. Eng. *45*, 45-65.

ANON. 1956. Some factors in location of a new chemical plant-panel discussion. Sewage Ind. Wastes *28*, 1247-1265.

ANON. 1957. Non-caustic chemical peels peaches in lab. tests. Food Packer *38*, No. 12, 19.

ANON. 1958. Foods now sterile-packed in drums. Canner Packer *127*, No. 7, 30.

ANON. 1960. State by State list of plant sites. Chem. Eng. Progr. *56*, No. 11, 85-110.

ANON. 1961A. Vacuum chamber used in new sulfuring method. Canner Packer *130*, No. 6, 61.

ANON. 1961B. One 4,000-gallon fabric tank replaces 80 50-gallon drums. Food Process. *22*, No. 9, 110.

ANON. 1962A. Storage, freezing, heat processing data. Food Eng. *34*, No. 3, 91-102.

ANON. 1962B. How to select your new plant location. Food Eng. *34*, No. 10, 78-79.

ANON. 1963. Key personnel—finding—training—keeping. Food Eng. *35*, No. 7, 73-84.

ANON. 1964. Breakthrough in rat poisons. Food Process. *25*, No. 11, 156-157.

ANON. 1965. Solves air pollution problem. Food Process. *26*, No. 5, 174.

ANON. 1966A. French dispersion drier offers speed, uniformity. Food Eng. *32*, No. 12, 68-70.

ANON. 1966B. Some frontiers in packaging. Food Technol. *20*, 1023-1030.

ANON. 1966C. International food packaging. Food Technol. *20*, 1453-1458.

ANON. 1967A. Ways to improve quality control. Food Eng. *39*, No. 7, 130.

ANON. 1967B. Stresses future growth. Food Eng. *39*, No. 9, 97.

ANON. 1968A. Tighten ingredient sanitation. Food Eng. *40*, No. 7, 128-129.

ANON. 1968B. Latest look into food plants. Food Eng. *40*, No. 9, 69-72.

ANON. 1968C. Five advances in plant construction. Food Eng. *40*, No. 9, 82-85.

ANON. 1969A. Waste disposal without pollution. Food Eng. *41*, No. 12, 103-104.

ANON. 1969B. Oxygen steps up waste treatment. Ind. Eng. Chem. *61*, No. 2, 5-6.

ANON. 1970A. Improve scrubbing efficiency. Food Eng. *42*, No. 4, 114-116.

ANON. 1970B. Commercial infra-red peeling process. Food Process. *31*, No. 1, 28.

ANTHONY, M. V. 1970. The Air Quality Act of 1967. Progress and problems. Chem. Eng. Progr. *66*, No. 3, 23-25.

ARMSTRONG, R. 1965. Tailoring building and space requirements to process requirements. Food Process. *26*, No. 2, 73-75.

ARTHUR, J. C., and MCLEMORE, T. A. 1955. Sweet potato dehydration; effects of processing conditions and variety on properties of dehydrated products. J. Agr. Food Chem. *3*, 782.

ASSELBERGS, E. A., and PAVRIE, W. D. 1956. Peeling of apples with infra-red radiation. Food Technol. *10*, 297-298.

ASSELBERGS, E. A., and PAVRIE, W. D. 1961. New developments in infra-red radiation. Food Can. *21*, No. 10, 36-38.

ASSOC. OF FOOD INDUSTRY SANITARIANS. 1952. Sanitation for the Food Preservation Industries, 1st Edition. McGraw-Hill Book Co., New York.

BAIER, W. E. 1961. Pros and cons of food additives. Food Technol. *15*, No. 11, 5-9.

BAKER, G. 1967. Tougher packaging laws. Food Eng. *39*, No. 3, 100.

BALL, C. O. 1970. Food packaging of the future. Food Eng. *42*, No. 3, 76-78; *42*, No. 5, 155-164.

BALLS, A. K. 1962. Catalysts and food technologists. Food Technol. *16*, No. 11, 17-20.

BARAIL, L. C. 1954. Packaging Engineering. Reinhold Publishing Corp., New York.

BARTLETT, P. G. 1966. Clean scientifically with today's detergents. Food Eng. *38*, No. 8, 84-89.

BAXTER, J. L., Jr. 1962. Disposal of potato wastes in Maine. 12th Natl. Potato Util. Conf. Proc., Bakersfield, Calif.

BEDROSIAN, K., NELSON, A. I., and STEINBERG, M. P. 1959, 1960. The effect of borates and other inhibitors on enzymatic browning in apple tissue. I. Food Technol. *13*, 722-726. II. Ibid. *14*, 480-483.

BIERWERT, D. V., and KRONE, F. A. 1955. How to find best site for new plant. Chem. Eng. *62*, No. 12, 191-197.

BITTING, K. G. 1917. Lye peeling. Natl. Canners Assoc. Bull. *10*.

BOMBEN, J. L., FARKAS, D. F., LAZAR, M. E., and DIETRICH, W. C. 1972. Reduces blancher effluent. Food Eng. *44*, 107.

BONEM, F. L. 1962. Solve seasonal waste disposal. Food Process. *23*, No. 2, 34-36.

BRODY, J. 1970. Ingredient water-analytical requirements. Food Eng. *42*, No. 5, 94-95.

BROWN, J. B. 1960. Obligations of food technologists to the consumer. Food Technol. *14*, No. 7, 4-8.

BURTON, L. V. 1943. Where to locate that dehydration plant. Food Ind. *15*, No. 2, 72-73.

CALDWELL, J. S. 1943. Variety and place of production as factors in determining suitability for dehydration in white potatoes. Canner *97*, No. 3, 43; No. 4, 14; No. 5, 15.

CAMP, W. J., and MASON, J. P. 1968. Building functional co-op complex. Food Eng. *40*, No. 9, 74-77.

CHILTON, C. H. 1950. "Six-tenths factor" applies to complete plant costs. Chem. Eng. *57*, No. 4, 112-114.

CLARK, J. P. 1970. WURRD'S task force on agricultural pollution. Proc. 1st Natl. Symp. Food Process. Wastes, Apr. 6-8, Portland, Ore.

CLARKE, F. E. 1962. Industrial reuse of water. Ind. Eng. Chem. *54*, No. 2, 18-27.

COLEMAN, J. R., and YORK, R. 1964. Optimum plant design for a growing market. Ind. Eng. Chem. *56*, No. 1, 28-34.

COMBINED FOOD BOARD (THE ADVISORY COMMITTEE ON DEHYDRATION). 1944. Survey of Vegetable Dehydration Factories in the U.S.A. and Canada. Washington, D.C.

COX, H. E., and PEARSON, D. 1962. Chemical Analysis of Food. Chemical Publishing Co., New York.

CROSS, F. L., Jr., and ROSS, R. W. 1967. Single pass drier reduces air and water pollution. Food Eng. *41*, No. 12, 83-85.

CRUESS, W. V. 1947. Blanching—its frozen pack importance. Canner *104*, No. 2, 62-64.

CYR, J. W. 1971. Progress report: Study on dry caustic peeling vs conventional peeling and the effect on waste disposal. Proc. 2nd Natl. Symp. Food Process. Wastes, Mar. 23-26, Denver.

DAY, A. D. 1960. A new plant comes to town. Chem. Eng. Progr. *56*, No. 11, 42-45.

DELUCHI, J., and ROBE, K. 1966. Automatic washing of conveyor belts. Food Process. *27*, No. 6, 126-128.

DENMAN, L. L.   1961.   Maximum reuse of cooling water.   Ind. Eng. Chem. *53*, No. 10, 817–822.

DESROSIER, N. W.   1970.   The Technology of Food Preservation, 3rd Edition.   Avi Publishing Co., Westport, Conn.

DIAMOND ALKALI CO., 1956.   Lye Peeling of Root Crops.   Cleveland, Ohio.

DIAMOND ALKALI CO., 1962.   Caustic Soda Handbook, 4th Edition.   Cleveland, Ohio.

DIMARCO, R. G.   1964.   Let detergents do your cleaning.   Food Eng. *36*, No. 10, 54–56.

DLOUHY, P. E., and DAHLSTROM, D. A.   1969.   Food and fermentation waste disposal.   Chem. Eng. Progr. *65*, No. 1, 52–57.

DOYLE, E. S., and STARK, E. B.   1961.   Sanitation in food products manufacture.   Canner Packer *130*, No. 8, 32–40.

DUCKWORTH, R. B., and TOBASNICK, M.   1960.   Diffusion of sulfite during dehydration.   J. Sci. Food Agr. *11*, 226–228.

DUNKLEY, S. J.   1921.   Apparatus and process for peeling fruits and vegetables.   U.S. Pat. 1,396,268.   Nov. 8.

DUNLAP, R. L.   1944.   Lye peeling pays off.   Food Ind. *16*, 969–971.

DUNSTAN, G. H., and LUNSFORD, J. V.   1955.   Cannery waste disposal by irrigation.   Sewage Ind. Wastes *27*, 827–834.

EIDT, C. C., and MACARTHUR, M.   1944.   The peeling of fruits and vegetables for processing.   Food Can. *4*, No. 7, 31.

ELIASEN, R.   1963.   What about water resources.   Chem. Eng. Progr. *59*, No. 11, 20–21.

EPSTEIN, R. J.   1965.   New solutions to site selection–building construction–supporting services.   Food Process. *26*, No. 2, 77–79, 102.

FARRELL, D. E.   1962.   Preventing delamination of multistructure laminations.   Food Process. *23*, No. 12, 73–76.

FOOD ENGINEERING STAFF.   1967.   Simple techniques control sanitation.   Food Eng. *39*, No. 9, 128–132.

FINLAYSON, K., and GANS, M.   1967.   Planning a successful start-up.   Chem. Eng. Progr. *63*, No. 2, 33–39.

FISHER, C. D., MRAK, E. M., and LONG, J. D.   1942.   Effect of time and temperature of sulfuring on absorption.   Fruit Prod. J. *21*, 175–176.

FULTON, M.   1964.   Selecting a plant site.   Food Eng. *36*, No. 9, 51–53.

GERBER, P.   1966.   Sanitary design of processing equipment.   Food Process. *27*, No. 8, 44.

GILDE, L. C.   1969.   Waste system tailored to Campbell plants.   Food Eng. *41*, No. 8, 80–83.

GILL, J. M.   1963.   Industry to get deeper into the act.   Chem. Eng. Progr. *59*, No. 11, 30–32.

GOODING, E. G. B., TUCKER, C. G., and MCDOUGALL, D. B.   1960.   Dehydration of carrots.   Food Manuf. *35*, No. 6, 249–254.

GOULD, G. A.   1962.   Waste water lagoon system.   Food Process. *23*, No. 11, 137–139.

GRAHAM, H. D.   1968.   The Safety of Foods.   Avi Publishing Co., Westport, Conn.

GRAHAM, R. P.   1970.   Dry caustic peeling of fruits and vegetables.   Proc. 1st Natl. Symp. Food Process. Wastes, Apr. 6–8, Portland, Ore.

GRAHAM, R. P. *et al.*   1969A.   Prevents potato peel pollution.   Food Eng. *41*, 91–93.

GRAHAM, R. P. *et al.*   1969B.   Dry caustic peeling of potatoes.   Food Technol. *23*, 195–200.

GRAY, J. A.   1960.   Physical aspects of plant location.   Chem. Eng. Progr. *56*, No. 11, 46–49.

HANNIGEN, K. J.   1969.   More functional than ever.   Food Eng. *41*, No. 3, 80–81.

HARD, M. M., and ROSS, E.   1959.   Flavor changes in some fruits and vegetables treated with pesticides.   J. Agr. Food Chem. *7*, 434–435.

HARRINGTON, W. O. *et al.*   1956.   Observations on peeling of potatoes.   Food Technol. *10*, 347–351.

HARRIS, R. S., and VONLOESECKE, H. W.   1971.   Nutritional Evaluation of Food Processing.   Reprinted by Avi Publishing Co., Westport, Conn.

HART, S. A., and MCGAUHEY, P. H.   1964.   The management of wastes in food processing and food producing industries.   Food Technol. *18*, 432–438.

HAVIGHORST, C. R.   1943.   New dehydration plant handles record quantities.   Food
Ind. *15*, No. 12, 82–85.
HAZELTON LABORATORIES.   1970.   Food and Color Additives Index.   Hazelton
Laboratories, Falls Church, Va.
HECK, J. P.   1964.   Paint your plant with flood lights.   Food Eng. *36*, No. 9, 101–102.
HEMMETER, G. T.   1946.   Device for peeling agricultural products.   U.S. Pat. 2,403,923.
July 16.
HEMMETER, G. T.   1948.   Apparatus for peeling onions, including a conical jet of gas.
U.S. Pat. 2,445,881. July 27.
HEMMETER, G. T.   1951.   Rotary cooker or blancher.   U.S. Pat. 2,537,053.   Jan. 9.
HENDEL, C. E. *et al.*   1960.   Direct process for producing potato granules.   USDA
Western Util. Res. Lab., Albany, Calif., Circ. *74-6.*
HENDEL, C. E., NOTTER, G. K., LAZAR, M. E., and TALBURT, W. F.   1961.
Production of dehydrated potato granules. U.S. Pat. 3,009,817. Nov. 21.
HESS, S. A., and WEAVER, J. B.   1961.   How big a plant.   Ind. Eng. Chem. *53*, No. 7,
47A–48A.
HEWITT, E. J., MACKAY, A. M., KOENIGSBACHER, K., and HASSELSTROM, T.
1956. The role of enzymes in food flavors. Food Technol. *10*, 487–489.
HIGGINS, R. C.   1969.   Continuous ion exchange of process water.   Chem. Eng. Progr. *65*,
No. 6, 59–62.
HLAVACEK, R. G.   1968.   Automatic cleaning saves 15–18 man hours per day.   Food
Process. *29*, No. 2, 16–19.
HOLLER, W., and MCCOLLOUGH, J. J.   1969.   Central cleaning system drops steam,
water use 60%. Food Process. *30*, No. 2, 14–15.
HUCKER, G. J., PETERSON, C. S., and BROOKS, R. F.   1943.   The sanitation of food
plants. N.Y. State Agr. Exp. Sta. 63rd Ann. Rept.
HUGE, T. L.   1961.   Mice are underrated in food plants.   Food Eng. *33*, No. 3, 79–81;
33, No. 4, 86–88.
HUXSOLL, C. C., and MORGAN, A. I., Jr.   1968.   Microwave dehydration of potato and
apple. Food Technol. *22*, 705–710.
IVES, M., and NAGLER, E. M.   1960.   Biological screening techniques for food additives.
Food Technol. *14*, 499–502.
JACKSON, M. L.   1962.   Utilizing the potato industrially.   Ind. Eng. Chem. *54*, No. 2,
50–56.
JANSEN, E. F.   1958A.   Inhibition of enzymes in plant tissue.   U.S. Pat. 2,857,282.
Oct. 21.
JANSEN, E. F.   1958B.   Process for inhibiting enzyme activity in plant tissue.   U.S. Pat.
2,860,055. Nov. 11.
JANSEN, E. F.   1961.   The stability and activity of bound versus soluble enzymes.
21st Ann. Meeting, Inst. Food Technologists, May 8.
JANSEN, E. F., JANG, R., and BONNER, J.   1960A.   Orange pectin esterase binding and
activity. Food Res. *25*, 64–72.
JANSEN, E. F., JANG, R., and BONNER, J.   1960B.   Binding of enzymes to Avena
Coleoptile cell walls. Plant Physiol. *35*, 367–374.
JENSTEAT, R., and ZIEMBA, J. V.   1969.   Orderly layout keeps production running
smoothly. Food Eng. *41*, No. 9, 70–71.
JOSLYN, M. A., and HEID, J. L.   1963–1964.   Food Processing Operations, Vol. 1, 2,
and 3. Avi Publishing Co., Westport, Conn.
KAHLER, W. H.   1951.   Lighting the food plant.   Food Eng. *23*, No. 8, 105–111.
KIDD, F., and WEST, C.   1950.   The refrigerated gas storage of apples.   G. Brit. Dept.
Sci. Ind. Res., Food Invest. Leaflet *6.*
KOHLER, G. O.   1970.   Animal feeds from vegetable wastes.   Proc. 1st Natl. Symp. Food
Process. Wastes, Apr. 6–8, Portland, Ore.
KOENIGSBACHER, K. S., HEWITT, E. J., and EVANS, R. L.   1959.   Application of
flavor enzymes to processed foods. I. Panel studies. Food Technol. *19*, 128–132.
KRAMER, A., and TWIGG, B. A.   1970, 1973.   Quality Control for the Food Industry, 3rd
Edition, Vol. 1 and 2. Avi Publishing Co., Westport, Conn.

LAMB, F. C. 1954. Plant lighting–for best eye performance. Food Eng. 26, No. 9, 56–60.
LANCE, S. W., and LANG, R. W. 1970. The versatility of fluid bed driers. Chem. Eng. Progr. 66, No. 7, 92–93.
LANKLER, J. G., and MORGAN, O. M. 1943. How wetting agent improves the chemical peeling process. Food Ind. 15, No. 1, 53–54.
LAWLER, F. K. 1959. Know your new additive law. Food Eng. 31, No. 1, 46–48.
LAZAR, M. E., BARTA, E. J., and SMITH, G. S. 1963. Dry-blanch-dry (DBD) method for drying fruit. Food Technol. 17, No. 9, 120–122.
LAZAR, M. E., CHAPIN, E. O., and SMITH, G. S. 1961. Dehydrofrozen apples: recent developments in processing methods. Food Technol. 15, 32–36.
LAZAR, M. E., LUND, D. B., and DIETRICH, W. C. 1971A. Reduces effluent from blanching. Food Eng. 43, No. 8, 54.
LAZAR, M. E., LUND, D. B., and DIETRICH, W. C. 1971B. A new concept in blanching. Food Technol. 25, 684–686.
LAZAR, M. E., and POWERS, M. J. 1959. Method of preparing unsulfured dehydrated fruit. U.S. Pat. 2,895,836. July 11.
LAZAR, M. E., SMITH, G. S., and CHAPIN, E. O. 1961. Preparation of dehydrated fruit having the characteristics of sun-dried fruit. U.S. Pat. 3,979,412. Apr. 11.
LEAVITT, P., and ZIEMBA, J. V. 1969. At Gerber water does triple duty. Food Eng. 41, No. 9, 90–91.
LEE, F. A. 1958. The blanching process. In Advan. Food Res. 8, 63–109.
LEINEN, N. 1966. Material handling. Food Process. 27, No. 6, 36–37.
LIUZZO, J. A. 1966. Quality control measures for irradiated food. Food Technol. 20, 1451–1452.
LIVINGSTON, G. E. 1955. Why not a food technologist in your plant? Food Eng. 27, No. 6, 105–106.
LOPEZ, A., WOOD, C. B., and JOHNSON, J. M. 1958. Trimming time and yield factors in processing applesauce. Food Technol. 12, 57–64.
LUND, D. B., BRUIN, S., Jr., and LAZAR, M. E. 1972. Internal temperature distribution during quick blanching. J. Food Sci. 37, 167–170.
MACKAY, D. A. M., and HEWITT, E. J. 1959. Application of flavor enzymes to processed foods. II. Comparison of the effect of flavor enzymes from mustard and cabbage upon dehydrated cabbage. Food Res. 24, 253–261.
MAKOWER, R. U. 1960. Chemical inactivation of enzymes in vegetables before dehydration. Food Technol. 14, 160–164.
MAKOWER, R. U., and BOGGS, M. M. 1960. Quality of cabbage dehydrated after chemical or steam inactivation of enzymes. Food Technol. 14, 295–297.
MAKOWER, R. U., BOGGS, M. M., and BURR, H. K. 1952. Development of off-flavor in shelled peas held in cold water. Food Technol. 6, 179–180.
MAKOWER, R. U., and WARD, A. C. 1950. Role of bruising and delay in development of off-flavor in peas. Food Technol. 4, 46–49.
MANOCK, J. J., VOLLER, J. P., HIGHTOWER, R., and ROBE, K. 1964. Meticulous cleaning process. Food Process. 25, No. 10, 160–162.
MANUFACTURING CHEMISTS ASSOC. 1961. Food Additives–What They Are and How They Are Used. Washington, D.C.
MASURE, M. P., BOHART, G. S., EASTMOND, E. J., and BOGGS, M. M. 1950. Value of starch coating in the preservation of quality dehydrated carrots. Food Technol. 4, 94–97.
MASURE, M. P., and CAMPBELL, H. 1944. Rapid estimation of peroxidase in vegetable extracts–an index of blanching adequacy for frozen vegetables. Food Prod. J. 23, 369–373, 383.
MAXCY, R. B. 1968. Concepts and challenges for sanitation. Food Technol. 22, 558–562.
MAZZOLA, L. C. 1943. New caustic peeling method reduces waste, saves labor. Food Ind. 15, No. 1, 53, 104.
MAZZOLA, L. C. 1946. Potato peeling methods analyzed and appraised. Food Ind. 18, 1708; 18, 1874.
MACDONALD, C. A., and LEOPOLD, H. 1968. Material handling key to Stouffers. Food Eng. 40, No. 9, 90–92.

MCILHENY, W. F. 1967. Recovery of additional water from industrial waste water. Chem. Eng. Progr. *63*, No. 6, 76–81.

MCINTOSH, G. H., and MCGEORGE, G. G. 1964. Year round lagoon operation. Food Process. *25*, No. 1, 82–86.

MELNICK, D., HOCHBERG, M., and OSER, B. L. 1944. Comparative study of steam and hot water blanching. Food Res. *9*, 148–153.

MIERS, J. C. *et al.* 1971. Field processing of tomatoes. 2. Product quality and composition. J. Food Sci. *36*, 400–404.

MILLEVILLE, H. P., and GERBER, P. 1964. Sanitary design of processing equipment. Food Process. *25*, No. 10, 93–114.

MINISTRY OF AGRICULTURE, FISHERIES, AND FOOD. (GREAT BRITAIN). 1958. Vegetable Dehydration Practice. H. M. Stationary Office, London.

MOHLMAN, F. W. 1950. Waste disposal as a factor in plant operation. Chem. Eng. Progr. *46*, 321–327.

MORGAN, A. I., Jr., BARTA, E. J., and GRAHAM, R. P. 1966. Chemical peeling of grain. Chem. Eng. Progr. *62* Symp. Ser. *69*, 138–141.

MORRIS, H. J. 1958. Rapid peroxidase test for better control of browning. USDA Agr. Res. Serv. *74-10*.

MORRIS, J. C. 1963. Conventional approaches not enough. Chem. Eng. Progr. *59*, No. 1, 34–36.

MOYER, J. C., ROBINSON, W. B., STOTZ, E. H., and KERTESZ, Z. I. 1952. Effect of blanching and subsequent holding on some chemical constituents and enzyme activities in peas, snap beans, and lima beans. N.Y. State Agr. Expt. Sta. Bull. *752*.

MOYER, J. C., and STOTZ, E. 1945. The electronic blanching of vegetables. Science *102*, 68–69.

MOYER, J. C., and STOTZ, E. 1947. The blanching of vegetables by electronics. Food Technol. *1*, 252–257.

NATIONAL CANNERS ASSOC. 1968. Laboratory Manual for Food Canners and Processors, Vol. II. Avi Publishing Co., Westport, Conn.

O'CONNELL, W. J., Jr. 1957. California fruit and vegetable cannery waste disposal practices. Sewage Ind. Wastes *29*, 268–280.

OLSON, H. V., and MISTELSKE, E. 1968. Designed to be super sanitary. Food Eng. *40*, No. 9, 78–81.

OLSON, I. T. 1941. Wetting agents speed chemical peeling. Food Ind. *13*, No. 4, 51–52.

PARKER, M. E., HARVEY, E. H., and STATELER, E. S. 1954. Elements of Food Engineering, Vol. II. Reinhold Publishing Co., New York.

PARKER, M. E., and LITCHFIELD, J. H. 1962. Food Plant Sanitation. Van Nostrand-Reinhold Books, New York.

PENNSALT CHEMICALS CORP. 1965. How to Remove Fruit Skins Easily. Philadelphia.

PHAFF, H. J., and MRAK, E. M. 1948. Sulphur house operation. Univ. Calif. Agr. Expt. Sta. Bull. *383*.

PILORZ, B. 1955. Peeling by hot air blast. Food Eng. *27*, No. 2, 68.

PINSENT, B. R. W. 1962. Peroxidase regeneration and its effect on quality in frozen peas and thawed peas. J. Food Sci. *27*, 120–126.

POTTER, J. R. 1966. Plant structural design accents sanitation. Food Eng. *38*, No. 1, 62–65.

POTTER, N. N. 1968. Food Science. Avi Publishing Co., Westport, Conn.

POWERS, M. J., and LAZAR, M. E. 1959. Method of preserving apples. U.S. Pat. 2,874,059. Feb. 17.

RASMUSSEN, C. L. 1967. Raw material yields. Food Technol. *21*, 1305–1308.

RATZESBERGER, L., Jr. 1964. Need enough clean water for all. Food Technol. *18*, 1895–1897.

RICHES, L. V., and FORBES, J. H. 1958. New technique averts site selection hazards. Food Eng. *30*, No. 4, 59–62.

ROBE, K. 1958. Breakthrough in bulk canning. Food Process. *19*, No. 11, 24.

ROHRER, D., and ROBE, K. 1970. Cold water cleaning system improves efficiency. Food Process. *31*, No. 3, 72–73.

ROLFE, E. 1965. Recent developments in food dehydration. Food Manuf. *40*, No. 7, 46–52.

ROSE, W. W. *et al.* 1970. Symp.-Clean up waste water. Food Eng. *42*, No. 7, 65–91.
SACHAROW, S. 1970. Food packaging in developing nations. Food Eng. *42*, No. 8, 80–81.
SACHAROW, S., and GRIFFIN, R. C. 1970. Food Packaging. Avi Publishing Co., Westport, Conn.
SAMUEL, O. C. 1965. Solves waste disposal problem. Food Process. *26*, No. 7, 92–97, 123.
SANBORN, N. H. 1953. Disposal of food processing wastes by spray irrigation. Sewage Ind. Wastes *25*, 1034–1043.
SCHEEL, H. A. 1968. Your plant can save water. Food Eng. *40*, No. 8, 92–95.
SCHOLLE, C. H. 1969. Pressure spraying improves cleaning. Food Eng. *41*, No. 10, 92–93.
SCHOMER, H. A., and SAINSBURY, G. F. 1957. Controlled atmosphere storage of Starking Delicious apples. USDA Agr. Marketing Serv. *178*.
SCHULTZ, H. W. 1960. Food Enzymes. Avi Publishing Co., Westport, Conn.
SCHULTZ, W. G. *et al.* 1971. Field processing of tomatoes. 1. Process and Design. J. Food Sci. *36*, 397–399.
SCOTT, L. E., WALLS, E. P., and HUNTER, H. A. 1945. How to prevent discoloration of sweet potato. Food Packer *26*, No. 8, 45.
SEMLING, H. V. 1967. FDA new emphasis on sanitation—the unseen. Food Process. *28*, No. 12, 94.
SHARPE, L. E. 1970. Two year training program. Food Technol. *24*, 247–248.
SHOCKLEY, R. T. 1962. Laminations suitable for packaging freeze-dried foods. Food Packer *23*, No. 12, 72–76.
SMITH, T. J. 1970. Pilot plant experience of USDA—Magnuson dry caustic peeling process. Proc. 1st Natl. Symp. Food Process. Wastes, Apr. 6–8, Portland, Ore.
SMOCK, R. M. 1949. Controlled storage of apples. Cornell Univ. Expt. Sta. Bull. *759*.
SMOCK, R. M. 1950. The storage of apples. Cornell Univ. Agr. Expt. Sta. Bull. *440*.
SMOCK, R. M., and SOUTHWICK, F. W. 1948. Air purification in apple storage. Cornell Univ. Agr. Expt. Sta. Bull. *843*.
STEPAN, D. G. 1963. Water renovation. Chem. Eng. Progr. *59*, No. 11, 19.
STRANIERO, D. 1956. Novel freeze-enzyme technique peels tomatoes at six tons per hour. Food Eng. *28*, No. 10, 58.
SWANSON, W. M. 1962. Disposal of potato wastes in Idaho. 12th Natl. Potato Util. Conf. Proc, Bakersfield, Calif.
SWAYNE, T., and ROBE, K. 1969. Sanitary blancher. Food Process. *30*, No. 10, 68–69.
TAGGART, R. S. 1967A. How to manage today's sanitation. Food Eng. *39*, No. 2, 87–89.
TAGGART, R. S. 1967B. Dry waste disposal. Food Eng. *39*, No. 7, 98.
TALBURT, W. F., and LEGAULT, R. R. 1950. Time lapse gets top blame for shelled pea off-flavor. Food Ind. *22*, 1021–1023.
THOMAS, L. R. 1966. Deep wells may answer water needs. Food Eng. *38*, No. 10, 96–99.
TOMB, J. O. 1952. Program for locating new plant. Harvard Business Rev. *30*, No. 11, 54–55.
TORREY, R. F. 1965. Transportation factors vital in selecting plant sites. Food Eng. *37*, No. 9, 88–89.
TUCKER, G. G. 1968. Designing a hot air drier. Food Manuf. *43*, No. 2, 34–35.
USDA. 1944. Vegetable and Fruit Dehydration—A Manual for Plant Operators. USDA Misc. Pub. *540*.
USDA. 1948. Experimental compression of dehydrated foods. USDA Misc. Pub. *647*.
USDA. 1959. Management Handbook to Aid Emergency Expansion of Dehydration Facilities for Fruits and Vegetables. Western Util. Res. Develop. Div., Agr. Res. Serv., Albany, Calif.
USDA. 1961. Dehydration of onion. USDA Agr. Res. Serv. *CA-74-10*.
U. S. DEPT. HEALTH, EDUCATION, WELFARE. 1949. Drinking Water Standards. Public Health Serv., Washington, D.C.
VAN ARSDEL, W. B. 1965. Food Dehydration: Recent advances and unsolved problems. Food Technol. *19*, 484–489.
VAN HEUVELEN, W. 1962. Disposing of potato processing wastes in the Red River

Valley of North Dakota and Minnesota. 12th Natl. Potato Util. Conf. Proc., Bakersfield, Calif.

VAN METER, W. R. 1962. Use a consultant profitably. Food Eng. *34*, No. 6, 55–57.

VAN METER, W. R., and EGAN, J. J. 1966. Insure quality via low count. Food Eng. *38*, No. 4, 92–96.

VON ALLMAN, E. 1960. Economics are basic for plant location. Chem. Eng. Progr. *56*, No. 11, 37–41.

WAGNER, J. R. 1970. In-field processing of tomatoes. Proc. 1st Natl. Symp. Food Process. Wastes, Apr. 6–8, Portland, Ore.

WARRICK, L. F., MCKEE, F. J., WIRTH, H. G., and SANBORN, N. H. 1959. Natl. Canners Assoc. Bull. *28-L*.

WEISER, H. H., MOUNTNEY, G. J., and GOULD, W. A. 1971. Practical Food Microbiology and Technology, 2nd Edition. Avi Publishing Co., Westport, Conn.

WILLOUGHBY, E. 1969. Select the right waste treatment system. Food Eng. *41*, No. 8, 74–79.

WOODROOF, J. G., ATKINSON, I. S., CECIL, S. R., and SHELDON, G. 1946. Studies in methods of scalding (blanching) vegetables for freezing. Georgia Agr. Expt. Sta. Bull. *248*.

WOODROOF, J. G., CECIL, S. R., SHELDOR, E., and CECIL, I. A. 1948. Peeling with lye. Food Ind. *20*, No. 6, 862–869.

WRIGHT, R. C., ROSE, D. H., and WHITEMAN, T. M. 1954. The Commercial Storage of Fruits, Vegetables, and Florist's and Nursery Stocks. USDA Handbook *66*.

ZIEMBA, J. V. 1960. Reduce plant waste by campaign. Food Eng. *32*, No. 12, 37–40.

ZIEMBA, J. V. 1967. Plant has many extras. Food Eng. *39*, No. 9, 71–73.

Symbols and Units

Most of the symbols used in this book are defined in terms of one consistent set of English engineering units. The symbol for a quantity remains the same, however, even if a different set of units is used; for example, heat transfer coefficient retains the symbol h whether its numerical value is given in (Btu)/(hr)(sq ft)(°F) or in (kcal)/(hr)(sq m)(°C).

The notation is, unfortunately, not completely consistent with any one standard system, because some symbols have become so firmly entrenched during the past 50 yr of engineering studies of drying that complete adoption of even such excellent systems as those of the American Standards Association for Letter Symbols for Chemical Engineering, ASA Y 10.12–1955, and Letter Symbols for Heat and Thermodynamics, Including Heat Flow, ASA Z 10.3–1943, would impose unnecessary burdens on many readers. The divergence from the standard usage is not extensive.

TABLE A.1

EXPLANATION OF SYMBOLS USED IN THIS VOLUME

Name	Symbol	Unit
General		
Area	A	(sq ft)
Density		
General	ρ	(lb)/(cu ft)
Bulk density	ρ_s	(lb/gross cu ft)
Density of dry substance	ρ_d	(lb dry)/(cu ft)
Diameter	D	(ft)
Differential operator	d	–
Diffusion resistance factor (Krischer)	ϕ	–
Distance, thickness, or other linear dimension	l	(ft)
Drying time constant (Jason)	τ	(hr)
Efficiency, thermal	η	–
Loading per unit area	L	(lb)/(sq ft)
Mass	m	(lb)
Molecular weight	M	–
Porosity	ψ	–
Radius	r	(ft)
Reynolds Number	**Re**	–
Spreading potential in adsorbed film	Π	$(lb_f)/(ft)$ or (lb)/$(hr)^2$
Surface tension	σ	$(lb_f)/(ft)$ or (lb)/$(hr)^2$
Time	θ	(hr)
Tunnel constant	b	(°F)

332

TABLE A.1 (*Continued*)

Name	Symbol	Unit
Velocity	u	(ft)/(hr)
Viscosity		
Dynamic	μ	$(\text{lb}_f)(\text{hr})/(\text{ft})^2$ or
		(lb)/(hr)(ft)
Kinematic	ν	(sq ft)/(hr)
Heat		
Chemical potential (Gibbs free energy change)	Δg	(Btu)/(lb mole)
Coefficient in recirculation Equation (21)	f	$(°F)^{-1}$
Cooling line slope ($\Delta t/1000 \ \Delta H$)	z	(°F)
Emissivity for radiation	ϵ	–
Energy of activation (Arrhenius)	E	(Btu)/(lb mole)
Enthalpy		
Moist air	E	(Btu)/(lb dry air)
Air saturated at the thermodynamic wet-bulb temperature	E^*	(Btu)/(lb dry air)
Condensed water	E_w^*	(Btu)/(lb water)
Entropy	S	(Btu)/(lb)(°R)
Gas constant	R	(cu ft)(atm)/(°R)
		(lb mole)
Gibbs free energy	g	(Btu)/(lb mole)
Heat quantity	Q_h	(Btu)
Heat transfer coefficient	h	(Btu)/(hr)(sq ft)
		(°F)
Heat transfer rate	q	(Btu)/(hr)
Heat usage of a dehydrator	F	(Btu)/(lb water
		evap'd)
Humid heat	c_s	(Btu)/(lb dry air)
		(°F)
Latent heat of evaporation at t °F	λ_t	(Btu)/(lb)
Mean specific heat of gas or vapor at constant pressure	c_p	(Btu)/(lb)(°F)
Mean temperature difference	$(\Delta t)_m$	(°F)
Specific heat (liquid or solid)	c	(Btu)/(lb)(°F)
Temperature		
Absolute (Rankine)	T	(°R)
Air	t_a	(°F)
Air entering drying section	t'	(°F)
Air leaving drying section	t''	(°F)
Adiabatic saturation	t^*	(°F)
Difference	(Δt)	(°F)
Outside air supply	t_0	(°F)
Surface	t_s	(°F)
Thermodynamic wet-bulb	t^*	(°F)
Wet-bulb (physical)	t_w	(°F)
Thermal conductivity	k	(Btu)/(hr)(sq ft)
		(°F/ft)
Thermal diffusivity	α	(sq ft)/(hr)

TABLE A.1 (Continued)

Name	Symbol	Unit
Total heat transferred	Q_h	(Btu)
Transfer coefficient, heat	h	(Btu)/(hr)(sq ft) (°F)
Wet-bulb depression	$t_a - t_w$	(°F)
Moisture		
Coefficient in constant-rate equation	a	—
Concentration of moisture in material	C	(lb)/(cu ft)
Diffusivity of water vapor in air	d	(sq ft)/(hr)
Diffusivity of moisture in material	D	(sq ft)/(hr)
Equilibrium moisture content	W_e	(lb)/(lb dry)
Fraction of total moisture removed	x	—
Humidity		
Absolute, or humidity ratio	H	(lb)/(lb dry air)
Absolute, of saturated air	H_s	(lb)/(lb dry air)
Absolute, of air sat'd at temp t^*	H^*	(lb)/(lb dry air)
Relative	r_h	—
Humid volume of air	V_h	(cu ft)/(lb dry air)
Moisture content—		
Material, "dry basis" or "moisture ratio"	W	(lb)/(lb dry)
Material, initial	W_0	(lb)/(lb dry)
Material, final	W_f	(lb)/(lb dry)
"Wet basis," percentage	ξ	(lb)/(100 lb) ("as is")
Mole fraction of water vapor in moist air	w	—
Permeability of water in moist solid	P	(lb)/(ft)(hr)(atm)
Permeability of porous material to gas flow	P_a	(lb)/(ft)(hr)(atm)
Recirculation, proportion of, in a dehydrator	r_d	—
Saturated volume of air	V_s	(cu ft sat'd air)/ (lb dry air)
Transfer coefficient mass		
Through gas film	k_g	(lb)/(hr)(sq ft) (atm)
Through liquid film	k_l	(lb)/(hr)(sq ft) (atm)
Pressure		
Partial pressure of water vapor in moist air	p_w	(atm)
Partial pressure of dry air in mixture	p_a	(atm)
Partial pressure difference	(Δp)	(atm)
Saturation vapor pressure of water	p_s	(atm)
Saturation vapor pressure of water at the wet-bulb temperature	p_{sw}	(atm)
Total or barometric pressure	P	(atm)
Vapor pressure of ice in freeze-drying piece	p_{ip}	(mm Hg)
Vapor pressure of ice on surface on condenser	p_{ic}	(mm Hg)
Volume or Flow		
Air flow rate	Q_a	(cu ft)/(hr)
Mass velocity	G	(lb)/(hr)(sq ft)
Saturated volume of air	V_s	(cu ft)/(lb dry air)
Specific volume of air	V	(cu ft)/(lb)

Moisture Determination in Dehydrated Foods

The magnitude of the "moisture content" of a dehydrated foodstuff or its raw materials depends in part upon the method used to determine it—i.e., all definitions of this term are operational. Many different methods of determination have been proposed, and several have some kind of status as "official" methods for one purpose or another. Choice of a method is based on the importance attached to accuracy, precision or reproducibility, time required for a determination, availability of necessary equipment, degree of skill or training required, and several other factors, as discussed by Stitt (1958). Purchase specifications frequently include definition of the moisture determination method that is to be accepted as conclusive, even though the method is a deliberate compromise between the accuracy demanded and the time required.

Methods used for various purposes are classed as (1) vacuum oven drying, (2) entrainment distillation, (3) Fischer volumetric, (4) nuclear magnetic resonance, and (5) dichromate oxidation. We give the detailed procedures only for the first three of these, which have been rather widely used either for procurement specifications (military, federal, or industrial) or in precise scientific investigations. Several kinds of "rapid" methods are also rather widely used for control purposes. Some of these employ the rapid heating of a small weighed sample for a specified arbitrary length of time. Others indicate the electrical resistance of a sample or its dielectric constant as that affects the tuning of a radio-frequency circuit. All such instruments are calibrated against samples of a similar product whose moisture contents have been determined independently. The catalogs of many laboratory equipment manufacturers describe commercial instruments of these kinds.

VACUUM-OVEN DRYING

Seven distinguishably different vacuum-oven procedures are currently specified or recommended for determining moisture content of various dry food commodities. The results they give differ from one another for reasons that are not entirely clear. We summarize the seven methods here in order to bring out the major distinctions between them.

(1) Drying to constant weight (about 5 hr) at the temperature of boiling water, oven pressure not over 100 mm mercury. (Used for dry milk, AOAC (1960) methods 15.101 and 15.102.)

(2) Drying to constant weight (about 5 hr) at 98°-100°C, oven pressure not over 25 mm mercury. (Used for egg solids, AOAC (1960) methods 16.002 and 16.003, and Quartermaster Corps specification MIL-E-25062, June 30, 1961.)

(3) Sample ground in blender 1 min, sifted through 20-mesh screen, caught

on 40-mesh screen. Drying 6 hr at 70°C, oven pressure not over 100 mm mercury. (Used for potato and for green beans, Quartermaster Corps specifications MIL-P-1073A, Dec. 12, 1950, and MIL-B-35011, Dec. 19, 1955, respectively.)

(4) Sample ground in blender 1 min. Drying 16 hr at 60°C, oven pressure not over 100 mm mercury. (Used for cabbage, Quartermaster Corps specification MIL-C-826A, Apr. 8, 1960.)

(5) Sample ground in a food chopper, Hobart mixer, or blender. Drying 6 hr at 70°C, oven pressure not over 100 mm mercury. (Used for dried and dehydrated fruits, AOAC (1960) methods 20.002c and 20.008; and for dehydrated onions, same AOAC methods.)

(6) Grind sample in Wiley mill through 40-mesh screen. Drying 30 hr at 60°C, oven pressure not over 5 mm mercury. (Research and reference methods for onions, cabbage, and leafy vegetables; Makower et al. 1946.)

(7) Grind sample in Wiley mill through 40-mesh screen. Drying 40 hr at 70°C, oven pressure not over 5 mm mercury. (Research and reference method for potatoes, carrots, beets, and sweet potatoes; Makower et al. 1946.)

We refrain from quoting all seven of these methods in full; the following directions for the dried milk method (AOAC 1960) and for the "40-hr, 70°C" reference method (Makower et al. 1946) provide a framework on which the specific variations prescribed for the other methods can be readily placed.

MOISTURE IN DRIED MILK PRODUCTS
(Official AOAC Methods No. 15.101 and 15.102)

Preparation of Sample

Sift sample through No. 20 sieve onto large sheet of paper, rubbing material through sieve and tapping vigorously if necessary. Grind residue in mortar, pass through sieve, and mix into sifted material. Discard particles that cannot be ground (wood, etc.). Sift sample two more times, mixing thoroughly each time. To avoid absorption of moisture, operate as rapidly as possible, and preserve sample in air-tight container.

Moisture

Weigh 1–1.5 gm sample into round flat-bottom metal dish (not less than 5 cm diameter and provided with tight fitting slip-in cover). Loosen cover and place dish on metal shelf (dish resting directly on shelf) in vacuum oven kept at temperature of boiling water. Dry to constant weight (about 5 hr) under pressure not over 100 mm Hg. During drying admit slow current of air into oven (about two bubbles per second), dried by passing through sulfuric acid. Stop vacuum pump and carefully admit dried air into oven. Press cover tightly into dish, remove from oven, cool, and weigh. Calculate percentage loss in weight as moisture.

MOISTURE IN DRIED POTATOES AND OTHER ROOT VEGETABLES
Preparation of Sample

Carefully sample the material, grind coarsely in a Wiley mill equipped with a U.S. 10-mesh sieve (Makower et al. 1946). Pass the ground material through a quartering funnel, regrind a 25-gm portion through the same mill with a 40-mesh sieve. Place subsamples of the reground material in weighing bottles with tightly fitting ground glass covers. If the material was so moist that it clogged the mill, predry prior to grinding, determining loss in weight quantitatively.

Moisture

Dry in a vacuum oven maintained at a pressure of 5 mm mercury or less. The temperature setting refers to the temperature of the oven shelf, which should be copper. Covers of the weighing bottles should be cocked. Dry potatoes, carrots, beets, or sweet potatoes for 40 hr at 70°C. Stop vacuum pump and carefully admit dried air. Close the weighing bottles tightly, cool in a desiccator, and weigh. Report loss in weight as moisture.

TOLUENE DISTILLATION METHOD
(Official method for dry milk products. American Dry Milk Inst. (undated))
Procedure

Transfer a 50-gm sample to a clean, dry 300 ml Erlenmeyer flask as quickly as possible and immediately pour approximately 75–100 ml toluene (technical, moisture-free) into the flask to cover the sample. Rinse down any milk particles on the inside of the flask when introducing the toluene.

Insert a dry distillation trap into the flask and fill the trap with the toluene. Note: Toluene is readily inflammable and the utmost care must be exercised to keep supplies of it away from flames and heating elements.

Shake the flask with the sample thoroughly before connecting the trap and flask to the condenser. Heat the contents to boiling, making sure that the sample does not scorch on the bottom of the flask. The amount of heat should be so regulated that the toluene will condense into the trap at a rate of about 4 drops per second.

Forty-five minutes after distillation has begun, and without interrupting distillation, dislodge water droplets in the condenser tube by means of a condenser brush. While the brush is in the upper part of the condenser, flush the tube with 10 ml of toluene.

Read the moisture level in the trap to the nearest half of a scale division (0.05 ml). Be sure that the meniscus between the toluene and water is sharp. Droplets of water in the toluene or droplets of toluene in the water may be dislodged by a long, stiff wire inserted down through the condenser into the trap.

Continue the distillation for an additional 15-min period (making a total time of 60 min) and again dislodge water droplets from the condenser tube as before and note the water level in the trap. If this reading agrees with the previous reading within 0.05 ml water in the trap, discontinue the distillation and report the determined moisture content. The milliliters of water in the trap multiplied by two equals the percentage of moisture in the sample.

If readings fail to agree as required, continue the distillation for additional 15-min periods until successive results agree within a half scale division.

MOISTURE DETERMINATION BY FISCHER REAGENT

Rapid method, suitable for use in a well equipped laboratory with skilled operator, gave good agreement with standard vacuum oven method in tests on beans, cake mix, egg powder, egg noodles, rolled oats, potato starch, rice, wheat, and garlic, onion, orange, and tomato powders (McComb and McCready 1952; McComb and Wright 1954).

Fischer Reagent

For each liter of reagent, dissolve 133 gm resublimed iodine in 425 ml of reagent-grade pyridine ($<$ 0.1% water) in a dry glass-stoppered bottle, add 425 ml of anhydrous methyl Cellosolve (Peters and Jungnickel 1955), and cool in an ice water bath. Add, in small increments, and with constant swirling, 70 ml of anhydrous sulfur dioxide from a graduated cylinder, and mix thoroughly, or add 100 gm of gaseous sulfur dioxide at a rate of about 40 gm per hr. Stopper the solution tightly and store for 2–3 days before use. The water equivalence of this reagent is approximately 6 mg of water per milliliter of reagent.

Water Equivalent of Reagent

Determine the water equivalent of the Fischer reagent and the blank titer of the formamide daily or each time a series of determinations is made. To determine the blank, titrate 10 ml of formamide in a 250 ml Erlenmeyer flask. To the same flask add, by means of a weight burette, 70–100 mg of water, and titrate. Calculate the water-equivalent of the reagent, milligrams of water per milliliter of reagent. The electrometric end point is used, employing a titrimeter whose indication should remain steady for approximately 30 sec.

Determination

Weigh a quantity of the sample, calculated to give a suitable titer, into a dry glass-stoppered 250 ml Erlenmeyer flask which contains a magnetic stirrer. Add 20 ml of formamide with slight agitation to disperse the sample and prevent clumping. Stir for 10 min, then titrate directly with the Fischer reagent.[1] The

---

[1] Beans, oatmeal, rice, and wheat must be heated with the formamide in the flask to 70°–80°C for from 5 to 30 min to complete the extraction of water, then cooled and titrated.

percentage water is calculated as follows:

$$\% = \frac{100 \ (\text{sample titer} - \text{blank titer})(\text{water equivalent})}{(\text{sample weight in milligram})}$$

BIBLIOGRAPHY

AMERICAN DRY MILK INST. (Undated) Standards for Grades and Methods of Analysis for the Dry Milk Industry. Bull. *916*. Am. Dry Milk Inst., Chicago.

AOAC. 1960. Official Methods of Analysis, 9th Edition, W. Horwitz (Editor). Assoc. Offic. Agr. Chemists, Washington, D.C.

MCCOMB, E. A., and MCCREADY, R. M. 1952. Rapid determination of moisture in dehydrated vegetables with Karl Fischer reagent by use of formamide as an extraction solvent. J. Assoc. Offic. Agr. Chemists *35*, 437–441.

MCCOMB, E. A., and WRIGHT, H. M. 1954. Application of formamide as an extraction solvent with Karl Fischer reagent for the determination of moisture in some food products. Food Technol. *8*, 73–75.

MAKOWER, B., CHASTAIN, S. M., and NIELSEN, E. 1946. Moisture determination in dehydrated vegetables. Vacuum oven method. Ind. Eng. Chem. *38*, 725–731.

PETERS, E. D. and JUNGNICKEL, J. L. 1955. Improvements in Karl Fischer method for determination of water. Anal. Chem. *27*, 450–453.

STITT, F. E. 1958. Moisture equilibrium and the determination of water content of dehydrated foods. *In* Fundamental Aspects of the Dehydration of Foodstuffs. Soc. Chem. Ind. (London) 67–88.

Moisture Contents of Various Foods, and Expected Ratios of Fresh to Dried Weights

Tables A.2 and A.3 represent somewhat different approaches to the important question of yield of acceptable product to be expected from a normal vegetable dehydration operation. Table A.4, covering the whole field of dehydrated foods, gives mean values for the moisture content of the edible portions of these foods, which of course is closely related to the yield of dehydrated product. The differences between values found in the three tables for the same commodity reflect mainly the wide variation of dry matter content in vegetables of the same variety under different conditions. Conservatism in use of these estimates is indicated.

TABLE A.2

DRYING RATIO AND OVERALL SHRINKAGE RATIO OF VARIOUS VEGETABLES

Commodity	Moisture in Fresh Commodity[1]		Computed Drying Ratio[2]	Overall Shrinkage Ratio[3]	
	Range	Mean	(Mean)	Range	Mean
Beans, lima	58.9–71.8	66.5	2.8/1	–	–
Beans, snap	78.8–94.0	88.9	8.5/1	–	–
Beets	82.3–94.1	87.6	7.6/1	10 to 15/1	13/1
Cabbage	88.4–94.8	92.4	12.4/1	17 to 25/1	20/1
Carrots	83.1–91.1	88.2	8.0/1	9 to 15/1	11/1
Celery	89.9–95.2	93.7	15.0/1	–	–
Chard, Swiss	89.9–92.9	91.0	10.5/1	–	–
Chili peppers	–	–	–	4 to 7/1[4]	5/1
Corn, sweet	61.3–86.0	73.9	3.6/1	–	–
Garlic	–	–	–	2.5 to 6/1[4]	3/1
Kale	81.4–91.2	86.6	7.0/1	–	–
Mustard greens	86.7–95.7	92.2	12.0/1	–	–
Onions	70.2–95.2	87.5	7.5/1	7 to 16/1	13/1
Parsnips	72.6–89.2	78.6	4.4/1	–	–
Peas, green	56.7–84.1	74.3	3.7/1	–	–
Potatoes (dice)	66.0–85.2	77.8	4.2/1	6 to 9/1	7/1
Rutabagas	86.1–91.8	89.1	8.6/1	–	–
Spinach	89.0–95.0	92.7	13.0/1	–	–
Sweet potatoes	58.5–82.7	68.5	3.0/1	5 to 7/1	5.3/1
Tomatoes	90.6–96.7	94.1	16.0/1	–	–

[1] In edible portion, uncut, unblanched. Source; Vegetable and Fruit Dehydration. Misc. Publ. No. *540*, USDA, 1944.
[2] Ratio of weight of prepared material entering drier to weight of product containing 6% moisture, assuming moisture content of prepared material entering the drier is the same as that of the uncut, unblanched fresh commodity. Computed from Column 3 above.
[3] Ratio of weight of unprepared commodity delivered to the plant to net weight of acceptable finished product. Unpublished estimates, private sources.
[4] From limited number of observations.

TABLE A.3

OVERALL SHRINKAGE RATIO, DRYING RATIO, AND REHYDRATION RATIO
OF VARIOUS VEGETABLES

Kind of Vegetable	Overall Shrinkage Ratio[1]	Drying Ratio[2]	Rehydration Ratio[3]
Asparagus, green	30	11	8.0
Beans, green	–	12.5	8.0
Beets (powder)	9.0	6.5	6.0
Cabbage	21.0	11.5	10.5
Carrots			
Dice	12.0	7.5	7.0
Granules	12.0	7.5	6.0
Cross-cut	12.0	7.5	5.0
Celery			
Stalk and leaf	20.0	16.5	9.0
Stalk	30.0	17.5	10.0
Garlic	8.0	5.0	4.0
Horse-radish	5.5	5.0	5.0
Leek	11.0	9.5	8.0
Onions (powdered, sliced, etc.)	8.0	7.0	5.5
Onions, green (flaked, minced)	14.0	10.5	9.0
Parsley	11.0	9.9	8.0
Peppers, sweet, bell			
Green	22.0	16.0	8.0
Red	19.0	12.0	6.5
Pimiento	28.0	10.0	7.0
Spinach	13.5	13.0	9.0
Tomato (flakes)	20.0	14.0	5.0

Source: 1963 Price List, California Vegetable Concentrates, Inc. All values are approximate.
[1] Overall shrinkage ratio, the number of pounds of fresh, untrimmed (as harvested) vegetable required to produce 1 lb of acceptable dry product at specification moisture content.
[2] Drying ratio, the number of pounds of fresh, fully prepared vegetable required to produce 1 lb of acceptable dry product.
[3] Rehydration ratio, the drained weight of product recovered by rehydrating 1 lb of dehydrated product under specified conditions of reconstitution.

TABLE A.4

MOISTURE CONTENT OF EDIBLE PORTION OF VARIOUS FOODS

Foodstuff	Moisture (%)	Moisture Content, Dry Basis[1] (Lb per Lb Dry)
Milk, fluid		
Whole	87	6.7
Nonfat	90	9.0
Egg, raw		
Whole, without shell	74	2.85
White	88	7.3
Yolk	51	1.04
Beef, lean, roasted	60	1.50
Chicken, broiled	61	1.56

TABLE A.4 (Continued)

Foodstuff	Moisture (%)	Moisture Content, Dry Basis[1] (Lb per Lb Dry)
Pork, lean, roasted	50	1.00
Crabmeat, canned	77	3.35
Shrimp, canned, meat	66	1.94
Beans, lima, immature, cooked	75	3.00
Beans, snap, green, cooked	92	11.5
Beets, diced, cooked	88	7.3
Cabbage		
Raw, Shredded	92	11.5
Cooked	92	11.5
Carrot		
Raw, whole	88	7.3
Diced, cooked	92	11.5
Celery, raw, diced	94	15.7
Corn, sweet, cooked	76	3.2
Mushrooms, canned	93	13.3
Onions, mature, raw	88	7.3
Parsley, raw, chopped	84	5.25
Peas, green, cooked	82	4.45
Peppers, sweet, raw	92	11.5
Potatoes, boiled, peeled	80	4.00
Spinach, cooked	91	10.1
Squash, winter, baked	86	6.15
Sweet potatoes, baked, peeled	64	1.78
Tomatoes, raw	94	15.7
Tomato juice	94	15.7
Turnips, cooked, diced	92	11.5
Apples, raw	85	5.7
Apple juice	86	6.15
Apricots, raw	85	5.7
Bananas, raw	76	3.2
Canteloups, raw	94	15.7
Cherries, sour, pitted, raw	83	4.9
Figs, raw	78	3.55
Grapefruit, raw sections	89	8.0
Grapefruit juice	90	9.0
Grapes, raw, European type	81	4.25
Lemons, raw	90	9.0
Lemon juice	91	10.1
Orange, Naval, raw	85	5.7
Orange juice, Florida Valencia	88	7.4
Peaches, raw	89	8.0
Pears, raw	83	4.9
Pineapple, raw, diced	85	5.7
Plums, except prunes, raw	86	6.15
Strawberries, raw, capped	90	9.0
Tangerines, raw	87	6.7
Watermelon, raw	92	11.5

Source: USDA, 1960. Nutritive Value of Foods. Home and Garden Bull. 72, Washington, D.C.
[1] Computed from values in second column.

Index

NOTES

NOTES

NOTES

NOTES

NOTES

NOTES

NOTES

NOTES

NOTES